REREADING EAST GERMANY

The Literature and Film of the GDR

EDITED BY

KAREN LEEDER

CAMBRIDGE
UNIVERSITY PRESS

CAMBRIDGE
UNIVERSITY PRESS

University Printing House, Cambridge CB2 8BS, United Kingdom

Cambridge University Press is part of the University of Cambridge.

It furthers the University's mission by disseminating knowledge in the pursuit of
education, learning and research at the highest international levels of excellence.

www.cambridge.org
Information on this title: www.cambridge.org/9781107006362

© Cambridge University Press 2015

First published 2015

Printed in the United States of America by Sheridan Books, Inc.

A catalogue record for this publication is available from the British Library

Library of Congress Cataloguing in Publication data
Rereading East Germany : the literature and film of the GDR / edited by Karen Leeder.
pages   cm
Includes bibliographical references and index.
ISBN 978-1-107-00636-2 (hardback)
1. German literature – Germany (East) – History and criticism.   2. Motion pictures –
Germany (East) – History.   3. Germany (East) – In literature.   I. Leeder, Karen J., editor.
PT3705.R44   2015
830.9′943109045–dc23
2015024724

ISBN 978-1-107-00636-2 Hardback

Contents

Illustrations

Notes on contributors

SEÁN ALLAN is Reader in German Studies at the University of Warwick. He has also been a visiting scholar at the DEFA Film-Library (University of Massachusetts, Amherst) and at Smith College. He is the co-editor of *DEFA: East German Cinema 1946–92* with John Sandford and has published widely on GDR and post-unification German cinema, including essays on Konrad Wolf, Kurt Maetzig and, most recently, the documentary work of Jürgen Böttcher.

GERRIT-JAN BERENDSE is Professor of Modern European Literature and Culture at Cardiff University. He has published *Die 'Sächsische Dichterschule'. Lyrik in der DDR der sechziger und siebziger Jahre* (1990) and *Grenz-Fallstudien. Essays zum Topos Prenzlauer Berg in der DDR-Literatur* (1999), as well as numerous articles on poetry in the GDR. In 2014 he edited a special number of *German Life and Letters* on German poetry. He is currently writing a monograph on surrealism in the GDR.

STEPHEN BROCKMANN is Professor of German at Carnegie Mellon University and was President (2011–2012) of the German Studies Association. He is the author, most recently, of *A Critical History of German Film* (2010), as well as of *Nuremberg: The Imaginary Capital* (2006), *German Literary Culture at the Zero Hour* (2004) and *Literature and German Reunification* (1999). From 2002 to 2007 he was the managing editor of the *Brecht Yearbook*, and in 2007 he won the DAAD Prize for Distinguished Scholarship in German and European Studies / Humanities.

CAROL ANNE COSTABILE-HEMING is Professor of German and Chair of the Department of World Languages, Literatures, and Cultures at the University of North Texas, in Denton, Texas. She has published widely on *Wende* literature and post-*Wende* Berlin, including *Textual Responses to German Unification: Processing Historical and Social Change in*

Literature and Film (2001) and *Berlin, The Symphony Continues: Orchestrating Architectural, Social, and Artistic Change in Germany's New Capital* (2004). In 2012, she was named the Outstanding German Educator for the Post-Secondary level by the American Association of Teachers of German.

BIRGIT DAHLKE is Visiting Professor of German Literature at the Humboldt University, Berlin. She is the author of *Wolfgang Hilbig. A Biography* (2011) and *Papierboot. Autorinnen aus der DDR – inoffiziell publiziert* (1997) and co-editor of volumes on *German Life-Writing in the Twentieth Century* (2010); *Kerstin Hensel* (2002); *Zersammelt. Die inoffizielle Literaturszene der DDR nach 1990. Eine Bestandsaufnahme* (2001); *LiteraturGesellschaft DDR. Kanonkämpfe und ihre Geschichte(n)* (2000) and the bi-annual journal for new literature, essays and criticism *Moosbrand. neue texte* with Klaus Michael, Lutz Seiler and Peter Walther (1996–99). She is currently setting up a new research centre on Gerhard and Christa Wolf at the Humboldt University, Berlin and investigating authors' personal libraries as the subject of research.

WOLFGANG EMMERICH is Professor Emeritus of German Literature, History and Culture at the University of Bremen. In 1989 he founded the Bremen Institute for German Cultural Studies (IfkuD). He is the author of *Kleine Literaturgeschichte der DDR* (1982/1989/1996), as well as volumes on Heinrich Mann (1980), *Paul Celan* (1998) and *Gottfried Benn* (2006) among others; co-editor of *Lyrik des Exils* (1985/1997), *Mythenkorrekturen. Zu einer paradoxalen Form der Mythenrezeption* (2005) and *Literarisches Chemnitz. Autoren – Werke – Tendenzen* (2008).

KAREN LEEDER is Professor of Modern German Literature at the University of Oxford, and Fellow and Tutor in German at New College, Oxford. She has published widely on GDR literature, especially poetry and the literature of the Berlin Republic, and has translated work by a number of German writers into English, including Volker Braun, *Rubble Flora: Selected Poems*, 2014. Her most recent outing with Cambridge University Press was *The Cambridge Companion to Rainer Maria Rilke* in 2010 (with Robert Vilain). An edited volume, *From Stasiland to Ostalgie: The GDR – Twenty Years After*, appeared in 2009, *Brecht & the GDR: Politics, Culture, Posterity* (with Laura Bradley) appeared in 2011 and the volume *Durs Grünbein: A Companion* (with Chris Young and Michael Eskin) appeared in 2013.

ALISON LEWIS is Professor of German in the School of Languages and
Literature at the University of Melbourne, Australia. She has published
widely in a number of areas of German Studies, especially on the GDR,
unification and post-communist writing. She is the author of three
monographs: *Subverting Patriarchy: Feminism and Fantasy in the
Works of Irmtraud Morgner* (1995), *Die Kunst des Verrats: der
Prenzlauer Berg und die Staatssicherheit* (2003) and *Eine schwierige Ehe:
Liebe Geschlecht und die Geschichte der Wiedervereinigung im Spiegel der
Literatur* (2009) and co-editor (with Alan Corkhill) of *Intercultural
Encounters in German Studies* (2014) and *Other Encounters: European
Writers and Gender in Transnational Context* (with Lara Anderson and
Heather Merle Benbow) (2014). She is co-editor of the Australian year-
book of German Literary and Cultural Studies *Limbus* (Rombach). She
is currently working on a project on the Stasi files: 'Secret Lives and the
Lives of Secrets: Secret Police Narratives' and co-editing a monograph
(with Valentina Glajar and Corina L. Petrescu), *Secret Police Files from
the Eastern Bloc: Between Surveillance and Life Writing*.

GEORGINA PAUL is Associate Professor in German at the University of
Oxford, and Fellow and Tutor in German at St. Hilda's College,
Oxford. She has an established reputation for her work on the literature
of the GDR and eastern German literature after 1990, including ground-
breaking articles on Christa Wolf. Her monograph *Perspectives on
Gender in Post-1945 German Literature*, which included chapters on a
number of GDR authors (Wolf, Müller, Köhler), appeared in 2009.
Most recently, she published an edited collection: *An Odyssey for Our
Time: Barbara Köhler's Niemands Frau* (2013). She has an active interest
in theories of gender and sexuality.

DENNIS TATE is Emeritus Professor of German Studies at the University
of Bath. His research interests are East German literature before and
after unification, autobiographical prose and competing forms of lit-
erary remembrance. His main publications include *The East German
Novel: Identity, Community, Continuity* (1984), *Franz Fühmann:
Innovation and Authenticity* (1995) and *Shifting Perspectives: East
German Autobiographical Narratives Before and After the End of the
GDR* (2007). He has recently co-edited *Dislocation and Reorientation:
Exile, Division and the End of Communism in German Culture and
Politics* (2009), *German Life Writing in the Twentieth Century* (2010)
and *Twenty Years On: Competing Memories of the GDR in Postunification
German Culture* (2011).

HOLGER TESCHKE is a German author and director born on the island of Rügen in the former GDR. He studied Theatre Directing and Dramaturgy at the Ernst-Busch-School for Acting and Directing in Berlin and held positions as Dramaturg at the Senftenberg Theatre from 1985 to 1987, author and Dramaturg at the Berliner Ensemble from 1987 to 1999 and Guest Professor at NYU, Mount Holyoke College and University of Notre Dame, USA, from 2000 to 2009. He is well known for his work as a poet, dramatist and writer of radio plays and essays. He has won numerous prizes including the 'Neruda-Preis für Lyrik' (2004) and the 'Hörspielpreis der Stadt Karlsruhe' (2007).

JILL E. TWARK is Associate Professor of German at East Carolina University in Greenville, North Carolina. She has published widely on the topic of humour and satire in post-unification East German novels, as well as an article on Günter Grass. Her major publications include the monograph *Humor, Satire, and Identity: Eastern German Literature in the 1990s* (2007); the edited volume *Strategies of Humor in Post-Unification German Literature, Film, and Other Media* (2011); and *Envisioning Social Justice in Contemporary German Culture*, co-edited with Axel Hildebrandt (2015).

Acknowledgements

This volume was made possible by the generosity of John Fell Oxford University Press (OUP) Fund. The editor would also like to acknowledge the assistance of The Faculty of Medieval and Modern Languages, Oxford, New College, Oxford, and the Ludwig Fund, New College, Oxford. The Goethe Institute, London, sponsored Durs Grünbein's visit to Oxford, for a symposium where contributors first aired the ideas, which would lead to this volume. The editor would like to thank Penny Black at the Goethe Institute, London, for making the visit possible, and Durs Grünbein himself for his generosity with time and ideas. Ralf Kukula from Balance Film, Berlin, allowed *Oktoberfilm* (2009) to have its first screening outside Germany at the same event and also allowed one of the images from the film to be used as the cover of this book. The book itself has had a long gestation and I am indebted to the contributors, whose enthusiasm for the volume and forbearance have ensured it comes into being. I am also grateful to the anonymous readers who offered such thoughtful support to the proposal, to Neil Leeder for the website and help with IT, to Nick Hodgin and Emily Spiers for help with translation, to Uwe Warnke for help in sourcing images and to Linda Bree along with Maartje Scheltens and Anna Bond from Cambridge University Press for their patience and careful advice along the way.

The photograph on the cover from *Oktoberfilm*, Balance Film, Berlin (2009), is printed courtesy of Balance Film and Klaus Thiele; the photographs from the series 'Frauen im Bekleidungswerk Treffmodelle' (Women at the Treff-Modelle Clothing Factory, Berlin, 1984) and from the series 'Müllfahrer' (Dustmen, 1974) in Chapter 6 are both reprinted ©Helga Paris VG Bildkunst; in Chapter 9 the invitation to the 'Zersammlung' event using a drawing by Cornelia Schleime (1984) is printed courtesy of Uwe Warnke and the image 'Autoren im Werkstatt von Wilfried Mass' (Authors at Wilfried Mass's Studio, 1981) is reprinted ©Helga Paris VG Bildkunst; in the final chapter the photograph of the

Berlin Television Tower by Christian Rudat is printed courtesy of
Christian Rudat; the photograph 'Potsdamer Platz' by Michael Wesely is
printed courtesy of Galerie Fahnemann, Berlin.

We are grateful to the following for permission to cite poems: Suhrkamp
Verlag for permission to cite Volker Braun, 'Das Eigentum' and 'Das
Lehen' from Braun, *Lustgarten Preußen: Ausgewählte Gedichte* (Frankfurt/
M.: Suhrkamp, 1996), ©Surhrkamp Verlag GmbH and Barbara Köhler,
'Rondeau Allemagne' and from Barbara Köhler, *Deutsches Roulette.
Gedichte 1984–1989* (Frankfurt/M.: Suhrkamp, 1991), © Suhrkamp
Verlag GmbH; Kerstin Hensel for permission to cite 'Schatten Riß' from
Kerstin Hensel, *Schlaraffenzucht. Gedichte* (Frankfurt/M.: Luchterhand,
1990), ©Kerstin Hensel; Andreas Koziol for permission to quote from the
poem 'addition der differenzen', from his *mehr über rauten und türme*
(Berlin: Aufbau, 1991), ©Andreas Koziol; and Druckhaus Galrev and
Andreas Koziol for permission to cite 'Tradition der Differenzen', from
Andreas Koziol, *Sammlung* (Berlin: Edition qwertzuiopü, 1996),
©Druckhaus Galrev and Andreas Koziol. We are grateful to Uwe
Warnke, for permission to quote from 'DIALEKTIK', from Uwe
Warnke, *wortBILD. Visuelle Poesie in der DDR* (Halle/S. and Leipzig:
Mitteldeutscher Verlag, 1990), ©Uwe Warnke; and to Michael
Wüstefeld for permission to quote from 'ABWANDLUNG des
DEUTSCHEN oder HERLEITUNG eines DEUTSCHEN', from
Heinz Ludwig Arnold (ed.), *Die andere Sprache. Neue DDR-Literatur der
8oer Jahre* (Munich: edition text + kritik, 1990), ©Michael Wüstefeld.

Chronology

1945	Potsdam Conference: USA, USSR and Britain agree to demilitarize, denazify and democratize Germany. The Allies assume control over Germany and divide it into zones.
1946	Formation of 'Sozialistische Einheitspartei Deutschlands' (SED) from Communist Social-Democratic alliance. Establishment of DEFA film company in Berlin.
1948	Currency reform. Berlin divided into two different currency zones. Berlin Blockade. The United States begins the Berlin Airlift to keep Berlin supplied with food and fuel. Brecht founds the Berliner Ensemble in Berlin.
1949	7 October: Foundation of German Democratic Republic (GDR).
1950	Walter Ulbricht elected General Secretary of the SED.
1951	SED campaigns against formalism and decadence in favour of the doctrine of socialist realism.
1952	Second Party Conference of the SED. Class War urged against churches, bourgeoisie and intelligentsia.
1953	17 June: Uprising of industrial workers in Berlin against raised work norms. Suppressed by Soviet tanks.
1956	Creation of the Nationale Volksarmee (NVA – People's Army of the GDR). Soviet revelations about Stalin. Hungarian Uprising fails and leads to renewed cultural repression. Death of Bertolt Brecht.
1957	Show trial of the so-called Harich group.
1959	24 April: Initiation of industrial campaign of 'Bitterfelder Weg'.
1961	13 August: Building of Berlin Wall. Borders with the West are closed.
1963	Introduction of 'New Economic System'.
1965	Eleventh Plenum of the Central Committee of the SED clamps down on media and signs of 'dissidence'.
1968	New constitution of GDR comes into effect. The GDR army participates in Warsaw Pact intervention in Czechoslovakia.

1970   Gradual regularization of relations with the Federal
        Republic (BRD).

1971   Erich Honecker replaces Walter Ulbricht as SED leader. He gives
        his 'No Taboos' speech, initiating greater freedom for artists and
        writers.

1972   Cultural liberalization heralded by reception of Ulrich Plenzdorf's
        Die neuen Leiden des jungen W. (The New Sufferings of Young
        W.) Signing of Basic Treaty between GDR and FRG.

1976   November: 'Ausbürgerung' (expatriation) of singer/songwriter
        Wolf Biermann. Reprisals for many who support him and gradual
        exodus of many writers and artists. Consolidation of 'under-
        ground' journals in many GDR cities.

1979   'Lex Heym' and expulsions from the Writers' Union; punitive
        measures taken against dissenting intellectuals.

1981   Cultural intelligentsia from East and West begin a series of peace
        conferences 'Berliner Tagung zur Friedensforschung'.

1983   After Soviet Union has stationed SS20 missiles in the GDR
        occasioning major demonstrations in 1982, peace campaigner
        Roland Jahn is expelled.

1985   Gorbachev's accession to power in the Soviet Union. His con-
        cepts of *glasnost* and *perestroika* promise to bring new political and
        cultural liberalizations.

1987   Writers, Congress debates censorship. A rock concert held in front of
        the Reichstag building in West Berlin leads to fighting with police.

1989   August onwards: Regular demonstrations outside Nikolai
        Church in Leipzig. 7 October: GDR celebrates 40 years.
        Demonstrations suppressed. 4 November: Over 1 million
        demonstrate in East Berlin's main square, Alexanderplatz, for
        freedom of the press and free elections. 7 November: Resignation
        of Politburo. 9 November: Opening of the Berlin Wall.
        Dissolution of the Stasi. 28 November: petition 'Für unser Land'
        (For Our Country) from artists and writers. 22 December:
        Opening of the Brandenburg Gate.

1990   SED becomes PDS (Party of Democratic Socialism) under
        Gregor Gysi. 18 March: First free elections to the Volkskammer
        with the CDU, the largest party. June: Christa Wolf publishes
        Was bleibt. Beginning of the 'Literaturstreit' (literary debate).
        Treuhand Agency set up to dispose of East German industry.
        3 October: Unification of Germany. GDR joins Federal Republic
        in accordance with Article 23 of the Basic Law.

Abbreviations, references and translations

Abbreviations and terms used

Bundesrepublik Deutschland (BRD)	Federal Republic of Germany (FRG)
Deutsche Demokratische Republik (DDR)	German Democratic Republic (GDR)
Deutsche Film-Aktiengesellschaft (DEFA)	GDR Film Company
Freie Deutsche Jugend (FDJ)	Free German Youth Movement
Inoffizieller Mitarbeiter (IM)	Unofficial Collaborator working for the MfS
Ministerium für Staatssicherheit (MfS) / (Stasi)	Ministry for State Security
Nationale Volksarmee (NVA)	GDR army (National People's Army)
Neues Forum	An influential citizens' initiative founded during the *Wende*
Das Neue Ökonomische System der Planung und Leitung (NÖS or NÖSPL)	New Economic System introduced into the GDR planned economy in 1963
Operativer Vorgang (OV)	Integrated surveillance operation mounted by the MfS
Ostalgie	Nostalgia after 1990 for aspects of life in the former GDR
Partei des demokratischen Sozialismus (PDS)	Party of Democratic Socialism, the successor to the SED, later to become known as *Die Linke* (the Left Party)

Sovietische Besatzungszone (SBZ)	Soviet-Occupied Zone
Sozialistische Einheitspartei (SED)	Socialist Unity Party
Volkseigener Betrieb (VEB)	Nationalized firm in the GDR (People's Enterprise)
Die Wende	Name given to the period of change in 1989–1990

On the first mention titles are given in German with an English translation; thereafter German is used. Quotations are generally given in English unless a special linguistic point is to be made. Such translations are by the individual contributors unless otherwise attributed.

Introduction

Karen Leeder

> Das Fabeltier Sozialismus
> Beißt sich selbst in den Schwanz und verschlingt sich
>
> (The fabled beast socialism
> Bites its own tail and swallows itself)[1]

On 18 March 1990, the day when the Volkskammer elections put an end to hopes of a reformed socialism in an independent German state, Stefan Heym famously claimed, 'There will be no more GDR. It will be nothing more than a footnote in world history.'[2] That prognosis might seem to have been refuted by the sheer volume of literature, film and analysis that continues to be devoted to exploring or reimagining the East German state. As Timothy Garton Ash commented,

> Yet, if the GDR has indeed become a footnote, it is without doubt the longest, best documented and most interesting footnote in world history. No dictatorship in history – not even the Third Reich – has been so rapidly, comprehensively and scrupulously documented and analyzed.[3]

When Garton Ash made these remarks in November 2009, two decades after the spectacular implosion of the socialist state, the controversy showed no signs of abating. Indeed the anniversary was the spur for a widespread stocktaking both in Germany and the wider world, revealing that an absolute majority of former East Germans felt that life had been better under communism. But that was not the only story. Garton Ash's comparison with the Third Reich is instructive. At one extreme was the former GDR remembered as 'Stasiland', that is, Anna Funder's memorable label for a country remembered through its repressive security network.[4] And this image has perhaps come to dominate in popular culture since 1990. At the other end of the spectrum, however, was the particular brand of nostalgia for the securities of the former Eastern bloc that had brought a new word to the German language: 'Ostalgie'. This dichotomy goes to the heart of the debate, for the two visions of the GDR do not exist in isolation, but are, in Peter Thompson's phrase, the 'conjoined twins of really existing socialism'.[5] This is important since the work of remembering and reinterpreting the GDR is also part of a larger task: that of coming to terms with the possibilities and catastrophes of utopian thinking writ large, and ultimately of the enlightenment project. David Bathrick was one of the first to identify the profound, if conflicted, critical investment in the project of GDR socialism that remained even after the state itself had disappeared.

> Thus, despite their basically critical view of repressive Stalinist state socialism, many critical leftists – and here we must speak of East and West German intellectuals – never overcame a strangely libidinal attachment to the GDR as a potential purveyor of a post-capitalist alternative, as a preservation reserve for the idea of a noncapitalist utopia.[6]

But there is also the diametrically opposed tendency, identified most memorably by Hans Mayer in his *Der Turm von Babel*, to evaluate the literature and history of the GDR solely in the light of its demise: 'all's bad that ends bad'.[7]

This raises a broader question that has troubled many commentators: how does one judge the products of the socialist state? They were at once sponsored by the utopian dream that inspired it, but also marked by the crippling reality of what it became. What is more, it is undoubtedly the case that for many years critical judgements in East and West were skewed more to political or moral considerations than aesthetic ones. Whatever the rights and wrongs of the so called 'German literary debate' of 1990 (see the chapter by Carol Anne Costabile-Heming in this volume), it revealed the extent to which GDR literature had been stymied by its need to act as an alternative to the public political realm. Few would go as far as Grünbein, in referring to his early work, written before unification, as 'poetry from the bad side'.[8] And yet it is clear that a radical re-reading of the GDR is necessary in order to feel one's way between the many political interests and prejudices. But it is also important to remember that this is not simply an academic debate. It is linked with the way a whole nation remembers and comes to terms with its own past. It is not easy to weigh the value of the culture of an unjust state (*Unrechtsstaat*) that was indissolubly indexed to a future that did not arrive. Equally, 'the question as to whether the German Democratic Republic was an "unjust state" is a question for historians. For the individual there was the everyday [den Alltag], that little eternity'.[9]

The fierce rejection of GDR culture in the aftermath of German unification (writers likened it to a state being dumped into a skip or put through the shredder) is only one story, however. There has also been a concerted attempt to recuperate and memorialize that culture, too, almost to the point of what has been called a musealization of the GDR. In the Berlin Republic the GDR is commemorated – one might say fetishized – in the Trabi tours, the Ostel design hotels, websites for GDR goods or the many GDR museums that boast an authentic experience of genuine GDR artefacts. But the fixation on a plethora of memory icons simultaneously raises two further aspects that go to the heart of how we remember: the extent to which our memory of the GDR is being constructed or simulated and how far it is also being commodified. These in turn feed into the broader memory contests of recent years.

Yet despite the sometimes overwhelming amount of information, there is also the possibility that the GDR reality will become impossibly remote, an indelibly lost country, the 'fabulous beast' of Grünbein's libretto to *Oktoberfilm*, that supplies a motto for this Introduction and an image for the cover of this volume. Stephen Brockmann, among others, has pointed out how distant to a contemporary reader the GDR and its culture can seem, that is, as if one is looking at it through the wrong end of telescope.[10] Moreover, it has also acquired the aura of myth or fairy tale. 'It has to be called Atlantis', says Hinrich Lobek, the protagonist of Jens Sparschuh's 1995 novel *Der Zimmerspringbrunnen* (The Indoor Fountain), after he has invented a kitsch fountain with a map of the former GDR and a model of East Berlin's television tower.[11] And Uwe Tellkamp's *Der Turm* (The Tower, 2008) describes the GDR as a socialist Atlantis, a mythical island state that operated by different rules and even used a different time system: 'the invisible realm behind the visible one, [. . .] ATLANTIS: The Second Reality'.[12] These things need not be mutually exclusive. The two visions of the GDR suggest an ambivalent even 'spectral' apprehension. It was, after all, a state founded on the spectre of communism; in its ideal form it existed as a spectre informing an inadequate reality; and it now haunts contemporary capitalism as unrealized aspiration, trauma or travesty.

Brockmann puts it thus: 'Now [. . .] that the socialist Atlantis has long since sunk under the waves, it has precisely the quality of a legend, something unreal that may or may not have really existed.'[13] Of course this is only a metaphor. The existence of the GDR is of no doubt to the many victims of its repressive reality. But it is a provocative formulation. In the same piece of 2009, Garton Ash also warned that East Germany might disappear: eclipsed within larger historical trajectories.

> The history of East Germany increasingly looks like one of those neglected
> country roads that used once to be a main highway, but is now a slightly

mysterious detour running more or less parallel to the motorway. More
particularly, it seems like an extended episode in the epoch that the historian
Tony Judt has described with the single word 'Postwar'.[14]

That possibility is even more acute today. Tackling the great paradox of
late capitalism's cultural amnesia, on the one hand, and the ubiquitous
'memory boom', on the other, Andreas Huyssen, both in *Twilight
Memories* (1995) and *Present Pasts* (2003), highlights the vital role of
memory:

> Memory and musealization are together are called upon to provide a bulwark
> against obsolescence and disappearance, to counter our deep anxiety about
> the speed of change and the ever shrinking horizons of time and space.[15]

And answering that call is the aim of this volume.

The culture of the 'other' Germany, that is, the German Democratic
Republic or East Germany, has long held a peculiar fascination for those
interested in Germany today. It is not simply that many authors considered
to be of world stature emerged from, or are identified with, it: from Bertolt
Brecht to his radical successor Heiner Müller, the novelists Stefan Heym and
Christa Wolf, and the poets Volker Braun and Durs Grünbein. Certainly a
number of works that would stand in any pantheon of twentieth-century
literature owe their genesis to the particular struggle between 'Geist' and
'Macht' (spirit and power) that characterized cultural production there.
However, the GDR also fascinates because it offers a case study in the way
literature, film and culture responded to the challenges of an authoritarian
regime, so often staking out the territories beyond what was permitted and,
to borrow a phrase from Wolf, 'stretching the boundaries of the sayable'.

This does not mean, though, that all GDR literature is only of historical
value, trading on what might be called its 'dissident bonus'. Nor does it
necessarily mean that all of it stands up to scrutiny today, freed from its
particular context. Rather, under the pressure of censorship, writers and
film-makers developed innovative strategies that negotiated between complicity, dissidence and autonomy. Works of prose, poetry, drama and film
of extraordinary intensity and invention were created that bear repeated
scrutiny for what they can tell us about the processes of literature itself. It is
significant, for example, that an alternative vision for a future German
culture emerged out of the ruins of the Second World War; that some of
the finest women's writing of the 1980s owed its existence to the cultural
climate of East Germany; that socialist writers were in the vanguard of the
subjective turn and the development of a sophisticated and self-
reflexive body of autobiography; that, in that most polluted of European

territories, literature was at the heart of ecological initiatives; or that the samizdat scene pioneered experimental collaborations between artists, writers, musicians and film-makers that are still admired today.

Ironically (or inevitably, perhaps), the great boom in GDR Studies has come after the GDR has ceased to exist. The contemporary literature and film, which engages with the existence of that state, and the disappointed hopes which sustained it, plays a central role in the extraordinarily rich output of the Berlin Republic today. And it is striking that many of the most important German cultural exports of recent years have been films documenting the socialist state or the processes of coming to terms with its loss: Wolfgang Becker's *Goodbye, Lenin!*, for example, or Florian Henckel von Donnersmark's *The Lives of Others*.

Astonishingly no single volume has been published in English that attempts to come to terms with the GDR as a cultural phenomenon. Today, some twenty-five years after the fall of the Berlin Wall, that absence is even more striking. The aim of this volume is, then, both to grasp the history and context of GDR literature and film as a particular historical entity but also to trace its repercussions in the period since its demise. The perspective gained from a contemporary vantage point allows research to take account of the important revisions and reflections on that legacy since 1989, but also to explore phenomena like *Ostalgie*, the retro-chic rebranding that has allowed GDR design items to become icons of high fashion; the emergence of Berlin as the cultural capital of Europe; and the fascination with the German Stasi, or secret police. It allows an insight into the various approaches which researchers have taken to this most contested legacy, from a generational schema to postcolonial models or the increasingly important paradigms of memory: cultural memory (Jan and Aleida Assmann), postmemory (Marianne Hirsch) or prosthetic memory (Alison Landsberg).

Fresh, often critical, readings of many of the major GDR authors who continue to be widely read today – from Brecht or Wolf to Müller and Braun – are integrated with critical overviews of the development of the different genres (film, poetry, drama, prose). But in addition the volume sets out to present a chronological overview of the development of the GDR: from the beginnings out of the rubble of the Second World War to the radical dissolution of the late 1980s. Within that broader arc, individual chapters home in on key debates (the so-called 'formalism debate' of the early years or the post-*Wende* 'German literary debate') or historical flashpoints – the *Aufbau* years, the liberalizations of the Honecker era, the expatriation of Wolf

Biermann in 1976 and the *Wende* itself – and situate them in their literary and political context. Finally, key contextual information is offered in chapters on autobiography, gender, satire, cultural opposition, the underground and the Stasi, together, attempting to carve out what is the distinctive contribution of GDR authors and film-makers to the larger sense of German literature today. The volume is rounded off by a view from 2015 – twenty-five years after the fall of the socialist state – that examines the afterlife of the GDR in the Berlin Republic. Cumulatively, it is hoped, that these chapters allow a new reading of the cultural legacy of the GDR, but also of the way it is has been read in the past and the way it is remembered today.

Notes

1. Durs Grünbein, libretto, *Oktoberfilm: Dresden 1989*, dir. Ralf Kukula (Balance film GmbH, 2009).
2. Hannes Bahrmann, Christoph Links, *Chronik der Wende: Stationen der Einheit. Die letzten Monate der DDR* (Berlin: Links, 1995), p. 174.
3. Timothy Garton Ash, 'Preface', in Karen Leeder (ed.), *From Stasiland to Ostalgie: The GDR – Twenty Years After*, Oxford German Studies, 38.3 (November 2009), 234–35, p. 234.
4. Anna Funder, *Stasiland. Stories from behind the Berlin Wall* (London: Granta, 2003).
5. Peter Thompson, 'Die Unheimliche Heimat', in Karen Leeder (ed.), *From Stasiland to Ostalgie*, 278–87, p. 283.
6. David Bathrick, 'Crossing Borders: the End of the Cold War Intellectual', *German Politics and Society* (Fall 1992), 77–87, p. 84.
7. Hans Mayer, *Der Turm von Babel: Erinnerung an eine Deutsche Demokratische Republik* (Frankfurt/M.: Suhrkamp, 1991), p. 17.
8. Thomas Naumann and Durs Grünbein, 'Durs Grünbein. "Poetry from the Bad Side". Ein Gespräch', *Sprache im technischen Zeitalter*, 30.124 (1990), 442–49.
9. Grünbein, libretto, *Oktoberfilm*.
10. Stephen Brockman, 'Remembering GDR Culture in Postunification Germany and Beyond', in Renate Rechtien and Dennis Tate (eds.), *Twenty Years On: Competing Memories of the GDR in Postunification Culture*, (Rochester, NY: Camden House, 2011), pp. 39–54.
11. Jens Sparschuh, *Der Zimmerspringbrunnen* (Cologne: Kiepenheuer & Witsch 1995), p. 24.
12. Uwe Tellkamp, *Der Turm: Geschichten aus einem versunkenen Land* (Frankfurt/M.: Suhrkamp, 2008), p. 9; *The Tower: Tales from a Lost Country*, trans. Mike Mitchell (London: Penguin, 2014), p. xiii.

13. Brockman, 'Remembering GDR Culture in Postunification Germany and Beyond', p. 40.
14. Garton Ash, 'Preface', p. 234.
15. Andreas Huyssen, *Twilight Memories: Marking Time in a Culture of Amnesia* (New York and London: Routledge, 1995) and Andreas Huyssen, 'Present Pasts: Media, Politics, Amnesia', in *Public Culture*, 12.1 (2000): 21–38, p. 23, also reprinted in his *Present Pasts: Urban Palimpsests and the Politics of Memory* (Stanford, CA: Stanford University Press, 2003).

CHAPTER I

The GDR and its literature
An overview

Wolfgang Emmerich

Twenty-five years on: a feeling of closeness

The ruling party of the GDR, the Socialist Unity Party (SED), decreed that the socialist state was always to be referred to in full as the German Democratic Republic. The three-letter abbreviation was almost taboo. This fact alone gives an indication of the strict demands governing this remarkable state that existed for some forty years. The GDR authorities sought to persuade people that the future belonged to their state alone, the only state on German soil which was based on true democratic and republican foundations, and that as such it would be a model for all Germans; West Germany, moreover, or the Bundesrepublik Deutschland (Federal Republic, FRG) as it was derogatively called, would follow suit sooner or later. History turned out otherwise; the GDR submitted, peacefully and without coercion, to the *Grundgesetz* (Basic Law), which had been the Federal Republic's constitution since 1949 – something that was unprecedented in world history.

More than twenty-five years have passed since that day. The GDR and the everyday life lived there is now as far in the past as the National Socialist regime was in 1965 or the end of the First World War was at the beginning of the Second World War in 1939. However, the distance to the epochal year of 1990 *feels* decidedly shorter: surely it was only yesterday that people danced on the Wall and 10,000 GDR Trabbis suddenly congested West German city centres? In fact, all the events that we have come to call the *Wende* happened more than twenty-five years ago and have already become history. Despite any 'feeling of closeness',[1] the GDR is now clearly recognizable as the crystallization of political and sociocultural developments, which from start to finish were governed by the global constellation that emerged out of the Cold War and competition between political systems.

Translated by Nick Hodgin

While the GDR was still in existence and West Germans were closely bound up with it through family and other relationships, this fact was much harder to identify. It is much more readily apparent today.

GDR chronotope

What are the distinctive characteristics of the GDR? One way of approaching this question, and it is the one I shall adopt here, is to employ Mikhail Bakhtin's key literary theoretical concept, the chronotope, as a tool for broader cultural analysis. For Bakhtin the notion of the chronotope, which he set out as early as 1937–38, is a significant category in the analysis of narrative prose.[2] Of central importance is the 'internal chronotope', that is, the 'time-space of their [the characters'] represented life' in the novel.[3] But Bakhtin is interested, too, in the 'exterior real-life chronotope',[4] from which the literary portrayal derives and in which it operates in the public sphere. Broadly speaking, it is the 'epoch-specific time-space structure of human world perception'.[5] My aim is twofold: first I wish to expand on Bakhtin's central concept in order to imagine the notions of (geographical) space and (historical) time, along with their respective social and cultural conditions, as far as possible as mutually interconnected. Second, I wish to apply this expanded concept of the chronotope to the specific political and social structure which lasted more than forty years and which we call the GDR, and to consider this closely intertwined realm of 'time-space' and its specific organizational structures as a basic premise of the GDR and also of GDR literature. This way of approaching the GDR chimes with the insights suggested by what has become known as the 'spatial turn' in culture more generally.[6] But what exactly does it entail?

1. The GDR was a coherent territory for over forty years, though it had an island at its centre – West Berlin – which naturally functioned as a constant disruption within the chronotope GDR.
2. The GDR was ethnically homogenous, being a Germanic-North German settlement area that was temporarily and partially settled by Slavs (a tiny Slavic minority continued to live there). The GDR territory stretched across two former states, Prussia and Saxony. This marks a regional, though not ethnic, distinction that could be acrimonious, though it was never critical during the GDR.
3. The GDR was religiously homogenous. In 1949, 90 per cent of the population was Lutheran Protestant. Catholics unquestionably constituted the diaspora. The consequence was what Max Weber called a

'protestant ethic of achievement', which in the end was also a significant factor for East German writers' self-understanding.

4. Despite some changes in policy and some attempts at reform and
    restoration, the GDR had the same political administration and the
    same socialist state-organized economy for over forty years. The struc-
    ture was hierarchical and subject to manifold control. Autonomous
    action in any area of society's value system (that is the hallmark of a
    genuinely modern society, according to Weber) was the exception
    rather than the rule in the GDR. Moreover, things were identical in
    the cultural sphere. To borrow terms from sociology, the GDR was a
    land of 'blocked', 'braked', 'partial' or 'halfway' modernization.[7]

5. The GDR's sociocultural and political traditions were not homoge-
    nous, but they nevertheless made a deep impression on the state. Along
    with the industrial heartland of West Germany, the Ruhrgebiet,
    Saxony was (with parts of Thüringia and Sachsen-Anhalt) the modern
    German industrial region par excellence, as well as one of the oldest
    centres of the workers' movement and the state where the SPD had
    once won its first seats in the German parliament. These regions
    (including Berlin), which had once been red, became brown during
    the Nazi period and then red again after 1945.

6. Last but not least, the GDR literary system was based on a state-
    sponsored notion of all-encompassing homogeneity. This was already
    evident in the legal and economic structures. There were no private
    publishers, and book publishing, both wholesale and retail, was con-
    trolled by the state. In particular, the SED's cultural and political
    education programmes, and the closely allied doctrine of socialist
    realism, were intended to ensure homogeneity in literature, which
    was certainly the case for the first twenty years in the GDR.

So, to summarize the GDR's characteristics: it was a coherent territory,
homogenous both in its ethnicity and religious orientation, always 'half
modern' in its political and economic structure, politically and sociocultu-
rally unambiguous and, last but not least, with a strictly homogenized
literary field at its core. Of course these fundamental characteristics are
only sketched out here. Nevertheless they all point towards a single conclusion: the GDR as a place remained structurally unchanged for a long period
of time. A further factor was the faltering increase in population size and its
eventual shrinkage. The population shrank decisively until 1961 as a result of
'Republikflucht' (flight from the Republic), which was largely the flight of
the educated elite – a fact that in turn resulted in the further homogenization

of the remaining population. From 1961 to 1989 the GDR population lived within sealed borders. In addition to the basic tendency towards homogenization of ethnicity, religion, political and economic structures and political traditions, there was a gradual assimilation of the diverse social groups which even transcended generations. Furthermore, there were few foreigners in the GDR. Those that did live there (Red Army soldiers, for example) or who were invited there (students, political asylum seekers from South Africa or Chile and later guest workers mainly from Vietnam and Mozambique) were generally kept apart from the East German population. Miscegenation was not encouraged and was for the most part uncommon.

One conclusion we can draw from these facts is that just as the term 'GDR' is a useful analytical category in historiographical terms, so is the term 'GDR literature' in literary historiography. It is most easily comparable with terms that define a particular period, such as 'the literature of the Weimar Republic', 'National Socialist literature' and 'the literature of the Federal Republic'. These connect a body of literature with a specific historically or politically defined period of time (in this case the forty years of the GDR, from 1949 to 1990), but simultaneously also refer to a specific geographical territory of the nation-state, as is the case with similar concepts such as Austrian or Swiss literature. All of these terms have a chronotopic aspect, in the sense that I have already outlined, since they draw together historical periods and their political systems with territories and their traditions. Such concepts do not, however, have any bearing on the aesthetic styles associated with such periods, and the same is true of such accounts of GDR literature.

The recurring controversies about the concept of a body of GDR literature (which are as old as the GDR itself) also demonstrate that, beyond the objective approach of the chronotope, any definition is determined by the particular standpoint of the observer and represents a theoretical construct. Since the beginning of the 1950s there has been a conflict between the concept of two (or more) German literatures, which includes GDR literature and the notion of a single, unified German literature that transcends states and the boundaries of political systems. Such polarization was, and continues to be, rooted in two different understandings of the relationship between art and society: one emphasizes the close, even causal, links between them; the other views art as entirely separate from society. It was political interests that initially determined which position was taken. In the 1950s, both conservative West German literary criticism and official GDR cultural policy claimed that there was only one German literature. The former automatically assumed socialist literature to be inferior and excluded it from their very traditional canon. Despite the existence of two states, SED

ideologues adhered – until at least 1956 – to the officially decreed 'unity of
the nation' in principle and this also extended to their concept of a single
literature. After the Berlin Wall was built in 1961, however, official GDR
literary criticism routinely spoke of the development of an independent
'socialist national literature', the founding principle of which was the 'revolutionary shift from capitalism to socialism and the establishment of a
socialist society'. Its style of writing was 'realistic, a method of representation
that facilitated and demanded revolutionary change'.[8] Exemplary propo-
nents of this method included Johannes R. Becher, Bertolt Brecht, Anna
Seghers, Erwin Strittmatter and Johannes Bobrowski. Other aesthetic
approaches were not countenanced. The GDR's socialist realist literature
was aggressively positioned against the literature of the Federal Republic,
which was seen as 'riven by class contradictions'.[9]

West German and other foreign literary criticism which only belatedly
acknowledged GDR literature in around 1970 provided diverse reasons for
and against the existence of a separate GDR literature and, in so doing,
acknowledged divergences and convergences in German-language literature
since 1945. Critical opinion followed the lead of the Leipzig-based literary
scholar Hans Mayer, whose pioneering essay (based on a series of lectures
given in 1963) pointed to the very different traditions and organizational
structures in East and West German literature. Above all, he emphasized the
enormous divergences in authors' biographies: 'The inner unity of this
[GDR] literature, of today's Writers' Union and its objectives, would be
impossible to imagine without the homogeneity of the political and literary
biographies of those concerned.'[10]

His comment refers to the fact that nearly all older East German authors
came from a communist background and that most of the younger authors
happily adopted their older colleagues' emphatic worldview. It was Jürgen
Link, above all, who developed Mayer's theory when he suggested in 1980
that a distinct lifestyle and cultural identity had already evolved in the 1950s
as a result of the GDR's socialist *Aufbau* (construction) programme. This
'cultural discontinuity', or disculturality (*Diskulturalität*), as he termed it,
between East and West Germany gave rise to bodies of literature fundamentally at odds with one another: a perspective which tallies with the
thesis outlined here of different chronotopes – of East and West Germany,
respectively.[11] Link also noted a corresponding and GDR-specific recourse
to pre-modern modes of expression.

But the period from the 1970s onwards also saw a noticeable and
increasing thematic and aesthetic rapprochement between West and East
German literature, marked by a 'Zivilisationskritik', or critique of existing

civilization. This transcended ideological systems, and made of the GDR an 'accessible other'[12] for those in the west. What is more it undoubtedly went some way to relativizing any actual cultural discontinuity.

All sense of clarity in the literary landscape was lost after Wolf Biermann's expatriation in 1976, following which more than a hundred writers, including some of the most prominent, left the GDR. By 1977, Fritz J. Raddatz was already talking of 'the second German exile literature',[13] and later, in 1987, even more confusingly, of 'a third German literature' – a term he used to describe the supposedly homogenous group of migrant authors whose work was realistic and socially critical.[14]

The controversies surrounding the question, 'how many German literatures?' continued after the *Wende*. In 1995, for example, Ursula Heukenkamp argued for the distinctive character of GDR literature, maintaining:

> The particular relationship with the state, entered into by the majority of authors with a mixture of reluctance, anguish and solidarity is indeed one of the singular features which developed in the GDR [. . .] Bonds were forged and maintained which were doubtless important to many authors: a sense of common cause into which readers were also drawn or allowed themselves to be drawn.[15]

In that same year Rainer Rosenberg came to quite the opposite conclusion, claiming, with little substantiation, that GDR literature would 'hardly be dealt with as an independent German-language literature [. . .] in the future', once the state's borders had disappeared.[16] Such an apodictic conclusion may seem surprising; the GDR, and its literature, does not after all automatically change simply because the state itself has ceased to exist. If it did, the same would also be true, for example, of the three literatures between 1933 and 1945.

There is, then, an irrefutable contradiction: on the one hand, for four decades the GDR was a time-space with reasonably homogenous structural characteristics. On the other hand, this homogenous chronotope of GDR socialism produced or provoked clearly defined political and aesthetic positions, which over time drifted apart and were located somewhere between the opposing poles of affirmation and subversion, although their reference point – that is, the GDR – always remained apparent.

The antifascist foundation myth and the 'workerly' society

A number of important structural differences between the Federal Republic and the GDR have been established, but there are several more that need to be considered.

The implantation of foundation myths in the GDR, which established the GDR as the diametric opposite of the new West German
state, was a decisive factor in the sociocultural homogenization of
the GDR.

It is widely accepted that (unlike any reasonably serious historiography)
the narratives that make up a foundation myth do not deal with 'the events
themselves, but rather with their significance for the course of history'.[17]
Foundation myths always emerge after wars, revolutions or other radical
transitions, when new rulers need to establish, justify or indeed 'found'
their existence – but they are also necessary when a nation or a community
is fatally damaged or has incurred a heavy burden of guilt and finds itself in
a crisis of moral legitimization.

Precisely these characteristics apply to the situation in East Germany
after 8 May 1945. In the Soviet Zone (SBZ), the ruling Communist Party,
the KPD (which merged with the SPD to become the SED in 1946), began
to promote two political myths. These became the literal foundation myths
in October 1949. These myths were, quite simply, 'antifascism' and 'socialism'. Of particular significance here is what Herfried Münkler has
appositely called the *Ansippung* (genealogical appropriation) of the newly
founded GDR state to the antifascist resistance.[18] Just as a family member
may search for a significant, morally respectable relative or ancestor either
within or outside the family as a role model, who may enhance his or her
reputation, or rather, who may increase his or her symbolic capital, so the
GDR sought out a 'godfather' in the antifascist (mainly communist)
resistance in order to confer on the new state a moral authenticity and
meaningful future prospects that might help it overcome the lowest point
of German history during the National Socialist regime and the Second
World War.[19] That resistance to the Nazi regime was hardly the norm and
in truth represented only a small minority was deliberately brushed aside.
Indeed, this founding myth constituted itself only by insisting that the
people had never really been Nazis at all. The mythical distortion of history
even went so far as to suggest that any remaining Nazis were in the Federal
Republic, while the whole GDR population were now 'Sieger der
Geschichte' ('history's victors'). Stephan Hermlin suggested (in 1979)
that 'this formula'

> immediately spread like ripples in still water, into which one has thrown a
> stone, with each GDR citizen now personally able to feel him – or herself to
> be the 'victor of history'. Flattering and exonerating the people in this way
> made it easier to govern. In the long term it is more difficult to govern a

people who feel guilty in some way. This formula also endowed the GDR with a certain authority.[20]

The founding myth of antifascism fraudulently obtained by means of the selective adoption of desirable traditions served, on the one hand, as an instrument of political power. On the other hand, it also 'effected a comprehensive cleansing of the GDR population's collective memory, unburdening many people of feelings of guilt and was for that reason a myth that was willingly adopted'.[21] The antifascist foundation myth thus served a dual function: as a national doctrine which would last for forty years *and* as a reassuring delusion, in that the majority of the citizens of the SBZ and later the GDR had no more been antifascists than the West Germans.

Closely entwined with this first foundation myth is the second myth, namely socialism. The SED characterized the capitalist west as the refuge of exploitation, repression, imperialist war-mongering and the 'new' fascists. The *Aufbau* or 'building' of a socialist (and later communist) society, following an interim stage of 'antifascist democratic new order', would be the only acceptable historical and ideological answer to the recently defeated National Socialism and subsequent capitalism. The watchwords 'Antifascism', 'Democratic New Order' and 'Socialist *Aufbau*' became intrinsic to the GDR's essential, quasi-mythical interpretive framework and pattern of ideological self-justification. Like antifascism, socialism was accepted without reservation by young people because it presented the absolute opposite of 'fascism' and implied a new beginning. National Socialism, which communists had a tendency to personalize by calling it 'Hitler-Fascism', was the ultimate evil. Antifascism, and socialism along with it, thus came to represent the ultimate in humanity and goodness per se and, what is more, introduced a new doctrine of salvation, following the collapse of the National Socialist agenda. However, at the same time, the twofold founding myth of the GDR, with its associated moral weight, proved to be a 'loyalty trap'.[22] Once caught up in it, it proved difficult to escape. Notwithstanding any criticisms or grievances one might wish to level against those in power, it was almost unimaginable to distance oneself from the union of antifascists (i.e., the unimpeachably good) and change sides. These structures created powerful and deeply rooted bonds that lasted until the *Wende* and indeed beyond, as is evident in the East Berlin appeal 'Für unser Land' (For Our Country). On 28 November 1989, only weeks after the opening of the Wall, activists called for the GDR to continue and to 'develop a socialist alternative to the Federal Republic' because, as they suggested, 'we are still conscious of the antifascist and humanitarian ideals with which we first began'.[23] Among the first signatories of this appeal were the writers Stefan Heym, Christa Wolf and Volker Braun, and also civil-rights activists like Ulrike Poppe, Friedrich Schorlemmer and Konrad Weiß. When, not long after, high-ranking SED functionaries like Egon Krenz and Hans Modrow added their voices to the appeal, the loyalty trap snapped shut for one last painful time.[24]

So a specific 'cultural memory', passed from one generation to the next, developed over the course of several decades. This memory differed significantly from that in the west with regard to central aspects of the Nazi dictatorship. While the concentration camp at Auschwitz (as a main site of the Holocaust) had since the mid-1960s become for the west a historical sign (*Geschichtszeichen*) in the Kantian sense, a 'signum rememorativum, demonstrativum, prognosticon',[25] the SED successfully set about instilling the concentration camp at Buchenwald in the minds of numerous generations of GDR citizens as the symbolic site of a supposedly successful proletarian communist resistance. It was at Buchenwald that many German and foreign communists in particular were interred. The communists' conduct, talent for organization and especially their attempt at insurrection shortly before the camp's liberation became the embodiment of a brand of heroic antifascism, to which all young GDR citizens in their enrolment in the Thälmann pioneers and the dedication ceremony, or 'Jugendweihe', were obliged to swear allegiance – especially after the publication of Bruno Apitz's *Nackt unter Wölfen* (Naked among Wolves), in 1958, which sold more than 600,000 copies within two years. The Holocaust was not denied in the GDR but it was marginalized by a wholly different view of fascism. It had only a peripheral role in public discourse and in cultural memory as was evident, not least, in literature.[26] Simply put, *Buchenwald replaced Auschwitz in the cultural memory of the GDR*.

The development and propagandistic nurturing of what Wolfgang Engler has rightly termed the 'workerly society'[27] is a further characteristic of the GDR chronotope. The GDR was from start to finish a society with a pronounced focus on work. For all the political slogans to the contrary, the working class was never the ruling class; but 'work' was nevertheless always highly valued and, what is more, across all GDR milieus. In a survey in 2000 only 34.7 per cent of West Germans identified work as an important area of their lives; family, friends and leisure time were their top priorities. By contrast 60.8 per cent of East Germans rated work as important (though likewise after family).[28]

This can certainly be explained by the fact that the SED promoted 'the ideology of labour', which, as part of the prescribed cultural memory, was an essential feature of 'really existing socialism'. But it was not ideology alone. Over the forty years of the GDR's existence a pattern emerged in which the 'myth of the working class [converged] with the dominant proletarian and petty bourgeois materialist culture of everyday life' to become what Engler calls the 'workerly society'. This resulted in a corresponding habitus (in Pierre Bourdieu's terms, those pre-existing social pressures and norms that we have unconsciously internalized and translated almost automatically into forms of behaviour and action), which became deeply ingrained in all sectors and classes in the GDR and was characteristic for the forty years of its existence.[29] The *Wende* and subsequent developments profoundly shook this habitus but it did not disappear altogether. Between 1990 and 2000, the number of those in work in East Germany fell by 48 per cent – that is, almost half of the workforce lost their jobs (today the number is still high). They experienced the devaluation of their professional skills, and to cite Pierre Bourdieu, their cultural and symbolic capital, but they also lost their social capital since the East Germans' social networks were far more connected with the workplace than they were in the old Federal Republic.[30]

If one takes all of the homogenizing factors in the GDR's sociocultural sphere into account, it is evident that, despite the problems and system fatigue which were taken up in the various citizens' initiatives from the mid-1970s on, the GDR enjoyed a remarkable period of solidity and continuity which lasted for more than forty years. This continuity existed not only at the level of the state but constituted a particular way of life and everyday environment for GDR citizens and, last but not least, a deeply rooted 'memory culture'. The mutual interpenetration of spatial and temporal determinants relating to everyday life and culture in the GDR is thus both enduring and far-reaching. And it is this collection of homogenizing characteristics that constitutes the striking distinctiveness of GDR literature as a body over and above the many underlying differences. All memory, as Maurice Halbwachs has noted, belongs to a place, and together the various places amount to something like a topography of memory. This is why Halbwachs says that the place

> a group occupies is not like a blackboard, where one may write and erase figures at will. [. . .] Place and group have each received the imprint of the

other. Therefore every phase of the group can be translated into spatial
terms, and its residence is but the juncture of all these terms.[31]

Applying Halbwachs's understanding of the close connection between
individual or collective memory and place, or rather space, we can see how
different GDR literature is in the uniqueness of its settings (internal
chronotopes in Bakhtin's sense) to West German literature, and the extent
to which this constitutes its distinctiveness. Certainly in the first twenty
years, the world of work, especially the industrial sectors, are frequent and
typical settings and sites of memory in GDR literature: from early production novels and plays to Bitterfelder Weg and works by Uwe Johnson,
Christa Wolf, Irmtraud Morgner or Angela Krauß (and even a later writer
like Antje Rávic Strubel). Places of agricultural production appear in works
by Peter Hacks, Heiner Müller and Erwin Strittmatter, among others. In
addition, there are, beyond the sphere of immediate production, those sites
of the GDR *Alltag*, or everyday life, to be found in works by Günter de
Bruyn, Christa Wolf, Ulrich Plenzdorf and many others. With regard to
the first category – the world of work – there are examples that could not be
found anywhere but in the GDR: three texts, for example, are devoted to
the construction of ring kilns for brick firing (by Eduard Claudius, Bertolt
Brecht and Heiner Müller); numerous texts treat large building projects
and brown coal mining (Erik Neutsch, Heiner Müller, B. K. Tragelehn,
Brigitte Reimann and Volker Braun); other texts are set in specific places
such as the Wismut uranium mines (which are the setting in Werner
Bräunig's novel *Rummelplatz* (Fairground), Konrad Wolf's film
Sonnensucher (Sunseeker) and in Lutz Seiler's post-*Wende* volume of
poems *pech & blende* (pitch & blende).

Certain historical sites were also prominent settings: the most important
are sites of antifascist resistance (Anna Seghers and Stephan Hermlin, though
Apitz's *Nackt unter Wölfen* remains *the* canonical text); and sites of the
Second World War that are made to conform to the GDR historical
perspective (Karl Mundstock, Harry Thürk, Franz Fühmann, Max Walter
Schulz and Dieter Noll, among others). Others set out early GDR history
(Anna Seghers, Max Walter Schulz and Dieter Noll). Hermann Kant's *Die
Aula* (The Auditorium) is representative of a number of works about
'Arbeiter-und Bauern Fakultäten' (worker and peasant universities); Uwe
Johnson's *Jahrestage* (Anniversaries), from the end of the second volume,
portrays space and time in the early GDR more vividly than any other book.

The internal chronotopes of GDR literature undoubtedly became more
differentiated in the final two decades of the state's existence. They became

more individual and sometimes consciously abandoned the GDR alto-gether, seeking out instead distant historical and mythical sites. Some texts, novels especially, portray chronotopes far removed from one another in a montage form as in Irmtraud Morgner's *Leben und Abenteuer der Trobadora Beatriz nach Zeugnissen ihrer Spielfrau Laura* (The Life and Adventures of Trobadora Beatrice as Chronicled by Her Minstrel Laura) and in novels by Fritz Rudolf Fries or Hans Joachim Schädlich. The GDR as a site of repression, for example, in the NVA (GDR army), spying and censorship were increasingly thematized in the period leading up to the state's collapse. And fifteen years after the end of the GDR, Uwe Tellkamp's *Der Turm* (The Tower) invokes a singular chronotope, the closed-off, educated middle-class milieu of Dresden's villa district, known as Weißer Hirsch, a single homogenous cultural space within the grand chronotope GDR.[32] That, too, was 'a place in time, at a particular time, neither before nor after', to borrow Ruth Klüger's terms.[33] The novel also confirms that in their themes and writing practice, both loyal and critical, even dissident, authors are unmistakeably GDR oriented – from Hermlin, Hacks, Müller und Wolf, or the whole 'Sächsische Dichterschule' (Saxon School of Poets), Wolf Biermann, Volker Braun and Wolfgang Hilbig, to Reinhard Jirgl, Jürgen Fuchs and Bert Papenfuß-Gorek.[34] Equally it would be impossible to imagine texts by writers like Martin Walser, Hans Magnus Enzensberger, Botho Strauß, Brigitte Kronauer or Martin Mosebach being included in a list like this. Different though they are, and along with many others, they can be identified with the West German chronotope.

Changes in the timeline: generations

As already established, the GDR literary system was intended to be structurally and ideologically homogenous from the start. The SED's cultural political education programme and the dogma of socialist realism provided the guidelines. Writers were expected to write in a way that was popular (*volkstümlich*), accessible, optimistic and 'activist in social terms'.[35] The same condition existed for membership of the Writers' Union and was thus the legal prerequisite for being active as a writer. The SED imagined its writers as educators of the people and sought to remove them once and for all from the garret, the much maligned ivory tower.[36] Most writers in the GDR accepted this role and internalized it – some of them until the GDR's demise and even beyond. Provided authors accepted and per-formed this role, they could enjoy intensive, wide-ranging support in the form of financial grants, generous royalties, invitations to read from their work, good foreign exchange revenues from publications in the west and opportunities to travel, as well as training at the Leipzig Literature Institute 'Johannes R. Becher'. If they did not keep to the prescribed ideological guidelines, an elaborate series of censorship strategies were quickly implemented, which could result in legal sanctions and even expatriation. Such censorship meant that some of the most significant works of GDR literature were either never published or only published years or even decades after the fact, including, for example, Hanns Eisler's *Johann Faustus*, Bertolt Brecht's *Das Verhör des Lukullus* (The Trial of Lucullus), Stefan Heym's *5 Tage im Juni* (Five Days in June) and *Collin*, Uwe Johnson's *Ingrid Babendererde* and *Mutmaßungen über Jakob* (Speculations about Jakob), Fritz Rudolf Fries's *Der Weg nach Oobliadooh* (The Way to Oobliadooh), numerous plays by Heiner Müller and Volker Braun and poems by Günter Kunert, Reiner Kunze, Wolf Biermann and others. Some books – such as Ulrich Plenzdorf's *Die neuen Leiden des jungen W.* (The New Sufferings of Young W.) – remained in the writer's drawer for years. Others were published in tiny print runs and panned in the official state journals so that they could never be given proper distribution, as was the case, for example, of Christa Wolf's *Nachdenken über Christa T.* (The Quest for Christa T.). It was not until the Tenth Writers' Congress in 1987 that the author Christoph Hein was brave enough to criticize censorship as 'out-of-date, useless, paradoxical, inhumane, hostile to the people, illegal and culpable'.[37]

Johannes R. Becher, the first GDR Minister of Culture and state poet, emphatically proclaimed the GDR to be a 'literary society' (*Literaturgesellschaft*). This idealistic slogan was representative of his aim to achieve the complete democratization and socialization of literature at all levels – authorship, material production, distribution and public reception of literature. And, like Japan and the Soviet Union, the GDR was indeed a country of readers, though at a price: the comprehensive management and control of all aspects of literary life, which explicitly excluded a free book market and the self-regulation of writers' and readers' needs within it. Time and again, various forms of censorship and other measures to keep writers in check choked the exalted intentions of this projected GDR literary society. At the same time, the constant threat of state intervention in writers' lives resulted in another distinctive characteristic of GDR literature: from the early days and increasingly over time, it bore the tell-tale signs of self-censorship or camouflage, that is, writing in the language of slaves (*Sklavensprache*).

The claim that GDR literature during the forty years of its existence can be considered a distinctive body of work does not of course preclude major changes over the course of time. Indeed, the internal historiography of this long period is unquestionably necessary and has hitherto been only carried out at a rather rudimentary level. The starting point is critical aspects of *Realpolitik* in East Germany and the Eastern bloc, more generally, and their implications for the cultural sector, in particular. Caesuras such as these do not automatically apply to literary production in any direct way, however. Equally important are those larger and more diffuse social and cultural shifts (e.g. the development of mass media, the spread of Western pop culture), which relate to international developments and also influence literature.

The importance of these and other shifts can be seen quite clearly in the succession of literary generations that shaped the cultural landscape of the GDR, whether they promoted a conservative or progressive agenda. In what follows the systemic approach to GDR literature adopted up until now is therefore supplemented by a differentiated historical approach, based on the different experiences and changes in view of four generations of authors. This is based on two hypotheses:

The first hypothesis is that the four different generations of authors are each shaped by what the sociologist Karl Mannheim, in his seminal essay 'The Problem of Generations' of 1928, termed a 'natural view of the world'. It is, according to Mannheim, 'early impressions' and the 'experiences of youth' that are critical in shaping individuals to the extent that they also pre-form all subsequent experiences and how they are processed (even if in the form of negation). For Mannheim, it is of considerable importance for the formation and relevance of every single experience,

> whether it is undergone by an individual as a decisive childhood experience, or later in life, superimposed upon other basic and early impressions. Early impressions tend to coalesce into a *natural view* of the world. As a result all later experiences then tend to receive their meaning from the original set, whether they appear as that set's verification and fulfilment or as its negation and antithesis. Experiences are not accumulated in the course of a lifetime through a process of summation or agglomeration, but are 'dialectically' articulated in the way described.[38]

Members of the different generations in the GDR therefore reacted very differently to key political events such as the end of the war, the foundation of the state in 1949, the 1953 uprisings, the demise of the demigod Stalin in 1956, the erection of the Wall in 1961 and Biermann's expatriation in 1976 – in so far as they actually experienced or could consciously process these events.

Second, writers are usually the ones who react like seismographs to changes in their community. In the first twenty years after 1945, the majority of initially loyal authors began to register the divergence between the declared claims and the reality of East German socialism. As a result, the literature produced after 1965 increasingly set itself up in opposition to the hegemonic political discourse and simultaneously favoured a programme of aesthetic modernization of what had been an overwhelmingly aesthetically conservative literature. Let us now consider the individual stages of GDR literature in the context of different generations.

The basic charter for GDR literature, even before the state's foundation, was its antifascist consensus. It united the writers of the first older generation, those such as Becher, Brecht, Seghers and Arnold Zweig, who had been in exile (one might also include younger writers such as Stefan Heym and Stephan Hermlin), with those of the second, younger generation, whose members had experienced the National Socialist regime and the war as members of the Hitler Youth, the BDM (the equivalent organization for girls), as members of the SA (Brown Shirts) or as regular soldiers, or generally as naive enthusiasts or *Mitläufer*. The members of this generation born in the 1920s now replaced a belief based on a total worldview with a new totalizing belief in Marxism. Antifascism, born out of bad political conscience, became the ideological umbrella – uniting writers such as Erwin Strittmatter, Franz Fühmann, Hermann Kant, Erich Loest, Christa Wolf, Heiner Müller, Günter de Bruyn and Erik Neutsch with those older writers whose exile or resistance was testament to their left-wing identity. Their voluntary commitment to really existing socialism, which increasingly became a shackle, lasted until the end of the GDR and in some cases beyond. Relatively few writers – such as Peter Huchel and Günter Kunert – were able to avoid the quasi-familiar debt of loyalty to the state as 'victor of history' and advocate of antifascism.

In retrospect this twofold enmeshment of an entire generation with the structures of power seems more significant than the oft-cited doctrine of socialist realism that was promulgated by Georg Lukács as a method for writing in 1948 and put into practice in 1951 (closely connected to the so-called Formalism campaign, which targeted all avant-garde, modernist Western currents). Certainly, it is the case that the majority of writers in the 1950s, and even into the early 1960s, not only tolerated but approved of the Party's aesthetic guidance, the dominance of socialist production as a literary theme and the political use of their literary work (especially for increasing productivity). The factory novels and 'Brigade' (brigade) plays, antiwar books and the poetry of *Aufbau* generally affirmed the political master discourse, and contributed to the prevailing monosemic discourse. There are exceptions which prove the rule, however: Brecht's *Buckower*

Elegien (Buckow Elegies), poems by Erich Arendt, Peter Huchel, Johannes Bobrowski, Inge Müller and Günter Kunert, as well as early plays by Peter Hacks and Heiner Müller. In addition there were protests by some intellectuals at the Fourth Writers' Congress in 1956. Even the proclamations of the so-called Bitterfelder Weg, made at the conference on culture at the Bitterfeld Chemical Combine in 1959, were initially accepted by authors such as Franz Fühmann and Christa Wolf. According to this directive, authors were, on the one hand, expected to go into factories and to report on the brigades' daily lives, which Wolf did, for example, in *Der geteilte Himmel* (Divided Heaven, 1963), and, on the other hand, manual workers were expected to 'take up the pen'.[39] Culture and life, manual and intellectual labour would thus be reconciled. The second Bitterfeld Conference in 1964 turned out to be a poorly disguised burial of this idealistic concept, which was always bound to fail. Ironically, the early 1960s benefited from the building of the Wall and the subsequent incarceration of the people within the GDR state, and were shaped by the optimistic literature of arrival or *Ankunftsliteratur* which featured socialist versions of the bourgeois *Bildungs-* or *Entwicklungsroman* (the novel of education or self-development). After a political learning process, the protagonists (in books by Wolf, Brigitte Reimann, Werner Bräunig, Karl-Heinz Jakobs and others) finally 'arrive' in socialism.

From today's perspective the radical shift that took place in GDR literature in the second half of the 1960s looks to be at odds with the political changes between 1961 and 1971, especially the Eighth Party Conference that resulted in the transition from Ulbricht to Honecker and some liberalization of cultural policy. The infamous Eleventh Plenum of the SED Central Committee in December 1965, at which authors including Manfred Bieler, Wolf Biermann, Stefan Heym, Günter Kunert and Heiner Müller were harshly criticized, sought to lay down a marker against what were seen as 'modernist' and 'nihilist' tendencies – but this was ultimately in vain. Following Uwe Johnson's exclusion from GDR literature – his debut was twice prohibited (in 1956 and 1959) – writers such as Heiner Müller, Fritz Rudolf Fries, Christa Wolf and Jurek Becker, as well as the older Erich Arendt, and Peter Huchel and Günter Kunert (who had both been effectively silenced though repeated censorship), and some younger poets (Volker Braun, Wolf Biermann, Karl Mickel, Sarah and Rainer Kirsch, Reiner Kunze, Richard Leising, Heinz Czechowski and Bernd Jentzsch) increasingly and ever more radically began to distance themselves from official political discourse and to use literature as a kind of counter text.

Though it still existed, the binding force of the dual foundation myth of antifascism and socialism diminished noticeably among the generation of writers born in the mid-1930s. The classical heritage (the literature of Goethe and Schiller as well as bourgeois realism, from Gottfried Keller to Thomas Mann), together with the associated traditional realist writing style, was no longer such a dominant role model. Instead, the literature of the Romantics, of Kleist, Hölderlin, Jean Paul and Georg Büchner, as well as much of the avant-garde literature since Baudelaire and Rimbaud, served as a projective space, enabling writers to articulate their own desires and dreams, inner turmoil and melancholy – even in an appropriately modern form. Writers made use of unconventional, eccentric or dislocated narrative perspectives, which reached the standards set by modernism decades earlier (self-reflexivity, discontinuity and lack of plot). Narrative genres such as the fantastical narrative, or use of grotesque or dystopian tropes, which until the mid-1960s would have been considered examples of a decadent heritage, were now evident (in works such as Ulrich Plenzdorf's *Die neuen Leiden des jungen W.*, Irmtraud Morgner's *Trobadora Beatriz*, Christa Wolf's *Kein Ort. Nirgends* (No Place on Earth) or her *Kassandra* (Cassandra) and Fritz Rudolf Fries's *Verlegung eines mittleren Reiches* (Transfer of a Middle Realm)). At the same time, a new everyday realism developed, which established a substitute public sphere and broke social and political taboos such as the largely suppressed legacy of the Third Reich and the experience of the Holocaust: Franz Fühmann's *Zweiundzwanzig Tage oder Die Hälfte des Lebens* (Twenty-two Days or Half a Lifetime), Christa Wolf's *Kindheitsmuster* (Patterns of Childhood), Erich Loest's *Es geht seinen Gang oder Mühen in unserer Ebene* (In a Rut or Travails in Our Plain) and Jurek Becker's *Jakob der Lügner* (Jacob the Liar). Stalinization in the GDR was addressed in Christoph Hein's *Horns Ende* (Horn's Death), and continuing authoritarian feudal-socialist structures found expression in Günter de Bruyn's *Neue Herrlichkeit* (New Glory), Volker Braun's *Unvollendete Geschichte* (Unfinished Story), Thomas Brasch's *Vor den Vätern sterben die Söhne* (The Sons Die before the Fathers), Reiner Kunze's *Die wunderbaren Jahre* (The Wonderful Years) and Hans Joachim Schädlich's *Versuchte Nähe* (Attempted Closeness).

More and more writers wrote about alienated lives in an industrial civilization that lacked perspectives and innovation, which was how they felt their lives in the GDR to be (in works including, among others, Franz Fühmann's *Saiäns-Fiktschen*, Klaus Schlesinger's *Alte Filme* (Old Films) and Christoph Hein's *Der fremde Freund* (The Distant Lover), which was entitled *Drachenblut* (Dragon Blood) in the west). The common denominator of this new non-conformist East German literature was *Zivilisationskritik*: the overriding belief that the civilizing design of really existing socialism was increasingly dominated not by Ernst Bloch's 'Principle of Hope' but more by the counter notion of apocalypse, or at least a 'dialectic of enlightenment' in the sense outlined by Max Horkheimer and Theodor W. Adorno.[40] And in this context there is a surprisingly widespread use of old myths, Greek myths in particular. Authors as different as Erich Arendt in his poetry volume *Ägäis* (The Aegean), Franz Fühmann in *Marsyas* and *Das Ohr des Dionysios* (The Ear of Dionysus), Irmtraud Morgner in *Amanda. Ein Hexenroman* (Amanda. A Witch-Novel), Christa Wolf in her *Kassandra* as well as Peter Hacks and Heiner Müller considered classical myths to be archetypes of a contradictory Western civilization. Stefan Heym, on the other hand, used biblical myth to chastise the authoritarian state in *Der König David Bericht*, also published in English in Heym's own version as *The King David Report*. For Christa Wolf, the 'mega machine' of destructive irrationality that is our world today had its origins in the circumstances surrounding the figure of Cassandra and gave rise to a masculine, bellicose and purpose-orientated form of civilization which still exists today.

New theatre also rejected the classical legacy, with its fable based on a 'rational idea', in favour of a fragmentation of events that went far beyond Brecht's concept of epic theatre. This was pursued especially by Heiner Müller, most radically in his *Die Hamletmaschine* (Hamletmachine); by Volker Braun in his *Die Übergangsgesellschaft* (The Transitional Society); and also by Thomas Brasch and Stefan Schütz. Perhaps it was the young poets of the late 1960s and 1970s, especially the so-called 'Volker Braun generation', who were most aware of literature's potential as subversive counter-discourse, in which they could practise diverse ways of speaking – heteroglossia, dialogism and intertextuality – and thus undermine the monosemy-affirming language environment.[41]

GDR literature was in the beginning a willing 'literature of conviction' (*Gesinnungsliteratur*); later, as many older writers' convictions narrowed to a blinkered worldview and as young writers emerged unencumbered by such beliefs, it became a 'literature that sought to give meaning' (*Sinngebungsliteratur*).[42] But even this is not adequate to describe literature at the end of the 1970s following the expatriation of the popular singer-songwriter Wolf Biermann, the expulsion of numerous important writers from the Writers' Union and the exodus of more than a hundred writers from the GDR. Conviction gave way to something that came close to despair and which increasingly led to a sense of hopelessness. But what

persisted until the end of the GDR and only became untenable at the time
of the *Wende* was the privilege, unique to the GDR, of the writer being
taken seriously, being needed, whether as the cog in the machine of a
planned really existing socialist society or whether later, more importantly,
as a substitute public sphere, and as a taboo-breaker in an authoritarian
system. Writers continued to identify with their role as active educators
and social pedagogues, sometimes even beyond 1990.

The other thing that persisted was the remarkable fact that the dissent
and opposition of the authors mentioned so far found expression almost
exclusively from a position of Marxism or socialism. David Bathrick has
explored why critical dissent in the political and literary field of the GDR –
unlike in the other Eastern bloc countries, especially Poland and the Soviet
Union – was a genuinely Marxist one. After twelve years of Nazi rule, and
the experience of Holocaust, critics of the system in the GDR could neither
draw on an 'uncompromised' national heritage nor were the religious
traditions of the country suitable for establishing a counter position, as
in Poland, for example. On the other hand, Marx's work, especially his
early work, like the *Paris Manuscripts*, offered philosophical maxims from
which a 'true' socialism, 'socialism with a human face', could be construed.
In Bathrick's words,

> Like Luther, their [the authors'] original intent was very much a move
> toward reformation and revision and not a total abandonment of doctrinal
> adherence or even a break with the institutional church. And again like
> Luther, the political consequences of such heresy led them far afield of their
> imagined political goals.[43]

Indeed this internal Marxist heresy in the late 1960s and 1970s provided the
impetus for what would become the independent citizens' movements of
the 1980s that joined forces with the Protestant church. In this sense the
'protestant' habitus or self-styling of authors within the Marxist fold (e.g. the
multiple references to conscience), who since the *Wende* are generally
referred to as 'reform socialists',[44] and who include Biermann (at least the
Biermann of those years), Braun, Fühmann, Hein, Hermlin, Heym, Müller
and Wolf, along with a number of authors close to them who had long-term
visas for the west, such as Kurt Bartsch, Jurek Becker, Karl-Heinz Jakobs,
Erich Loest and Klaus Schlesinger, played a significant part in rendering the
continued existence of the GDR impossible. The *Wende* of 1980–90 presented a number of such reform socialist authors with a peculiar paradox.
With the collapse of the GDR they lost their symbolic capital and privileged
position as mouthpieces for the dissemination of 'true' socialism and a kind

of therapeutic counselling almost overnight. When they fell from their pedestals and were heaped with public scorn and mockery during the German literary debate of 1990, they definitively lost the representative status they had clung on to for so long.[45] Some, it must be said, were not particularly successful at resisting the temptation to cast themselves as martyr figures in the new literary and political field and to behave accordingly. One should not, however, forget that there was a quite different category of real martyrs created in the GDR: those who had been exposed to the whims of the authorities or those who were imprisoned or expatriated, such as Wolf Biermann, Rudolf Bahro, Jürgen Fuchs, Hans Joachim Schädlich, Wolfgang Hilbig and many others who are less well known.

Few fates are more telling with regard to the effects of the socialist illusion on the life and work of GDR authors than that of Christa Wolf. Very early, in childhood or youth under the Nazi regime, a habitus had developed – continued 'patterns of childhood' so to speak – the chief characteristics of which were a need for security, a desire to identify with authority, a susceptibility to mobilization (*Begeisterungsfähigkeit*) and moral rigour. In the early post-war years this habitus became synonymous with the teleology of Marxism. But gradually, with increasing disillusionment over the decades, not only did this become questionable as an ideological credo but the deeply rooted habitus itself also crumbled – at least in part. What remains are certain moralizing and self-legitimizing tendencies that persist in modes of speech or her writing style, as does what Jan Assmann calls 'binding' or 'connective memory' (*Bindungsgedächtnis*),[46] anchored in the antifascism of the early years. The author remains tied to a specific discourse (genetically linked with Marxism but not really actually Marxist) and to central concepts like 'alienation' or 'utopia', as demonstrated by the final entries in her diary publication *Ein Tag im Jahr. 1960–2000* (One Day a Year. 1960–2000) of 2003.[47] Although rare in the years leading up to her death in 2011, all the authors' media pronouncements and appearances, or to put it another way, her acts of self-stylization, bear the characteristic traces of this disposition, which developed over decades.

In the 1980s, a fourth generation of writers who had been born in the 1950s and 1960s began to write and finally abandoned this demanding role. These authors had only ever experienced socialism as a 'deformed reality' rather than as a 'hope of something else' (Heiner Müller).[48] In contrast to the preceding 'integrated generation' of the 1940s and early 1950s, they came to be known as the 'distanced generation'.[49] The experimental texts written by these 'young barbarians' (including Uwe Kolbe, Bert Papenfuss-Gorek,

Katja Lange-Müller, Jan Faktor, Stefan Döring), which were available only in small print runs in samizdat journals, made a crucial contribution to dismantling the assumed meaning in 'really existing socialism', their texts both undermining and lampooning ideological rhetoric. The lasting impact of these authors – Wolfgang Hilbig counts as an important forerunner – is that they broke free from the self-imposed fealty to the GDR system, something that older writers were never quite able to do. Of course, the scene was infiltrated by informers working for the Ministry of State Security or Stasi (Sascha Anderson and Rainer Schedlinski), which undermined their credibility considerably.

From chronotope to third space. East Germany and its literature after 1990

The *Wende* of 1989–90 seemed, on the face of it at least, to spell the end of GDR literature. The GDR's model of a *Literaturgesellschaft* collapsed very quickly and almost completely, and was replaced by Western institutions and structures with the literary market at their centre. Within a very short time in the 1990s other spaces appeared instead of the generally closed time-space that had characterized the GDR. These new spaces require some brief explanation.

The 9th of November 1989 marked the beginning of the end of the GDR's spatial and temporal borders; by October 1990, when the two German states were unified, these borders had ceased to exist entirely. The new West-plus-East Germany that came into being – the title of Christian Kracht's 1995 novel *Faserland* is appropriate here[50] – resembles a (virtual) third space in the sense described by Edward W. Soja[51] and Homi K. Bhabha,[52] in which different ideologies, mentalities, forms of habitus, writerly self-understanding and approaches to writing come together, as well as more fundamental differences such as ethnicity, religion and language. As Arjun Appadurai has said, ' groups are no longer tightly territorialized, spatially bounded, historically unselfconscious, or culturally homogenous'.[53] They do not come into contact with one another in an abstract or accidental fashion but rather in the daily lives of all people living in Germany and are thus in the consciousness of each individual author. In an age characterized by immigration and globalization, what once con-stituted GDR literature is being constantly reintegrated into the field of 'German literature', which itself has been homogenized by economic factors and the media as well as in people's minds. Moreover, the distinc-tive quality of such literature is increasingly dissipating as a result of a daily proliferation of styles in a literary landscape that is more and more vast and unclearly differentiated. Authors from the former GDR are now only a small, albeit important, group among many. The older East German authors in particular had to recalibrate their identities as authors; others sealed themselves off within their old identities (as was the case with Hermann Kant and Peter Hacks, for example). In a period that has seen the German nation become more transcultural, the West German memory space and the cultural memory that had developed there, and which previously seemed so fixed, have now also changed. The conflict between the two German post-war cultures and literatures that dominated the early 1990s, and to which we can apply Aleida Assmann's threefold notion of legitimization, delegitimization and distinction,[54] still continues but is certainly less intense or existentially loaded than it was fifteen or twenty-five years ago. For the older GDR authors (those over sixty), it is still a matter of 'distinction': that is, whether they preserve or surrender the symbolic capital which shaped their identity or attempt complex assimilation. Younger authors, on the other hand, have long since developed hybrid identities as writers. This was only to be expected – since the majority of them have by now spent long periods in the west, whether in France, Italy or New York. Even authors of the 'distanced generation' such as Angela Krauß, Katja Lange-Müller, Thomas Brussig, Durs Grünbein and Ingo Schulze, and especially those born in the 1970s like Antje Rávic Strubel, Jenny Erpenbeck, Jochen Schmidt and Jakob Hein, operate as effortlessly in the globalized world as do fish in water. These younger authors, whether from East or West Germany, are not at all disturbed by the growing number of authors of other ethnicities and religions or even from other parts of the world who write and publish in German – with, in some cases, exceptional results. Nor are they or their readers concerned by the number of translated texts from all over the world, novels especially, which have intruded into and broadened the German literary sphere. The notion of a national literature is increasingly questionable. Salman Rushdie's phrase, 'We all are translated men' is apposite.[55] Within trans-cultural discourse, there is already talk of a 'translational turn'.[56] And of course in this new chronotope, which is open on all sides, and which we may call the 'third space', all relationships to the past will be renegotiated far beyond guilt and sin, without false identification with victims or trite moralizing. The German family novel, which will soon span four genera-tions, will need to be written anew.[57]

As far as the now historical body of GDR literature is concerned, it will presumably be read less in the context of its time or assessed in ideological terms even though the wide range of prose that emerged there is still valuable because of its documentary significance. GDR literature will also be increasingly considered in European and Western contexts, and its aesthetic standards will come to be discussed in the context of international trends such as modernism and postmodernism. One consequence of this will be that GDR literature's failings will become more apparent (e.g. many authors' tendency to indulge a specifically German tradition, the speculative, moralizing literature of ideas); and similarities within German-language literature since 1945 will be more evident (as in the similarities between East and West German authors born around the same time, Böll and Grass on one side, for example, and Fühmann and Christa Wolf on the other). And if asked to provide a canon, one might, with twenty-five years' hindsight, say that GDR literature produced one playwright of world stature – Heiner Müller – and a wealth of extraordinarily accomplished and dynamic poetry; whereas its prose literature, which has been more widely discussed, and is more defined by its time and the system in which it was produced, may well be found wanting. Moreover, alongside some of the works of Günter de Bruyn, Christa Wolf, Jurek Becker and Christoph Hein that will endure, perhaps, the masterly novels of Stefan Heym will one day be rediscovered.[58]

Notes

1. This is also the title of Harald Martenstein's novel, *Gefühlte Nähe. Roman in 23 Paarungen* (Munich: Bertelsmann, 2010), though it has little to do with the issues addressed in this chapter.
2. Mikhail M. Bakhtin, 'Forms of Time and of the Chronotope in the Novel: Notes toward a Historical Poetics' (1937–38), in Michael Holquist (ed.), *The Dialogic Imagination: Four Essays* (Austin, London: University of Texas Press, 1981), pp. 84–254.
3. Ibid., p. 131.
4. Ibid.
5. Michael C. Frank and Kirsten Mahlke, 'Nachwort', in Mikhail M. Bakhtin (ed.), *Chronotopos*, trans. into German from the Russian by Michael Dewey (Frankfurt/M.: Suhrkamp, [1973] 2008), pp. 201–42; p. 205.
6. For more on this see Jörg Döring and Tristan Thielmann (eds.), *Spatial Turn. Das Raumparadigma in den Kultur- und Sozialwissenschaften* (Bielefeld: Transcript, 2008).
7. See, for example, Peter Christian Ludz, *Mechanismen der Herrschaftssicherung. Eine sprachpolitische Analyse gesellschaftlichen Wandels in der DDR* (Munich, Vienna: Hanser, 1980), pp. 58–65.

8. Horst Haase et al. (eds.), *Geschichte der deutschen Literatur von den Anfängen bis zur Gegenwart*, vol. xi: *Literatur der Deutschen Demokratischen Republik* (Berlin-Ost: Volk und Wissen, 1976), pp. 21–22.

9. Ibid., p. 23.

10. Hans Mayer, 'Über die Einheit der deutschen Literatur', in Hans Mayer (ed.), *Deutsche Literatur seit Thomas Mann* (Reinbek: Rowohlt, 1967), p. 111.

11. Jürgen Link, 'Von der Spaltung zur Wiedervereinigung der deutschen Literatur? (Überlegungen am Beispiel des Produktionsstücks)', *Jahrbuch zur Literatur in der DDR*, 1 (1980), 59–78; p. 61.

12. Heinrich Mohr, 'Entwicklungslinien der Literatur im geteilten Deutschland', *Jahrbuch zur Literatur in der DDR*, 1 (1980), 1–58; p. 54.

13. Fritz J. Raddatz, 'Die zweite deutsche Exillitertur', *Die Zeit*, 12 August 1977. Though those involved, including Sarah Kirsch, Hans Joachim Schädlich and Wolf Biermann, objected to the term.

14. Fritz J. Raddatz, *Eine dritte deutsche Literatur. Stichworte zu Texten der Gegenwart. Zur deutschen Literatur*, 3 (Reinbek: Rowohlt, 1987).

15. Ursula Heukenkamp, 'Eine Geschichte oder viele Geschichten der deutschen Literatur seit 1945? Gründe und Gegengründe', *Zeitschrift für Germanistik*, NF 1.1 (1995), 22–37; p. 30.

16. Rainer Rosenberg, 'Was war DDR-Literatur? Die Diskussion um den Gegenstand in der Literaturwissenschaft in der Bundesrepublik Deutschland', *Zeitschrift für Germanistik*, NF 1.1 (1995), 9–21; p. 19.

17. Herfried Münkler, 'Politische Mythen der DDR', in *Jahrbuch 1996 der Berlin-Brandenburgischen Akademie der Wissenschaften*, pp. 123–56; p. 124. See also Wolfgang Emmerich, *Kleine Literaturgeschichte der DDR. Erweiterte Ausgabe* (Berlin: Aufbau, 2000), pp. 34–39.

18. Münkler, *Politische Mythen der DDR*, p. 127.

19. Christoph Hölscher has described 'the exclusion of large groups of NS victims from the canonized "victims of Fascism" in official commemorations as the "birth defect of East German Antifascism"': Hölscher, *NS-Verfolgte im 'antifaschistischen Staat'. Vereinnahmung und Ausgrenzung in der ostdeutschen Wiedergutmachung (1945–1989)* (Berlin: Metropol, 2002), p. 229.

20. '"Wo sind wir zuhause?" Gespräch [von Klaus Wagenbach] mit Stephan Hermlin', *Freibeuter. Vierteljahreszeitschrift für Kultur und Politik*, 1 (1979), 47–55; p. 49.

21. Münkler, *Politische Mythen der DDR*, p. 53.

22. Annette Simon, 'Antifaschismus als Loyalitätsfalle', *Frankfurter Allgemeine Zeitung*, 1 February 1993.

23. 'Für unser Land', reproduced in Christa Wolf, *Im Dialog. Aktuelle Texte* (Frankfurt/M.: Luchterhand, 1990), pp. 170–71; p. 171.

24. There are innumerable texts on 'Antifascism in the GDR': among them Antonia Grunenberg, *Antifaschismus – ein deutscher Mythos* (Reinbek: Rowohlt, 1993); Sigrid Meuschel, 'Antifaschistischer Stalinismus', in Brigitte Rauschenbach (ed.), *Erinnern, Wiederholen, Durcharbeiten. Zur Psycho-Analyse deutscher Wenden* (Berlin: Aufbau, 1992), pp. 163–71. See also the

volume of case studies by Simone Barck, *Antifa-Geschichte(n). Eine literarische Spurensuche in der DDR der 1950er und 1960er Jahre* (Weimar, Vienna: Metzler, 2003).

25. Immanuel Kant, *Der Streit der Fakultäten*. Zweiter Abschnitt [1798], in Immanuel Kant, *Werke*, ed. Wilhelm Weischedel, vol. vi (Frankfurt/M.: Insel, 1964), p. 357.

26. Wolfgang Emmerich, 'Fast eine Leerstelle – Über die verleugnete Präsenz des Holocaust in der DDR-Literatur', *Jahrbuch des Simon-Dubnow-Instituts*, 9 (2010), 57–84.

27. Wolfgang Engler, *Die Ostdeutschen. Kunde von einem verlorenen Land* (Berlin: Aufbau, 1999), p. 200 and passim.

28. Jürgen Gerhards and Jörg Rössel, 'Familienkultur in den USA und in West- und Ostdeutschland', in Gerhards (ed.), *Die Vermessung der kulturellen Unterschiede. USA und Deutschland im Vergleich* (Wiesbaden: Westdeutscher Verlag, 2000), pp. 235–70; p. 239.

29. The term 'habitus' is fundamental to most of Bourdieu's work. See especially Pierre Bourdieu, *Distinction: A Social Critique of the Judgement of Taste*, trans. Richard Nice (Harvard University Press, 1987) and his survey essay 'The Forms of Capital', trans. Richard Nice, in *Handbook of Theory and Research for the Sociology of Education*, ed. J. Richardson (New York: Greenwood, 1986), pp. 241–58.

30. Dietrich Mühlberg, 'Schwierigkeiten kultureller Assimilation. Freuden und Mühen der Ostdeutschen beim Eingewöhnen in neue Standards des Alltagslebens', *Aus Politik und Zeitgeschichte* (B 17/26 April 2002), 3–11; pp. 4–5.

31. Maurice Halbwachs, 'Space and the Collective Memory', in Halbwachs, *Collective Memory*, with an introduction by Mary Douglas (New York: Harper-Colophon Books, 1950), Chapter 4.

32. Compare David Clarke, 'Space, Time and Power. The Chronotopes of Uwe Tellkamp's *Der Turm*', in *German Life and Letters*, 63.4 (2010), 490–503. Clarke's essay, which became known to me only after I had formulated my own position, uses Bakhtin's category of the chronotope above all in a literary sense in order to uncover 'the politics of space in the city' of Dresden (p. 490).

33. Ruth Klüger, *weiter leben. Eine Jugend* (Göttingen: Wallstein 1992), p. 78. I am grateful to Matías Martínez for this suggestion. Here Klüger is explicitly referring to the concentration camp as a particular site (which is more than simply a place or landscape), but I consider the transferred meaning permissible in this context.

34. On the 'Sächsische Dichtershule' see the chapter by Gerrit-Jan Berendse in this volume.

35. Uwe Johnson in a discussion about 'Two German Literatures?' documented in *alternative. Zeitschrift für Literatur und Diskussion*, 7. 38/39 (October 1964), 97–100; p. 98.

36. Manfred Jäger suggested the term 'Sozialliteraten' in his *Sozialliteraten.*
    Funktion und Selbstverständnis des Schriftstellers in der DDR (Düsseldorf:
    Bertelsmann Universitätsverlag, 1973).
37. Christoph Hein, 'Arbeitsgruppe IV Literatur und Wirklung', *X.*
    Schriftstellerkongreß der Deutschen Demokratischen Republik. Arbeitsgruppen
    (Cologne: Pahl-Rugenstein, 1988), pp. 225–47; p. 228.
38. Karl Mannheim, 'The Problem of Generations', trans. Edith Schwarzschild
    and Paul Kecskemeti, in *From Karl Mannheim*, ed. Kurt H. Wolff, 2nd exp.
    edn (New Brunswick: Transaction, 1993), p. 373.
39. For a fuller account of the Bitterfelder Weg see the chapter by Stephen
    Brockmann in this volume.
40. Ernst Bloch, *The Principle of Hope* (1959), trans. Neville and Stephen Plaice
    and Paul Knight (Cambridge, MA.: MIT Press, 1995); Max Horkheimer and
    T. W. Adorno, *Dialectic of Enlightenment* (1947), ed. Gunzelin Schmid Noerr,
    trans. Edmund Japhcott (Stanford University Press, 2002).
41. Compare Gerrit-Jan Berendse's chapter in this volume.
42. I introduced this term at the beginning of 1990 before Ulrich Greiner
    and others started writing GDR literature off as 'Gesinnungsästhetik'
    (literature governed by an aesthetic of conviction). Wolfgang Emmerich,
    'Die Schrift der Freiheit', in *LIBER. Europäische Kulturzeitschrift*, 2.1
    (January 1990), 9, and Ulrich Greiner, 'Die deutsche
    Gesinnungsästhetik', *Die Zeit*, 2 November 1990. For more on what has
    been called the 'German-German literature debate' see Thomas Anz
    (ed.), *'Es geht nicht um Christa Wolf'. Der Literaturstreit im vereinten*
    Deutschland (Munich: edition spangenberg, 1991).
43. David Bathrick, 'Language and Power', in Michael Geyer (ed.), *The Power of*
    Intellectuals in Contemporary Germany (University of Chicago Press, 2001),
    pp. 138–59; p. 146.
44. Horst Domdey, 'Volker Braun und die Sehnsucht nach der Großen
    Kommunion. Zum Demokratiekonzept der Reformsozialisten', in
    Deutschland Archiv, 23 (1990), 1771–74. See also Wolfgang Emmerich, *Kleine*
    Literaturgeschichte der DDR, where the term is used throughout.
45. On the 'Literaturstreit' see Carol Anne Costabile-Heming's chapter in this
    volume.
46. Jan Assmann, *Religion und kulturelles Gedächtnis. Zehn Studien* (Munich:
    Beck, 2000), pp. 34–38, 40–41 and 108–14.
47. See the last entry of 27 September 2000, in Christa Wolf, *Ein Tag im Jahr.*
    1960–2000 (Munich: Luchterhand, 2003), pp. 618–24.
48. Heiner Müller, '"Wie es bleibt, ist es nicht". Zu Thomas Brasch *Kargo*', in
    Müller, *Rotwelsch* (Berlin: Merve, 1982), p. 154.
49. Annegret Schüle, Thomas Ahbe and Rainer Gries (eds.), *Die DDR aus*
    generationen-geschichtlicher Perspektive. Eine Inventur (Leipzig:
    Universitätsverlag, 2006), especially the contributions by Mary Fulbrook,
    Bernd Lindner and Thomas Ahbe and Rainer Gries.

50. Christian Kracht, *Faserland* (Cologne: Kiepenheuer & Witsch, 1995). The title plays on the English word 'fatherland', but spoken with a German accent (with the sound 's' instead of 'th') and calls to mind the association with a frayed ('zerfasert' from 'fasern') German fatherland.

51. Edward W. Soja, *Thirdspace. Journeys to Los Angeles and Other Real-and-Imagined Places* (Oxford: Blackwell, 1996).

52. Homi K. Bhabha, *The Location of Culture* (London: Routledge, 1994) among other works by the same author.

53. Arjun Appadurai, *Modernity at Large. Cultural Dimensions of Globalization* (Minneapolis/London: University of Minnesota Press, 1996), p. 48.

54. Aleida Assmann, *Erinnerungsräume. Formen und Wandlungen des kulturellen Gedächtnisses* (Munich: Fink, 1999), p. 138 and passim.

55. Salman Rushdie, *Imaginary Homelands. Essays and Criticism 1981–1991* (London: Penguin Books, 1992), p. 17.

56. Doris Bachmann-Medick, 'The Translational Turn', *Translation Studies. Special Issue*, 2.1 (London: Routledge, 2009), 2–16.

57. See, for example, Simone Costagli and Matteo Galli (eds.), *Deutsche Familienromane. Literarische Genealogien und internationaler Kontext* (Munich: Fink, 2010).

58. Hermlin, a German Jewish and also (from 1935 to 1951) American author, was adept both in German and English: for example, *Hostages* (1943) and *The Crusaders* (1948), which both appeared first in the USA; *5 Tage im Juni* (1974); *König David Bericht* (1973); *Collin* (1979) and *Ahasver* (1981). See Peter Hutchinson's introduction *Stefan Heym. The Perpetual Dissident* (Cambridge University Press, 1992).

CHAPTER 2

Resurrected from the ruins
The emergence of GDR culture

Stephen Brockmann

Like its West German counterpart, the Federal Republic of Germany
(FRG), the German Democratic Republic (GDR) emerged out of the
complete devastation wrought by twelve years of Nazi dictatorship and
four years of brutal war. On 30 April 1945 the Nazi dictator Adolf Hitler
committed suicide in Berlin, not far from where Red Army soldiers were
fighting against German troops for control of the capital, and a week later
German officials signed an unconditional surrender, first in Reims, France,
on April 7 in the presence of American officers, and the next day, at Soviet
insistence, in Berlin-Karlshorst in the presence of Soviet officers. Most of
the territory that was later to become the GDR was occupied by Soviet
troops; however, American troops had reached the Elbe River to the
northeast of Leipzig, at Torgau, and therefore a significant chunk of future
East German territory that included the cities of Leipzig, Erfurt and
Eisenach was initially occupied by Americans. The entire city of Berlin,
in contrast, was occupied by Soviet troops. A few months later, in July of
1945, as decided at the Yalta conference in January of 1945 – where
Roosevelt, Stalin and Churchill had agreed to divide Germany and its
capital Berlin into clearly demarcated zones of occupation – American
troops withdrew to the borders of the future FRG, making room for Soviet
occupiers; and in return Soviet troops withdrew from the western sectors of
Berlin, making way for American, British and French troops there.

At the end of the Second World War Germany lost large chunks of its
previous territory in the east, including the provinces of East Prussia, Silesia
and eastern Pommerania, and almost all of the ethnic Germans living in
those territories – well over ten million – fled westward, into what was left
of Germany, both the future GDR and the future FRG. When the war
ended, Allied authorities declared the German state to be non-existent and
proclaimed that all political power lay in their hands alone. The end of the
Second World War in Germany thus differed significantly from that of the
First World War, in which German troops had still occupied large swathes

35

of territory outside Germany, Germans had not been forced to leave their homes on a mass scale and a functioning German government maintained control of the homeland. In contrast, at the end of the Second World War Germany was occupied by foreign powers, it contained large numbers of German and non-German refugees and any central government controlled by Germans had ceased to exist. Moreover, most of the country's major cities, including Berlin, Hamburg, Cologne, Frankfurt, Nuremberg, Munich, Leipzig and Dresden, had been badly damaged by massive bombing raids in which tens of thousands of civilians had been killed. When he returned to Berlin on 2 May 1945 after spending the years of the Hitler dictatorship in Moscow, the German communist Wolfgang Leonhard found, as he later recalled, 'a picture of hell – flaming ruins and starving people shambling about in tattered clothing'.[1] And in the midst of these ruins defeated Germans, as Leonhard was to remember, were hanging 'white or red flags [. . .] from the windows. It could be seen that the red ones had been recently converted from swastika flags'.[2]

The utter military and political defeat of Germany at the end of the Second World War went along with a moral and cultural catastrophe that can hardly be overemphasized and that is only hinted at in Leonhard's words. Although at the end of the Second World War the word 'Holocaust' was not yet being used to refer to the systematic murder of millions of European Jews by Nazi authorities, many Germans, as well as members of the occupying armies, were acutely aware of the many atrocities and war crimes committed by uniformed Germans – whether ordinary soldiers or members of the SS (Schützstaffel) that ran the concentration camps. From his exile in California, Thomas Mann, Germany's most famous living writer, proclaimed on the BBC on 8 May 1945 that 'our shame lies open to the eyes of the world', and that 'everything German, everyone who speaks German, writes German, has lived in German, is affected by this shameful revelation'. As overblown as this rhetoric may sound today, Mann was not exaggerating. Although he was referring primarily to the death camps, the shame of which Mann spoke included all the crimes of the Nazi regime, with which even German anti-Nazis were associated. 'Humanity shudders in horror at Germany!' he declared.[3] Mann's ideological opponent, the socialist playwright Bertolt Brecht, wrote thus in August 1945: 'Of course we who would not have been victors if Hitler had won, are defeated along with him.'[4]

The country's moral catastrophe was also a catastrophe for German culture, of which Germans had been justifiably proud. It was clear at the end of the war that a high level of cultural development did not necessarily guarantee a correspondingly high level of morality. The fact that the same nation had produced both Beethoven and the Nazi death camps, both the Goethe of Weimar and the Buchenwald concentration camp only a few miles away from Weimar, was widely noted. The exiled Germanist Richard Alewyn proclaimed in 1949, the 200th anniversary year of Goethe's birth, 'Between us and Weimar lies Buchenwald.' A German patriot might try in various ways to dissociate himself from Germany, Alewyn argued, but 'what will not work [. . .] is to boast about Goethe while denying Hitler. There are only Goethe *and* Hitler, humanity *and* bestiality'.[5]

It is important to bear all of these factors – Germany's military, political and cultural devastation, and its lack of control over its own affairs – in mind when studying the emergence of the GDR and its culture. Germany's division into two countries and involvement in the Cold War that followed the Second World War was to acquire a sense of inevitability in later years, but at the beginning of May 1945 nothing seemed inevitable but German defeat at the hands of the Soviet Union, the United States and their Allies. While the division of Germany into military zones of occupation had been decided on at Yalta in January of 1945, there had been no decision to create two separate German states, and many Germans hoped that the four zones of occupation (American, British, Soviet and French) would eventually become part of a unified German state – as indeed they ultimately did in 1990, far later than most had imagined at the end of the Second World War. When, at the German writers conference that was held in Berlin in October of 1947, during a period of increasing tension between the United States and the Soviet Union, the assembled authors approved a resolution proclaiming the 'irrevocable unity' of the fatherland and declaring literature itself to be a 'band of unity above and beyond all zonal boundaries and political positions', they were expressing the heartfelt wishes of many patriots, not just literary intellectuals.[6]

The Germany that emerged out of the ruins of the Second World War was, German leaders hoped and proclaimed, to be a peaceful Germany in which the factors that had made Nazism possible would be eliminated or at least rendered powerless. This meant that in both the east and the west, German politicians' approach to the formation of a new German state was dependent on their beliefs about the reasons for Nazism's triumph – or, alternatively, that German politicians adjusted their beliefs about the reason for Nazism's triumph to the nature of the state in which they lived or hoped to live. In the west, Nazism was seen above all as a turning away from Christianity, and therefore one of the major responses to Nazism was the creation of the Christian Democratic Union (CDU) as a political party explicitly committed to a Christian worldview; the CDU was to become the governing party of the FRG for most of its history. For communists and socialists, however, the Nazi regime had above all been a capitalist regime, in accordance with the so-called Dimitrov thesis – named after Georgi Mikhailov Dimitrov, the major twentieth-century leader of the Bulgarian Communist Party and the General Secretary of the Communist International (Comintern) from 1934 to 1943 – which defined the Nazi dictatorship as 'the open terrorist dictatorship of the most reactionary, chauvinist, and imperialist elements of finance capitalism'.[7] This meant that for communists the most effective way to ensure that Nazism would never again triumph in Germany was to fight for socialism.

It was precisely this that Walter Ulbricht, the leader of the so-called 'Gruppe Ulbricht' (Ulbricht Group), undertook to do when he and nine other exiled members of the German Communist Party (KPD), including the future renegade Wolfgang Leonhard, Karl Maron (the father of the East German writer Monika Maron) and Fritz Erpenbeck (the father of the German scientist and writer John Erpenbeck and grandfather of the writer Jenny Erpenbeck) flew from their exile in Moscow back to Germany on 30 April 1945, which was, coincidentally, also the day of Hitler's suicide. It was Ulbricht's task to organize the restructuring of the KPD – which of course had been illegal under the Nazi dictatorship – in the defeated country and to work towards what was termed an antifascist-democratic transformation of Germany. As Leonhard later recalled, 'All we knew was that, according to our directives, we had a political mission to carry out, the target of which was Fascism and its remnants, and the purpose of which was the transformation of Germany into a democracy.'[8] Ulbricht's official brief, at least in the first instance, was *not* to create a socialist dictatorship. As Ulbricht put it many years later, he and his fellow communists believed that their primary goal ought to be the 'creation of antifascist-democratic administrative units' and 'cooperation in the removal of the remnants of fascism and in overcoming the distress of the population'.[9] Leonhard's recollections are not significantly different: 'I believed that after the destruction of Hitler's army the Soviet Union would selflessly help the German antifascists and democrats to build up a new, democratic Germany. [. . .] Wasn't our mission itself – initiated even before the conclusion of hostilities! – proof of the fact that the Soviet Union did not want to behave like a conqueror but rather as a power that was willing to help the German antifascists in the struggle against Nazism?'[10]

A little over a month after the Ulbricht group's return to Germany, on 10 June 1945, the communist writer Johannes R. Becher, who like so many other leading communists had spent the years of the Nazi dictatorship in exile in Moscow, also flew back to Germany to help reorganize cultural life in the defeated Germany generally and in the Soviet zone specifically. Becher immediately went about setting up an antifascist cultural organization called the Cultural Federation for the Democratic Renewal of Germany (Kulturbund zur demokratischen Erneuerung Deutschlands), which was officially recognized in all of Berlin's sectors by mid-July. The Kulturbund was to play a major role in the GDR's cultural life for the next four decades; and Becher himself was one of the dominant figures in East German cultural development for over a decade, becoming the nation's first Minister of Culture in 1954. Also playing a key role in cultural development at this time was the communist functionary Anton Ackermann, who, in an official manifesto of June 1945, proclaimed the KPD to be the 'protector of the vital interests of the German nation' and emphasized the party's interest in working not just with socialists and communists but with all forces opposed to Nazism, with the ultimate political goal being the establishment of parliamentary democracy, not a communist dictatorship.[11] Less than a year later, Ackermann was to proclaim his belief that Germany could and should develop its own special path to socialism, and that Germany should not have to slavishly follow the example of the Soviet Union.[12] Other key figures in the cultural landscape of the Soviet zone in the immediate aftermath of the Second World War were Becher's colleague Alexander Abusch, who had spent the years of the Nazi dictatorship in exile in France and Mexico, as well as the Soviet officers Colonel Sergei Tulpanov, an economist with excellent German language skills who ran the Soviet Military Administration's (SMAD) propaganda department and operated as one of Soviet Marshall Georgi Zhukov's right-hand men, and Major Alexander Dymschitz, also a Germanist, who led the cultural section of the SMAD. Both of these Soviet military men brought with them an appreciation for the accomplishments of German culture coupled with the determination to transform Germany into a country that would no longer pose a threat to Soviet security. As Tulpanov later recalled, 'Our goal was to preserve all the treasures of German culture', especially 'what the fascists had appropriated and besmirched. We could not give up everything that the fascists had claimed for themselves. We had to purify it.'[13]

To what extent the Soviet government under Stalin was serious about permitting real democracy in Germany is unclear. Ultimately the German Democratic Republic, which was founded in October of 1949, over four years after the end of the war, became a socialist dictatorship governed almost exclusively by one party (although other parties did exist); but it is possible that if the western powers had been willing to preserve German neutrality and guarantee reparations payments from the west to the Soviet Union the latter might have been willing to accept a democratic, unified Germany. After all, it is not clear whether the mere fact of the existence of a socialist Germany was really that important to Soviet leaders – more important, for instance, than reparations payments from the far wealthier western part of the country, which was where Germany's major industrial region, the Ruhr, was located. The Soviet zone, in contrast, was far less heavily industrialized. At any rate, as the 'hot' Second World War between Germany and the Allies was rapidly supplanted by the Cold War between the United States and the Soviet Union, Stalin's intentions with respect to Germany were never seriously put to the test by western powers, and by the end of 1947 the division of Germany became increasingly inevitable.

German communists' determination to transform Germany into a peaceful, unthreatening country, and their desire to work with other antifascists, predated the end of the Second World War. Already in the mid-1930s, not long after Hitler's accession to power in January of 1933, the communists had worked towards what they called a Popular Front (Volksfront), which was intended to involve all antifascists – from the relatively conservative but democratic bourgeoisie to the communists' left-wing rivals, the Social Democrats – in the common struggle against Nazism. In order to make this effort convincing, communists needed to downplay their long-range goal for a dictatorship of the proletariat under the leadership of the KPD and instead stress the common element that connected them to bourgeois and Social Democratic antifascists: opposition to Nazism. Since, until Hitler's accession to power, the KPD had been involved in an extremely bitter internecine feud with the SPD (Social Democratic Party of Germany), even calling the Social Democrats 'social fascists', it is clear that the communists' proclamation of a *Volksfront* in the mid-1930s was to a large extent a tactical move intended to preserve and expand communist influence in a period of great danger, when both the KPD and the SPD were banned in Germany, along with any other non-Nazi political party. However, even though much of the *Volksfront* rhetoric was tactical, it had a powerful impact in the 1930s and 1940s, and many Germans – communists as well as non-communists – took it seriously.

The first major goal of the KPD in the Soviet zone, after the refounding of the party, was unification of the KPD with the SPD, a goal that was achieved in the Soviet zone – but not in the western zones – in April of 1946, with the cooperation of the SPD leader Otto Grotewohl and with the exertion of considerable pressure on any members of the SPD who opposed the conjoining of the two parties. The unification of the two socialist parties resulted in the creation of the Socialist Unity Party (SED), which was to become the ruling party of the GDR during the four decades of its existence. Walter Ulbricht and other communists trumpeted this unification as one of the signal achievements of German history more generally, since in their view it meant the unification of a working class whose bitter division, they believed, had helped make Hitler's triumphs possible; they hoped that the fusion of the two parties would make it possible to create a more progressive Germany and prevent a return to Nazism. As Walter Ulbricht was to put it later, 'the unification of the SPD and the KPD to form the Socialist Unity Party of Germany became the turning point in Germany's history, making it possible to prevent the revival of the rule of monopoly capitalism, of neo-Nazism, and of colonialism in one part of Germany and to create a strong bastion of peace in Germany'.[14]

In addition to working on the unification of the working class, however, the communists also wanted to involve non-socialists in the political transformation of the country, and hence their *Volksfront* rhetoric extended well beyond the newly formed SED. It is this *Volksfront* rhetoric that one hears in many of the proclamations of German communists from the mid-1940s, and that led to the establishment of the Democratic Block – an umbrella organization for all legal antifascist parties – in July of 1945; five years later the Democratic Block was to become the National Front, which was responsible for carrying out the GDR's elections. The GDR was never officially a one-party state; the National Front included representatives not just of the SED but also of the Christian Democratic Union (CDU), the Liberal Democratic Party (LDPD), the Democratic Farmers' Party of Germany (DBD) and even the NDPD (National Democratic Party of Germany), a party created especially for nationalists and former Nazis in order to integrate them into the politics of the Soviet zone. The National Front also included the leaders of major antifascist organizations, such as Johannes R. Becher's Kulturbund and the FDJ (Freie Deutsche Jugend or Free German Youth, the GDR's mass youth organization). Communist tactics in the immediate post-war period were based on at the very least the appearance of inclusiveness, and this emphasis on inclusiveness was to last until the end of the GDR, even if in practice it was always the SED that pulled the strings. Also, leading cultural figures like Johannes R. Becher were generally willing to go along with the tactics of the SED even when they disagreed with them because of their support of the SED's proclaimed overall strategy, that is, the creation of a socialist Germany. This was true even of a writer as critical as Brecht, who, although he disagreed, for instance, with the SED's brutal response to the 1953 uprising against new work norms, kept his criticisms to himself and did not make public his critical poem 'Die Lösung' (The Solution).

Culture always played an important role in the thinking of communist leaders for a number of reasons. For tactical political reasons an emphasis on culture was well suited for the creation of broad constituencies that would include not just communists but other Germans as well. Not all Germans were in agreement on the need for a dictatorship of the proletariat, but most Germans could agree on respect and esteem for the accomplishments of German culture, and in the assessment that Germany at the end of the Second World War had reached a historical and cultural nadir. In many of the proclamations of major communist cultural figures from the mid-1940s, one sees virtually no specific mention of communism but instead much broader mentions of the need for a democratic transformation of German culture. In September of 1944, at a meeting of German communist intellectuals in Moscow, Becher gave a speech on the 're-education of the German people', proclaiming that this would be both political and cultural: a 'national work of liberation and construction in the largest sense at the level of ideology and morality. [...] Our goal is to liberate the German people from all the reactionary detritus of its history, revealed in its crassest form in Hitler, and to bring to the German people, out of its own history and out of the histories of other nations, all the positive energies that make it capable of surviving and that will prevent it from once gain falling prey to imperialist adventures'.[15]

These sentiments were incorporated into the foundation of the Kulturbund in July 1945. At the ceremonial meeting marking the organization's creation, Becher proclaimed that the guiding star of cultural policy in the new Germany should be respect for the great accomplishments of German culture, coupled with an insistence that culture and politics should no longer be in opposition to each other but rather complement each other:

> In the political and moral attitude of our people we must now give clear, strong, convincing, shining expression to this rich heritage of humanism, of classicism, to the rich heritage of the workers' movement. Our classicism never corresponded to a classical politics. On the contrary, in our political actions we always acted against our best traditions. We were never able to find a political expression that corresponded to those high cultural achievements. We must now get beyond this unholy contradiction between intellect and power, which has led to the worst catastrophe in our history, and which ultimately even destroyed any free intellectual activity.[16]

What this meant was that cultural policy in the Soviet zone and later in the GDR was above all conservative, oriented toward preserving and promoting the heritage of German classicism, a heritage that communist leaders – and many others as well – believed had been betrayed by the Nazis; this was the implication of Tulpanov's later statement: 'We could not give up everything that the fascists had claimed for themselves. We had to purify it' (quoted above). As Becher argued in 1949, on the occasion of the 200th anniversary of Goethe's birth, 'if Goethe had been alive among the German people, then his living strength would have engendered such an overpowering hatred of Nazi barbarism that the movement would have failed at the very beginning'.[17] Victor Klemperer, an ethnically Jewish scholar of French literature who had survived both Nazi antisemitism and the firebombing of Dresden in February of 1945, agreed. Klemperer wrote in 1946 that the solution to Nazism had to be a renewed emphasis on German cultural traditions. The Nazis, Klemperer argued, represented 'the most extreme opposite of the basic views of the German classical era', and therefore the response to Nazism's devastation of the country had to be 'Further down the path of culture!'[18] The emphasis on traditional culture was something that communists like Becher and non-communists like Klemperer could agree on, and, furthermore, it dovetailed with the approach of many leading intellectuals in the western occupation zones, such as the great historian Friedrich Meinecke and the renowned literary scholar Ernst Robert Curtius. Nevertheless, the relatively uncritical celebration of traditional German culture in the GDR did separate its culture from that of the FRG, where attacks by Alewyn or the existentialist philosopher Karl Jaspers, not to mention the Frankfurt School theorist Theodor W. Adorno, on cultural smugness began to have a major cultural impact by the 1960s. In contrast, the classical heritage was celebrated and upheld in the GDR; this celebration informed, for instance, the career of the great GDR playwright Peter Hacks and was to find an echo, many years after the GDR's demise, in the complaint by a character in Uwe Tellkamp's novel *Der Turm* (The Tower, 2008) that Goethe is 'the generalissimo of opinions and the prince of feelings; because he is the engraving-king of the quotation-coins'.[19]

In conformity with such pro-classical sentiments, cultural policy in the Soviet zone was never about eliminating bourgeois culture or proclaiming the triumph of new artistic forms and genres. Instead, communist literary intellectuals, for the most part, wanted to use traditional literary and artistic forms in order to support a radically new social and economic structure; this created a tension between political radicalism, on the one hand, and artistic conservatism, on the other, that was difficult for many progressive intellectuals, such as Brecht, to put up with; but put up with it he and many others did.

Many of the debates among GDR literary intellectuals during the 1950s, such as the debate about formalism, harked back to similar debates of the 1920s and 1930s about Expressionism and other modernist cultural and literary movements. Although writers like Brecht championed modernism and artistic innovation, the dominant trend in literature and literary criticism was much more conservative, in line with the influential Hungarian critic Georg Lukács's celebration of the traditions of nineteenth-century realism. Lukács and his many disciples in the GDR tended to uphold conservative cultural values and to argue against extreme modernism or avant-gardism, against 'formalism', which was an epithet that could be applied to virtually any attempt at formal experimentation. Movements like Expressionism were politically and aesthetically suspect because they were believed to represent decadence and decline rather than strength and optimism, and any literary intellectuals who questioned the validity of German cultural traditions were likely to come in for stinging criticism. The irony of this, of course, was that artistic and literary experimenters had been subjected to eerily similar criticisms during the so-called 'Third Reich'. Although similarities between literature and literary criticism in the 'Third Reich' and the GDR should not be exaggerated – because there were significant differences, especially the focus in the GDR on realism and on economic and work life, as well as the virtually total absence of real literary or artistic battles within the 'Third Reich' – these similarities are nevertheless disturbing. In the run-up to the celebrations of the 200th anniversary of Goethe's birth, when Karl Jaspers expressed scepticism about the relevance of Goethe for the post-Holocaust world, the Soviet military officer Alexander Dymschitz castigated Jaspers and proclaimed Goethe to be 'the herald of Germany's national unity'. Johannes R. Becher, who succeeded in luring Thomas Mann to Weimar for the Goethe celebration that year, also spoke out against 'the existentialist blather about' Goethe's 'inability to grasp the whole problematic of the human being', arguing that, in contrast to the misery 'of existentialism, we find in Goethe that fear has been overcome', so that human beings can raise themselves 'in triumph even over death'.[20] Such sentiments frustrated Brecht and came in for criticism much later, in Tellkamp's *Der Turm*, but they had a profound impact on the development of East German culture.

Given the relatively conservative cultural predilections of German communist literary intellectuals, as well as communists' proclaimed wish to cooperate with all other antifascists, including bourgeois intellectuals, in the rebuilding of Germany, it is no coincidence that one of the first major literary-cultural battles in the young GDR occurred in 1953 over a work that was perceived as criticizing Goethe's most famous work, *Faust*. Hanns Eisler, a distinguished leftist composer and writer who had spent the years of the Nazi dictatorship in exile in the United States – like Eisler's friend and colleague Brecht, with whom Eisler frequently collaborated – had published excerpts from the libretto to his planned opera *Johann Faustus* in the second half of 1952. In contrast to Goethe, who had ended his complex two-part play with the salvation, not the damnation, of Faust, Eisler depicted Faust in a highly negative way: as the epitome of the German intellectual who betrays the poor and downtrodden for his own personal gain. As Eisler interpreted his own drama, 'He who rejects and betrays his people, the movement of his people and the revolution, by making a pact with the rulers, is the Devil's prize. He is rightly destroyed.'[21] For Eisler this pact with the devil had ultimately led to Nazism.

For more traditionalist communist intellectuals, Eisler's drama represented an intolerable attack on Germany's proud cultural heritage. Three meetings were held at Berlin's Academy of the Arts in the spring of 1953 to discuss Eisler's *Johann Faustus*, and most of the speakers were fiercely critical of it. Alexander Abusch proclaimed that 'certain of our artists have not thought deeply enough about the fundamental questions of our patriotic struggle and have thus not developed a genuine relationship with the great inheritance of our national literature', and he called Goethe's Faust 'a great, positive hero of our classical national drama' (even though Goethe's Faust had by no means been an unambiguously positive figure). The communist intellectual Wilhelm Girnus attacked Eisler in the SED national newspaper *Neues Deutschland* (whose cultural section Girnus edited) the following day, calling *Johann Faustus* 'pessimistic, élitist, hopeless, anti-national', and also 'unsuitable as the basis of a new national opera'. In Girnus's view, 'A conception which sees German history as nothing but "Misere", and which lacks an appreciation of the creative potential of the people, is false. This false conception necessarily goes hand in hand with a false understanding of questions of realism in artistic form and aesthetics.'[22] Largely as a result of these attacks, Eisler stopped work on the opera and never completed it. As he wrote in a letter to the SED's Central Committee in October of 1953, 'After the attacks on *Faustus*, I noticed that I had lost any impulse to write music.'[23] The attack on Eisler and Eisler's reaction to it demonstrate how the GDR's own cultural establishment often wound up stifling the country's most creative artists, even (or especially) ones who were sympathetic with communism itself. Such artists' devotion to the goal of a socialist Germany is evident in Eisler's letter to the Central Committee: 'Yet I cannot hope to find the motivation to write music again, which is what keeps me alive, anywhere but in the German Democratic Republic.'[24] Such artists wanted to support a socialist Germany, which they believed offered hope for a better future, but they inevitably came into conflict with the contradictory and often changing desires of the SED's leaders.

The primary aesthetic approach championed by communists from the 1930s onward was socialist realism, which was associated in the Soviet Union with Stalin's ideological henchman Andrei Alexandrovich Zhdanov. Socialist realism, promulgated in the Soviet Union in 1932, was also adopted in the Soviet occupation zone of Germany and in the later GDR, and it was championed by most communist writers as well as by party intellectuals like Alexander Abusch, who would succeed Johannes R. Becher as Minister of Culture in 1958. Socialist realism was supposed to provide a realistic depiction of human life from a socialist perspective; antirealism and antisocialism were frowned upon. Socialist-realist literature was also supposed to feature a 'positive hero' (the kind of hero that Abusch had seen in Goethe's Faust – in practice such a figure was often a member of the working class) that the reader could identify with and look up to; and, since socialism implied an optimistic philosophy of history, socialist-realist literature was supposed to convey optimism about the future. In practice there were often conflicts between realism, on the one hand, and optimism, on the other, since the real situation of Germany in the immediate aftermath of the Second World War was hardly a pleasant one. The emphasis among party intellectuals on socialist realism also led to predictable disagreements not only between socialist and non-socialist writers but also between the party's own ideologues, such as Becher and Abusch, and the GDR's most famous and talented writers and artists – people like Brecht and Eisler, who favoured a more modernist approach than most party ideologues were comfortable with, and who tended to be, as demonstrated by Eisler's *Johann Faustus*, more critical of traditional German culture. In spite of such disagreements, both Eisler and Brecht supported the socialist German state, and both created art that explicitly supported it. In the 1950s, for instance, when the dictates of socialist realism – not to mention the need to rebuild Germany, which found expression in the title of the Kulturbund's journal *Aufbau* (literally: building) and in the GDR's major publishing house, the Aufbau-Verlag, which continues to exist to this day – often meant a primary focus in literature and art on the world of work and its problems and triumphs, there were plays like Karl Grünberg's *Golden fliesst der Stahl* (The Golden Flow of Steel, 1950), about the struggle for production in a steel mill. Such works, not surprisingly, tended to dispense with psychological complexity even as they celebrated the world of labour; but

Brecht, during this period, also toyed with the idea of creating a much more complex picture of the world of work in his project about Hans Garbe, a highly productive East German worker who was much-praised in the GDR press. Although Brecht never completed this project, his successor Heiner Müller did complete a play with a similar theme, about the complexities and problems of the push for higher production, *Der Lohndrücker* (The Scab, 1958). The emphasis on the world of work ultimately led to the Bitterfeld Conference of 1959 and the so-called 'Bitterfelder Weg' in the 1960s, in which GDR writers were encouraged to focus on production, while GDR workers were encouraged to write. While western stereotypes of socialist realism tend to imagine it as simplistic and celebratory, the examples of Brecht and Müller demonstrate that this was not always the case. At its best, socialist realism was able to focus on the world of work and production in ways rarely equalled by the literature of the west.

In 1950, after the foundation of the GDR, Eisler composed the music to the GDR's national anthem, with words by none other than Johannes R. Becher:

> Auferstanden aus Ruinen
> Und der Zukunft zugewandt,
> Laß uns dir zum Guten dienen,
> Deutschland, einig Vaterland.
> Alte Not gilt es zu zwingen,
> Und wir zwingen sie vereint,
> Denn es muß uns doch gelingen,
> Daß die Sonne schön wie nie
> Über Deutschland scheint.

(Resurrected from the ruins and / Turned toward tomorrow, / Let's say goodbye to our sorrow, / Germany, united fatherland. / We must overcome old woe / And overcome it as one / For we already know: An even brighter sun / Will soon shine over German lands.)[25]

One of the many historical ironies of GDR culture is that after Erich Honecker succeeded Walter Ulbricht as the GDR's paramount leader in 1971, this national anthem ceased to be sung at official events, although Eisler's music continued to be played. The problem with Becher's words after 1971 was that the words 'Deutschland, einig Vaterland' (Germany, united fatherland), which had corresponded to communist policy in 1950, no longer corresponded to the SED's approach in the 1970s and 1980s, which emphasized the GDR's self-sufficiency rather than German unity. Since the GDR was typically one of the most prolific winners of medals at Olympic events, an international audience thus got to witness the spectacle of the best East German athletes standing in silence while Eisler's music was played. The GDR is probably the only case in world history of a country in which the words to its own official national anthem were in effect banned.

Most of the best German writers – such as Thomas Mann and his brother Heinrich, Bertolt Brecht, and the great novelist Anna Seghers – had left the country during the Nazi dictatorship. After the end of the Third Reich, one of the primary questions for German culture was whether these writers would return to their homeland, and if so, to which part of Germany: the socialist east or the capitalist west. One of Johannes R. Becher's great accomplishments as leader of the Kulturbund was that he encouraged such people to return. In November of 1945 the Kulturbund issued a proclamation to German emigrants, who, it claimed, had pre-served Germany's honour, and who, 'in word and deed have publicly vouched for the fact that the true, free German spirit still lives and breathes and that its victory is certain'.[26] The Kulturbund's invitation to emigrant writers stood in stark contrast to the situation in the west, where exiles like Thomas Mann – who never did return permanently to Germany but chose instead to relocate from California to neutral Switzerland – were often vilified in the press for supposedly having left the country in its time of need. Anna Seghers returned to Germany in 1947 and Bertolt Brecht returned in 1948. Both supported the SED and the creation of socialism in the Soviet zone, and both settled in the GDR. Seghers wrote some of the most moving fictional depictions of German history in the twentieth cen-tury, and her novels *Das siebte Kreuz* (The Seventh Cross, 1942) and *Die Toten bleiben jung* (The Dead Stay Young, 1949), both about the communist resistance to the Nazi dictatorship, became standard reading in the GDR. After his return to Berlin, Brecht together with his wife Helene Weigel established the Berliner Ensemble from 1954 on in Berlin's Theater am Schiffbauerdamm, and it was in this and other Berlin theatres that Brecht, after fifteen years of exile from his homeland, was finally able to produce some of the plays that he had written during his years of exile: masterpieces like *Mutter Courage und ihre Kinder* (Mother Courage and Her Children), *Der gute Mensch von Sezuan* (The Good Person of Sezuan), *Der kaukasische Kreidekreis* (The Caucasian Chalk Circle) and *Leben des Galilei* (Life of Galileo), which exerted a powerful influence on the development of world theatre in the 1950s and 1960s. In the arena of culture, then, it is fair to say that the GDR and not the West German Federal Republic was able to attract the most famous and influential exile writers. As Brecht wrote in response to the West German writer Wolfgang Weyrauch, who had criticized him for writing lyrics in support of the East German state, 'I have my opinions not because I am here; rather, I am here because I have my opinions.'[27]

It was Anna Seghers who, in her brilliant novella *Der Mann und sein Name* (The Man and His Name, 1952), was able to capture the cultural situation of the GDR in the immediate aftermath of the war. The novella is about a former SS man who once worked in a Nazi concentration camp, where he almost certainly participated in the oppression of anti-Nazi resistance fighters. Like so many other real and fictional Nazis at the end of the Second World War, this man does not quite know how to respond to the utter defeat of Nazism, a movement that had previously been so triumphant and that had worshipped power and success. The protagonist's world is both literally and figuratively shattered. In order to hide from justice, he takes on a false name: that of a communist resistance fighter who he knows was killed in the concentration camp where he worked. Ultimately the protagonist even becomes a communist and a member of the SED, but over time it becomes increasingly difficult for him to live a double life, especially when the entire meaning of history seems to be opened up to him through his study of Marxism-Leninism. In other words, increasingly the Nazi protagonist becomes a communist, and this transformation is not just one of convenience but one of deep conviction. In the end the protagonist's deception is discovered, and he is stripped of his party membership and must begin all over again, using his real name. This figure is hardly the stereotypical 'positive hero' that critics in both the east and the west tended to expect from socialist realism; rather, he is a deeply problematic, flawed, but, therefore, also realistically portrayed human being. In this novella the real 'positive hero', the resistance fighter whose name the protagonist has appropriated, is dead and therefore never able to make an appearance. Seghers's novella depicts an archetypal situation of the immediate post-war period. The GDR was a socialist state founded on the ruins of a Nazi state dedicated to the elimination of what its leaders perceived as 'Jewish' socialism, and many of its citizens had been ardent Nazis prior to the foundation of the GDR. Just as Seghers's protagonist is trying to transform himself from a Nazi into a communist, so too the German Democratic Republic proclaimed a desire to transform a Nazi Germany into a socialist Germany. That this transformation would be difficult is admitted in the conclusion to the novella: 'Es wird nicht leicht sein' (It won't be easy).[28] History, of course, proved that Seghers was right.

Notes

1. Wolfgang Leonhard, *Child of the Revolution*, trans. C. M. Woodhouse (Chicago: Regnery, 1958), p. 373.

2. Ibid., p. 374.

3. Cited in Stephen Brockmann, *German Literary Culture at the Zero Hour* (Rochester, NY: Camden House, 2004), p. 92.

4. Bertolt Brecht, Journal entry from 3 August 1945, *Werke: Große kommentierte Berliner und Frankfurter Ausgabe*, 30 vols., ed. Werner Hecht, Jan Knopf, Werner Mittenzwei and Klaus-Detlef Müller, vol. 27, *Journale 2* (Berlin, Weimar, and Frankfurt: Aufbau and Suhrkamp, 1995), p. 228. Here and elsewhere, translations from German-language sources are my own unless otherwise noted.

5. Cited in Brockmann, *German Literary Culture at the Zero Hour*, p. 132.

6. Carsten Gansel, *Parlament des Geistes: Literatur zwischen Hoffnung und Repression 1945–1961* (Berlin: BasisDruck, 1996), p. 91.

7. Cited in Wolfgang Fritz Haug (ed.), *Historisch-Kritisches Wörterbuch des Marxismus*, vol. 4 (Hamburg: Argument, 1999), p. 157. This definition of fascism became official at the thirteenth plenum of the Executive Committee of the Communist International in December 1933.

8. Leonhard, *Child of the Revolution*, p. 360.

9. Walter Ulbricht, 'Wie kam es zur Vereinigung von KPD und SPD?', in Walter Ulbricht *Reden und Aufsätze* (Hamburg: Blinkfüer, 1968), pp. 115–27; p. 123.

10. Wolfgang Leonhard, *Die Revolution entlässt ihre Kinder* (Cologne: Kiepenheuer & Witsch, 1957), p. 340. My translation; this passage is not in the published English-language translation.

11. Dietrich Orlow, 'The GDR's Failed Search for a National Identity, 1945–1949', *German Studies Review*, 29.3 (October 2006), 537–58; p. 539.

12. Ibid., p. 539.

13. Cited in Gerd Dietrich, *Politik und Kultur in der SBZ 1945–1949* (Bern: Lang, 1993), p. 15.

14. Ulbricht, 'Wie kam es zur Vereinigung von KPD und SPD?', p. 127.

15. Wolfgang Schivelbusch, *Vor dem Vorhang: Das geistige Berlin 1945–1948* (Frankfurt/M.: Fischer, 1997), pp. 120–21.

16. Johannes R. Becher, 'Auferstehen!', in Becher, *Gesammelte Werke*, vol. 16, *Publizistik II 1939–1945* (Berlin and Weimar: Aufbau, 1978), pp. 454–62; p. 461.

17. Johannes R. Becher, 'Aus: Der Befreier', in Karl Robert Mandelkow (ed.), *Goethe im Urteil seiner Kritiker: Dokumente zur Wirkungsgeschichte Goethes in Deutschland Teil IV 1918–1982* (Munich: Beck, 1984), pp. 318–32; p. 321.

18. Victor Klemperer, *Kultur: Erwägungen nach dem Zusammenbruch des Nazismus* (Berlin: Neues Leben, 1946), p. 6; p. 12.

19. Uwe Tellkamp, *Der Turm* (Frankfurt/M.: Suhrkamp, 2008), p. 347.

20. Cited in Brockmann, *German Literary Culture at the Zero Hour*, p. 129.

21. Cited in Peter Davies, 'Hanns Eisler's "Faustus" Libretto and the Problem of East German National Identity', *Music & Letters*, 81.4 (November 2000), 585–98; p. 592.

22. Ibid., pp. 595–96.

23. Ibid., p. 598.

24. Ibid.
25. Johannes R. Becher, 'Auferstanden aus Ruinen', in Becher, *Gesammelte Werke*, vol. 6, *Gedichte 1949–1958* (Berlin: Aufbau, 1973), p. 61. Brecht, tellingly, wrote a much less celebratory alternative to this national anthem entitled 'Kinderhymne' (Children's Anthem), which emphasized not triumphalism but the ordinariness of German post-war aspirations: 'Neither over nor yet under / Other peoples will we be / From the Oder to the Rhineland / From the Alps to the North Sea'. Brecht, 'Children's Anthem' trans. Edith Roseveare, in Brecht, *Poems 1913–1956*, ed. John Willett and Ralph Manheim (London: Methuen, 1987), p. 423.
26. Dietrich, *Politik und Kultur in der SBZ 1945–1949*, p. 238.
27. Bertolt Brecht, 'Antworten auf Fragen des Schriftstellers Wolfgang Weyrauch', Brecht, *Werke: Große kommentierte Berliner und Frankfurter Ausgabe*, vol. 23, *Schriften 3*, pp. 216–20; p. 220.
28. Anna Seghers, 'Der Mann und sein Name', in Seghers, *Der Bienenstock: Gesammelte Erzählungen in drei Bänden*, vol. 3 (Berlin: Aufbau, 1963), pp. 56–153; p. 153.

CHAPTER 3

DEFA's antifascist myths and the construction of national identity in East German cinema

Seán Allan

On 17 May 1946 the director of the Soviet Military Administration's Propaganda Division, Sergei Tulpanov, formally issued the Deutsche Film-Aktiengesellschaft (DEFA), with its licence to resume film production at the Babelsberg studios in Potsdam. Outlining the Soviet Union's vision of a programme of de-Nazification and political re-education in Germany, he left his audience in no doubt of the importance of developing a new generation of filmmakers committed to a democratic antifascist cinema.[1] Not surprisingly, these views on the ideological importance of film and other related art forms dovetailed perfectly with those of the exiled members of the KPD (German Communist Party), for whom, in the words of Johannes R. Becher, peace was 'the continuation of the war against fascism by other means, mainly ideological means'.[2] However, the rapid resumption of film production in the east reflected not only the Soviets' understanding of cinema's key role in the post-war ideological struggle but also their realization that any unnecessary delay would give rival studios in Munich and Hamburg greater opportunities to entice leading filmmakers to the west.

The situation for left-leaning German filmmakers at the end of the Second World War was very different to that with which the writers of fiction and poetry were confronted. Whereas the latter could draw on an existing tradition of antifascist literature produced in exile, progressive film-makers had to look back to the era of Expressionism and to the proletarian cinema of the Weimar Republic for their inspiration. Although the majority of filmmakers working for DEFA (most of whom lived in the western sectors of Berlin) were ideologically committed to an antifascist agenda, there was very little consensus as to the form such films should take, and this lack of agreement is reflected in the stylistic diversity of the films released in the period 1946–49. If there is indeed any common denominator linking such proto-antifascist films such as Wolfgang Staudte's *Die Mörder sind unter uns*

(The Murderers Are among Us, 1946), Kurt Maetzig's *Die Buntkarierten* (Girls in Gingham, 1949) and Staudte's *Rotation* (1949), then it is the rejection of war mediated, in some cases, via psychologically traumatized male returnees. And while everyone agreed that the model to be avoided was the aesthetic legacy of Ufa (Universum Film AG – the principal German film company during the Weimar Republic) with its infamous 'factory of dreams', embarking on a new direction was to prove problematic, not least because most of those recruited to the early DEFA production teams had learned their craft at Ufa during the 1940s.

Just how difficult breaking with the past could be is exemplified by Kurt Maetzig's *Ehe im Schatten* (Marriage in the Shadows, 1947). In it we witness the tragic story of a successful actor named Hans Wieland, whose Jewish wife, the actress Elizabeth Maurer, is banned from appearing on stage by the Nazis. Having achieved fame for their pre-1933 performances of the eighteenth-century dramatist Friedrich Schiller's play *Kabale und Liebe* (Love and Intrigue), the couple find themselves forced to perform their stage roles in real life when, in a melodramatic quasi-Schillerian *Liebestod* at the end of the film, Hans poisons Elizabeth's tea before drinking from the same cup himself. Yet despite being one of the first films to address questions of Jewish victimhood during the Nazi period, its exaggerated pathos obscures, rather than clarifies, the historical reasons for Elizabeth's persecution.[3]

At a thematic level, Maetzig's film breaks new ground by highlighting the disastrous consequences of conceptualizing art as a transcendent realm in which artists might seek refuge from the contingencies of everyday politics; formally, however, it remains firmly stuck in the aesthetics of 1940s Ufa melodrama. A resounding success with the viewing public across all four sectors of divided Berlin when first released on 3 October 1947, it was, perhaps inevitably, condemned by Brecht as 'terrible kitsch!'[4] Indeed Maetzig himself subsequently acknowledged that 'genuine emotions are [. . .] obscured by the performers' unnecessarily sentimental style of acting [. . .] and stylistically, the film owes much to Ufa'.[5] That this should be so is hardly surprising, for the production credits read like a 'who's who' of German cinema from the early 1940s. The author of the treatment on which the film had been based, Hans Schweikart, had directed *Das Fräulein von Barnhelm* (Minna von Barnhelm, 1940); cameraman Friedl Behn-Grund had been the cinematographer for Wolfgang Liebeneiner's Nazi propaganda film *Ich klage an* (I Accuse, 1941); art director Otto Erdmann had acted as set-designer for Helmut Käutner's melodrama *Romanze in Moll* (Romance in a Minor Key, 1943); and composer

Wolfgang Zeller had written the score for Veit Harlan's infamous anti-
Semitic film *Jud Süß* (Jew Süss, 1940). Nonetheless, as the popularity of *Ehe
im Schatten* demonstrated, breaking with the past placed demands not only
on filmmakers but on audiences too: 'I adopted this style of cinematography partly out of a sense of uncertainty', Maetzig conceded, '[b]ut also
from a desire to meet the expectations of my target audience'.[6]

With the transformation of the SED into an explicitly Stalinist organization at the start of 1949 and the founding of the GDR on 7 October that
same year, the mythologization of the state's allegedly antifascist origins
came to play an increasingly important role in the construction of the
GDR as the 'Other' of fascism, and in shoring up the leading role of the
party within the newly created state. Not surprisingly, filmmakers at
DEFA soon found that the fuzzy definitions of antifascism with which
they had been working hitherto were to be subjected to a much greater
degree of ideological control. In contrast to filmmakers of a liberal political
persuasion in the west, who portrayed fascism as a form of political
totalitarianism that could only be countered through guarantees of individual freedom backed up by the promotion of a system of liberal parliamentary democracy, antifascist filmmakers in the east found themselves
increasingly under pressure to follow the so-called 'Dimitrov doctrine' of
1935. Named after the Bulgarian communist Georgi Dimitrov, this theory
portrayed fascism as an essentially economic phenomenon, defining it as
'the open terrorist dictatorship of the most reactionary, most chauvinistic
and most imperialist elements of finance capital'.[7] Seen in this light, the
GDR's rejection of capitalism could be seen as a radical break with
Germany's fascist past, while the use of the terms 'fascist' and 'antifascist'
(rather than Nazi and anti-Nazi) obscured the historical specificity of
German fascism and facilitated the rehabilitation of former members of
the NSDAP in East German political life. An early casualty of this shift in
cultural policy was Falk Harnack's *Das Beil von Wandsbek* (The Axe of
Wandsbek, 1950), a film about a Hamburg butcher recruited by the Nazis
to execute four members of the antifascist resistance. Withdrawn by the
DEFA studio management, ostensibly because of its failure to condemn
the central character outright, Harnack's film served as a warning that such
psychologically oriented approaches to the question of Nazi collaboration
(to say nothing of the questions the film raised about the appointment of
former Nazis to positions of political prominence in the GDR) would no
longer be tolerated.

By contrast, Kurt Maetzig's *Der Rat der Götter* (Council of the Gods,
1950) – the first concerted attempt in either East or West Germany to offer

a sustained analysis of the causes of German fascism – is a film dominated by economics rather than individual or social psychology. Drawing on Richard Sasuly's study *I.G. Farben* (1947) and documents from the Nuremberg trials, Maetzig and his scriptwriters, Friedrich Wolf and Philipp Gecht, set out to expose the company's involvement in supporting Hitler. In keeping with the prevailing Dimitrov doctrine, the film posits a link between monopolistic capitalism and fascism; and as in many DEFA productions of the 1950s, Hitler is portrayed as a weak individual, wholly dependent for his political survival on the grace and favour of the 'gods' of monopoly capitalism. Yet while few questioned the role played by heavy industry in supporting Hitler during the 1930s, what made Maetzig's film so controversial (and led to it being banned in the Federal Republic) was its depiction of the agreement struck between the firm I.G. Farben and the American corporation Standard Oil during the Second World War. By exchanging a range of lucrative patents for an assurance that, in the event of an aerial war, the German industrial plant will be spared, each company ensures its continued economic survival in the post-war period. As the chairman of I.G. Farben, Mauch, and his American counterpart, Mr Lawson, meet in Switzerland to discuss the division of the post-war world into spheres of influence, the film depicts a world dominated not by politicians, but by global capitalists whose common enemy is the Soviet Union and the international labour movement.

At the time of its release and for long afterwards Maetzig insisted that his film was not a work of propaganda targeted at the Federal Republic, but an accurate account of historical events.[8] Here, as in so many other DEFA antifascist classics, the fetishization of historical 'authenticity' plays a crucial role in masking the film's ideological agenda. Not only does *Der Rat der Götter* begin with an intertitle reminding us that 'the plot is based on facts taken from the minutes of the Nuremberg trials of war criminals from I.G. Farben and other American sources', but its claim to authenticity is further heightened through the interpolation of documentary material at a number of key moments such as when we see newsreel footage depicting the construction of an autobahn juxtaposed with similar footage of Göring delivering a speech on rearmament. Yet throughout the film, this type of visual montage is constantly undercut by a modernist soundtrack (composed by Hanns Eisler) with the result that the film assumes the form of a cinematic *Lehrstück*, or didactic work, on the relationship between capitalism and military aggression.

As Maetzig acknowledged, it is scarcely possible to do justice to the complex relationship between monopoly capitalism, fascism and military conflict in a film lasting just 107 minutes. However, his claim that *Der Rat der Götter* could not be construed as an attack on the Federal Republic because the events depicted in it date back to 1933 seems disingenuous. Although the intertitles indicate that the action takes place in the 'Rhineland industrial zone in 1933', the first clearly recognizable image is a shot of the I.G. Farben building in Frankfurt am Main. As cinema-viewers in 1950 knew only too well, not only had that building survived the Allied air raids, but it had also served as the centre of the US European Command; and also it was there that the introduction of the Deutschmark had been announced on 20 June 1948. In inviting viewers to draw a link between the past and the present, and between militarism and capital, *Der Rat der Götter* went further than perhaps any other antifascist film at the time and played a key role in promoting the use of the term 'fascist' to refer to the Federal Republic and the United States in GDR political discourse. By portraying fascism as a global economic phenomenon, *Der Rat der Götter* underlined both the antifascist credentials of the GDR and the SED's depiction of its German neighbour as an aggressively militaristic regime in which the spirit of Hitler's Germany lived on.

While *Der Rat der Götter* posited a link between the economic basis of German fascism and the post-war Federal Republic, cinematic representations of antifascist resistance produced by DEFA in the 1950s were to play an increasingly important role in the construction of a founding myth of national identity for the GDR in so far as they suggested that its origins could be traced back to the antifascist resistance fighters imprisoned in Buchenwald, to the international brigades fighting in the Spanish Civil War of 1936–39 and to the radical political activists of the Weimar Republic. In this respect, the significance of the murdered communist leader Ernst Thälmann for the construction of a distinctively East German historical imaginary can hardly be overstated and, of all the films produced by DEFA, perhaps no other has been quite so overtly deployed in the service of political self-legitimation by the SED as Kurt Maetzig's two-part epic *Ernst Thälmann – Sohn seiner Klasse* (Ernst Thälmann – Son of the Working Classes, 1954) and *Ernst Thälmann – Führer seiner Klasse* (Ernst Thälmann – Leader of the Working Classes, 1955). Endowed with a huge budget, Maetzig's 'Thälmann-project' was one of the few productions of the 1950s to be filmed in colour, and during the first four weeks of its release it was seen by over 3 million people in the GDR.

During its production, Maetzig and his scriptwriters Willi Bredel and Michael Tschesno-Hell, both of whom had been appointed to the project as early as 1949, found themselves under constant pressure to abandon their original more biographically oriented treatment of Thälmann's life in favour of one that reflected Ulbricht's wish to show the protagonist not simply as 'the leader of the German working classes in their struggle for peace, democracy and socialism' but more importantly as 'the leader of that party which today [. . .] represents the decisive political force in the GDR'.[9] Further evidence of the extent to which this mythologization of the past was intended to serve the needs of the present is evident in the prominent roles assigned to Walter Ulbricht and Wilhelm Pieck, both of whom are closely associated with Thälmann throughout the film. However, adapting Thälmann's biography to harmonize with the historical imaginary of the SED in the mid-1950s required a number of substantial alternations to well-known facts: the first part – *Sohn seiner Klasse* – shows Thälmann as part of a revolutionary group of German soldiers on the western front in 1918, and as the charismatic leader of the Hamburg shipyard strikes of 1923 – two sequences so obviously at odds with the historical facts that even Sepp Schwab, the SED hardliner in charge of DEFA, argued for their omission.[10] Nor did this process of re-editing the past end with the film's release; having been instructed in the early 1950s to give Stalin a more prominent role in the film, the filmmakers were subsequently compelled to remove all references to him following Khrushchev's denunciation of the former Soviet leader in 1956.

As in Maetzig's earlier film, *Der Rat der Götter*, German fascism in *Ernst Thälmann – Führer seiner Klasse* is presented as an effect of monopoly capitalism, and Hitler and the Nazis are portrayed as puppets manipulated by the German and American entrepreneurs Hauck and McFuller. Yet the real enemy in the film is not Hitler and his capitalist backers, but rather the SPD – the social fascists ('Sozialfaschisten') – whose failure to endorse the radical economic policies of the KPD is instrumental in facilitating Hitler's rise to power. Whereas in the earlier DEFA productions during the founding years almost all the protagonists who undergo a 'road-to-Damascus' style conversion switch their allegiance from the NSDAP to the KPD, in Maetzig's 'Thälmann-project' such conversions invariably involve the rejection of the SPD in favour of the KPD. However, what makes *Ernst Thälmann – Führer seiner Klasse* so fascinating for film historians is not its predictably schematic rewriting of German history, but rather the de-historicizing aesthetic it mobilizes in the service of such propaganda. Thälmann's status as the iconic embodiment of an abstract political idea rather than an individual of flesh and blood is accentuated by an almost complete lack of psychological interiority and character development. This mythologization of the central protagonist is further enhanced through the use of low camera angles and/or extreme close-ups that situate Thälmann on a pedestal in relation to the viewer. Whereas in Maetzig's *Der Rat der Götter*, the discordant tones of Eisler's modernist soundtrack were used to underscore the contradictions of capitalism, the very absence of such a musical commentary in *Ernst Thälmann – Führer seiner Klasse* stands in the way of a similar analysis of the contradictions within the GDR historical imaginary. Instead, Wilhelm Neef's highly emotive score enhances both the idealized image of Thälmann as a revolutionary martyr and the pathos of the film generally.

It is not difficult to identify the aesthetic models underpinning Maetzig's Thälmann-project; the use of a predominantly red colour palette, on the one hand, and quasi-religious iconography, on the other, point unmistakably to the influence of the Soviet filmmaker Mikhail Chiaureli and his monumentalist films *Padeniye Berlina* (The Fall of Berlin, 1946) and *Kliatva* (The Oath, 1946).[11] Just as in *The Oath*, Chiaureli's biography of Stalin, the personal history of the bolshevik peasant Vavara is intertwined with the wider history of the Soviet Union, so too in Maetzig's Thälmann-films the sub-plot of Fiete and Änne Jansen offers ordinary East German viewers a point of identification and a means of linking their own memories of history with the greater historical narrative of the SED embodied in the transcendent figure of Thälmann. However, as Sabine Hake has argued, 'the formal debts to the genius films from the Third Reich are undeniable', and a comparison of Maetzig's *Ernst Thälmann – Führer seiner Klasse* and Wolfgang Liebeneiner's 1940 production *Bismarck* underlines just how similar these films are stylistically.[12] Not only are *Bismarck* and *Thälmann* shot in almost identical fashion but their status as messianic figures transcending the contingency of their immediate historical context is reflected in a transfigured gaze constantly directed above and beyond the camera. Seen in this light, the subsequent rejection of the Thälmann-films (by both audiences and director alike)[13] serves as a reminder of the contradiction that lies at their very heart, namely the attempt to render a materialist conception of history using a profoundly ahistorical idealist aesthetic.

While Thälmann's biography was exploited by the SED to provide the GDR with a pre-history extending back to the Weimar Republic and beyond, the Spanish Civil War of 1936–39 also lent itself to a similar process of mythologization, albeit one with an internationalist dimension. Although references to the Spanish Civil War (usually in the form of the celebrated 'Jamara Song') adorn many DEFA films, the first feature film specifically about the international brigades, Karl Paryla's *Mich dürstet* (I'm Thirsty, 1956), did not appear until the 20th anniversary of the conflict. In *Mich dürstet* the arrival of Republican soldiers from Madrid helps the peasant boy Pablo transform his village into an effective antifascist force. When Pablo's lover, Magdalena, is killed by a German bomb he is filled with a hatred of everything German; nonetheless, his subsequent encounter with the International Brigades teaches him that not all Germans are fascists. While the didactic thrust of Paryla's rather wooden production was hardly subtle, it did reflect the changing landscape of German-German politics during the Cold War. East German cinema-viewers could hardly have failed to map the contrasting representations of German military action in Paryla's film onto the political developments of 1955 and, in particular, the recent integration of the Federal Republic into the NATO alliance. For, as Stefan Soldovieri has argued, the release in the west of Harald Reinl's *Solange du lebst* (As Long As You Live) in 1955 – an anti-communist film inspired by the climate of McCarthyism in which a young German pilot helps 'liberate' a Spanish village from the 'oppressive' rule of the Republican forces – had addressed the need to provide citizens in the Federal Republic with positive images of German suffering and sacrifice in military combat.[14]

While the representation of the Spanish Civil War in Paryla's *Mich dürstet* is, aesthetically speaking, rather conventional, the same cannot be said of Frank Beyer's *Fünf Patronenhülsen* (Five Cartridges) of 1960. Since the release of *Mich dürstet* in 1956, the cultural significance of the Spanish Civil War in the East German historical imagination had undergone a number of changes.[15] Following Khrushchev's denunciation of Stalin, the Soviet Union had become increasingly open about its military involvement in the Spanish Civil War. Up until then GDR historians had denied any knowledge of Soviet involvement in Spain (and there are no references to the Soviet Union in Paryla's *Mich dürstet*). By contrast, in Frank Beyer's *Fünf Patronenhülsen* the Soviet communications officer Wasja dies the death of an heroic martyr. Even more important for an understanding of the film's presentation of military conflict, however, were developments in the East German Ministry for National Defence and the creation of the National People's Army (NVA) in 1956. Although the NVA remained a voluntary professional army up until 1962, compulsory military service had already been introduced into the FRG in 1956. Fearful that rumours of compulsory military service in the GDR would swell the ranks of those already emigrating to the west, the SED also sought to use the Spanish Civil War as a source of inspiring images of military action for East Germans that were untainted by any association with the Second World War, and which could be exploited to bolster feelings of solidarity in the Cold War and ongoing struggle against global fascism.

Directed by the twenty-eight-year-old Beyer (who had worked as an assistant to Maetzig during the making of the Thälmann-films), and starring a young Armin Müller-Stahl and an even younger Manfred Krug, *Fünf Patronenhülsen* is a film firmly rooted in the second generation of DEFA filmmakers. It shows the German Commander Witting (played by the archetypal antifascist actor Erwin Geschonneck) entrusting five members of his International Brigade with what they (mistakenly) believe to be part of a document outlining the fascist forces' plan of attack. When they finally reach the headquarters of their retreating brigade, they discover that contained within the spent cartridge each has been carrying is not the enemy's battle plan, but a message from their dying commander which, when reassembled, reads, 'Stay together. That way you will survive.'

Working for the first time with a so-called 'optisches Drehbuch' – a storyboard on which details of the camerawork were meticulously planned – Beyer and his team explored new ways in which the drama of Walter Gorrish's screenplay could be conveyed not through dialogue, but through a visual language based on the stylized depiction of the heroic masculine body. The depth of field provided by a 28 mm lens of the kind usually used for long shots enabled the cameraman Günter Marczinowsky to generate a series of highly expressive images depicting the suffering body locked in a struggle with the unremittingly harsh Sierra landscape (see Figure 1). This modernist approach to film aesthetics that combined elements of neorealism and quasi-Expressionist cinematography was further enhanced through the use of montage, most notably in the Russian Wasja's stream of hallucinatory images as he searches for water. It is, of course, tempting to see this departure from conventional socialist-realist aesthetics as a rejection on Beyer's part of the grand filmic narratives of DEFA's antifascist cinema. Yet, as Sabine Hake has argued, it is important not to fall into the trap of equating filmic experimentation with expressions of political dissent.[16] Whereas the conventionality of a film such as *Mich dürstet* might be seen as a stagnation of the antifascist genre, Beyer's achievement in embedding a simple, but emotionally powerful antifascist narrative within a modernist aesthetic framework represents not a rejection, but rather a creative renewal, of the genre. And as the closing sequence suggests – a sequence in which the face of the old communist Witting is blended into close-up shots of the young survivors – the antifascist torch has been transferred successfully from one generation to the next, not only from Witting to his comrades but also from the first generation of East German filmmakers like Maetzig and Geschonnek, both born before the First World War, to the new generation of Beyer, Müller-Stahl and Krug, all of whom were born during the 1930s.

Figure 1 The suffering antifascist body. Erwin Geschonneck as Heinrich Witting. From: *Fünf Patronenhülsen* (*Five Cartridges*, 1960) dir. by Frank Beyer, DEFA, 1960. DVD capture.

While the modernist elements of *Fünf Patronenhülsen* are part of an affirmative cinema of affect that sought to update and revitalize early 1950s paradigms of heroic antifascism, the new wave aesthetic of Konrad Wolf's films of the late 1960s serves a quite different function. In part, this change of direction can be explained in terms of the traumatic legacy of the infamous Eleventh Plenum of the Central Committee of the SED in December 1965, a process that saw twelve films banned and a number of writers and filmmakers subjected to scathing attacks. The mood after 1965/66 was in stark contrast to that of the early 1960s. Following the building of the Berlin Wall in 1961 and the landmark Kafka conference of 1963 in Liblice, a number of filmmakers felt sufficiently confident to explore ways in which the antifascist genre might be reworked aesthetically. One of the boldest undertakings in this respect was Ralf Kirsten's *Der verlorene Engel* (The Lost Angel, 1965/71), a screen adaptation of Franz Fühmann's novel about the Expressionist sculptor Ernst Barlach. Barlach had always been a controversial figure in the GDR, and the first major exhibition of his work had been prematurely closed in 1952. Kirsten's film sought to rehabilitate Barlach and make a case for incorporating his Expressionist figures within a new paradigm of modernist antifascist aesthetics that would challenge the reductionist approach of socialist realism. However, *Der verlorene Engel* had the distinction of being the only film not set in the contemporary GDR to be banned in the wake of the Eleventh Plenum. As the newly appointed president of the East German Academy of Arts, Konrad Wolf was well acquainted with the fate of Kirsten's film. Anxious that DEFA should not be cut off from developments in new-wave cinema in both Western and Eastern Europe, and keen to build on the modernist agenda he had embraced with his own *nouvelle vague*-inspired adaptation of *Der geteilte Himmel* (Divided Heaven, 1964), Wolf chose to return once again to what many regarded as the safe haven of the antifascist genre with his next film *Ich war neunzehn* (I Was Nineteen, 1968). However, in embedding the narrative of *Ich war neunzehn* within a modernist aesthetic, Wolf sought to address a new generation of East German cinema audiences who had come to take an increasingly sceptical view of the heroic master narratives of antifascism.

Both thematically and formally, *Ich war neunzehn* is a film that invites the viewer to reflect on the role played by the media and indeed all forms of representation in constructing history and memory.[17] The clearest example of this is to be found in the propaganda work of the young Gregor and the two Soviet officers, Sascha and Vadim, as they travel through the bleak landscape of the eastern front announcing the German defeat over loudspeakers to an accompaniment of German music in an attempt to win over the minds and hearts of potential deserters. The crucial role played by the radio in mediating knowledge of the course of the war is emphasized during the discussions that take place between Gregor, Vadim and the *Wehrmacht* officers in the Spandau citadel: when informed by Vadim that their situation is hopeless, the officers respond by quoting German radio reports to the contrary, a telling reminder that, in the context of modern warfare, there is no unmediated access to reality and that, in reaching strategic and ethical decisions, the individual is always at the mercy of competing representations. By contrast, a more low-key example of the interplay between memory and representation is to be found when Gregor enters the room of an elderly woman who has committed suicide, and we follow his gaze as his eyes wander over a collection of photographs attempting to piece together the victim's life from the still images of relatives and events from the past. Filmed in the manner of a documentary using a handheld camera, the seemingly unmediated objective film record is overlain with Gregor's subjective view of this past life.

What is most striking about *Ich war neunzehn*, however, is the way in which, by presenting the viewer with a multiplicity of perspectives, the film probes the tensions in German-Soviet relationships more critically than any other DEFA film up until then. This issue is highlighted when a young German girl comes to seek refuge in the military headquarters, or Kommandatura, in Bernau. Not surprisingly the issue of German women raped by Soviet troops had been a taboo subject in conventional antifascist discourses of the 1950s and 1960s in the GDR. The issue of rape (though never explicitly mentioned as such) was considerably more prominent in Wolf's original treatment for the film than in its final realization; there we read that the Kommandatura was besieged not by one, but by 150–200 women seeking shelter.[18] Right from the outset the studio management was uneasy and eventually succeeded in having the original sequence replaced with one in which just a single German girl turns up and addresses Gregor, saying, 'I'd rather sleep with one, than with all of them!' At the same time, during the violent quarrel that erupts between her and the young female Soviet soldier, the juxtaposition of the German girl's anxiety and protestations of innocence, on the one hand, and the account of the Russian girl's suffering, on the other, focuses the viewer's attention on the underlying and unresolved tensions not only within the bond between the GDR and the Soviet Union, but within the very concept of victimhood itself.

This episode is just one of a number of sequences in which the film highlights the effects of war on children; others include the child-soldier decorated by the SS officer in the Spandau citadel, the young Soviet soldier shot when a group of Germans commandeer a battalion of T34 tanks, and the little girl stranded in the midst of the firefight in the final episode of the film. In each case, the vulnerability of the children is underscored in Wolf's stylized presentation of the body and in the use of long static shots that open up a discursive space for a process of melancholic reflection. No one embodies this child-like vulnerability more clearly than the film's central protagonist Gregor played by the young student-actor Jaecki Schwarz. At one level, such images allude to the horrors of war for Soviets and Germans alike; but at another, these images can also be read intertextually as a sceptical allusion to, and critique of, the masculinist fantasies of the heroic antifascist body that are so prevalent in earlier antifascist films such as Frank Beyer's *Fünf Patronenhülsen* and *Nackt unter Wölfen* (*Naked among Wolves*, 1963) (see Figures 2 and 3).

What makes *Ich war neunzehn* one of the most enduring German war films is precisely its refusal to ignore the complexities of victimhood; and in

Figure 2 The heroic antifascist body. Erwin Geschonneck as Walter Krämer. From: *Nackt unter Wölfen* (*Naked among Wolves*, 1963), dir. by Frank Beyer, DEFA, 1963. DVD capture.

Figure 3 Re-imagining the antifascist body. Jaecki Schwarz as Gregor Hecker. From: *Ich war neunzehn* (*I Was Nineteen*), dir. by Konrad Wolf, DEFA, 1968. DVD capture.

one of the most memorable sequences in which extracts from *Todeslager Sachsenhausen* (Death Camp Sachsenhausen, 1946) are intercut with images of Gregor showering, we are presented with an image of what Gertrud Koch has described as the threefold threat of death: 'the threat of death as a Jewish German, as a German communist, and as a Soviet soldier'.[19] In suggesting that this image be read as a reference, however oblique, to Jewish victimhood, Koch highlights one of the most problematic issues for historians of East German cinema, namely the representation of the Holocaust in DEFA. Interpreting fascism as an essentially economic phenomenon constituted an almost insuperable obstacle to historiographical explanations of Jewish persecution grounded in racial theory and led to the privileging of communist members of the antifascist resistance (rather than Jews) as the victims of the Third Reich. Moreover, all too often such references as there were to the Holocaust in East German political life were exploited not as an opportunity to embark upon a process of introspection within the GDR, but as a means of denigrating the neighbouring Federal Republic. Finally, Soviet-inspired anti-Zionist policies of the early 1950s, including the notoriously anti-Semitic trial of Rudolph Slánský in Czechoslovakia in 1952, played a key role in ensuring that the Holocaust and Jewish victimhood remained a largely marginalized issue in GDR political discourse.

Despite such limitations, it is important nonetheless to remember that throughout its history DEFA produced a number of films tackling Jewish persecution and, in some cases, the deportation of Jews to concentration camps.[20] While it is easy to criticize Maetzig's *Ehe im Schatten* for its melodramatic format and failure to analyse anti-Semitic policies in terms of racial ideology, its subject matter together with the fact that it was seen by over twelve million viewers made its release a landmark moment in post-war German cinema. Although released over forty years later, Siegfried Kühn's *Die Schauspielerin* (The Actress, 1988) – a film set during the Third Reich in which a German actress assumes a (fake) Jewish identity in order to perform together with her Jewish actor-husband at the Jewish Theatre in Berlin[21] – underlines the lasting impact of Maetzig's pioneering work. While the roots of anti-Semitism in Imperial Germany are explored in Erich Engel's *Die Affäre Blum* (The Blum Affair, 1948), the deportation of Greek Jews to Auschwitz lies at the heart of Konrad Wolf's groundbreaking film *Sterne* (Stars, 1959). Although Wolf's German-Soviet background is central to an understanding of so many of his films, it should not be forgotten that his Jewish roots are evident not only in *Sterne* and *Professor Mamlock* (1961) but also in *Der nackte Mann auf dem Sportplatz* (The Naked Man on the Playing Field, 1974), a film in which the central character, the sculptor Kemmel,

reflects on how to represent the horror of the Jewish massacre of 1941 at Babi
Yar within the prevailing aesthetic paradigms.

   The two best-known East German films about the plight of Jews during
the Second World War, however, remain Frank Beyer's *Nackt unter Wölfen*
and *Jakob der Lügner* (Jacob the Liar, 1975), two adaptations of highly
successful novels by Bruno Apitz and Jurek Becker, respectively. Released
in 1963, *Nackt unter Wölfen* was the first DEFA film to be set specifically
within a concentration camp and, as Bill Niven has argued, the timing of
its release coincided with the SED's attempts to develop the Buchenwald
concentration camp into a site of antifascist memory.[22] Revolving around
the attempts of a group of antifascist prisoners to save the life of a young
Jewish boy smuggled into Buchenwald in a suitcase, *Nackt unter Wölfen*
ends with the boy's survival and, quite contrary to historical fact, the
liberation of the camp by the communist inmates themselves. Yet despite
the formal inventiveness of Marczinovsky's camerawork and Beyer's genuine attempt to focus the film on the conflict of reason and feeling in the
contrasting reactions of the inmates triggered by the child's arrival, the
viewer is left with a sense of unease. For in portraying the members of
the antifascist resistance simultaneously as both masters of their own destiny
and saviours of the Jewish 'victim', the film also lays itself open to the charge
of instrumentalizing Jewish issues in the service of an altogether different
political agenda.

   The contrast with *Jakob der Lügner* of 1974 could hardly be greater.
Beyer's first cinema film following the furor over his filming of Erik
Neutsch's novel *Spur der Steine* (Trace of Stones) in 1966, *Jakob der Lügner*
is a superlative example of what Daniela Berghahn has termed 'unheroic
resistance'.[23] A celebration of the power of the imagination to combat
adversity, the film explores the attempts of the physically diminutive Jakob
to distract those in the Jewish ghetto (including the young Jewish girl Lina)
from a seemingly inevitable fate. Yet what renders Beyer's film so radical is
the way in which it refuses to sentimentalize its subject matter; and at the end
of the film, it is clear that there is no escape from the destination in which the
train containing Jakob and the other deported Jews is heading. By contrast,
Peter Kassovitz's Hollywood remake of 1999, *Jakob the Liar*, casts the central
protagonist (played by Robin Williams) as an heroic figure of individual
resistance and supplies an artificial 'happy ending' in which the Jews incar-
cerated on the train are rescued by Russian troops.

   Often dismissed – unfairly – as one-dimensional propagandist works,
DEFA's antifascist films offer a unique insight into the shifting paradigms
of both GDR cultural politics and East German film aesthetics. In contrast

to films set in the contemporary GDR, antifascist films about the past offered filmmakers a position of security from which to embark on a process of formal experimentation. While early examples of antifascist cinema revealed an often remarkable degree of continuity with the traditions of Ufa, the introduction of new technology and the influence of new-wave aesthetics in the work of Beyer and Wolf served to both affirm and call into question existing myths of antifascism in the GDR. By the late 1970s and early 1980s, however, the antifascist genre appeared to have run its course as filmmakers found themselves increasingly unable to respond to the dilemma touched upon in Konrad Wolf's *Der nackte Mann auf dem Sportplatz*, namely the need to find new aesthetic forms conducive to a more differentiated approach to questions of victimhood and memories of the antifascist past. In this respect Ulrich Weiss's *Dein unbekannter Bruder* (Your Unknown Brother, 1982) is a notable exception. However, Weiss's less-than-flattering depiction of the antifascist resistance as a web of paranoia, betrayal and mutual distrust (a reading that inevitably invited parallels to be drawn with the Stasi and the surveillance society of the GDR in the final phase of its existence) represented both the logical conclusion of the antifascist genre and, at the same time, its demise.[24]

Notes

1. The speeches delivered at the occasion are (partially) reproduced in Christiane Mückenberger and Günter Jordan, *'Sie sehen selbst, Sie hören selbst . . .'. Die DEFA von ihren Anfängen bis 1949* (Marburg: Hitzeroth, 1994), pp. 37–40.
2. Johannes R. Becher, 'Zu unseren Kulturaufgaben', cited in Horst Haase (ed.), *Johannes R. Becher. Leben und Werk* [Schriftsteller der Gegenwart 1], 2nd edn (Berlin: Volk und Wissen, 1987), p. 187.
3. Cf. Robert R. Shandley, *Rubble Films. German Cinema in the Shadow of the Third Reich* (Philadelphia, PA: Temple University Press, 2001), pp. 81–90; p. 84.
4. Martin Brady, 'Discussion with Kurt Maetzig', in Seán Allan and John Sandford (eds.), *DEFA. East German Cinema, 1946–92* (Oxford, New York: Berghahn, 1996), pp. 77–92; p. 82.
5. Günter Agde (ed.), *Kurt Maetzig: Filmarbeit. Gespräche, Reden, Schriften* (Berlin: Henschel, 1987), p. 36.
6. 'Neuer Zug auf alten Gleisen. Kurt Maetzig über die Ufa-Tradition', in Hans-Michael Bock and Michael Töteberg (eds.), *Das Ufa-Buch* (Frankfurt/M.: Zweitausendeins: 1992), pp. 470–73; p. 471.
7. Georgi Dimitrov, 'The Fascist Offensive and the Tasks of the Communist International in the Struggle of the Working Class against Fascism. Main Report Delivered at the Seventh World Congress of the Communist

International, August 2, 1935', in Jane Degras (ed.), *The Communist International 1919–1943: Documents* (Oxford University Press, 1965), 3 vols., vol. 3 (1929–43), p. 296.

8. 'Discussion with Kurt Maetzig', p. 77.

9. 'Stellungnahme der DEFA-Kommission zum Drehbuch des *Thälmann*-Films von Willi Bredel und Michael Tschesno, 20.08.1951' [= BArch Abt. DDR (Kultur) DR 117/A025]. For a discussion of the production history, see Russel Lemmons, '"Great Truths and Minor Truths". Kurt Maetzig's *Ernst Thälmann* Films, the Antifascism Myth, and the Politics of Biography in the German Democratic Republic', in John Davidson and Sabine Hake (eds.), *Framing the Fifties. Cinema in a Divided Germany* (Oxford, New York: Berghahn, 2007), pp. 91–105.

10. See Dagmar Schittly, *Zwischen Regie und Regime. Die Filmpolitik der SED im Spiegel der DEFA-Produktionen* (Berlin: Christoph Links, 2002), pp. 66–67.

11. Kurt Maetzig was well acquainted with Chiaureli's work having overseen the dubbing of *The Oath* in 1947. See 'Der preisgekrönte *Schwur*', *Der Spiegel*, 15 February 1947.

12. Sabine Hake, *German National Cinema*, 2nd edn (London and New York: Routledge, 2008), p. 102.

13. See 'Christiane Mückenberger im Gespräch mit Kurt Maetzig', in Torsten Musial and Nicky Rittmeyer (eds.), *Kurt Maetzig* [Archiv-Blätter 22] (Berlin: Akademie der Künste, 2011), pp. 53–61; p. 55.

14. Stefan Soldovieri, 'Germans suffering in Spain. Cold War Visions of the Spanish Civil War in *Fünf Patronenhülsen* (1960) and *Solange du lebst* (1955)', *Cinémas*, 8.1 (2007), 53–69.

15. For a detailed account of the changing valency of the Spanish Civil War in East German cultural policy, see Josie McLellan, *Antifascism and Memory in East Germany: Remembering the International Brigades, 1945–1989* (Oxford University Press, 2004).

16. Sabine Hake, 'Political affects: Antifascism and the Second World War in Frank Beyer and Konrad Wolf', in Paul Cooke and Marc Silberman (eds.), *Screening War. Perspectives on German Suffering* (Rochester, NY: Camden House, 2010), pp. 102–22; p. 106.

17. For a detailed discussion of this aspect of the film, see Marc Silberman, 'Remembering History: The Filmmaker Konrad Wolf', *New German Critique* 49 (1990), 163–91.

18. See Wolfgang Jacobsen und Rolf Aurich, *Der Sonnensucher Konrad Wolf* (Berlin: Aufbau, 2005), pp. 319–21. For a discussion of this aspect of the film, see also Anke Pinkert, *Film and Memory in East Germany* (Bloomington and Indianapolis: Indiana University Press, 2008), pp. 163–67.

19. Gertrud Koch, 'On the Disappearance of the Dead among the Living. The Holocaust and the Confusion of Identities in the Films of Konrad Wolf', *New German Critique*, 60 (1993), 57–76; p. 74.

20. For a wider discussion of this issue, see David Bathrick, 'Holocaust Film before the *Holocaust*. DEFA, Antifascism and the Camps', *Cinémas*, 18.1

(2007), 109–34, and Frank Stern, 'Ein Kino subversiver Widersprüche. Juden im Spielfilm der DDR', *a propos: Film 2002. Das Jahrbuch der DEFA-Stiftung* (2002), 8–23.

21. The Jewish Theatre in Berlin (in which only non-Aryan actors and technicians could work) was established by the Jewish Cultural Federation (Jüdischer Kulturbund) in 1933. Most productions were at the Berliner Theater (Charlottenstraße 90/92) until the theatre's closure in 1935. The Jewish Cultural Federation was disbanded by the Gestapo on 11 September 1941.

22. Bill Niven, *The Buchenwald Child. Truth, Fiction, and Propaganda* (Rochester, NY: Camden House, 2007), p. 124.

23. Daniela Berghahn, *Hollywood behind the Wall. The Cinema of East Germany* (Manchester and New York: Manchester University Press, 2005), p. 89.

24. Inevitably the films selected for discussion represent only a fraction of the DEFA studio's output, and I am grateful to Barton Byg, Sabine Hake and Larson Powell and the participants at the DEFA Summer Film Institute 2009 for a wealth of stimulating perspectives on these films, many of which are reflected in this survey.

CHAPTER 4

From Faust III *to* Germania III
Drama in the GDR between 1949 and 1989
Holger Teschke

The smoke from the battle for Berlin had barely cleared and the ink on the capitulation document of the German Reich had barely dried when the official newspaper of the Soviet Military Administration in Germany, the *Tägliche Rundschau*, announced, on 17 May 1945, that four theatres were ready for business. Initially, classics and popular plays from the Weimar Republic were performed, including Brecht's *Dreigroschenoper* (Threepenny Opera). It is ironic that Brecht, the first playwright forced to flee Berlin after the burning of the Reichstag in February 1933, was one of the first exiles to be performed and that Hans Albers, one of the most beloved Ufa stars (Universum Film AG – the principal German film company during the Weimar Republic) during the Nazi era, now stood on stage as the gangster boss Macheath. At the time, Brecht was still in Santa Monica working on a new version of his *Leben des Galilei* (Life of Galileo) for Charles Laughton and writing a hexameter version of the *Communist Manifesto*. It would be another three years before he returned to Berlin in October 1948 to continue his theatre work after an interruption of twelve years. Shortly thereafter, he found himself caught up in the middle of Soviet and American cultural politics. This battle between the GDR and FRG would play a major role in GDR drama until the opening of the Wall in November 1989.

The development of theatre in the GDR can only be understood in light of the debates about Brecht's epic theatre and his work at the Berliner Ensemble (BE). Part of this revolved around the pros and cons of appropriating the legacy of German classics, Goethe, Schiller, Kleist and Büchner, within the prescribed aesthetic of socialist realism, demanded from Moscow.[1] This debate continued throughout the lifetime of the GDR with Goethe's *Faust* at its centre.[2] In 1948 the newly

Translated by Karen Remmler and Holger Teschke.

founded National Theatre in Weimar was the first theatre under Soviet occupation to perform the first part of Goethe's *Faust*. Amid wide-ranging discussions about the appropriate forms of engagement with Classical 'Erbe', or heritage, it was hailed as the model for the socialist appropriation of the classics. On 22 October 1946, Brecht and Helene Weigel returned to Berlin from Switzerland to test the possibilities for their work in the young socialist state. Just two months later, they were both celebrated for their production of Brecht's *Mutter Courage und ihrer Kinder* (Mother Courage and Her Children) at the Deutsches Theater (DT). However, the production also unleashed the first major debate in the cultural politics of the Soviet-occupied zone and would continue to accompany Brecht until his death in August 1956. Fritz Erpenbeck, the chief editor of the newly established journal *Theater der Zeit*, used the production to claim that Brecht's mode of epic theatre was inferior to authentic drama in its original form. With this, Erpenbeck was promoting socialist realism based on the Soviet model; – itself a synthesis of Stanislavsky's theatre method and Stalinist ideology.[3] On 28 August 1949 *Faust* premiered under Wolfgang Langhoff during the celebration of the 200th anniversary of Goethe's birth at the DT. Coincidentally, exactly forty years later, the last *Faust* production took place in Dresden under Wolfgang Engel. The GDR was baptized and then carried to its grave by the tragedy of a German idealist, who sought the philosopher's stone and ended up a victim of his own hubris.[4]

In 1954 Heiner Kipphardt became the chief dramaturge at the DT and put contemporary GDR playwrights, such as Alfred Matusche, Peter Hacks and himself, onto the programme. The Kammerspiele even took a stab at non-socialist theatre with a German-language version of Jean-Paul Sartre's 1946 play *La Putain Respectueuse* (The Respectful Prostitute) and *Zum Goldenen Anker* (The Golden Anchor) by Marcel Pagnol, based on his 1929 play *Marius*. The Workers' Uprising on 17 June 1953, first in Berlin and then for a few days throughout the GDR, which was halted by Soviet tanks, gave Brecht the idea for a new play about the worker Hans Garbe. Garbe had been a highly praised, model activist worker after a spectacular repair of a defect industrial ring oven. The real circumstances of Garbe's action were documented in a script about the introduction of the Soviet Stachanow movement in the GDR, in order to raise the working productivity in the planned economy. Brecht, however, was interested in the actual story, which he worked up into a play fragment with his collaborator Käthe Rülicke, as a narrative by Garbe. In his *Arbeitsjournal* (Work Journal) on 30 October 1953, Brecht notes that the projected play 'in the play type of the histories' and in 'fatzer verse' would include 'a full act on

17th June'.[5] This idea remained a fragment, first realized by Heiner Müller
as part of his radio play, *Der Lohndrücker* (The Scab) in 1956, and two years
later as a play. Brecht also tried to create a play about the socialist transformation in agriculture by adapting Erwin Strittmatter's 1953 *Katzgraben*.
However, this project brought him into conflict with the SED (Socialist
Unity Party), and even with some in his own Ensemble. After 1953, however,
he had no illusions about the possibilities for his form of epic theatre in the
GDR: 'our performances in Berlin have almost no resonance any more',
wrote Brecht as early as March 1953 in his *Arbeitsjournal*; 'the effort will only
be worthwhile, if the manner of acting can be taken up later, i.e. when its
didactic value has been realized'.[6] While Langhoff, at the DT, and Fritz
Wisten, at the newly opened Volksbühne, turned to classical plays after
17 June, Brecht opened an adaptation of Molière's *Don Juan* at the Berliner
Ensemble in March 1954, a play about a reckless despot who places himself
unabashedly above every law and moral code and ends up in hell. Brecht
adapted the Chinese play *The Day of the Great Scholar Wu*, together with
Carl Weber and Peter Palitzsch, as an attempt to outsmart the party censorship. The audience will have recognized the letters 'W' und 'U' as the
initials of the party leader, Walter Ulbricht, who loved to lecture artists
and scientists like his role model Stalin. In January 1956, at the Fourth
Congress of the Writers' Union of the GDR, Brecht attacked the cultural
politics of the SED on account of its provincialism, praising instead the
theatre of the Russian avant-garde and demanding the small, flexible
forms of theatre which were more able to take on contemporary issues.
He called for the travelling stages of the agitprop tradition to be built
into the contemporary GDR repertoire and championed plays by Erwin
Strittmatter and Peter Hacks, Martin Pohl and Vera Skupin at the BE. As
a result of Khrushchev's first and tentative critique of Stalin at the
Twentieth Party Meeting of the Communist Party of the Soviet Union
in February 1956, Brecht's challenge was surprisingly enough taken up by
the Third Party Conference of the SED and *Wanderensembles* (travelling
ensembles) were instigated to bring plays to the rural areas of the GDR.

The Berliner Ensemble's guest performance in London of *Mutter
Courage und ihre Kinder*, *Der kaukasische Kreidekreis* (The Caucasian
Chalk Circle) and the adaptation of George Farquhar's late Restoration
comedy *The Recruiting Officer* as *Pauken und Trompeten* (Drums
and Trumpets) was an international triumph for Brecht's theatre and
influenced British contemporary theatre in a lasting way. This success
carried over to the GDR as well. In 1956, Benno Besson and Manfred
Wekwerth were finally able to produce Brecht's *Die Tage der*

Commune (The Days of the Commune) in Karl-Marx-Stadt, and
Wolfgang Langhoff seized the opportunity to produce Peter Hacks's *Die
Schlacht bei Lobositz* (The Battle of Lobositz), a play that focuses on the
problem of remilitarization and obedience in period garb, but is nonetheless recognizable as a statement about the question of rearmament in
the GDR.

After Brecht's death, his *Das Leben des Galilei* premiered in its first GDR
performance at the BE in January 1957. Under the direction of Brecht and
later Erich Engel, Ernst Busch's Galileo was portrayed as a scientist whose
conflicts with power resembled contemporary struggles in the shadow of
the atomic threat in East and West. Critics on both sides of the iron curtain
were impressed and the production became a model for modern European
theatre worldwide.

Despite its success, however, sobering restrictions returned. In the wake of
the crushing of the Hungarian Uprising in November 1956, the SED called
for a meeting of all the GDR theatre directors in March 1957. At this
meeting, Alexander Abusch, the Deputy Minister for Culture and one of
the most opportunistic ideologues of the Party apparatus, warned against
'misdirected discussions'[7] at the Twentieth Party Meeting. Clearly, this
meant an immediate end to any critique of the Party and the government.
Abusch attacked Wolfgang Langhoff especially pointedly, as well as the DT
and the Leipziger Schauspielhaus, for allegedly producing 'bourgeois comedies based on West European and American models', without the requisite
socialist realism. Abusch did not mention Brecht, Hacks and Strittmatter
explicitly, but his criticism was clearly also aimed at them. After a guest
performance in Moscow's Vakhtangov Theatre and the premiere of Brecht's
Der gute Mensch von Sezuan (The Good Person of Szechwan) at the BE,
Abusch, at the Cultural Conference of the SED in October 1957, once again
took a number of GDR theatres to task for 'tolerating enemy influences and
bourgeois decadence'.[8]

Langhoff did not allow this to deflect him, however. In March 1958 he
produced Peter Hacks's 1957 play *Der Müller von Sanssouci* (The Miller of
Sanssouci) – another play that deals with the subordinate mentality of the
Germans. After the publication of Heiner Müller's *Der Lohndrücker* in the
official literary journal *Neue deutsche Literatur*, the Leipzig Theatre took a
chance and premiered it that same year. When even the *Theater der Zeit*
responded positively, the Berlin Maxim Gorki Theatre staged the double
premiere of his *Der Lohndrücker* and *Die Korrektur* (The Correction),
in September. Even though the conflicts in both plays are tempered and
more or less clothed in traditional realism, Siegfried Wagner, the head of

the cultural division of the SED's Central Committee, launched a fero-
cious attack on the plays and became one of the most dogmatic critics of
Müller's work.

From this point on, the battle lines were clearly drawn. At a conference
in May 1959, Wagner criticized the plays and adaptations produced by
Heiner and Inge Müller, Heinar Kipphardt and Peter Hacks as 'didactic
learning plays' and demanded the involvement of young dramatists and
directors from the working class.[9] In the summer of 1959, Kipphardt left
the DT and the GDR. His calls for a dialectic theatre disappeared from the
vocabulary of contemporary dramaturgy. The dominant mood was politically and culturally conservative under the auspices of socialist realism.
Langhoff, for example, was forced to produce and direct a dramatization of
the Russian writer Mikhail Sholokhov's widely praised novel *Neuland
unterm Pflug* (Virgin Soil Upturned), a glorification of the collectivization
of the Soviet farmers that conformed to the Party line. The first theatre
conference of the GDR in January 1956 set as a goal the representation of the
Seven-Year Economic Plan and the creation of a Socialist National Theatre
in collaboration with state-owned businesses and other Party organizations.
The adaptation of classical plays was expected to create a platform to model
the socialist image of man. Party functionaries warned against 'subjective
interpretations' and 'unreliable attempts at updating', two concepts that
became slogans, which could cut short any argument on the part of directors.

However, the next conflict was not far away. Peter Hacks was working as
a dramaturge at the DT when a performance of his *Die Sorgen und die
Macht* (Anxieties and Power, 1958–60) at the Senftenberg Miners' Theatre
ran into trouble. The love relationship between the foreman Max Fidorra
and the glass worker Hede Stoll contained more reality than the socialist
realism of the comrades would tolerate. As a result Peter Hacks left the DT
and continued as an independent writer. In contrast, comedies free of
conflict, like the 1953 *Weiberzwist und Liebeslist* (Wenches' Quarrel and
Love's Cunning) by the prize-winning dramatist and cultural functionary
Helmut Sakowski, celebrated simultaneous openings throughout the
GDR, and Helmut Baierl's 1961 comedy *Frau Flinz*, a play about a stub-
born farmer's wife who loses her sons to socialism, was declared, in all
seriousness, to be the new *Mutter Courage*. At the same time, the BE under
Brecht's widow Helene Weigel was also following the prescribed forms.
The Swiss-born actor and director Benno Besson, who had come to the
GDR at Brecht's invitation, left the BE in disgust and ended up at the DT,
where he at first played it safe by directing Strittmatter's antifascist play of
1959, *Die Holländerbraut* (The Dutch Bride).

The erection of the Berlin Wall on 13 August 1961 led at first to a sense among the theatre groups that now, with the threat of the enemy under control, a new era of political and cultural openness would ensue. This initial hope was soon quashed. According to Heiner Müller, Otto Gotsche, the Secretary of the GDR State Council, declared, 'Now we have the Wall we will stamp out anyone who is against us.'[10] With this in mind, a number of theatres quickly changed their programmes. The BE, for example, postponed the premiere of Brecht's adaptation of Shakespeare's *Coriolanus* and, instead, premiered his play about the French Revolution *Die Tage der Commune* in October 1961. On 30 September 1961, the planned premiere of Heiner Müller's *Die Umsiedlerin* (The Resettler Woman) in the student theatre of the College for Economics in Berlin-Karlshorst, directed by the young B. K. Tragelehn, was declared 'reactionary and hostile to the Republic' and banned.[11] In a detailed and well-planned tribunal, Müller was expelled from the GDR Writer's Union. Only the composer Paul Dessau and Peter Hacks were brave enough to support him and his play.

With this action the SED had flexed its muscles in a bid to demonstrate the new direction of its cultural politics. The most important stage for the SED was now GDR television, praised by Walter Ulbricht at the Fourteenth Meeting of the Central Committee of the SED for its loyalty to the party line: 'The success of GDR television shows us what could have been achieved in theatre and film.'[12] The only problem, however, was that in all the parts of the GDR where West German television could be received, the antennae were facing west and no one watched the uplifting television dramas about the successful rise of socialism peddled on East German TV. After the erection of the Wall, more and more GDR citizens turned exclusively to the West German TV stations ARD and ZDF. Theatres noticed the difference. The audience numbers sank in 1962–63 from seventeen to thirteen million and then in 1965–66 they fell again to eleven million. As a consequence, a number of provincial theatres either closed or were amalgamated, including theatres in cities like Güstrow, Meissen, Wismar and Zittau, or were open for guest performances only.

The increased repression enacted in state cultural politics after 1961 also had another far-reaching effect upon contemporary GDR drama. After a new version of Hacks's *Die Sorgen und die Macht* had been attacked and closed down by the Party Central Office after only twenty-two performances due to its 'democraticism, hostile to the Party', Hacks took leave of contemporary drama in an essay entitled 'Versuch über das Theaterstück von morgen' (Essay on the Theatre Play for Tomorrow) and invented a post-revolutionary dramaturgy which he called 'socialist classicism'.[13] He delivered the repertoire for this new direction himself. With the opening of his adaptation of Aristophanes's *Der Frieden* (Peace), for example, on 14 October 1962, directed by Besson, he celebrated one of his most successful plays.

Similarly, Heiner Müller took refuge in ancient Greek myths and wrote an adaptation of Sophocles's *Ödipus, Tyrann* (Oedipus the King) for Benno Besson, followed shortly after by his *Herakles 5* (Heracles 5), *Der Horatier* (The Horatian), *Prometheus* and *Philoktet* (Philoctetes). In contrast, however, to Hacks's very successful *Die schöne Helena*, a version of *La belle Hélène* after Henri Meilhac and Ludovic Halévy in 1964, or *Amphitryon* of 1967, Müller's adaptations of Greek classics were all tragedies. Moreover, they all explored the tragedy of individuals trapped in tyrannical settings. The contrasting aesthetic as well as political approaches of Hacks and Müller set out here played a major role in defining GDR dramaturgy and theatre from 1962 to the end of the GDR, although Hacks's influence began to wane in the late 1970s, just as Müller's popularity began to grow.

The effects of the attacks on Müller and Hacks were felt immediately. Between 1963 and 1965 the programmes were flooded with comedies and musicals, including Horst Kleineidam's harmless farce *Urlaub im Glück* (Happy Vacation), which enjoyed a simultaneous premiere on four GDR stages, or a flat adaptation of Shakespeare's *As You Like It* by Günter Deicke and Klaus Fehmel. In spring 1963, Langhoff was forced to leave the DT and was replaced by the former director of the Volksbühne, Wolfgang Heinz. Nonetheless Langhoff's chief dramaturge, Gerhard Piens, remained at the DT and continued to support Hartmut Lange's adaptation of Molière's *Tartuffe*, which opened under the direction of Besson in December, 1963. Lange's clear criticism of hypocrisy and dogmatism was not only understood by the audience, however, and such courageous experiments appeared against the backdrop of many more conservative productions that furthered the goals of socialist realism. Such productions included the dramatic poem *Terra incognita* by KuBa (the party functionary Kurt Bartel) and Horst Salomon's *Katzengold* (Fools' Gold). Both plays followed Ulbricht's dictum, and exemplified 'the representation of the economic, social and political successes of the socialist community'.[14]

But although *Katzengold*, for example, won its author the National Prize Third Class, not even the critics from *Theater der Zeit* were convinced. These 'alibi plays' were clearly meant to function as a smoke screen in order to make more contentious projects like Hartmut Lange's *Tod und Leben des Herrn Marski* (Death and Life of Herr Marski) and Heiner Müller's adaptation of Erik Neutsch's novel *Spur der Steine* (Trace of Stones) possible. These plays were listed in the theatre programme for 1964–65, but in the event not produced after all.[15] Benno Besson's production of the Soviet dramatist Yevgeni Schwarz's *Der Drache* (The Dragon) with Horst Sagert's set on 21 March 1965 was nevertheless a great success. Even though the criticism of Stalinism and its consequences appeared under the guise of a fairy tale, the audience and the Party clearly understood who the dragon and the despotic politicians represented. Looking back in his memoir, *Krieg ohne Schlacht* (War Without Battle), Heiner Müller called the production the 'end of political theatre in the GDR'.[16] He pinpointed the fundamental problem of using fairy tale motifs that had become acceptable to the SED functionaries and, like Brecht's parables, had come to replace the real theatrical confrontation with the present.

The Party countered any possible confrontation to its policies by falling back once again on Goethe's *Faust*. The director of the Leipzig theatre, Karl Kayser, for example, was allowed to stage both parts of the tragedy in a monumental and pathos-ridden production in September 1965. One month later, Fritz Bennewitz's premiere of *Faust* in Weimar led to an intense discussion about both productions and gave the SED the opportunity to declare that 'national drama' could serve as a marker for the aesthetic of socialist theatre. Kayser's claim, that 'the Faustian man had come into his own in the classless society of socialism', echoed Ulbricht's speech in 1962 before the National Council of the National Front, at which the General Secretary of the SED declared that the workers of the GDR had begun to write the third part of *Faust* with their work for peace and socialism.[17]

The 1965 premiere of Peter Hacks's *Moritz Tassow*, a play about a pig herdsman who, after twelve years of silence under the Nazis, suddenly holds a visionary sermon, chases away the estate owners and establishes a 'commune of the third century', gave the Party apparatus a new reason to get to grips with contemporary drama. After all, this Moritz Tassow, like Hacks himself, exhibited utopian ideas about the future of socialism; and both were therefore suspect. In preparation for the Eleventh Plenum of the Central Committee in December 1965 and to bolster the Politburo's statement against the critical voices in theatre, film and literature, the Cultural Division of the Central Committee of the SED prepared analyses of Müller's *Der Bau* (The Construction Site), Hacks's *Tassow* and a number of critical films, like Frank Beyer's 1966 version of *Spur der Steine* and Kurt Maetzig's 1965 *Das Kaninchen bin ich* (I Am the Rabbit). After the failure of Ulbricht's 'New Economic System of Planning and Leadership', the SED desperately needed scapegoats which could serve to justify the introduction of centralized economic policies and stricter cultural politics. Critical films and plays were exactly what they needed in order to demonstrate the apparent failure of some comrades in the arts and to blame them for the 'false representation of Party and government policies'.[18] Erich Honecker led the way as Ulbricht's successor and delivered the keynote address at the Eleventh Plenum under the motto 'A clean state with unshakeable moral standards'.[19]

In this atmosphere even cautious criticism on the part of filmmakers, playwrights and directors became aligned by the authorities with a 'disregard for the dialectic, decadence and attacks against the leading role of the Party'.[20] The Eleventh Plenum became a form of 'Kahlschlag-Plenum' (Clearance Plenum) and led to a number of cleansing actions in theatres, publishing companies and the DEFA, the East German film studios. At the same time, it signalled a further definitive stage in the failing belief among theatre artists and playwrights in the cultural politics of the SED. It is not without irony that, from 1966 on, many theatres turned to West German playwrights, such as Peter Weiss, Rolf Hochhuth and Martin Walser, or the Swiss playwrights, Max Frisch and Friedrich Dürrenmatt, in order to avoid getting embroiled in the controversies surrounding contemporary GDR drama.

This trend, however, did not last very long. The journal *Theater der Zeit* stepped in to censure the practise and some theatres also began to hire so-called *Entwicklungsdramaturgen*, or development dramaturges, whose task it was to create present-day socialist dramas in line with the Party's ideology. The journal *Sinn und Form* even dedicated a special volume to this theme in June 1966 and published excerpts from plays by Müller, Baierl and Alfred Matusche. More and more plays were produced in which apparent conflicts were solved by collective happy ends, like Manfred Freitag's 1967 musical comedy *Seemannsliebe* (Sailor's Love) at the Maxim Gorki Theatre or Horst Salomon's successful *Ein Lorbaß* (A Good for Nothing) of the same year at the DT.

The production of *Faust* II at the German National Theatre in Weimar in April 1967 became the impetus for Manfred Nössig's declaration, in the May edition of *Theater der Zeit*, that the 'unity of the intellectual and cultural efforts in the theatres of the two German states' had come to an end.[21] The 'progressive ideas of this national drama' were reclaimed by the GDR, and, in contrast, it became clear in which part of Germany hell and damnation were supposed to reside. Once again, Goethe's *Faust* became the touchstone for proclaiming a cultural political shift. A year later, at the 'Brecht Dialogue 1968', the philosopher Wolfgang Heise responded by coining the description of theatre 'as a laboratory for social imagination', a term that became popular among critical dramaturges and directors.[22] But the concrete experimentation with political alternatives, like the attempt of Alexander Dubček and other Czech socialists to establish 'socialism with a human face' in August 1968, was brutally ended by the Red Army. The GDR Writers' Union and the Union of Theatre Workers supported this military intervention and thereby discredited themselves worldwide.

In September 1968, Ingrid Seyfahrt of *Theater der Zeit* criticized Volker Braun's play *Hans Faust*, inspired by Hans Mayer and featuring a proletarian Faust figure, which premiered in the same month in the German National Theatre in Weimar, as an example of 'disturbed dialectic between the people and the leadership'.[23] On 12 December Adolf Dresen and Wolfgang Heinz directed *Faust* I starring Fred Düren at the DT. Once again, Faust became the centre of a controversy. The Party launched a polemical critique of the productions in Leipzig and Weimar, describing them as an attack on the official cultural politics dedicated to working through the 'legacy of the classics'. Once again, Alexander Abusch called for a Faust that embodied 'the Marxist interpretation of a strong personality and a Renaissance figure' rather than the deplorably torn and despairing Faust in the DT version. Abusch criticized the production itself, too, comparing it to the 'fascist destruction of Goethe's humanism'.[24] As a result, this version of *Faust* was quickly removed from the DT's programme. Heinz stepped down as director of the theatre and Dresen left the GDR for the Vienna Burgtheater.

Heinz's successor, the Rostock artistic director Hanns Anselm Perten, installed in January 1970, was charged with bringing the theatre programme of the DT back into line with the Party ideology. Within two years, however, the good comrade from the Baltic Sea admitted defeat in the face of strong resistance from the DT ensemble. His attempt to champion contemporary GDR plays by Günther Rücker, Claus Hammel, Rolf Schneider and Helmut Baierl for the theatre programme convinced neither the audiences nor the critics. Benno Besson responded by leaving the DT for an artistic directorship at the Volksbühne. There his adaptation of Heiner Müller's rendition of Gerhard Winterlich's play *Horizonte* (Horizons) created a completely new method of engaging the audience directly in the performances, thus establishing a new form of contemporary drama. Besson hired the young directors Manfred Karge and Mathias Langhoff and the author Christoph Hein as dramaturge.

He was also successful in wooing Müller and Fritz Marquardt to come work at the theatre. In addition to directing Brecht, Molière and Gozzi, Besson also created a series of what he called 'Spektakel', or theatre spectacles, in the 1970s that included French farces and one-act plays, as well as works by André Müller, Anne Leonhardt and Christoph Hein. The

Volksbühne building was opened up with productions occurring in parallel throughout the day, in different (sometimes unorthodox) venues, and the audience was invited to choose between the plays as they pleased. The public responded with enthusiasm to this invitation to the theatre as a kind of *Volksfest*, or peoples' party, while the response of politicians and critics was more mistrustful. They were worried not only about controlling the reactions of the public but also about any direct participation in the theatrical process, a participation that could very well lead theatregoers to expect greater participation in political and economic decisions. More to the taste of the party was the premiere of *Faust I* in Halle in October 1970, directed by Horst Schönemann with a group of German academics. It was hailed as the 'correct and party-true appropriation of cultural legacy'.[25] Heiner Müller's sarcastic comment on GDR theatre of the moment, that there had 'never been so much dramaturgy and so little drama', rightly pinpoints the failed translation of a political mandate into convincing art.[26]

In June 1971, at the Eighth Party Conference of the SED, Erich Honecker was voted in as the First Secretary of the Central Committee. He reversed Ulbricht's motto of the 'socialist community' and demanded instead more *Volkstümlichkeit* and 'conceptual clarity'.[27] This led some theatre artists to hope for more political and aesthetic differentiation. The premieres of Heiner Müller's *Weiberkomödie* (Women's Comedy) based on a radio drama by his wife Inge, at the Volksbühne, Volker Braun's *Kipper* (Dumpers) in Leipzig and a theatre version of Ulrich Plenzdorf's *Die neuen Leiden des jungen W.* (The New Sorrows of Young W.) in Halle seemed to confirm this hope.

After the unspectacular end of Perten's directorship at the DT, Gerhard Wolfram, the former artistic director in Halle, produced a number of bold contemporary plays by GDR playwrights that were rich in conflict: Braun's *Kipper*, Plenzdorf's *Die neuen Leiden des jungen W.* and Müller's *Philoktet*, a formidable production with the actors Alexander Lang, Christian Grashof and Roman Kaminski. The premiere of Müller's *Zement* (based on Fjodor Gladkow's novel *Cement*) at the BE in October 1973, under Ruth Berghaus's direction, continued the sensational return of critical plays. The story of the bloody conflicts awaiting the revolutionary Gleb Tschumalow, on his return to his homeland, that threaten to tear his family apart represented an entirely new approach to illustrating the Great Socialist October Revolution in the Soviet Union.

A similarly productive era for contemporary drama began at this time, with Christoph Schroth as the new director at the Mecklenburg State Theatre in Schwerin. Authors such as Braun, Müller, Kurt Bartsch and later Lothar Trolle celebrated premieres, and Besson's dramaturgy of 'spectacle' continued there after 1976 with the avant-garde project *Entdeckungen* (Discoveries), based on Besson's model of simultaneous parallel productions. Between 1975 and 1980 works by other young playwrights were also produced, such as Stefan Schütz's *Fabrik im Walde* (Factory in the Woods) in Potsdam, Klaus Poche's *Befragung Anna O.* (Questioning Anna O.) in Rudolstadt, Albert Wendt's fairytale *Vogelkopp* (Birdbrain) in Leipzig and Jürgen Groß's *Match* at the Maxim Gorki Theatre in Berlin.

At the same time, however, two things happened that mark a shift in the apparent loosening of the cultural politics in the GDR: the expatriation of the songwriter Wolf Biermann after his concert in Cologne in 1976 and the subsequent wave of protests and departures from the GDR by writers, actors and directors. Dramatists such as Müller, Braun and Thomas Brasch signed petitions of protest, while Hacks, Baierl and Rainer Kerndl welcomed the decision publicly. Over one hundred other authors and theatre workers left the GDR out of protest and found employment on stages in West Germany, Austria and Switzerland. Plays written by the signatories of the Biermann petition disappeared overnight from the theatre programmes in the GDR and were replaced by harmless farces like Rudi Strahl's *Ein irrer Duft von frischem Heu* (A Heady Smell of Fresh Hay) and *Arno Prinz zu Wolkenstein* (Arno Prince of Wolkenstein). Strahl's plays became the most produced and performed plays in GDR theatres and were typically sold out. Nonetheless, they no longer reached their target audience of workers and farmers. Instead, schoolchildren, students, soldiers and retirees made up the majority of the theatregoers.[28]

In April 1979, after a struggle with the SED and the cultural ministry, Volker Braun's *Der Großer Frieden* (The Great Peace) opened at the BE, directed by Manfred Wekwerth and Joachim Tenschert. The drama, set in 'Asia before the European era', tells the story of the farmer Gau Dsu, who rises from the position of a revolutionary soldier to Emperor. The play demanded the 'transformation of the existing conditions from the bottom up',[29] reigniting the discussions that had been interrupted after Müller's *Zement* and opening a new phase of contemporary drama. At the beginning of October 1979, Schroth produced his third *Entdeckungen* project in Schwerin in tandem with unconventional versions of *Faust* I and II, Reiner Bredemeyer's 1970 *Lenin* composition and a dramatic version of Maxie Wander's much discussed women's protocols, *Guten Morgen, du Schöne* (Good Morning, You Beauty). In April 1980, Christoph Hein's *Cromwell* premiered in Cottbus. The play tells the story of the rise and fall of the historical revolutionary that is nonetheless meant to parallel the discussions

about the then still taboo issue of the effect of Stalinism. At the BE Piet
Drescher directed the premiere of Braun's dramatic collage *Simplex
Deutsch*, a play that illuminates the 'German Misery' from the beginning
of the social democratic workers' movement to the conflicts in the contemporary 'Worker's and Farmer's Nation'. Despite its critical stance, the
play completed its opening without incident. Apparently, the Party had
decided to greet controversial or problematic plays with silence, instead of
running the risk of creating more popularity for them by loud protest and
restrictions.

The Volksbühne performed the much delayed premiere of Müller's *Der
Bau*, directed by Fritz Marquardt, in September 1980 without a hitch. The
play had been put on ice for fifteen years after the Eleventh Plenum and yet
the conflicts depicted in the play still retained their importance. This was
also the case for the Volksbühne's production of Müller's 1979 play *Der
Auftrag* (The Mission) that Müller himself directed with his then wife
Ginka Tscholakowa in November 1980. In the following January, the
theatre was even permitted to hold a Colloquium on Müller, at which
many of the issues portrayed in the production were discussed openly.

However, despite the limited success of some theatres to champion contemporary GDR writing, in December 1981, the theatre critic Christophe
Funke published an essay in which he pointed out that plays by contemporary GDR playwrights, such as Braun, Müller, Hein, Trolle and Jochen Berg,
were still rarely seen in GDR theatres and that young dramatists were
discouraged as a consequence.[30] This bold essay had little effect and only a
few plays, such as Volker Braun's *Schmitten* in Leipzig and his prelude
'Totleben' for his drama *Lenins Tod* (Lenin's Death), were produced thereafter. The issue was briefly discussed at the third Workshop for Theatre in
1982 by a number of directors and playwrights, but only led to scenic readings
of plays by Georg Seidel, Lothar Trolle, Jochen Berg and Peter Brasch.
Notable exceptions were productions of Müller's *Der Auftrag* in Anklam
and Karl-Marx-Stadt in 1983 by Frank Castorf and Axel Richter, respectively,
both part of a new generation of directors.

Nevertheless, according to the statistics of the Theatre Union, the plays
with the largest audiences at this time included the musical *Wirtshaus in
Spessart* (The Pub in the Spessart) and *Hänsel und Gretel* and in drama the
Karl-Marx-Revue *Salut an alle!* (Salute to All!) by Hans Pfeiffer and Günter
Kaltofen. In October 1983 the critic Martin Linzer claimed in *Theater der
Zeit* that despite a few premieres in Karl-Marx-Stadt and Schwerin, con-
temporary plays were all but absent from the GDR theatre programmes.[31]
Planned premieres of plays by Braun, Plenzdorf and Trolle had been

cancelled without explanation and replaced with farces like Brandon Thomas's 1892 *Charley's Aunt*. Linzer also pointed out that the increased influence of important GDR directors in West Germany and their absence in GDR had led to a lack of engagement for contemporary theatre. Young theatre workers organized themselves more and more into so-called 'Lieder-Theater' (Song Theatres), such as *Karls Enkel* under the direction of Steffen Mensching and Hans-Eckardt Wenzel, the *Brigade Feuerstein* under Gerhard Gundermann and Bernd Rump's *Schicht-Theater*. Independent revues and puppet theatres, such as *Lumpensack* or *Zinnober*, attempted to create new theatre forms that fell under the radar screen of the state-controlled and state-subsidized city theatre system in order to escape political and aesthetic censorship.[32]

In December 1983, Alexander Lang broke the drought by directing Christoph Hein's *Die wahre Geschichte des Ah Q* (The True Story of Ah Q) at the DT. Along with Horst Sagert's production of *Urfaust-Szenen* (Scenes from Urfaust), adapted from Goethe, at the BE in March 1984, Hein's play marked a shift in the history of GDR theatre that began to influence the work of young directors and playwrights. Once again, a production of *Faust* broke new ground in the GDR by exposing the weakness of an imposed socialist realism. In 1986 and beyond, the church began to organize and support theatre productions, including Freya Klier's *Steinschlag* (Rockfall) or the cabaret performances of *Zinnober*. At the same time, productions like Frank Castorf's direction of Müller's *Der Bau* or Werner Buhss's *Die Festung* (The Fortress) under the circumspect artistic director Siegfried Meyer in Karl-Marx-Stadt were more the exception than the rule. In 1987, in Potsdam, the director Bernd Weißig was able to produce Müller's *Wolokolamsker Chaussee* II (Volokolamsk Highway II) even though it focused on the workers' protest of 17 June 1953, a theme that had not been handled publicly or artistically before. During the 750th anniversary of Berlin, the Volksbühne produced Müller's 'Horror-story' *Leben Gundlings Friedrich von Preußen Lessings Schlaf Traum Schrei* (Gundling's Life Frederick of Prussia Lessing's Sleep Dream Scream) and the premiere of Trolle's anarchistic *Weltuntergang Berlin* (The End of the World in Berlin). In Dresden in July 1987, Wolfgang Engel took a chance and produced Müller's bloody 'Shakespeare commentary', *Anatomie Titus Fall of Rome* (Anatomy Titus Fall of Rome), to great success, leading to a surge of audience pilgrimages to the Elbe.

Christoph Hein's new play *Passage* (Passage) was even produced in a simultaneous premiere involving theatres in Essen in West Germany and in Zürich. At the beginning of 1988, the only publishing company for plays, the Henschel Verlag in Berlin, published a volume with Müller's *Mauser*, *Hamletmaschine* (Hamletmachine) and the long-derided *Germania Tod in Berlin* (Germania Death in Berlin), making these plays accessible to the GDR public for the first time. Nevertheless, the theatre had forsaken its role as a space for dialogue about societal contradictions and conflicts. While the Party ideologues and their cultural interpreters continued to debate whether or not antagonistic contradictions existed in socialism, a whole generation of young theatre workers had removed themselves from this system by leaving the GDR or by retreating to alternative niches.

After members of the GDR Peace and Civil Rights Movement marched openly during the official commemoration activities for Karl Liebknecht and Rosa Luxemburg in Berlin-Friedrichsfelde in 1988, a number of artists made the street the stage for open confrontation between a new spirit of protest and the state. The state reacted immediately, by arresting the undesirable protestors and expelling a number of them against their will. In this atmosphere, Schroth's productions of new plays by Irina Liebmann, Trolle, Brasch and Müller were hailed as new discoveries in Schwerin in January 1988. Thomas Langhoff's production of Braun's *Die Übergangsgesellschaft* (The Transitional Society) at the Maxim Gorki Theatre sparked once more heated debates. Nevertheless, the real discussions about the future of the GDR had already shifted to church, academic and private spaces, where civil rights protestors, scientists, artists and environmentalists gathered. The mood at the Sixth Theatre Workshop in Leipzig was resigned, even though a number of directors promised to produce more contemporary plays. It was too late. The large 'Heiner Müller Retrospective' that took place during June and July 1988 was held in West Berlin, not in the GDR. Gorbachev's sensational reforms in the Soviet Union were bitterly resisted by the Party heads of the SED. They censored films and plays that emerged in Moscow during this period altogether or scheduled them for late-night broadcast, and took the journal *Sputnik*, which documented current debates about Stalinism in the Soviet Union, off the newspaper stands. It became clear that theatre artists in the GDR could no longer practice 'constructive criticism' and had to show their true colours.

Beginning in January 1989, a number of productions took place that would have been unheard of previously. The BE led the way with a production of Müller's *Germania Tod in Berlin*, directed by Fritz Marquardt, followed by the entire cycle of *Wolokolamsker Chaussee* in Potsdam, directed by Bernd Weißig. The climax of this movement occurred with the premiere of Christoph Hein's *Ritter der Tafelrunde* (The Knights of the Round Table) on 12 April 1989, directed by Klaus Dieter Kirst in Dresden. The aged knights, exhausted by their failure to find the Holy Grail, clearly represented the end of an era and a political system. Curiously, the theatre critic of *Neues Deutschland* saw these sad figures as representatives of a new beginning – a statement which marked one of the most absurd highpoints of this Party newspaper.[33] But the majority of the GDR public were no longer interested in such ironies.

By the time of the Monday demonstrations in the autumn of 1989, the theatres in the GDR, which had already joined the protests with a series of resolutions and open letters, used their stages to demand far-reaching political reforms under the banner 'We cast off our roles'.[34] The directors and actors were joined by stage hands, technicians and administrators. The large demonstration on 4 November 1989 in Alexanderplatz, initiated by a group of theatre workers, called for the implementation of the rights guaranteed on paper by the GDR constitution, including freedom of speech and assembly. Over a half million people gathered to hear the speeches by Christa Wolf, Heiner Müller, Christoph Hein, Stefan Heym and the actor Steffi Spira – speeches that created the atmosphere of a huge people's party. This demonstration was the last great theatrical production in the spirit of the ideal vision of Goethe's Faust: 'to stand upon free ground with a free people'.[35] For one unforgettable moment the barrier between the auditorium and the stage, as well as between the masses and the intellectuals had disappeared, and the hope for a society beyond Stalinism and capitalism emerged. But this moment lasted only for an instant. In the wake of German unification on 3 October 1990, the GDR theatres traded the dictatorship of ideology for the dictatorship of the market. *Faust* III was never written in the GDR, just as Müller, during his directorship at the BE, never finished his *Germania* III, the projected conclusion of his 'Germania trilogy'. After his death only the controversial synthetic fragment *Germania 3. Gespenster am toten Mann* (Germania 3. Ghosts at the Dead Man) remained.[36] What remains today is the memory of a time when theatre served as a place of political discourse, a chance of which it can only dream today. But perhaps there are still lessons to be learned from an era when theatre understood itself as a critical place in society, not just as an event for an elite desiring only entertainment and forgetfulness.

Notes

1. As background see Petra Stuber, *Spielräume und Grenzen. Studien zum DDR–Theater* (Berlin: Links, 2000).

2. This discussion will focus for the most part on the East Berlin theatre scene, since most of the major battles within the cultural politics of the GDR took place here. After the expulsion of the songwriter Wolf Biermann in 1976, censorship became determined by region. For a useful account in English which also addresses the provinces see Laura Bradley, *Cooperation and Conflict: GDR Theatre Censorship 1961–1989* (Oxford University Press, 2010).

3. Fritz Erpenbeck, 'Formalismus und Dekadenz', in Elmat Schubbe (ed.), *Dokumente zur Kunst-, Literatur- und Kulturpolitik des SED* (Stuttgart: Seewald, 1972), pp. 109–13. On the debates about Brecht's legacy in the GDR see Laura Bradley, 'Remembering Brecht: Anniversaries at the Berliner Ensemble', in Laura Bradley and Karen Leeder (ed.), *Brecht & the GDR: Politics, Culture, Posterity, Edinburgh German Yearbook*, vol. 5 (Rochester, NY: Camden House, 2011), pp. 125–44.

4. On the importance of *Faust* in the GDR see Deborah Viëtor-Engländer, *Faust in der DDR* (Frankfurt/M.: Lang, 1978).

5. Brecht, *Journals 1934–1955*, ed. John Willett, trans. Hugh Rorrison (London: Methuen, 1993), p. 456.

6. Ibid., p. 454.

7. Alexander Abusch, *Kulturelle Probleme des sozialistischen Humanismus* (Berlin: Dietz, 1957), p. 40.

8. Ibid., p. 56.

9. *Theater der Zeit*, Henschel Verlag Berlin, 8 (1959), Supplement, pp. 5–10.

10. Heiner Müller, *Gespräche 3: 1991–1995* (2008), in Frank Hörnigk (ed.), *Werke*, vol. 12 (Frankfurt/M.: Suhrkamp, 1998–2008), pp. 277–78.

11. Heiner Müller, *Krieg ohne Schlacht: Leben in zwei Diktaturen* (Cologne: Kiepenheuer & Witsch, 1992), pp. 170–72.

12. Walter Ulbricht, *Zur Geschichte der deutschen Arbeiterbewegung. Reden und Aufsätze*, vol. 10 (Berlin: Dietz, 1966), p. 196.

13. Peter Hacks, *Versuch über das Theaterstück von morgen* (Berlin: Henschel Verlag, 1978), pp. 53–70.

14. Ulbricht, *Zur Geschichte der deutschen Arbeiterbewegung*, p. 120.

15. Compare Manfred Durzak, *Der Dramatiker und Erzähler Hartmut Lange* (Würzburg: Königshausen & Neumann, 2003).

16. Müller, *Krieg ohne Schlacht*, p. 207.

17. Walter Ulbricht, 'An alle Bürger der DDR! An die ganze Nation', in *Zur Geschichte der deutschen Arbeiterbewegung*, 10, p. 457.

18. Erich Honecker, *Bericht des Politbüros an das 11. Tagung des ZK der SED* (Berlin: Dietz, 1965), p. 15.

19. Ibid., p. 21.

20. Ibid., p. 25.

21. *Theater der Zeit*, 5 (1967), 20.

22. 'Dialog der Theaterleute mit Philosophen, Politikern und Naturwissenschaftlern', in Sekretariat des Brecht-Dialogs (ed.), *Brecht-Dialog 1968. Politik auf dem Theater. Dokumentation 9.–16. Februar 1968* (Berlin: Henschelverlag, 1968), pp. 207–36; p. 222.

23. *Theater der Zeit*, 9 (1968), 25.
24. *Schriften des Verbands der Theaterschaffenden der DDR*, 1 (1969), supplement to *Theater der Zeit*, 2 (1969), 25. Compare Christoph Funke, 'Faust in der Diskussion', in *Theater der Zeit*, 24 (1968), 25 and Friedrich Dieckmann, 'Wieder Mal im Faust', *Theater der Zeit*, 2 (1969), 10.
25. *Programmheft*, Faust Theater, Halle, October 1970.
26. Heiner Müller, 'Sechs Punkte zur Oper' in *Schriften* (2005) in *Werke*, vol. 8, ed. Frank Hörnigk (Frankfurt/M.: Suhrkamp, 1998–2008), pp. 161–3; p. 163.
27. Erich Honecker, 'Hauptaufgabe umfaßt auch weitere Erhöhung des kulturellen Niveaus', in Gisela Rüß (ed.), *Dokumente zur Kunst-, Literatur und Kulturpolitik der SED 1971–1974* (Stuttgart: Seewald, 1976), pp. 287–89.
28. *Theater der Zeit*, 6 (1979), 38.
29. Berliner Ensemble, *Almanach 1977–1987* (Berlin: Berliner Ensemble, 1988), p. 20.
30. *Theater der Zeit*, 12 (1981), 15.
31. *Theater der Zeit*, 10 (1983), 23.
32. Compare David Robb, *Protest Song in East and West Germany since the 1960s* (Rochester, NY: Camden House, 2007).
33. *Neues Deutschland*, 3 May 1989; www.berliner-schauspielschule.de/tafel runde.htm.
34. The motto of the Initiative 4 November, which organized the 4 November demonstration on Alexanderplatz. Compare *Wir treten aus unseren Rollen heraus: Dokumente des Aufbruchs Herbst '89*, Theaterarbeit in der DDR, 19, ed. Angela Kuberski (Berlin, Zentrum für Theaterdokumentation und -information, 1990). For a more critical reading see Loren Kruger, '*Wir treten aus unseren Rollen heraus*: Theater Intellectuals and Public Spheres', in Michael Geyer (ed.), *The Power of Intellectuals in Contemporary Germany* (Chicago and London: University of Chicago Press, 2001), pp. 183–211.
35. Johann Wolfgang von Goethe, *Faust* II Bibliothek der Klassiker (Berlin and Weimar: Aufbau, 1988), p. 563.
36. Compare Jonathan Kalb, *The Theater of Heiner Müller*, 2nd rev. edn (Chicago: Academic Publishers, 2001).

CHAPTER 5

Autobiographical writing in the GDR era

Dennis Tate

Continuity and narrative breadth

Wolfgang Emmerich's historical point of departure in his indispensable literary history of the GDR – that there was no 'zero hour' marking the beginning of East German literature[1] – is particularly apposite in the context of autobiographical writing. To search amidst the harsh political and economic circumstances of 1949 for the origins of the literary form in which some of the most enduring works of East German literature were written would be a particularly fruitless task. How could anything as apparently self-indulgent as autobiography have gained a foothold at a time when ideological debate in the newly established GDR was preoccupied with exploiting the potential of culture to inspire a demoralized workforce facing a daunting task of industrial reconstruction? It is no surprise that there was little serious writing in a subjective vein published in the GDR's first decade, but it would be difficult to explain its emergence in the 1960s, not to mention its increasing importance in the 1970s and 1980s, without some awareness of the longer-term impact of experiments in autobiographical writing that occurred well before the establishment of the GDR.

My use of the broad term 'autobiographical writing' to categorize this distinctive aspect of East German literature is both deliberate and necessary.[2] The degree of narrative ambiguity that has always existed between self-styled autobiography and first-person fiction provided crucial room for manoeuvre for left-wing German authors working under the ideological pressures that bore down on them from 1933 onwards, once Hitler's rise to power had driven an entire literary generation into exile. When Christa Wolf used the term 'Prosa' (prose) in her 1968 essay 'Lesen und Schreiben' (Reading and Writing) to encompass the same diffuse narrative territory, she was both acknowledging its importance in historical terms and setting the parameters for East German writing in this mode in the following two decades (and beyond). Viewing all writing in this largely autobiographical vein as part of the same genre, using the definition produced by Wolf in her

88

highly influential essay – that is, 'inventing truthfully on the basis of one's own experience'[3] – helps to illuminate important continuities, both within the work of individual authors and across East German culture as a whole.

Wolf's focus on 'Prosa' was motivated by political as well as aesthetic factors. She was well aware of the suspicion with which explicit autobiography had been viewed by communism's all-powerful cultural policymakers from the 1930s onwards. They regarded it as the preferred medium of 'renegades' who had abandoned their commitment to the cause once it became clear how brutally all forms of dissent were being suppressed – a phenomenon illustrated in Michael Rohrwasser's monograph *Der Stalinismus und die Renegaten*.[4] This made it politically prudent for Wolf – still a committed author in 1968, although increasingly alienated by the continuing abuse of power that was to lead to the military suppression of the Prague Spring a few months after she wrote her essay – to insist that her own creative writing was not directly based on real people and events, as exemplified by the disclaimer she used to preface her innovative prose-work of 1969, *Nachdenken über Christa T.* (The Quest for Christa T.):

> Christa T. is a fictional character. Several of the quotations from diaries, sketches, and letters come from real-life sources. I did not consider myself bound by fidelity to external details. The minor characters and the situations are invented: any resemblance between them and living persons or actual events is accidental.[5]

In the era of socialist realism, the literary doctrine codified in the Soviet Union in 1934 that was formally adopted by the GDR in 1949 and never explicitly abandoned, any creative writing suspected of moving too close to autobiographical independence was deemed to be guilty of 'subjectivism', in other words, of failing to devote sufficient attention to the 'objective' social and historical context of inexorable progress towards communism.[6] Any condemnation of subjectivist tendencies by cultural bureaucrats carried considerable political force, even when the judgement was reached in a manifestly arbitrary way, and Christa Wolf would have been acutely aware of this danger in 1968. This did not, however, save *Nachdenken über Christa T.* from being attacked in precisely these terms.[7]

East German authors nevertheless had more room for creative manoeuvre than their counterparts in the Soviet Union. They benefited from a concession negotiated during the mid-1930s, when the question of whether the rigid rules of Soviet socialist realism should be imposed upon the work of left-wing exiles from Hitler's Germany was a fiercely debated ideological issue. The theorist Georg Lukács, concerned about the mediocre quality of

the Soviet Union's first wave of 'great proletarian novels', argued successfully that German authors had a special responsibility to build on their
unique cultural heritage of humanistic *Entwicklungsromane*, or novels of
self-development. The focus on representative individuals striving to
achieve a socially responsible identity during periods of political upheaval
that characterized canonical works by Goethe, Hölderlin and Keller was
seen by Lukács as an equally important priority for Germany's exile
authors.[8] For the reasons already indicated, this was no plea for explicit
autobiography, which Lukács saw as little more than the raw material for
the carefully composed *Entwicklungsromane* he admired, where 'the
tangled and complex interrelations between society and the individual'
were properly illuminated.[9] His recognition that subjective experience was
the starting point for Germany's classical *Entwicklungsromane* was nevertheless just as welcome in the early GDR years as it had been under the
harsh conditions of the Hitler era. In the exile years it had created the
opportunity for Johannes R. Becher, a cultural ally of Lukács, to publish
his self-revelatory first-person novel *Abschied* (Farewell, 1940), and for
Anna Seghers, Christa Wolf's mentor-to-be, to write *Der Ausflug der
toten Mädchen* (The Excursion of the Dead Girls, 1944), a deeply personal
meditation on the fate of her Jewish school friends. In the GDR era the
Entwicklungsroman was the medium in which many members of the new
generation of authors who went on to write with increasingly autobiographical directness – notably Brigitte Reimann, Günter de Bruyn and Franz
Fühmann as well as Christa Wolf – made their creative debut. However
conventional and predictable the majority of these early novels were, they
all contained a core of authentic personal experience on which their
authors were able to expand in their more subtle later work.

   Opening up this line of approach to East German autobiographical
writing suggests that it shares some key characteristics of the genre of life-
writing as a whole, as defined by the American scholar James Olney in his
monograph *Memory and Narrative: The Weave of Life-Writing*. The creative evolution of Christa Wolf's generation of authors shows them constantly reworking and refining the story of their lives in a variety of narrative
modes from the 1950s onwards, a process that has continued into the post-
unification era for those who lived beyond 1989. In the course of biographies
deeply marked by successive waves of historical turbulence – the Third
Reich, the Second World War, the division of Germany and the many crises
of the communist era that preceded the collapse of the GDR – they have
regularly needed to reconfigure earlier experience in the light of their
dramatically changing personal circumstances. For this reason it is also

important not to overplay the importance of the dramatic events of 1989–90 for their creative development, however fundamental this upheaval was in political terms. This phased approach chimes with Olney's argument that a striking variety of authors in diverse social and historical circumstances have become so preoccupied with writing the story of their life that it has turned into the 'all-encompassing endeavor' of their creative careers.[10]

The aim of this chapter is to highlight this pattern of recurring crises, deceptive hopes and intensified disillusionments as it has emerged in the work of the two literary generations that span the forty-year lifetime of the GDR. It will look first at the so-called '*Aufbau* (or construction) genera-tion', of which Christa Wolf is a key representative, socialized in the Third Reich before being entrusted as young adults with the formidable task of helping to create a viable GDR.[11] As optimistic debut authors of the 1950s, they then had to come to terms creatively with the existential shocks represented by events like the building of the Berlin Wall (1961) and the crushing of the Prague Spring (1968), finding themselves increasingly in conflict with the cultural policy of a state with which they still strongly identified. Their gradual disaffection is presented here in three historical phases, taking the systemic crisis of Eastern European communism in 1968 and the GDR-specific cultural crisis of 1979 as key crisis points. I will look in detail at one autobiographical work from each phase that particularly merits rereading from today's perspective.

The first phase is exemplified by Franz Fühmann's story *Böhmen am Meer* (Bohemia by the Sea, 1962), viewed in terms of its autobiographical inspiration in the summer of 1955, during the short-lived Eastern European 'Thaw', and not just – its usual fate – as a piece of state propaganda published just after the erection of the Wall. The second phase focuses on the most acclaimed autobiographical work of the 1970s, Christa Wolf's *Kindheitsmuster* (Patterns of Childhood, 1976), her pioneering account of the continuing impact of her socialization in the Third Reich on her socialist identity. It is revisited here in the light of Wolf's increasing problems with retrospective stocktaking, as exposed by her final experiment in auto-biography, *Stadt der Engel* (City of Angels, 2010). The third phase spans the GDR's final decade. In this section I argue that much of the autobiographical writing conceived, if not always completed, in the 1980s anticipated the demise of the state, a point obscured by the subsequent media-led determi-nation to view 1989 as the dramatic moment not only when the GDR collapsed but also when its supposed ban on writing autobiographically ceased to be a problem.[12] Günter de Bruyn's *Zwischenbilanz* (Interim Report), a work largely written by the autumn of 1989 but not published until 1992, will be used to illustrate the anticipatory quality of this last wave of GDR life-writing.

It also needs to be stressed that the preoccupation with writing autobiographically was not restricted to the '*Aufbau* generation'. Its cross-generational importance is indicated in the final section of my analysis by a discussion of the work produced in the 1980s by authors of the 'integrated generation', born in the war or early post-war years. Their entry into creative life largely coincided with the cultural crisis of 1979 that had such a fateful impact on the work of their elders, and this gave them the opportunity to shed significant new light on the earlier political failures of the system, from their perspective as the children and young adults of those years – a critical task they have been generally better equipped to pursue since unification than their elders, as they had less of an emotional stake in the survival of the GDR. The focus on 1968 in Angela Krauß's *Der Dienst* (Service), her prize-winning literary breakthrough of 1988, makes it invaluable for this comparative purpose.

1949–68: experiments and setbacks in the first two decades

The belated emergence of the first East German *Entwicklungsromane* in the 1960s was, as already indicated, an inevitable result of the ideological insistence, for most of the 1950s, on affirmative literature on contemporary industrial themes. While it would be misleading, as Georgina Paul's analysis of Eduard Claudius's *Menschen an unsrer Seite* (People at Our Side, 1951) in this volume shows, to dismiss all of these early industrial novels as optimistic fantasies of individuals transformed by working for the new state, they nevertheless generally relied on ideological stereotypes that left little scope for the subjective concerns of individual authors. It was rare for autobiographical structures to slip through the net, and the few exceptions tended to be special cases, such as *Auf andere Art so große Hoffnung* (Great Hope of a Different Kind, 1951), the volume of reflections compiled during the GDR's first year by Johannes R. Becher, the author who was soon to become its Minister of Culture. Not surprisingly under these circumstances, Becher's diary of 1950 was a hotchpotch of narrative and thematic contradictions. While it was heaped with official praise as a celebratory record of the GDR's beginnings, it was valued by aspiring authors for the way it illuminated the unresolved identity issues of the post-war period, as Christa Wolf later acknowledged.[13] Another early first-person text was *Hans Garbe erzählt* (Hans Garbe Tells His Story, 1952), ostensibly the testimony of an 'industrial hero', a stonemason who had almost single-handedly repaired a malfunctioning coal furnace in the depths of winter. On closer inspection it turned out to be ghostwritten for him in a manner that fully confirmed the propaganda of an SED-inspired industrial revolution.[14] In the later 1950s a book series entitled 'Autobiographien' (Autobiographies) was launched by the Verlag der Nation, but it was restricted to memoirs of the political and military elite, thus avoiding all risk of confusion with the life-stories of disillusioned renegades regularly published in the Federal Republic.[15]

There was as yet little opportunity for the ambitious authors of the '*Aufbau* generation' to make their mark. Their subsequently published prose-works and essays show, however, that they had all committed themselves in 1945 to telling their story of how they had been exposed to indoctrination in the Third Reich, as a warning to future generations.[16] This had generally been accompanied by a commitment to serve the self-styled antifascist GDR, as a means of making personal amends for the destruction of Europe and the Holocaust. What inevitably had to take priority was the task of serving the state, mostly by working for its political and cultural organizations. The first of these young authors to make a mark in their secondary creative role was Franz Fühmann, who was initially willing to reduce his life-story to a parable in verse, *Die Fahrt nach Stalingrad* (Journey to Stalingrad, 1953), dutifully presenting his first-person protagonist's progress from convinced fascist to equally committed communist as a dramatic transformation. This was just one of many creative compromises that later drove Fühmann to the brink of self-destruction. But he was also the author of an intriguingly hybrid autobiographical text, *Böhmen am Meer*, inspired by an entirely different sequence of personal and political circumstances just two years later, which sets out to tell an authentic personal story of the kind we associate with East German writing of the 1970s and 1980s.[17] If he had written it then, in the way he first conceived it, it could have helped to accelerate the movement towards autobiographical openness. When it was finally published, in 1962, it had been reframed in order to transmit a propagandist message.

Böhmen am Meer opens with a strikingly frank depiction of the identity conflicts of a first-person protagonist clearly based on the author. It is given a precise temporal setting, in May 1955, just as the post-Stalin 'Thaw' in Eastern European political and cultural life was providing a first opportunity to question the rigidity of the Cold War attitudes that had prevailed since 1949. The narrator has travelled to the Baltic coast for an overdue holiday, after five years' unstinting service to the state as an aspiring author, and he finds his new surroundings hugely liberating, as his ecstatic atmospheric depiction of them shows. Not only had Fühmann himself just made the same journey; he was also about to travel to his native Czechoslovakia for the first time since 1945, breaking the ban he had imposed on himself from ever returning home (his *Heimatverbot*) as a self-punishment for becoming a Sudeten German fascist in his youth.[18] This seaside holiday, as depicted in *Böhmen am Meer*, provided a first opportunity to reflect on the creative damage he had been doing to himself by denying his identity as a German-speaking Czech – or 'Bohemian', the politically incorrect term he chooses to use throughout his text. What it does above all is to release memories of the pre-1945 past that author and narrator alike had tried to suppress as irrelevant to a new life as a committed GDR citizen, from the everyday sounds and smells of a rural childhood to the triumphal celebrations of 1938, when the Sudetenland was annexed by the Third Reich. The text shows how such memory fragments are unlocked and depicts some of them in an autobiographical stream of consciousness other-wise foreign to early GDR literature. Although there is no archival evidence of these experiences having been written down in 1955, Fühmann recreated them with something close to their original immediacy when he came to write *Böhmen am Meer* in 1960–61.

The problem was that the political and creative hopes associated with the 1955 'Thaw' had by then disappeared from sight. The crushing of popular revolts in Poland and Hungary in 1956 put a bloody end to Eastern European dreams of liberalization and was followed in the GDR by heavy-handed cultural repression, of which Fühmann himself was a victim. Even though he was not deterred from placing rigorous self-analysis at the centre of his later work, he accepted for some time, as Cold War tensions reignited, the need to combine it with partisan political messages. However clear Fühmann might have been from 1955 onwards about his need to engage critically with his fascist past, he was more concerned in 1960–61 about the danger posed by pressure groups representing German expellees from Eastern Europe, who appeared ready to use military force to reclaim their homelands. This led him to use his encounter with other émigrés from his Czech homeland during the 1955 holiday on the Baltic coast as the narrative stimulus for an attack on the activities of their militant West German counterparts, viewed as neo-fascists threatening post-war European stability. The polemical excesses of this attack, arising from the depiction of a mass rally of expellees in West Berlin, helped to ensure, when *Böhmen am Meer* was finally published, that little attention was paid to the authenticity of its narrative starting point. Rereading it today, more than two decades after German unification, it is easier to appreciate the historical potential of these autobiographical aspirations. Fühmann, always his own most ruthless critic, later borrowed a phrase from the Russian poet Vladimir Mayakovsky, 'stepping on the throat of one's own song', to describe the effects of creative aberrations like this one on all of his work up to 1968.[19] It is a fitting metaphor for this phase in the history of East German autobiographical writing as a whole.

The same tensions are evident in the wave of *Entwicklungsromane* conceived in the later 1950s and early 1960s by Fühmann's contemporaries – notably Günter de Bruyn's *Der Hohlweg* (The Ravine, 1963), Christa Wolf's *Der geteilte Himmel* (Divided Heaven, 1963) and Brigitte Reimann's *Franziska Linkerhand* (1974) – in which their end of war imperative to tell a personal story in its full complexity was progressively compromised by the combined effects of self-censorship and state control of publications. Fühmann's contribution to the genre, *Das Judenauto* (The Jews' Car, 1962), completed just after *Böhmen am Meer* but, with its narrative focus restricted to his pre-GDR experience, has stood the test of time better. None of these authors were satisfied with the outcomes, but their semi-autobiographical works of fiction are not as worthless as some of their later scathing comments about them would tend to suggest.[20] They establish a basic thematic core of material that is successively refined in their subsequent attempts at life-writing, a process that is particularly visible in the case of Reimann's *Franziska Linkerhand.*[21] Its ten-year gestation process and steadily shifting emphasis from supposedly typical experience to something close to autobiographical openness can be fully reconstructed with the help of the mass of new material that has become available since the end of the GDR, including her diaries, correspondence and the uncensored text. While it remains an example of the limitations of the 1960s *Entwicklungsroman* it can also be seen as heralding the insistence on subjective perspectives that was to distinguish the best products of the next phase of development, the 1970s.

1968–79: self-realization under socialism as political hope and aesthetic programme

By the late 1960s there was a deep mood of crisis in East German literature. Those members of the '*Aufbau* generation' who sought to place self-analysis at the centre of their creative writing had abandoned the illusion that this could be combined with the promotion of the GDR's political interests. The state's attempt to breathe new life into socialist realism by encouraging writers like them to gain first-hand experience of working life and then produce *Entwicklungsromane* set in industrial locations (the much-publicized 'Bitterfelder Weg') had itself been discredited. There was still little scope, however, for a new literature that would look critically at why the Marxian utopia of free self-development under socialism was still so far from realization. The internal cultural repression imposed at the SED Central Committee's infamous Eleventh Plenum in December 1965, followed by the crushing in August 1968 of the transnational reformist aspirations of the Prague Spring, had generated widespread disillusionment. It was between these two dates that Christa Wolf, once praised by the cultural policy-makers as an exemplary young author, had faced such hostility, after attempting in *Nachdenken über Christa T.* to provide an authentic overview of her generation's confused sense of identity over the previous two decades. Only after Erich Honecker came to power in 1971, and following his unexpected promise that there would no longer be cultural taboos for committed East German authors, was the validity of self-reflexive writing like *Christa T.* finally acknowledged.

The 1970s thus became the decade in which serious autobiographical writing, articulating a competing range of views of how successfully its authors had integrated into GDR society, was allowed to flourish. The plurality of narrative forms in which this creative debate took place extended from the loosely structured reflections of Fühmann's *Zweiundzwanzig Tage oder Die Hälfte des Lebens* (Twenty-two Days or Half a Lifetime, 1973), via fictionalized life-stories such as Hermann Kant's *Der Aufenthalt* (Enforced Absence, 1977), to Stefan Heym's novel *Collin* (1979) – a work banned in the GDR because it suggested that it was still impossible to publish credible autobiography there. The need to face up to the continuing impact of socialization in the Third Reich and the Stalin era on contemporary behaviour patterns was gradually being recognized in the process. The work that best represents that significant leap forward, but also its limitations, is Christa Wolf's *Kindheitsmuster* (1976).[22]

Kindheitsmuster is a work that spans my first two historical phases, although it belongs firmly in the second in terms of its narrative structuring and its social impact. Wolf had been nurturing an autobiographical project with the working title 'Mein Buch über 1945' (My Book about 1945) since the 1950s, traces of which can be detected in her debut publication *Moskauer Novelle* (Moscow Novella, 1959). A diary entry from 1964 makes it clear that this was her top priority after completing *Der geteilte Himmel*. The fact that *Nachdenken über Christa T.* intervened proved a blessing in disguise, since it meant that Wolf's serious work on this more ambitious project did not begin until the Honecker era. Her original conception, however, with its clear emphasis on 1945 as the definitive turning point in her life, became more problematic as the distance between the end of the war and the narrative present grew. The aftermath of 1945 was difficult enough in terms of the suffering experienced by millions of uprooted Germans (who included Wolf's family as well as Fühmann's) during their long trek westwards, much of it at the hands of the Red Army. Subsequent existential crisis points such as 1956, 1961 and 1968 nevertheless also cried out for inclusion in a retrospective rooted in the 1970s – a need that Wolf found impossible to meet in *Kindheitsmuster*. Having drawn attention in *Christa T.* to her generation's post-war difficulties in achieving identity under socialism, Wolf placed herself under narrative and political pressure in *Kindheitsmuster* to mark a point in the narrative present when that identity was at least on the brink of being achieved.

This was a work she desperately wanted to be published in the GDR, not least because of her focus on the continuing impact of Third Reich socialization on her generation's attitudes, and there was an element of compromise in her desire to end on a positive note. Wolf's rigorous and graphic self-analysis as a child of the Third Reich is what readers in both German states most admired then and makes it worth rereading today. The way Wolf illuminated her sense of split identity at the narrative level, through her subtle use of three competing autobiographical voices, is a further pointer to the sophistication of *Kindheitsmuster*. Its weak point is its ending, located in May 1975. It links together the thirtieth anniversary of the end of the Second World War and the American defeat in Vietnam as harbingers of a new 'post-war era' when international socialism is beginning to prevail, just as her divided narrative self approaches its moment of harmonization. What might have been acceptable in the mid-1970s as an aspiration of the era of East–West détente now looks increasingly like a partisan standpoint at odds with both historical and subjective experience. Although Wolf continued to structure her major autobiographical works after *Kindheitsmuster* – *Sommerstück* (Summer Interlude, 1989), *Leibhaftig* (In the Flesh, 2002) and *Stadt der Engel* (2010) – around the tensions between present and past narrative perspectives, she appeared in her final years incapable of moving beyond the parameters of the GDR era. The dissolution of her utopian hopes of the mid-1970s left her clinging, in an increasingly embattled way, to the short-lived alternative models of socialism that emerged before the collapse of the GDR. This led even sympathetic reviewers of Wolf's *Stadt der Engel* – a text which views the popular demonstrations of the autumn of 1989 as a last futile attempt to keep the destructive forces of Western civilization at bay – to question the validity of

her whole autobiographical project, since it was based on the idea of a
narrative self always ready to question past assumptions in the light of new
insights.[23] The structural weakness at the heart of *Kindheitsmuster* now
appears more significant than it did at the time.

Ironically, it rapidly became clear to Wolf herself, from the way she was
demonized as an author by members of the SED hierarchy for her suggestion that the shadow of the Third Reich still hung over the GDR, that her
optimism regarding the dawning of the 'post-war era' was unfounded.
Matters were made worse by the Biermann Affair, which began just a few
weeks before the publication of *Kindheitsmuster* and blighted intellectual
life in general between the autumn of 1976 and the dispiriting cultural
tribunal in June 1979, when a group of alleged dissidents was expelled from
the Writers' Union.[24] Wolf was not alone in finding herself in the untenable position of being persecuted for her creative convictions while continuing in public to assert her loyalty to the antifascist principles on which
the GDR claimed to be founded.

1979–89 (1): subjective anticipations of historical breakdown in the work of the '*Aufbau* generation'

The impact of the repression that culminated in the 1979 Writers' Tribunal is
evident in Wolf's *Leibhaftig* (2002), where she depicts it symbolically as a
confrontation between her narrative self and a Mephisto-like cultural functionary cynically attempting to buy her allegiance. If she is prepared to
abandon her 'unattainable hopes' and her 'unproductive resistance', she is
promised a quiet life.[25] In her portrayal of this moment as a cultural breaking
point Wolf is in good company, since there is a wealth of autobiographical
writing by her contemporaries, published on one side or the other of divided
Germany in the 1980s or in united Germany thereafter, which also represents
the crisis of 1976–79 as the definitive break in their relationship with the SED
regime. This anticipatory moment deserves to be highlighted in the face of
the widespread assumption that it was not until the Wall came down that
disillusioned life-writing of this kind could be published. On closer inspection it turns out that many post-1989 publications were also conceived and at
least partly written before the demise of the GDR itself. Thoughts of 1979
provoke a mixture of pain – a dominant metaphor in the work of authors like
Wolf and Fühmann – and contempt for authority, as exemplified by Stefan
Heym's reference in his autobiography *Nachruf* (Obituary, 1988) to 'the
Lilliputians at their auto-da-fé'.[26] There were some rapid responses to this
complete loss of confidence in the SED regime with apocalyptic titles such as

Erich Loest's *Durch die Erde ein Riß* (The Riven Earth, 1981) and Fühmann's *Vor Feuerschlünden* (Facing the Inferno, 1982). In other cases there was a lengthy period of personal crisis, what Heym referred to euphemistically as a 'pause for thought',[27] before the stocktaking autobiography appeared, sometimes on the eve of the political collapse, such as *Nachruf* itself and Wolf's *Sommerstück*. And it is striking that many works published after unification – Klaus Schlesinger's *Fliegender Wechsel* (Rapid Changeover, 1990), Adolf Endler's *Tarzan am Prenzlauer Berg* (Tarzan in Prenzlauer Berg, 1994) or Günter Kunert's *Erwachsenenspiele* (Adult Games, 1997), for example – maintain this focus on 1979 as the turning point in their lives and say little about the intervening decade.

Günter de Bruyn's *Zwischenbilanz* (1992) offers revealing insights into the tensions between post-1979 and post-1989 autobiographical writing. As the first part of the life-story continued in his *Vierzig Jahre* (Forty Years, 1996) it finishes three decades before 1979 in its historical narrative, but there is no shortage of other evidence that this was the breaking point for him as well.[28] Even though he seeks to argue in *Vierzig Jahre* that he was a literary outsider throughout the GDR era, his attitude to the state hardens more gradually than this suggests, as the analysis of his evolution as a prose-writer since *Der Hohlweg* shows. De Bruyn tells us in his preface to *Zwischenbilanz* that he began this new autobiographical project in 1986, when he turned sixty, and the textual evidence indicates that much of it was written before 1989, even if he was convinced it would be unpublishable in the GDR. As an account of his life up to 1945 it is a brilliantly constructed narrative, self-consciously written in the tradition of Goethe's autobiographical *Dichtung und Wahrheit* (Poetry and Truth) and largely free of Wolf's concerns about the fragmentation of their generation's identity. In presenting himself as a social outsider from his Third Reich childhood onwards, inherently resistant to all forms of ideology, de Bruyn is able to claim a degree of scepticism in 1945 that is poles apart from Wolf's willingness to start afresh. It is already abundantly clear that he is not committed to the pursuit of self-realization as a GDR socialist.

What comes as a surprise, in the light of de Bruyn's achievements over his three decades as an East German author, is the tone of his post-unification preface, written at the point when his initial sympathies for ex-colleagues caught up in the so-called 'Literaturstreit' of the early 1990s[29] had begun to fade. The idea that he is only now, after years as a 'professional liar', attempting to speak the truth does scant justice to the integrity of most of his earlier work. Furthermore, his suggestion that authors should only write autobiographies at the very end of their careers (which is why he has entitled this volume *Zwischenbilanz*) disregards both the sense of personal mission that made him want to become an author in 1945 and the strong sense of continuity in East German autobiographical prose as a whole.[30] But the discourse of truth-telling after decades of repression dominated the early 1990s and evidently influenced the way in which de Bruyn sought to frame his autobiography as it approached publication. The comments he made a couple of years later in the course of his work on the sequel *Vierzig Jahre* are almost apologetic about the extent to which 'politics' would take centre stage in his more rapidly written account of his GDR years.[31] Most commentators would agree that the quality of his writing suffered as a result. The unevenness of these two volumes of de Bruyn's autobiography serves to underline the importance, especially in relation to these years of transition, of taking careful account of the duration and the changing circumstances of the writing process.

1979–89 (2): the autobiographical voice of the 'integrated generation'

From the late 1970s on there is a parallel process at work in East German autobiographical writing, as representatives of the generation brought up in the early GDR years also begin to write autobiographically. Authors such as Christoph Hein, Angela Krauß, Irina Liebmann and Monika Maron are primarily associated with the post-unification era, but they all made significant debuts in this vein in the GDR's last decade.[32] Their stimulus to do so was to some extent political, in the sense that the personal crises they experienced as children and young adults sometimes coincided with major upheavals, such as the repressive aftermath in the GDR of the Hungarian uprising, which has an obvious contextualizing function in Hein's *Horns Ende* (Horn's Death, 1985). The difference is that the narrative focus tends to be restricted to the subjective responses of their young protagonists to these as yet incomprehensible external events. Although authors of this generation were at too early a point in their literary careers to become victims of the Biermann Affair or the Writers' Tribunal, the widespread disillusionment of the late 1970s also had a perceptible impact on the direction their subsequent writing took. It was in 1979 that Hein, who started his career as resident dramatist at Berlin's famous Volksbühne theatre, had the dispiriting experience of having fifteen productions of his plays across the GDR banned, obliging him to give up his theatre post. This became, as he commented laconically at the time, 'a good reason to write prose'.[33] In 1979 too Angela Krauß – the author chosen here as representative of this literary generation – graduated from the GDR's Literaturinstitut in Leipzig, an organization whose staff and students were regularly accused during her time there of subverting its official function as a training ground for loyal working-class talent. It was therefore no surprise that the industrial placement in Saxony for which Krauß then volunteered resulted in a first novel, *Das Vergnügen* (Pleasure, 1984), which took a subtly ironic approach to the clichés of the 'Bitterfelder Weg'.

When Krauß made her literary breakthrough, near the end of the GDR era, it was with *Der Dienst*, a work with an unmistakeable autobiographical basis.[34] In a series of 'Lectures on Poetics', published in 2004 under the title *Die Gesamtliebe und die Einzelliebe* (Universal and Individual Love), she reconstructs the creative process that led to the writing of *Der Dienst*, for which she was awarded the prestigious Ingeborg Bachmann prize in 1988, although it did not appear in book form until 1990. Krauß's crucial formative experience came late in 1968, against the backdrop of the crushing of the Prague Spring, when her father committed suicide. She had little idea what his increasingly responsible police duties involved or why he had taken his life. This traumatic personal loss gave rise to Krauß's literary vocation and her prolonged search for a form that would allow her to explore the reasons for her father's suicide and its significance for her life. Only in 1986 did she find a creative way forward, by placing her childhood relationship with her father in the physical setting of the uranium mining area where he worked and she had spent much of her childhood, the Erzgebirge. Using the labyrinthine geology of the mountains as the metaphor for her literary approach to an absent father, Krauß structured her text on the principle that patient excavation will gradually expose previously hidden rhythms and movements, in the life of her first-person narrator as well as the father figure. As a form of what Krauß calls both 'subjective historiography' and 'life-writing',[35] *Der Dienst* establishes a distinctive narrative technique that she has continued to refine in all her post-unification writing.

Krauß's overriding need in *Der Dienst* to come to terms with the loss of her father inevitably led her, however, to neglect other aspects of her childhood. She was soon intent on adjusting her narrative perspective, in the same way that older East German authors engaged on long-term autobiographical projects had done throughout their careers but with the greater sense of urgency of the immediate post-GDR period. Within a year she had produced an expanded version of her text, now entitled *Dienst Jahre* (Years of Service, 1991), including several new fragments relating to her first-person narrator's childhood in the Erzgebirge, and especially her close relationship with her grandmother.[36] The new version evokes the narrator's own developmental processes and the workings of her subjective memory in a manner that now underlines her father's career-determined *absence* from so much of her growing up. It has become more fully the narrator's own story without diminishing the pathos of her father's unspoken suffering. Krauß's autobiographical 'lectures', delivered well over a decade later, reveal an additional political dimension that underlines why the collapse of the GDR was not crucial to her creative development: the alienation from state authority that had given rise to it had happened long before 1989. While the original text ends with the shock of the narrator's sudden bereavement in 1968, Krauß's lectures spell out its political consequences. 'The death of my father twenty years before the end of the socialist era had taught me to observe and look beyond appearances. After my father's failure I experienced the failure of the system. I observed it rolling towards the abyss.'[37] The continuing willingness to modify her narrative focus that she displays in her lectures has been integral to her autobiographical project from the outset.

The broad conclusion to be drawn from this comparative study of the autobiographical writing of these two generations of authors is that the political collapse of the GDR was not a significant creative watershed in either case. Disillusionment had set in earlier and subjective narrative structures were being widely used across the generational divide during the 1980s as a means of establishing critical distance from the state and its ideology. The divisions that have been exposed since 1989, most strikingly between Wolf and de Bruyn as figureheads of the '*Aufbau* generation', relate to the question of what, if anything, remains of the GDR's socialist project in unified Germany. For Krauß, as for most members of the 'integrated generation', the issue is rather the one signalled by the title of her stocktaking narrative of 2006, *Wie weiter* (How to Move On).[38]

Notes

1. See Wolfgang Emmerich, 'Kein Nullpunkt', *Kleine Literaturgeschichte der DDR: Erweiterte Neuausgabe* (Berlin: Aufbau, 2000), pp. 70–95.
2. For a detailed discussion of issues of genre and terminology see my monograph *Shifting Perspectives: East German Autobiographical Narratives before and after the End of the GDR* (Rochester, NY: Camden House, 2007), pp. 1–36. Translations into English are mine, except where otherwise indicated.
3. Christa Wolf, 'Lesen und Schreiben', in Wolf, *Essays, Gespräche, Reden, Briefe 1959–1974, Werke*, vol. 4, ed. Sonja Hilzinger (Munich: Luchterhand, 1999), pp. 238–82; p. 258.

4. Michael Rohrwasser, *Der Stalinismus und die Renegaten: Die Literatur der Exkommunisten* (Stuttgart: Metzler, 1991).

5. The quotation is taken from the preface to *Nachdenken über Christa T., Werke*, vol. 2, ed. Hilzinger (Munich: Luchterhand, 1999), and cited from *The Quest for Christa T.*, trans. Christopher Middleton (London: Virago, 1982).

6. Compare the entries 'Realismus, sozialistischer' and 'Subjektivismus' in what was intended as the authoritative work of reference, the *Kulturpolitisches Wörterbuch* (Berlin: Dietz, 1970), pp. 449–56 and 498–99.

7. See the 1969 verdict of the ideologue Hans Koch, in Angela Drescher (ed.), *Dokumentation zu Christa Wolf 'Nachdenken über Christa T.'* (Hamburg: Luchterhand, 1991), p. 158.

8. See Georg Lukács, '*Wilhelm Meisters Lehrjahre*' [1936], 'Hölderlins *Hyperion*' [1934] and 'Gottfried Keller' [1938], in *Deutsche Literatur in zwei Jahrhunderten, Werke*, vol. 7 (Neuwied: Luchterhand, 1964), pp. 69–88, 164–84 and 334–419.

9. Ibid., p. 395.

10. James Olney, *Memory and Narrative: The Weave of Life-Writing* (Chicago University Press, 1998), p. XIII. Although Christa Wolf is one of his chosen subjects (pp. 255–61), Olney unfortunately fails to do justice to the complexity of her life-writing; he focuses on how she comes to terms with her upbringing in Hitler's Germany without reference to the changing GDR context in which she was working.

11. For an overview of the generational categories used here see Wolfgang Emmerich, 'Autobiographical Writing in Three Generations of a GDR Family: Christa Wolf – Annette Simon – Jana Simon', in Renate Rechtien and Dennis Tate (eds.), *Twenty Years On: Competing Memories of the GDR in Postunification German Culture* (Rochester, NY: Camden House, 2011), pp. 141–57.

12. This section builds on my article 'Subjective Anticipations of Historical Breakdown: East German Literary Autobiography before the End of the GDR', in Heinz-Peter Preußer and Helmut Schmitz (eds.), *Autobiografie und historische Krisenerfahrung* (Heidelberg: Winter, 2010), pp. 107–15.

13. Wolf used an unresolved question from Becher's diary – 'What does it mean to "achieve identity"'? – as her motto for *Nachdenken über Christa T.*, signalling her intention to pursue this fundamental issue for East German authors more rigorously.

14. It was written by Käthe Rülicke, an actor in Bertolt Brecht's Berliner Ensemble, and published in Helmut Hauptmann (ed.), *DDR-Reportagen: Eine Anthologie* (Leipzig: Reclam, 1969), pp. 33–41. Garbe's story had already been fictionalized in 1951 by Claudius in *Menschen an unsrer Seite*.

15. A typical example was Rudolf Petershagen's *Gewissen in Aufruhr* (Conscience in Turmoil, 1957), the story of a Wehrmacht general's conversion to communism; among the most enduring of the post-1945 renegade memoirs is Wolfgang Leonhard's *Die Revolution entläßt ihre Kinder* (Cologne: Kiepenheuer & Witsch, 1955), published as *Child of the Revolution*, trans. Margaret Woodhouse (London, Collins, 1957).

16. See, for example, Günter de Bruyn, *Das erzählte Ich: Über Wahrheit und Dichtung in der Autobiographie* (Frankfurt/M.: Fischer, 1995), p. 15.

17. Fühmann, *Böhmen am Meer*, in Fühmann, *Erzählungen 1955–1975, Werkausgabe*, vol. 2 (Rostock: Hinstorff, 1977), pp. 283–318.

18. This discussion is based on recent work carried out on the genesis of *Böhmen am Meer*, focused on textual variants and related correspondence held in the Academy of Arts archives in Berlin. See also my article 'Böhme am Meer, Bohemien mit Heimweh: Franz Fühmanns literarische Begegnung mit Thomas Mann im identitätsstiftenden Frühsommer 1955', in Roland Berbig, Stephan Krause and Volker Scharnefsky (eds.), *Literarisches Bergwerk: Arbeitswelt und Bibliothek Franz Fühmanns* (Berlin: Zentral- und Landesbibliothek, 2014), pp. 51–67.

19. See the 1982 interview with Wilfried F. Schoeller reprinted in Fühmann, *Den Katzenartigen wollten wir verbrennen: Ein Lesebuch*, ed. Hans-Jürgen Schmitt (Munich: dtv, 1988), p. 279. The quotation is from Mayakovsky's poem 'At the Top of My Voice'.

20. See, for example, Günter de Bruyn's dismissal of *Der Hohlweg* as a 'Holzweg' (false track) in his autobiography *Vierzig Jahre: Ein Lebensbericht* (Frankfurt/M.: Fischer, 1996), pp. 115–21.

21. Brigitte Reimann, *Franziska Linkerhand*, ed. Angela Drescher (Berlin: Aufbau, 2000). See also Georgina Paul's chapter in this volume.

22. Christa Wolf, *Kindheitsmuster, Werke*, vol. 5, ed. Hilzinger (Munich: Luchterhand, 2000).

23. Christa Wolf, *Stadt der Engel oder The Overcoat of Dr Freud* (Frankfurt/M.: Suhrkamp, 2010). See especially the reviews by Wolf's biographer Jörg Magenau, *Tageszeitung*, 26 June 2010, and Christine Cosentino in the internet journal *glossen*, 31 (2011).

24. Joachim Walther's documentary volume *Protokoll eines Tribunals: Die Ausslchüsse aus dem DDR-Schriftstellerverband 1979* (Reinbek: Rowohlt, 1991) provides insights into the despair provoked by this futile act of repression.

25. Christa Wolf, *Leibhaftig* (Munich: Luchterhand, 2002), pp. 181–84.

26. Stefan Heym, *Nachruf* (Frankfurt/M.: Fischer, 1997), p. 834.

27. Ibid., p. 836.

28. Günter de Bruyn, *Zwischenbilanz: Eine Jugend in Berlin* (Frankfurt/M.: Fischer, 1992) and de Bruyn, *Vierzig Jahre*.

29. See the chapter by Carol Anne Costabile-Heming in this volume.

30. De Bruyn, *Zwischenbilanz*, p. 7.

31. De Bruyn, *Das erzählte Ich*, pp. 56–60.

32. Astrid Köhler's monograph *Brückenschläge: DDR-Autoren vor und nach der Wiedervereinigung* (Göttingen: Vandenhoeck & Ruprecht, 2007) gives a detailed account of these continuities.

33. Christoph Hein, *Öffentlich arbeiten: Essais und Gespräche* (Berlin: Aufbau, 1987), p. 101.

34. Angela Krauß, *Der Dienst* (Frankfurt/M.: Suhrkamp, 1990).

35. Angela Krauß, *Die Gesamtliebe und die Einzelliebe: Frankfurter Poetikvorlesungen* (Frankfurt/M.: Suhrkamp, 2004), pp. 72, 76.
36. Angela Krauß, *Dienst Jahre und andere Prosa* (Berlin: Aufbau, 1991).
37. Ibid., p. 46.
38. Angela Krauß, *Wie weiter* (Frankfurt/M.: Suhrkamp, 2006).

CHAPTER 6

Gender in GDR literature

Georgina Paul

Studies of gender in the GDR have tended to focus on the situation of women in the East German state. This emphasis is understandable, since the GDR's policies on women – the constitutional commitment to equality between men and women from the founding of the state in 1949 onwards, the creation of a social environment which enabled women to combine work and family, together with the broadly successful state promotion of women's further education and professional qualification – meant that over the course of the state's existence women's lives in East Germany became distinctively different from the lives of women in Western European countries. By contrast, as historian Mary Fulbrook has commented, 'Official conceptions of masculinity changed very little during the forty years of the GDR. [...] If East Germany was a more "working class" society in its official imagery and rhetoric than West Germany, then it was also in many respects more "male" in a very traditional construction of masculinity.'[1] The interest in the topic of gender would seem, then, to lie with the study of women, and it is notable that Fulbrook's chapter on 'Gender' in her study *The People's State* (2005) is almost exclusively concerned with this aspect of East German gender politics. The present chapter proceeds from a different premise. In the first place, gender as a social construction, regulating as it does the interaction between men and women in the interests of the social whole, is always necessarily relational, and to take masculinity as read – as Fulbrook does – is to miss important information about how a society conceives of itself. Taking a closer look at the patterns of representation of masculinity in GDR literature will reveal a more complex picture than Fulbrook's assumption about traditional 'working class' masculinity would lead us to expect. In addition, it is widely accepted among social historians that women's emancipation was restricted in the GDR because of the authoritarian and paternalistic nature of the state, in which women's social progress was always defined and determined from above, in the higher echelons of the state bureaucracy where women were notably under-represented.[2] This does not altogether square with the literary historians' viewpoint, which sees the contribution made by women writers in speaking to their women readers' self-awareness and challenging the state's paternalistic notions as a major aspect of GDR literature in the 1970s and 1980s.[3] Considering gender in terms of the literary representation of both men and women and their relations to each other will bring a more multifaceted picture into view than the one familiar from the social historians' narratives, while at the same time raising questions of class difference and generational shifts to complement those of the symbolic function of gender in GDR texts selected from four decades.

The 1950s: a hierarchy of masculinities and the dual image of women

As an instrument of agitation and propaganda, explicitly understood in accordance with Leninist principles as a medium for communicating the objectives of the ruling party, the socialist-realist literature of the founding years of the GDR displays the gender politics underlying the young socialist state. Central to the rebuilding of the post-war economy, as well as to the ideology of socialist collectivism, was the physical strength, the professional expertise and the complementary skills of the working-class *Brigade*, the smallest unit in the competitively organized shift work of the state-owned East German factory or plant.[4] The brigade lent itself to literary representation, in that it provided a limited cast of characters who could be used to depict a range of differing attitudes typical of the society at large and the antagonisms between them. The common focal protagonist in early factory-based plots is the working-class *Aktivist*, a worker of particular ambition and energy who galvanizes his more reluctant colleagues in the brigade, raising production norms for the collective social benefit in opposition to the individual worker's personal interest in defending his own wage-packet by maintaining existing norms. Typically, the fictional *Aktivist* is a physically strong man with a particular professional skill (such as bricklaying, metal-work and so on), but otherwise little education. He represents a raw force and practical vision for how the job at hand can best be done, which, however, also needs the guidance of committed direction, especially that of the Socialist Unity Party (SED), whose 'leading role' in society was asserted in the GDR constitution. Thus the *Aktivist* and his brigade are not represented in isolation, but in relationship to the factory and Party management, men of superior training and overview.

These masculine models can be seen in Eduard Claudius's exemplary work of early socialist realism, *Menschen an unsrer Seite* (People at Our Side, 1951). The central *Aktivist* figure is Hans Aehre, based on a historical bricklayer named Hans Garbe, who gained the socialist accolade of 'hero of labour' (*Held der Arbeit*) for his feat in repairing a ring furnace while it was still firing at the Siemens-Plania works (later the state-owned electro-carbon works at Lichtenberg) in 1949–50. Claudius, himself a former brick-layer, had published a work of reportage about Garbe in 1950.[5] Claudius's fictional Aehre is a forceful person who must persuade his brigade of doubt-ers that they are capable of working collectively on the furnace without shutting it down, which would cost the factory six months' lost production. At points, Aehre is portrayed as the symbolic representative of all socialist workers whom the novel encourages to think of themselves as the 'ruling class' in the state, no longer subordinate to the capital-owning class or to factory managers:

> Yes, we are workers, Comrade Backhans. We are workers. Even if an engineer or a foreman or the contractor is present – it's we who build the furnace, we! And if there is no foreman who wants to help us or no engineer, well then, we'll build it anyway . . . of course we will . . . it must be possible for us to do it by ourselves.[6]

Elsewhere, however, Aehre is shown to require the restraining guidance of the Party. The Party instructor Schadow sees him as 'a wild colt, which doesn't care to wear a bridle and yet which, if it's going to draw the cart, will definitely need to be kept in rein'.[7] Schadow is one of a number of characters in positions of authority in the plant whose decision-making creates the context for Aehre's heroic act. Another is the factory director Carlin, a former mechanic who has risen to his position without substantial training but who nonetheless possesses the necessary personal qualities to guide the factory through turbulent times, a 'hard hand, when it's needed', 'an unerring eye for people and things', and whose leadership 'is purposeful and not to be deflected', as the haut-bourgeois director of research Doktor von Wassermann (himself a throwback to an earlier model of bourgeois masculinity) notes appreciatively.[8] While the narrative is focused on the *Aktivist* plot, in a manner intended to invite the identification of the ordinary working-class reader, in fact the novel presents a hierarchy of masculinities, with the higher echelons portrayed in terms reminiscent of the positively connoted characteristics of nineteenth-century bourgeois entrepreneurialism, now transferred to the SED leaders: rationality, good judgement, the capacity for hard work, goal-orientation and effective governance.

The representation of the women in the novel, meanwhile, is notable for its dual aspect. Katrin Aehre, Hans's wife, is, on the one hand, the source of sexual reward for masculine purposiveness and, on the other hand, is the firer of Aehre's sexual desire, the strikingly infernal source of the energy that drives him, at least in his imagination: 'The heat rose up in him, and hunger for her. He thought: the work, is it me that does it? No, not me! Her! A real devil, she sits on my back and drives me onward.'[9] The combination of fiery heat and sexualized, devilish energy inspired by the woman in the man makes of the *Aktivist* a kind of reconceived genius figure.[10] But the rather conventional female role presupposes that the wife remains confined to the domestic sphere, leaving the field of public action to her husband. In the course of the novel, Aehre is compelled to take leave of his inherent conservatism with regard to his wife and watch her move into his sphere of industrial production, enabled by the state childcare system which provides their child with a kindergarten place. In the face of his resistance, Katrin lays claim to her desire to be 'a whole human being', grasping the opportunities provided by the state to 'learn something, too, and do something which I can see and which is durable' rather than being defined solely as a woman and a wife.[11] Suse Rieck, meanwhile, the sole female character in the brigade of men, is presented, 'blackened by the coal and streaming with sweat', as a modern socialist working-class woman, at home in the industrial environment, while simultaneously fulfilling a more conventional role as the corporeally present Muse to the artist figure Andrytzki.[12]

The symbolic system of gender in *Menschen an unsrer Seite* is, then, a complex one. Working-class male physicality, the strength needed to build the state, is aligned with the female as the conventional source of inspiration and male sexual energy – symbolic terms familiar from the bourgeois literature of modernity.[13] As in the literature of the bourgeois era, raw physicality needs the guidance of conventionally masculine-connoted intelligence and purposiveness, characteristics now associated with the higher echelons of the socialist hierarchy: the Party leadership is constructed as quasi-bourgeois. The female figures, meanwhile, are moving into a double role, both sexualized body, affirming the male's connection to the physical world and acting as the source of his inspiration and sexual reward, and the ambivalently genderless or masculine-connoted 'Mensch' (human being), seeking fulfilment through work on the same terms as men, as encouraged and endorsed by the East German state. The same structural pattern can be seen in other literary works of the 1950s. In Elfriede Brüning's *Regine Haberkorn* (1955), for example,

Erwin Haberkorn provides a similar model of ambitious male working-class energy, needing the guidance of the works director Hintze, the union leader and foreman Mielke and the Party secretary Sasse in order for that energy to be targeted in such a way as to make it more than just a means to personal gratification. The latter is by implication the working-class man's main motivation if left unguided by the Party. Like Aehre, Erwin is conservative in his attitudes towards his wife, the eponymous Regine, and needs to be educated in the course of the novel to appreciate that she, too, wishes to realize her talents within the socialist collective, not remain constrained as a wife and mother at home – moreover, the state is in need of women's participation to boost the labour force. Part of the aim in this female-authored novel is to negotiate male sexual expectations of women in this new era, where men and women are also potentially equal working part-ners. The moral high ground is taken by Regine as burgeoning *Aktivistin* and brigade leader, at times too busy to fulfil Erwin's sexual needs, not the manipulative seductress Käthe Behnert, who lures Erwin away by soothing his masculine ego, but loses out in the end.

The majority of the works of the 1950s are transparently moralizing in this way and idealizing in their representation of the positive development of workers and the superior visionary wisdom of the Party leadership. The early works by the dramatist Heiner Müller, who would become the GDR's most important successor to Brecht, present a refreshing exception in their more rigorous realism and challenging open-endedness, although the stock char-acters remain recognizably similar. In *Der Lohndrücker* (The Scab, 1957), another version of the Hans Garbe story, the *Aktivist*, here called Balke, is less sentimentally presented. A clear-sighted man who understands that his 'heroic' action is for the greater good within the present economic system, he is also shown to have accepted Nazi rule when he worked in a munitions factory during the war, denouncing a communist saboteur back then who turns up in his present factory as the new Party secretary. This raises issues of recent national history, political commitment and personal trust more overtly than Claudius's novel does. The focus of the play is also more on the contest between the different brigade members and their attitudes to their work, offering a palette of masculinities jostling (sometimes violently) for pre-eminence, while the factory director and Party leadership are depicted as more compromised by the struggle to build up the works in less-than-ideal historical conditions.

The aspect of the advancement of women is quite absent in Müller's treatment of the Garbe material. It does feature, however, in one of his best (and most controversial) works of his early period: *Die Umsiedlerin oder*

Figure 4 Helga Paris. From: 'Müllfahrer' [Dustmen] (1974). © Helga Paris
VG Bildkunst.

Das Leben auf dem Lande (The Resettler Woman, or Country Life, 1956/
1961, 1964). The eponymous resettler Niet, for most of the play an unas-
suming character shown fetching beer for her wastrel lover, Fondrak,
decides at the end not to follow the latter in his flight to the west, nor to
accept the advances of another of the villagers, but to take the offer of a farm
from Flint, the communist mayor, and work it independently.[14] It is a subtle
sign of the changing times, as is the political criticism of Flint for neglecting
his wife for a younger woman, since the Party must be seen to be above
reproach.[15] But these are passing moments in an otherwise largely male-
dominated play, where the women are mostly seen as sexualized objects of
desire for their menfolk. The Party secretary (*Sekretär*) and the district
administrator (*Landrat*) are portraits of efficient, clear-sighted leaders in
the standard socialist-realist mould, and Flint is depicted positively, despite
his womanizing. Nonetheless, Müller delivers a markedly realistic assessment
of the competing interests within the rural community which make the
building of communism such a tough objective. The play was strongly
criticized for its 'counter-revolutionary, anti-communist, anti-humanistic'
tendencies,[16] as a result of which Müller suffered an effective work ban which
lasted until the 1970s. In terms of his generally less-than-idealizing account of
the Party leadership and eye for the insubordinate working-class man who is
not easily persuaded by state propaganda, Müller anticipated the more
interesting developments in socialist realism in the 1960s.

The 1960s and 1970s: triangles

By the late 1950s, criticism of mechanistic plot construction in the socialist-
realist novel was being voiced by even the strongest adherents of SED
cultural policy, and by the early 1960s, the kind of crude idealization of the
Party leadership and of working-class activism that had characterized the
literature of the founding years was receding. Paradoxically, the period
following the building of the Berlin Wall in August 1961 was one of
increasing openness to criticism in the GDR's socialist literature. In part,
this was because the Wall screened the state off, making politicians and
committed writers alike feel less exposed to the judgements of the west and
able to concentrate on the problems at hand in the consolidation of the
socialist system. But it was also because a generation of younger writers
began to move onto the scene, coming up through the Bitterfelder Weg,
the cultural-political initiative started in 1959 to bring the intelligentsia into
the workplace to gain first-hand experience of life in production. For
writers such as Christa Wolf and Brigitte Reimann, seen as up-and-coming

youngsters, it was an eye-opening encounter with the struggle to build the economy in the face of persistent supply shortages, cash-flow problems, a sometimes overly dogmatic Party leadership and a workforce often resistant to the ideological frameworks imposed by the regime.

Striking in the literature of the 'era of arrival', as the early 1960s came to be called after Brigitte Reimann's 1961 novel *Ankunft im Alltag* (Arrival in the Everyday), is the plot device of situating a young woman between two significant alternatives in her choice of love relationship. Recha, the Jewish orphan in *Ankunft im Alltag*, must choose between the Party official's son, Curt, and the artist, Nikolaus, as they all work out their practical year in a power plant before going on to study. Curt is revealed to be a self-interested opportunist, whereas Nikolaus, ostensibly less politically engaged, shows commitment to the workers' collective at the risk of his own personal goals. Predictably, it is Nikolaus who gets the girl as the symbolic sexual reward for his right social instincts. In Wolf's *Der geteilte Himmel* (Divided Heaven, 1963), Rita Seidel relives in memory her love affair with Manfred, a talented chemist who, after a new lease of life brought on by Rita's optimistic belief in him, slips back into cynicism when his innovative work does not receive due recognition from the Party authorities and eventually flees to the west just before the building of the Berlin Wall separates the lovers forever. At the end of the novel, it is hinted that Rita will find a more apposite partner in the Party functionary Wendland, a man honestly committed to the socialist collective as she is.[17] There are further variants on this triangular plot structure in the literature of the 1970s. Ulrich Plenzdorf's *Die neuen Leiden des jungen W.* (The New Sufferings of Young W., 1974), following the model of Goethe's *Die Leiden des jungen Werthers* (The Sorrows of Young Werther, 1774), is narrated from the perspective of the tearaway youth Edgar, but at issue is the contest for the affections of the female character, Charlotte (Charlie), fought out between him and her unimaginative, conformist fiancé, Dieter. Karin, the central character in Volker Braun's *Unvollendete Geschichte* (Incomplete Story, 1975), is torn between her boyfriend, Frank, a socially marginalized character who is viewed with suspicion by the authorities but who really loves Karin, and her father, the Party functionary with tunnel-vision who demands of his daughter that she reject Frank, with disastrous consequences: implied is a strong critique of the state's paternalistic standards. As becomes evident from this list, at issue in these triangular plots is the moral opposition of opportunism, self-interest or political conformity versus the genuine energy, imagination and commitment needed for social transformation. The female characters validate the male characters when they behave with integrity, maintaining the conventional symbolic role of the woman as sexual reward. However, the moral validation shifts towards the more marginalized male figures as literature consolidates its critical role in the course of the 1970s vis-à-vis the stultifying effects on society at large of a too rigidly dogmatic political system. Interestingly, in Christa Wolf's major novel of 1968, *Nachdenken über Christa T.* (The Quest for Christa T.), it is the marginalized *female* figure who is validated in her own right, without reference to a male figure as the rewarded lover.

Two novels show particularly illuminating parallels in their organization of the triangular relationship, both of them landmarks in the history of GDR literature: Erik Neutsch's *Spur der Steine* (Trace of Stones, 1964) and Brigitte Reimann's *Franziska Linkerhand* (1974). Both feature the same tension between the transformative physical energy of the working-class man versus the judgement and leadership of the quasi-bourgeois Party man as was evident in the literature of the 1950s, but now with the socialist-trained professional woman caught between them. In their different solutions to this triangular contest, they display the changing politics of literature from the early 1960s to the mid-1970s, as well as the different gender perspectives of the male and female authors.

In *Spur der Steine* the conflict is between the dynamic but wayward brigade leader Hannes Balla (played in Frank Beyer's 1966 film of the novel by the charismatic actor Manfred Krug[18]) and the Party secretary Werner Horrath, sent to instil discipline, who, in falling as an already married man for the female engineer Katrin Klee, impregnating her and not having the courage to stand by her, emerges as duplicitous and compromises his authority. In *Franziska Linkerhand* the triangle is formed by the dumper truck driver Wolfgang ('Ben') Trojanowicz, the quasi-bourgeois architect Horst Schafheutlin (secretly and unrequitedly in love with Franziska) and the vibrant, temperamental and sexually attractive Franziska, a trained architect who is also the locus of the novel's utopian energy. Both works play on major building sites which stand for the construction of the socialist state:[19] in *Spur der Steine* it is a fictional chemical plant essential for the industrial future of the GDR so that it is of the essence that the teams of builders and engineers identify the most time- and cost-efficient building methods; in *Franziska Linkerhand* the symbolically named Neustadt (literally, 'new town'), where industrially prefabricated units are used to build apartment blocks to house the workers from the local power plant (based on the Schwarze Pumpe at Hoyerswerda, where Reimann was writer-in-residence). Neutsch's novel endorses scientific method as the key to the future of the socialist state; Reimann's criticizes the development of a socialist architecture from which human individual creativity has been eradicated, with its consequence of soulless urban living.

In *Spur der Steine*, the physically dominant Balla, a 'mixture between robber captain and cowboy',[20] is drawn to the female figure; but she, educated and qualified and so transformed from the locus of sexual energy alone, chooses the physically weaker quasi-bourgeois male figure, the symbolic representative of attained culture. Indeed, she recoils from the 'raw force'[21] of Balla, before whose gaze she feels stripped naked at their first encounter.[22] Nonetheless, her feminine influence is instrumental in gradually taming Balla, imposing the discipline on him to settle for her friendship alone as a preparatory step for his eventual acceptance of the discipline of Party membership, towards which he is patiently led by Horrath. The quasi-bourgeois man, meanwhile, the bringer of discipline and purposiveness to others, fails with regard to himself. Placing his own (physical) desires above the claims of the Party, Horrath stands in the end as a morally discredited figure. Neutsch's novel and especially Beyer's film implicitly posit the continuing need for Balla's virile force to build up the state, and, interestingly, what draws Kati Klee to Horrath is his energy and determination and his dedication to achieved action, even if it involves bending the rules, characteristics he shares with Balla. Kati is represented as loving 'real life' which 'cannot be squeezed to fit a formula',[23] and it is this which motivates the symbolic validation through her of both of the less-than-conformist men who desire her. But she is also the locus of clear moral judgement. She loves truth[24] and is incapable of duplicity,[25] so that her love for Horrath fades as he proves unable to declare his love for her publicly when it matters. So, too, though, does her belief in the Party's authority when its rulings become driven by dogma rather than by acknowledgement of achievement. The ending of the novel shows both Horrath and Kati Klee deprived of their agency through their treatment at the hands of the Party bureaucracy, an implied criticism of SED dogmatism, which is characteristic of much of the better GDR literature of the 1960s and beyond.

Reimann's novel organizes the vectors of energy differently. Here, the simultaneously sexualized and intellectually trained and qualified woman chooses not the quasi-bourgeois Party man, but the virile working-class man. This is emphatically not a formulaic choice. Reimann's novel is differentiated in its depiction of the working-class characters, including strikingly negative portraits of Franziska's estranged husband and his family, the grotesquely reactionary Exß clan, with their 'mistrust of those above them, their little-man-on-the-street ideology, their scams with their wage-packets'.[26] The gang of rowdy, bellicose characters who populate the pub in Neustadt also stand apart from the usual idealizing representation of the working class in GDR literature. Among the great virtues of Reimann's novel, alongside its vibrant style, are its author's eye for what life was really like in the GDR's dismal, often socially dysfunctional provinces and her talent for authentic characterization. Franziska's lover, Ben, is partially based on a real-life lover of Reimann's, and the love represented between the two figures is personal and psychologically believable, albeit symbolically also an expression of Franziska's predilection for the 'whiff of adventure and proud, wild independence'[27] which is validated above Schafheutlin's subservience to order. Ben proves elusive, not faithful – not tameable – in contrast to Balla, who is so disappointingly tamed in Neutsch's novel. But neither is Franziska's vital and utopian force tamed by a relationship with a man who is not daring or imaginative. Rather, she opens up a new dimension in the overly organized and conformist mindset of Schafheutlin, initially focused, as his name suggests, on the realistically possible achievements of today rather than the greater vision of the socialist future, which propels Franziska's work: 'It must, it must exist, the intelligent synthesis of today and tomorrow, of dismal prefabricated blocks and cheerfully dynamic streetscene, between the necessary and the beautiful, and I'm on the hunt for it, arrogant as I am and, oh, how often fainthearted, and one day I'm going to find it.'[28]

The 1970s and 1980s: women in the vanguard

Reimann began writing *Franziska Linkerhand* around the time of the publication of *Spur der Steine*, when as yet little of the radical writing by women which would come to be associated with the GDR had been thought of. By the time the novel appeared posthumously in 1974, the same year as Irmtraud Morgner's *Leben und Abenteuer der Trobadora Beatriz nach Zeugnissen ihrer Spielfrau Laura* (The Life and Adventures of Trobadora Beatrice as Chronicled by Her Minstrel Laura) and two years after the reissue of Christa Wolf's *Nachdenken über Christa T.*, which had been withdrawn from circulation under political pressure shortly following publication, it entered a context in which women writers were making their mark as the bearers of challenging and utopian thinking, embracing what Julia Hell calls the 'feminine imperative of change'.[29]

Wolf and Morgner were among the GDR's foremost literary innovators who, as committed progressive socialists, were intent on using their works to contribute critically to the development of GDR socialism, while simultaneously drawing consciously on their status as women. Early works such as Morgner's *Hochzeit in Konstantinopel* (Wedding in Constantinople, 1968) and Wolf's short stories published in the early 1970s, especially 'Selbstversuch' (Self-Experiment) and 'Neue Lebensansichten eines Katers' (New Life Attitudes of a Tom Cat) launched a defence of the imagination vis-à-vis a GDR regime enthralled in the late 1960s by scientific planning and cybernetics as the route to social progress,[30] and this in turn maps onto the texts' gender symbolism. The quasi-bourgeois male characters, dedicated to scientific investigation, appear emotionally stunted and motivated only by their own career advancement, whereas the female characters are visionary and hold the key to the rethinking of social relations.[31] This function of female characters set a trend. By the mid-1970s, Wolf's Christa T., Reimann's Franziska Linkerhand, and Morgner's Trobadora Beatriz were all exemplifying women's desire for both self-fulfilment and a different, more productive way of conceiving of social community. As Dorothee Schmitz-Köster comments, 'In the early 1970s, women evidently see it as their role to initiate movement, to break through conformism, to articulate genuinely socialist aspirations – for the development of the personality, for self-fulfilment, for happiness – and to battle for their realization.'[32]

Both Wolf and Morgner emphasized what had been achieved in the GDR in terms of creating the conditions for women's emancipation, and in this sense affirmed state policy. But they also used their women characters to communicate criticism of inherited modes of social behaviour, including gender norms. Morgner's compendious *Trobadora* novel fuses realist elements with a highly inventive (and very funny) confabulation of Romantic, mythical and magic motifs in a tale of a strong-willed medieval troubadour who, awaking from an 800-year sleep, comes to live with a female tram-driver and her son in East Berlin, introducing into the household a host of imperious female figures from classical myth. The novel marked a breakthrough to a more overt literary representation of erotic relations between men and women than had been considered admissible before, and even included hints at lesbian desire, a major taboo in the prudishly heterosexist GDR.[33] Together with its 1983 sequel, *Amanda. Ein Hexenroman* (Amanda. A Witch-Novel), it was intended by Morgner to engender 'self-confidence, courage, even "megalomania"' in her female readers,[34] challenging the persistence of complacent patriarchal thinking. Wolf's work of the late 1970s and early 1980s on the women Romantics – essays on the poet Karoline von Günderrode (1780–1806) and the novelist and political activist Bettina von Arnim (1785–1859), written to accompany re-editions of their work[35] – and her imaginative account of a fictive meeting between Günderrode and her contemporary Heinrich von Kleist

Figure 5 Helga Paris. From: 'Frauen im Bekleidungswerk Treffmodelle' [Women at the Treff-Modelle Clothing Factory, Berlin] (1984). © Helga Paris VG Bildkunst.

at a party in 1804, *Kein Ort. Nirgends* (No Place on Earth, 1979), were, on the one hand, part of a trend within the East German literature of the 1970s to look to the Romantic tradition as a medium of veiled criticism of the political present. On the other hand, they also reflected upon the historical conditions of forms of post-Enlightenment subjectivity and gender identity, highlighting personal and emotional restriction as the price men paid for their public standing, validating female friendship and its utopian potential and showing the disenfranchised women as paradoxically more intellectually free.[36] Wolf's work on Günderrode also had the effect of restoring this largely forgotten writer to the nineteenth-century German literary canon.

Wolf continued her efforts to counteract what she perceived as the alienation of human individuals under patriarchy with her work of the early 1980s on the ancient Greek legend of the siege of Troy, as told in the Homeric epic, *The Iliad*. Her 1983 novel *Kassandra* (Cassandra), a fictional monologue of considerable lyrical force, retells Homer's story from the perspective of the female seer who was fated to foresee the fall of Troy but not to be believed. In the accompanying four lectures, Wolf addressed the history of women's exclusion from political agency and raised issues of feminist aesthetics, but also contextualized the fictional project within the Cold War stand-off of the 1980s. *Kassandra* was at its heart an anti-war work, tracing the international bellicosity of the Cold War back to the aggrandizement of aggressive and self-alienated masculinity in Western culture's foundational literature and positing the disastrous consequences of women's historical removal from positions of social power.

The 1970s saw the rise of the New Women's Movement in the West, and Western feminism provided a very productive frame for the reading of these GDR works, assuring their authors an international reputation, at least within the discipline of German Studies.[37] This synergy between the GDR women writers and Western feminism remained somewhat ambivalent, however. There was no organized feminism in East Germany as there was in West Germany – the GDR authorities would not permit special interest groupings to form which might challenge their monopoly of political debate – and East German writers were generally keen to distinguish their stance from that of Western feminists. In the author's preface to her hugely influential 1977 volume of interviews with GDR women, *Guten Morgen, du Schöne* (Good Morning, You Beauty), which was widely read in both East and West Germany, Maxie Wander locates the utopian impulses of her book in the GDR context of achieved gender equality and stresses the benefits for the whole of society, men and women alike, of the rethinking of customary gender roles: 'We cannot emancipate ourselves in opposition to men, but only in discussion with them, for what we are looking for is liberation from the established gender roles, for human emancipation more generally.'[38] This must, at least in part, be read as a jibe at Western feminist separatism, and it is highly characteristic of the GDR's specific brand of feminism, with its emphasis on the social collective, not on the gains to be made for women alone. Nonetheless, there is evidence of the reception of Western feminist writing by women writers and thinkers in the GDR,[39] especially visible in the case of Wolf's *Kassandra* project,[40] and the status of the GDR women writers at home was surely helped by the fact that their works achieved such good sales abroad where they *were* read in a feminist context.

Following in the wake of Reimann, Wolf and Morgner came a number of younger women writers who entered the literary scene in the course of the 1970s and early 1980s and whose work differed from their predecessors' in terms of a greater focus on personal, less parabolic narratives.[41] Helga Königsdorf, Helga Schubert, Rosemarie Zeplin, Christine Wolter, Charlotte Worgitzsky, to name but a few, all published well-received volumes of prose fiction which dealt with aspects of women's day-to-day experiences – in their domestic and sexual relationships, as working mothers juggling childcare and housework with their professional commitments, dealing with abortion or with illness. These fictions can be seen as negotiating expectations of women in the social sphere and vis-à-vis policy-makers.[42] In that the female figures have a less socially or culturally symbolic role in these fictions, they mark, too, a kind of normalization of women's experiences as the material of literature. In a sense, this had already been achieved much earlier by the notable women poets of the GDR. Sarah Kirsch's poetry of the late 1960s and early 1970s appeared so radical at the time precisely because it eschewed any political posturing, instead articulating private concerns, including emotional conflict within the male–female couple, sketched against acutely observed scenes of rural domesticity. Elke Erb's work, too, attained a high degree of autonomy from the pressure to be political in the GDR context, instead making precise observations of the interactions of subjects and their lived environments, captured in distinctive verse forms.

The 1980s: a diverse landscape

Up until the 1980s, the representation of gender and gender's symbolic import in GDR literature can be understood in relation to the politics of the state, as endorsing, criticizing or inciting debate on it, even though the prominence of the GDR's major women writers is attributable in part to their reception in the context of Western feminism. The picture in the GDR's last decade is more diffuse, a symptom of the growing diversity of GDR literature itself as the state's notion of what constituted 'socialist' literature came to seem increasingly outmoded. No prominent trend in gender representation and gender symbolism characterizes the 1980s, though a number of developments are worthy of note.

The 1980s saw the rise of environmental depredation as a major concern in the GDR, something that was made the more acute by the spectre of nuclear fallout after the Chernobyl nuclear reactor disaster in April 1986. Several GDR writers were also active in the peace movement, as the stationing of a new generation of nuclear missiles on German soil brought Cold War tensions to a head. These political issues form the backdrop to works such as Monika Maron's *Flugasche* (Flight of Ashes, FRG 1981), Wolf's *Kassandra*, discussed above, and *Störfall* (*Accident*, 1987), which responded directly to the Chernobyl incident, and Helga Königsdorf's *Respektloser Umgang* (Disrespectful Conduct, 1986), which tells of a hallucinatory encounter between a narrator-figure and Lise Meitner, the woman member of the team of physicists which discovered nuclear fission in 1938. All build on the female figure's propensity to generate a moral 'critique of civilization' (*Zivilisationskritik*), since she occupies a position somehow disassociated from a supposedly male-created social order or from male-generated science and as such could reach out to readers beyond the GDR. But while these works continued, in a feminist vein, to suggest the transformative potential of the feminine, Christoph Hein's novella *Der fremde Freund* (*The Distant Lover*, 1982) brilliantly used a female protagonist to tell a story about self-alienation in modern society, an important corrective to the role of the fictional female as the mediator of alternative ways of being.

Volker Braun made a mark with his more locally relevant *Hinze-Kunze-Roman* (Every Tom, Dick and Harry Novel, 1985), a cleverly critical representation of the symbiotic relationship between a manipulative Party functionary Hinze and his exploited chauffeur Kunze, a final, negative stocktaking on the relationship between the working-class man and the GDR quasi-bourgeois and the regime's failure to overcome class hierarchy.

The success of Maxie Wander's *Guten Morgen, du Schöne* spawned further ventures in the genre of 'protocol literature'.[43] Two volumes of interviews with men, both edited by women, were published in the course of the 1980s, Christine Müller's *Männerprotokolle* (Men: Protocols, 1985) and Christine Lambrecht's *Männerbekanntschaften: freimütige Protokolle* (Male Acquaintances: Candid Protocols, 1986), neither of which had anything like the resonance of Wander's book. Yet they did begin to address the self-understanding of men in the GDR, which had hitherto not really been closely examined (and which remains a notable gap in the scholarship on the GDR and on GDR literature).

Uwe Saeger's *Nöhr* (1980) is a novel about a male identity crisis and it also cautiously addresses male homosocial bonding, if not explicitly homosexuality. The latter was still a taboo topic. However, the formation of interest groups under the umbrella of the Protestant Church in the 1980s enabled gays to make some headway at last against the state authorities' negative attitude to homosexuality.[44] The first GDR film about gay experience, Heiner Carow's *Coming Out* (1989), ironically received its première on the night the Berlin Wall was opened. Gay literature remained marginalized until the end of the GDR.[45]

Finally, the writers who emerged after unification from the so-called 'unofficial scene' of the 1980s deserve mention. While gender was not a prominent theme in general in the work of the GDR's youngest generation, nonetheless a number of women writers made their debuts in this context for whom gender and gender relations were a significant issue. Gabriele Stötzer-Kachold wrote radically feminist, overtly erotic poetry, deploying experimental linguistic techniques and bringing the female body to the fore in a manner not hitherto seen in GDR literature.[46] Barbara Köhler, already in the 1980s thinking about what it means to write as a woman in a tradition shaped by men,[47] in her work after 1990 went on to explore the way in which the conventions of grammar fix gender and, notably in the essays in *Wittgensteins Nichte* (Wittgenstein's Niece/Noughts, 1999) and her poems responding to Homer's *Odyssey* in *Niemands Frau* (Nobody's Wife, 2007), sought to raise to conscious awareness the conventions according to which subjectivity is thought of in oppositionally gendered terms in a manner which owes something at least to the GDR's specific tradition of feminist-inflected *Zivilisationskritik*.

Notes

1. Mary Fulbrook, *The People's State. East German Society from Hitler to Honecker*, paperback edn (New Haven and London: Yale University Press, 2008), p. 141.
2. See Fulbrook, *The People's State*, Chapter 7; Michael Schwartz, 'Emanzipation zur sozialen Nützlichkeit: Bedingungen und Grenzen von Frauenpolitik in der

DDR', in Dierck Hoffmann and Michael Schwartz (eds.), *Sozialstaatlichkeit in der DDR. Sozialpolitische Entwicklungen im Spannungsfeld von Diktatur und Gesellschaft 1945/49–1989*, Schriftenreihe der Vierteljahrshefte für Zeitgeschichte (Munich: Oldenbourg, 2005), pp. 47–87; Susanne Kranz, 'Women's Role in the German Democratic Republic and the State's Policy towards Women', *Journal of International Women's Studies*, 7.1 (November 2005), 69–83.

3. See Dorothee Schmitz-Köster, *Trobadora und Kassandra. Weibliches Schreiben in der DDR* (Cologne: Pahl-Rugenstein, 1989); Lorna Martens, *The Promised Land? Feminist Writing in the German Democratic Republic* (Albany: State University of New York Press, 2001).
4. Julia Hell's *Post-Fascist Fantasies. Psychoanalysis, History, and the Literature of East Germany* (Durham and London: Duke University Press, 1997) looks at early family narratives from the GDR rather than novels of industrial production, which produces a different gender narrative from the one presented here, focused on the antifascist father (Chapter 1).
5. Eduard Claudius, *Vom schweren Anfang* (The Difficult Beginning, 1950).
6. Eduard Claudius, *Menschen an unsrer Seite* (Berlin: Volk und Welt, 1951), pp. 171–72.
7. Ibid., p. 96.
8. Ibid., p. 35.
9. Ibid., pp. 53–54.
10. See Christine Battersby, *Gender and Genius. Towards a Feminist Aesthetics* (London: The Women's Press, 1989).
11. Claudius, *Menschen an unsrer Seite,* pp. 274–75.
12. Ibid., p. 62.
13. See Georgina Paul, *Perspectives on Gender in Post-1945 German Literature* (Rochester, NY: Camden House, 2009), Chapter 1.
14. Heiner Müller, *Die Umsiedlerin oder Das Leben auf dem Lande*, in Müller, *Die Stücke I*, ed. Frank Hörnigk (Frankfurt/M.: Suhrkamp, 2000), p. 281.
15. Ibid., pp. 234–35. On socialist morality, see Josie McLellan, *Love in the Time of Communism. Intimacy and Sexuality in the GDR* (Cambridge University Press, 2011).
16. See editorial commentary in ibid., p. 545.
17. Julia Hell persuasively reads Wendland as an 'ego ideal' and brother figure to Rita, rather than a future lover: *Post-Fascist Fantasies*, pp. 177–85.
18. The film was banned a few days after its premiere. See Joshua Feinstein, 'Constructing the Mythic Present in the East German Cinema: Frank Beyer's "Spur der Steine" and the 11th Plenum of 1965', *Central European History*, 32.2 (1999), 203–20.
19. See Detlev Schöttker, 'Die Wirklichkeit unserer Städte: Wiederaufbau, Kulturkritik und Literatur', *Merkur*, 62.4 (April 2008), 318–27.
20. Erik Neutsch, *Spur der Steine* (Halle/S.: Mitteldeutscher Verlag, 1964), p. 223.
21. Ibid., p. 97.

22. Ibid., p. 76.
23. Ibid., p. 84.
24. Ibid., p. 852.
25. Ibid., p. 84.
26. Brigitte Reimann, *Franziska Linkerhand* (Berlin: Neues Leben, 1974), p. 111.
27. Ibid., p. 161.
28. Ibid., p. 582.
29. Hell, *Post-Fascist Fantasies*, p. 67.
30. See Brigitte Rossbacher, *Illusions of Progress. Christa Wolf and the Critique of Science in GDR Women's Literature* (New York: Lang, 2000).
31. See Martens, *The Promised Land?*, p. 31.
32. Schmitz-Köster, *Trobadora und Kassandra*, p. 51.
33. See Beth V. Linklater, *Und immer zügelloser wird die Lust: Constructions of Sexuality in East German Literatures, with Special Reference to Irmtraud Morgner and Gabriele Stötzer-Kachold* (Bern: Lang, 1998); Georgina Paul, '"Über Verschwiegenes sprechen": Female Homosexuality and the Public Sphere in the GDR before and after the *Wende*', in Elizabeth Boa and Janet Wharton (eds.), *Women and the Wende. Social Effects and Cultural Reflections of the German Unification Process*, German Monitor 31 (Amsterdam, Atlanta, GA: Rodopi, 1994), pp. 226–37.
34. Martens, *The Promised Land?*, p. 58.
35. Christa Wolf, 'Der Schatten eines Traumes. Karoline von Günderrode: Ein Entwurf', in Sonja Hilzinger (ed.), *Werke*, vol. 6 (Munich: Luchterhand, 2000), pp. 107–75 and 'Nun ja! Das nächste Leben geht aber heute an. Ein Brief über die Bettine', in ibid., pp. 177–221.
36. Wolf, 'Der Schatten eines Traumes', pp. 141–44.
37. See Angelika Bammer, 'The American Feminist Reception of GDR Literature (with a Glance at West Germany)', *GDR Bulletin* 16 (Fall 1996), 18–24.
38. Maxie Wander, *Guten Morgen, du Schöne. Protokolle nach Tonband* (Munich: Deutscher Taschenbuchverlag, 2003), p. 9.
39. See Martens, *The Promised Land?*, pp. 10–12, 18–22; also the sociologist Hildegard Maria Nickel's account of the study of Western feminist literature in the interdisciplinary research group at the East German Academy of Sciences under the aegis of Irene Dölling in Gerda Szepansky, *Die stille Emanzipation. Frauen in der DDR* (Frankfurt/M.: Fischer, 1995), pp. 106–7.
40. See Wolf, 'Frankfurter Poetik-Vorlesungen', in Wolf, *Werke*, vol. 7, p. 161.
41. See Cheryl Dueck, *Rifts in Time and the Self. The Female Subject in Two Generations of East German Women Writers* (Amsterdam, New York, NY: Rodopi, 2004); Julia Petzl, *Realism and Reality in Helga Schubert, Helga Königsdorf and Monika Maron* (Frankfurt/M.: Lang, 2003).
42. See Martens, *The Promised Land?*, Chapter 5.
43. See Reinhard Andress, *Protokolliteratur in der DDR. Der dokumentierte Alltag* (New York: Lang, 2000).
44. See McLellan, *Love in the Time of Communism*, Chapter 5.

45. See Denis M. Sweet, 'A Literature of "Truth": Writing by Gay Men in East Germany', *Studies in Twentieth Century Literature*, 22.1 (Winter 1998), 205–25; Denis M. Sweet, 'Renegade Lit: Gay Writing at the End of Socialist East Germany', in Christoph Lorey and John L. Plews (eds.), *Queering the Canon: Defying Sights in German Literature and Culture* (Columbia, SC: Camden House, 1998), pp. 293–308.
46. See Linklater, *Und immer zügelloser wird die Lust*, Chapters 4 and 5.
47. See Birgit Dahlke, '"... auf einem Papierboot bestehen". Schreiben in der DDR der 80er Jahre', in Georgina Paul and Helmut Schmitz (eds.), *Entgegenkommen. Dialogues with Barbara Köhler* (Amsterdam, Atlanta, GA: Rodopi, 2000), pp. 45–61.

CHAPTER 7

Negotiating the politics and aesthetics of satire
Satirical novels in the GDR and beyond

Jill E. Twark

In his Introduction to 'A Contribution to the Critique of Hegel's Philosophy of Right' of 1843–44, a young Karl Marx wrote with reference to the proletarian revolution he was promoting at that time in Germany:

> History is thorough, and passes through many phases when it conveys an old form to the grave. The final phase of a world-historical form is its *comedy*. The Greek gods, already once mortally wounded, tragically, in Aeschylus' *Prometheus Bound*, had to die once more, comically, in the dialogues of Lucian. Why does history proceed in this way? So that mankind will separate itself *happily* from its past. We claim this *happy* historical destiny for the political powers of Germany.[1]

A hundred years later, after the Second World War had ended and the Soviet occupation zone was reorganized as the Marxist-Leninist German Democratic Republic (GDR), however, its citizens found little to laugh about. The country lay in ruins and millions were homeless and hungry. Nevertheless, from the start the socialist administration recognized the need for humorous entertainment and for a satire that would vilify its capitalist enemies in the west while extolling socialism's benefits. Art was to serve as a tool for changing attitudes and values in order to develop a new socialist society. Texts and performances should root out an 'antiquated' capitalist, imperialist ideological consciousness and any unsocialist behaviour; supply state-supported and condoned means of entertainment; and provide outlets for readers and spectators to 'let off steam', diverting frustration and discontent with the socialist system. Humorous and satirical modes first appeared in the form of a satirical magazine titled *Frischer Wind* (est. 1946), a few film comedies based on literary or operatic precedents[2] and several cabaret theatres. *Frischer Wind*, later renamed *Eulenspiegel* after a left-wing satirical magazine published in the Weimar Republic from 1928–33, was quite popular in East Germany, with readers passing copies to relatives and friends because it sold out quickly at newsstands; following unification it counted over 100,000 subscribers. The Berlin publishing house Eulenspiegel Verlag also began printing a colourful palette of humorous, satirical and later also erotic literature beginning in 1954. A year earlier the first state-supported cabaret theatre, the East Berlin *Distel*, had been founded, followed by the Leipzig *Pfeffermühle* (1954) and the *Herkuleskeule* (1955) in Dresden, among others. Testifying to their having become embedded in the East German collective psyche over the years as popular sources of entertainment and socio-political criticism, all of these cultural institutions except DEFA survived unification by privatizing and still exist to this day.

This chapter will address official East German political policies towards its nation's satirists, as well as significant East and West German theories of the genre and key satirical novels from the 1960s to the 1980s. East German satire focused primarily on the unequal relationship between the state, its representatives and ordinary citizens; deficiencies in the socialist planned economy; labour conditions in factories and other workplaces; male-female relationships; and environmental destruction. Perhaps surprisingly, despite the repressive nature of the GDR regime, satirists eventually managed to expose the major political, economic and social problems in East German society. Whether authors named problems openly or hid them in their texts, readers could find their grievances aired. For many years, such critiques buttressed state power by functioning as a kind of 'safety valve', but they eventually helped usher in the autumn 1989 protests that led to the GDR's dissolution by displaying its atrophied condition with ever greater distortion. This chapter suggests a new approach to interpreting East German satirical novels: categorizing them based not on their political contents, but rather on their narrative and linguistic structures, which at times adhered to an 'ironic realism'[3] and at others were conspicuously experimental. It furthermore draws connections between GDR and post-1989 satirical novels and examines how far this particular legacy will survive beyond the context out of which it emerged.

How East and West German scholars viewed satire under socialism

State-supported scholars in the GDR characterized satire as a weapon in the revolutionary struggle to build and spread socialism. Interestingly enough, the related genre of humour was not discussed as frequently, for it was not perceived to be as political and thus a less dangerous tool for regime critics. The first East German to define socialist satire was Georgina

Baum, who served throughout the 1960s first as editor, then chief editor, at the prolific Berlin publishing house Volk und Welt. Baum assumed a strict Marxist position and reproved philosophers like Immanuel Kant and Arthur Schopenhauer for having emphasized humour's 'subjective' nature.[4] According to Marxist theory, based on Hegel's philosophy, the most significant function of the comical is to provoke laughter at real, 'objective' discrepancies in bourgeois society and thereby to eradicate them.[5] Whereas bourgeois theorists had valued humour above satire because of the former's assumed abstract, aesthetic and apolitical nature, Baum asserted that by refusing to acknowledge satire's value as a critical *and* aesthetic art form, these theorists contributed to the perpetuation of stratified social inequalities in capitalist countries.[6] She argued that in a socialist context both satire and humour possess revolutionary power, and she used her editorial position to further the publication of satirical texts in the GDR.[7]

In 1966 the literary scholar and SED party member Werner Neubert put Baum's theories into practice by investigating both pre-1945 German and post-1945 West and East German prose satire. Ironically, Neubert's definition of a 'new satire', employed in order to support socialist society, echoes Baum's critique of bourgeois theories.[8] Neubert criticized the Soviet and GDR governments for their vapid use of satire as party propaganda; satire, he argued, does not distinguish between public and private spheres: '[Satire] wants to root a man out and give him no place to hide, because the personal, the way of life, the commitment to marriage and the family, for example, are an expression of one's political, societal position.'[9] Like Baum, however, Neubert argued that 'objective' contradictions between capitalist and socialist practices should be satire's focus, not the individual's 'subjective' perception of what is worthy of satirical critique, although the individual must reflect on these criticisms and strive to improve society.

By the early 1970s, after Erich Honecker's speech calling for an end to taboos, GDR satirists like Ulrich Plenzdorf and Wolf Biermann began to test the limits of satirical critiques, and by the mid-to-late 1980s, satire theorists were rebelling openly against the way satire was viewed and treated by the Party. In 1986 the SED party journalist Mathias Wedel, himself a satirist and cabaret text writer (since 2009 chief editor of the satirical magazine *Eulenspiegel*), had still sought to use Marxist theory to argue that subjective criticism of socialist society's imperfections be allowed.[10] Nevertheless, as the GDR neared its demise in 1987/88, a significant re-evaluation of satirical texts and performances beyond the orthodox interpretation finally took place. At this time Wedel teamed up with the satirist and former cabaret writer Matthias Biskupek[11] to write the self-reflexive, satirical and theoretical essay collection *Streitfall Satire* (Disputed Case Satire). An ironic, self-deprecatory Preface poking fun at other GDR authors' use of historical settings to camouflage their criticisms introduces the essays as if they had been discovered at a future date. By this time, the restrictive circumstances of which they write purportedly would have long since disappeared. Biskupek and Wedel exposed the government's term for 'liberating laughter' (befreiendes Lachen) as a covert form of control, because it was supposed to 'free' or purge citizens from their frustrations temporarily so that these frustrations would not swell and citizens act subversively.[12] Attacking official attitudes and policies towards satire and the censorship process, they contended that artists and critics needed to pay more attention to 'reading pleasure' along with 'usefulness and timeless value'.[13] Calling for playfulness not to be denounced in favour of satire's instrumentalization, Biskupek and Wedel promoted a view of literature and literary criticism that considers a text's aesthetic form to the same degree as its content. Without calling the Marxist-Leninist ideology into question, they openly refuted the politics, regulation and practice of literary criticism and censorship in the GDR.

This brief summary of GDR satire theory demonstrates how orthodox socialist views of satire prior to the 1980s precluded it from being perceived as a 'free' art form and made it difficult for socialist authors to produce texts that can lay claim to universal, timeless value beyond their context. Along with such overarching 'rules' for writing subsumed under the heading 'socialist realism'[14] and moral guidelines such as Walter Ulbricht's 'Ten Commandments of Socialist Morality'[15] put forth in 1958, GDR writers were restricted in what they were officially allowed to publicize or perform. For these reasons, West German scholars like Joachim W. Jaeger and Manfred Jäger labelled and thereby disparaged them (mainly *Eulenspiegel* contributors and cabaret writers) in the mid-1980s as 'state licensed gag writers', who did not produce real humour or satire.[16]

It also took until the mid-1980s for the West German scholar Barbara Meyer to assess East German satire in a more differentiated manner. She distinguished three categories: 'angepasste' (conformist), 'kritisch-auf-bauende' (critically-constructive) and 'vernichtende' (destructive) satire. She laid out how authors of conformist satire judged their subject matter from a really existing socialist standpoint, adhering firmly to its underlying ideology. Their satire was supposed to serve a conciliatory function, convincing GDR citizens that the socialist system was worth supporting despite its failings. Meyer proposed Hermann Kant as a prime example of 'conformist' satire. His novels such as *Die Aula* (The Auditorium, 1966),

Das Impressum (The Masthead, 1972) and *Eine Übertretung* (A Transgression, 1975) openly discuss 'taboo' topics such as the lack of consumer goods or the slow pace of the bureaucratic system, but they do not call socialism into question.[17]

Satires considered 'critically-constructive' also did not impugn the Marxist-Leninist ideology, but rather the fact that its ideals were never realized fully in GDR society. Meyer lists satirical treatments of women's emancipation – never achieved there, despite an equal rights clause in the constitution – as examples of critiques intended to further socialist progress. According to Meyer the short story anthology *Blitz aus heiterem Himmel/Geschlechtertausch* (Bolt from the Blue, GDR 1975/Sex Change, FRG 1980), including works by Christa Wolf, Irmtraud Morgner, Sarah Kirsch, Günter de Bruyn and others, along with Irmtraud Morgner's novel *Leben und Abenteuer der Trobadora Beatriz nach Zeugnissen ihrer Spielfrau Laura* (The Life and Adventures of Trobadora Beatrice as Chronicled by Her Minstrel Laura, 1974) 'sketch out a positive alternative to the prevailing circumstances. Satire and utopia converge. The critique of the status quo contains an anticipation of what should come. Satire is a trailblazer here. By insinuating its consciousness-altering power, its effects are assumed to reach beyond the literary context into reality'.[18]

Contrasting with the optimism of these first two groups, GDR authors producing the third type of satire, what Meyer called 'destructive' satire or 'absolute negation', called the entire East German sociopolitical system into question. Such authors did not wish to educate GDR citizens, but rather to negate the predominant system of values and norms under really existing socialism.[19] Meyer lists Günter Kunert, Stefan Heym, Erich Loest, Klaus Schlesinger, Lutz Rathenow, Roger Loewig and Hans Joachim Schädlich as this group's representatives and, predictably, many of their texts could only be published in the west. Indeed many of these authors defected to West Germany or suffered from the censorship or banning of their works in the GDR. Like Baum's and Neubert's theoretical treatises, however, Meyer's categorization of East German satire was based on a scale attuned to political critique, that is, to the works' contents rather than to aesthetic criteria.

While scholars like Baum and Neubert were working to define socialist satire from a theoretical perspective, GDR government officials at all levels – from Socialist Unity Party (SED) representatives to members of the Ministry for State Security (known as the MfS or Stasi) to publishing house editors – worked more or less actively to delineate an often arbitrary set of boundaries inside of which GDR satirists could express critiques. Beyond the cry for 'objective' criticism, socialist realism and Ulbricht's

'Ten Commandments', for example, the government expected satirists to aim their attacks primarily at Western imperialism and capitalism's short-comings like high unemployment, as well as at the 'Bonner Ultras', that is, 'reactionary' West German politicians. Socialist ideology, the SED, all government leaders, the military and the border, including the Berlin Wall, were all taboo topics, as well as any other words with negative or revealing political connotations.[20] The very word 'Zensur' (censorship), for example, was forbidden.[21] Vulgar sexual references and representations of homosexuality were also frowned upon. Thus authors needed to cloak their critiques in ambiguous language, called a *Sklavensprache* (slave language), to circumvent the censors, or 'Verlagslektoren', who worked in publishing houses to edit and improve texts stylistically and attempt to block the publication of subversive statements. Nevertheless, the most successful GDR satirists learned how to circumvent these controls and, like other artists and authors, they became ever more critical of the state throughout the GDR's existence. When asked in a 1999 interview about the relationship between socialist realism and published texts in the GDR, the East German satirist and film script writer Bernd Schirmer (b. 1940) revealed that 'socialist realism did not exist any longer when I began [writing]. [...] One ignored it more or less, dealt with it critically or dismissed it with irony'.[22] And, in fact, the best GDR satires were tragicomedies that did not endorse socialist-realist 'positive heroes'. Although some politicians and lectors strove to, and believed they could, control the content and reception of satire in East Germany, from the start this goal proved unattainable.

The origins of the popular satirical novel in East Germany: Erwin Strittmatter's *Ole Bienkopp*

By the early 1960s controversies erupted surrounding a number of revealing satires that were published and/or performed on stage. The forerunner in both severity and number of books sold in East Germany was the 1963 novel *Ole Bienkopp*, a *Bauernroman*, or rustic novel, written by the baker, farmer and later public administrator, newspaper editor and secretary of the GDR Writers' Union Erwin Strittmatter.[23] Titled after its main character's nickname, this novel provoked a public debate that lasted from December 1963 to mid-1965. Appearing in prominent newspapers and journals such as *Neue deutsche Literatur, Sonntag, Sinn und Form*, and even the farmers' newspaper *Neue Deutsche Bauern-Zeitung*, the arguments centred predictably on the question of whether or not *Ole Bienkopp* fulfilled socialist-realist criteria and promoted socialist goals. The novel depicts the problematic history of farm collectivization in the GDR, which had just taken place in the mid-to-late 1950s, focusing on the fictional farmer Ole Bienkopp and his struggle to establish a collective farm in order to even out inequalities produced by the redistribution of land (*Bodenreform*) initiated by the Soviet Union in its occupied zone a decade earlier. Forced on the farmers by the East German government, this move to collectivize was difficult to justify and to incorporate into the optimistic ideology of a country wishing to understand itself as antifascist and democratic. Strittmatter's collective farm offers an alternative to forced collectivization in that his protagonists initiate it themselves.

Looking back at *Ole Bienkopp* today, one can see that Strittmatter strove to produce a novel that would appeal to working-class farmers and factory workers by telling truths, albeit in fictional form, about problems with agricultural policies in East Germany. He used satire and humour to represent farmers and SED bureaucrats as engaged in an archetypal battle between the forces of good and evil. Ole's 'old' enemies, the 'Altbauern', or midsize farmers, are depicted as greedy capitalists, while his 'new' enemies are socialist officials who blindly follow directives 'from above', either because they believe too strongly in the party, are ignorant of the farmers' actual needs or harbour personal grudges. Major points of contention for critics were the ways Strittmatter depicted these party bureaucrats and how he concluded the novel by having his protagonist work himself to death in order to save his new collective farm. Ole's suicide was viewed as his anarchical, selfish rejection of the socialist system, and critics debated the extent to which a negative hero can be a catalyst for readers to learn a positive lesson.[24]

Despite and perhaps because of the controversy surrounding *Ole Bienkopp*, it became one of the most popular novels ever written in the GDR, selling more copies than any other and still being read today, mostly by eastern Germans because of their feelings of *Ostalgie* (nostalgia for the GDR) and Strittmatter's popularity and high reputation there.[25] East German cultural politics contributed to the novel's success by including it from 1969 until unification on the list of books that could be selected to fulfil secondary school curriculum requirements. Further reasons for this particular novel's popularity, however, do derive from the style in which it was written. From a post-*Wende* perspective, *Ole Bienkopp* can be seen to fit the mould of a popular cultural melodrama 'driven by the experience of one crisis after another, crises involving severed familial ties, separation and loss, misrecognition of one's place, person, and propriety'.[26] Moreover, as in conventional melodramas, it is connected to 'a vision of the world as a scene of polarized moral conflict'.[27] The novel thus provided the 'total package' for East German citizens who had worked hard to build a functioning socialist economy: it criticized GDR politics and governmental structures; affirmed a collective socialist vision; and provided melodramatic, occasionally hilarious, entertainment. Its topic of farm collectivization furthermore endeared it to government officials, because agriculture was 'the poster child of "socialism in the colours of the GDR". [. . .] [I]f no one in the GDR suffered from hunger, it could be traced to the engagement of the collective farmers'.[28]

Ole Bienkopp's wider significance for East German cultural history lies in the fact that it was one of the first pro-socialist novels to reveal how the SED used humiliation as a means to control its members' and other citizens' behaviour.[29] Additionally, it broke new ground by suggesting through its narrator that the party might be fatally flawed because of its adherence not only to Stalinist but also to Leninist principles and practices, and that a rejection of the Leninist elements would inevitably lead to its downfall. This prophecy in *Ole Bienkopp* was proved right by what happened in the GDR in the late 1980s. Along with early satirical stage dramas like the controversial *Die Sorgen und die Macht* (Anxieties and Power, 1958–60) by Peter Hacks and the unsatirical novel *Spur der Steine* (Trace of Stones, 1964) by Erik Neutsch, among others, it paved the way for future GDR authors to take a critical stance toward socialism's repressive leadership structures.[30] Viewed from a twenty-first-century perspective, however, Strittmatter's terse, choppy language, contrasting ironically with his drawn-out, winding plot and flat, typified characters, precludes it from holding much literary value beyond its East German historical context. By contrast, Strittmatter's short stories, children's books and novels, especially the trilogy *Der Laden* (The Shop, 1983; 1987; 1992) and a made-for-television film of it from 1998, have continued to receive much positive media and scholarly attention, not slowed by the recent discovery that Strittmatter served in the Second World War as a member of an SS-led Mountain Infantry Regiment that engaged in atrocities against partisans in Slovenia.[31] Like the author, the GDR government hid this fact from the East German public in order to be able to hold him up as an official state writer.

Ironic Realist satire: Günter de Bruyn's *Neue Herrlichkeit*

Although satirists, like other GDR writers and artists, suffered from repeated verbal and written admonishments and censorship, they received more public praise overall for their works than one might expect. Newspaper and scholarly reviews of such scathing novels as Morgner's *Trobadora Beatrice*, de Bruyn's *Märkische Forschungen* (Brandenburg Investigations, 1978) or Ulrich Plenzdorf's *Die Legende vom Glück ohne Ende* (The Legend of Happiness without End, 1979) – an extended and more socially critical version of his 1973 cult film *Die Legende von Paul und Paula* (The Legend of Paul and Paula), directed by Heiner Carow – were mostly positive. The few minor, mostly ideologically framed comments directed against them indicated that their works were too subjective or not socially engaged enough.[32] The otherwise generally positive reviews they received must have contributed to the works being read by some GDR citizens, and their being read produced a cycle of endorsement of the readers' complaints, which then fuelled writers to be ever bolder in their criticisms.

One prominent example of a satirist who suffered from various forms of state persecution for daring to criticize contemporary problems in the GDR and yet managed to publish satirical novels of high literary quality was Günter de Bruyn. On the one hand, de Bruyn was able to get away with biting criticisms, partly by placing them in a historical context, as in *Das Leben des Jean Paul Friedrich Richter* (The Life of Jean Paul Friedrich Richter, 1975), and partly by couching them in complex metaphors or symbols or simply changing the verb tense from the simple past to the present in order to indicate a critique of the GDR.[33] After having published the schematic, conformist novel *Der Hohlweg* (The Ravine, 1963); the critically acclaimed, witty novel exploring the psyche of an errant husband entitled *Buridans Esel* (Buridan's Ass, 1968); and the equally praised Richter biography, de Bruyn established a reputation for himself as a respected writer. By this time schooled in circumventing censors, de Bruyn thus had an easier time than some of his contemporaries in publishing most of his later, more critical works. On the other hand, as York-Gothart Mix discovered when granted access to secret police files in the 1990s, the Stasi approached de Bruyn clandestinely on several occasions, telling him fabricated stories (called by the MfS the 'legend' method) in efforts to convince him to spy on his fellow writers,[34] and his novel *Neue Herrlichkeit* (New Glory, FRG 1984 / GDR 1985) had to be published in the west before it could appear in the east a year later.

Tightly written and structured, de Bruyn's novels resemble nineteenth-century Realist novels and classical tragedies in their narrative composition. Their strengths lie especially in the author's differentiated, not fully typical character portraits and the way he balances satirical and sympathetic humour to amuse and demand reflection from the reader. After unification, de Bruyn has received more critical attention and acclaim than he had before 1990, for reasons Dennis Tate offers in the Introduction to his edited volume *Günter de Bruyn in Perspective* (1999).[35] Tellingly, the international scholars here focus largely on de Bruyn's and his colleagues' political battles or characters and plot developments, without reassessing his writing from an aesthetic perspective. And yet, de Bruyn's ironic Realist writing style, like that of his contemporaries Ulrich Plenzdorf or Christoph Hein, provides possibilities for reinterpretation based on his novels' strategies and subtexts.

Neue Herrlichkeit,[36] for example, plunges its protagonist Viktor Kösling, the son of an upper-level party functionary, into a carnivalesque situation (particularly interesting, once again, because Bakhtin was forbidden in the GDR as his theories were considered subversive). When Viktor is sent by his parents to the exclusive inn for Party functionaries called New Glory to focus on writing his doctoral dissertation, he enters a topsy-turvy world of blinding snowstorms, family drama, alcohol-induced revelry and a love affair, all of which suspend his feelings of responsibility to his parents, the university and the Party for several weeks. Fitting Bakhtin's theories of the carnivalesque and folk laughter, Viktor overcomes his anxiety and alienation from the Other – here, the working class – as he intermingles with people from different social strata and they unite in what resembles a play without a stage. Sacred and profane, high and low, great and small are coupled together and have a liberating and regenerative effect on Viktor at a time when he feels insecure about his future and afraid that he will not be able to live up to his parents' and Party expectations. For several weeks, Viktor's official worldview undergoes a Bakhtinian profanization, or blasphemous degradation, in which institutions and rituals Viktor has held sacred, such as his parents, career ladder or the East German state, could be parodied, 'turned inside out' and thereby temporarily superseded.[37] The novel is framed blatantly and yet artfully with carnivalesque images of the dead. A nearby cemetery and a landfill that threatens to engulf the very land on which the inn stands, both located on a road named 'Totenweg' (Way of the Dead), usher in the novel (p. 14). It then closes with grotesque images of an eldercare facility resembling a concentration camp (p. 182, pp. 195–98), juxtaposed with the inn's reorganization after the dispersal or burial of some of its caretakers, and Viktor's conformist decision to assume a position with the government as foreign diplomat, thus extinguishing his love affair with one such caretaker. Using carnivalesque and often humorous situations and images, de Bruyn connects flaws in the GDR to those found in other modern, industrialized societies, and presents inequalities between social strata in a universal manner with which an international audience can identify.

Experiments with narrative complexity: Irmtraud Morgner

Much East German satire was written in an ironic Realist mode throughout the GDR's existence. Along with older authors like de Bruyn, Erwin Strittmatter, Erich Loest and Hermann Kant, younger authors like Ulrich Plenzdorf and Christoph Hein later produced ironic Realist satires. In the 1970s, however, other East German authors, such as Adolf Endler, Fritz Rudolf Fries and Irmtraud Morgner, began trying out new forms of writing. Irmtraud Morgner's *Trobadora Beatrice* stood out in particular because of its narratively experimental 'operative montage' format. Consisting of a compilation of short stories, letters, scientific reports and sections of her novel *Rumba auf einen Herbst* (Rumba for Autumn; written 1965, published 1992), as well as other types of texts and fantastical characters, Morgner defines this new type of novel as a genre befitting her female characters, who lead busy lives and thus face constant distractions.[38] Morgner's East German protagonist Laura describes the 'operative montage' method to an editor at the esteemed Aufbau publishing house as a way for hard-working women and mothers to write and compile short pieces whenever possible and thereby capture events taking place during the 'appalling information explosion' of the late twentieth century, a time of great unpredictability during which global and local events 'constantly shift her views of the world'.[39] The 'operative montage' form is a future-oriented, 'indestructible genre' that places a high value on 'the encounters and experiences of the epic "I"', going against the otherwise advocated 'objective' perspective in socialist art. It contextualizes and communicates 'truths' about the main characters' lives, while allowing for experimentation, 'interventions' (ambiguously alluding to distractions from the outside world, as well as to the author's engagement in subversive acts) and reading pleasure.[40] The novel's diverse texts are strung along a central plot strand focusing on a friendship between an 800-year-old troubador named Beatrice de Dia and her 'minstrel', an East German tram driver, mother and writer named Laura Salman, both of whom struggle to support themselves financially while seeking fulfilment through the production and contemplation of literary texts.

A new way of looking at Morgner's novel that connects it to novels produced elsewhere and a few produced in Germany since 1989 is to see it as what Thomas J. Rice calls a 'novel of complexity'.[41] Using the scientific theory of 'complexity' as a means of looking at otherwise 'uninterpretable' novels, Rice proposes that scholars and authors look to the sciences for interdisciplinary answers to questions of life and art. 'Complexity theory' grants insights into disjointed, nonlinear structural networks by allowing them to be viewed like a complex science model and, therefore, 'not embodiments of a top-down, preconceived reading of a simplified reality but rather bottom-up attempts to generate a simulation of the complex real'.[42] Morgner's narrative develops in bits and pieces, some of which push the plot forward and others of which interrupt it, interjecting apparently inconsequential or otherwise unrelated information. It also engages in the technique of 'oscillation', derived from the structuring principle in Umberto Eco's *Foucault's Pendulum* (1988), by conflating and distorting genres and zigzagging between characters, plots, authenticity and fictionality and philosophical or scientific ideas. Its meandering structure prompted the satire theorist Werner Neubert to disparage it misogynistically: 'The fable does not "hound" [jagen] a person. On the other hand, one needs tremendous time and patience in order to get through it; there are stretches when one would like to give up, yell at Morgner: "Lord God, others knit endless scarves and you do this!"'[43] Because of its quirky originality, socially critical and philosophical wisdom and deep insights into East German women's lives, *Trobadora Beatrice* is one of a handful of GDR literary works, like those by Christa Wolf, Christoph Hein and Heiner Müller, to have been translated into English.

Linguistic playfulness: Volker Braun

A third group of GDR satirists experimented extensively with language in their texts. Many such authors, like Hansgeorg Stengel or Peter Ensikat, gained fame in the GDR by writing texts for cabaret shows and the *Eulenspiegel*. The most prominent representative of this group, however, is the now canonical author Volker Braun, whose puns and other wordplays contort his prose, rendering it rich in signification and at times challenging to read. Whereas de Bruyn turned to writing autobiographical and historical texts after 1990, and Morgner did not live to see unification, Braun continues to produce satirical texts to this day. In the 1960s he had written enthusiastically pro-socialist, 'conformist' poetry and plays to spur socialist progress, but after the Soviets suppressed the Prague Spring democracy movement in 1968 and Wolf Biermann was expatriated from the GDR in 1976, Braun's writings came to reflect his disillusionment. His poetry, drama and prose from the 1980s are arguably some of the most searing and structurally – though not thematically or politically – postmodern pieces produced by any GDR author.

Completed in 1981 but not permitted to be published until 1985, the *Hinze-Kunze-Roman* (Every Tom, Dick and Harry Novel) is a satirical tour de force. Like Morgner, Braun employs the rhetorical devices of incongruity, repetition and seemingly binary opposites, which turn out to be two sides of a complex whole, humorously to critique social stratification and patriarchy. As the working-class chauffeur Hinze drives his boss, the SED functionary Kunze, around East Berlin, they engage in philosophical discussions about whether their sexual exploits, eating habits, vocations and other behaviour can be considered acting 'in the interest of society'.[44] Braun thereby mocks GDR dictates that life and art always be directed 'objectively' towards building socialism. Injecting himself as a fictional author into the novel and personifying society as a brazen woman, he exposes the circular logic of this demand by using the verb 'to think' repetitively: 'Society, a poor but talkative hussy, always sat with me at the table (like now at my desk). She demanded that one think of oneself, in thinking of her, in thinking of oneself; it only became problematic when she relieved one of one's thinking' (p. 60). Braun's post-unification satirical works *Der Wendehals* (The Turn-Throat, 1995) and *Machwerk oder Das Schichtbuch des Flick von Lauchhammer* (Botched Job or the Shift Book of Flick of Lauchhammer, 2008) employ similar dialectical character constellations and playful but biting linguistic strategies in order to deconstruct problems of globalization and capitalism's tragedies like mass unemployment, excessive materialism, ageism, xenophobia and environmental destruction.[45] Braun ends *Machwerk* by having an unemployed 'expert' set the employment officer's desk on fire and by commenting on his own role as author:

> He has perhaps overfished the ocean, but not exhausted the topic. He acted with the urgency that he observes. Perhaps humanity needs to spell itself anew, and the new beginning of history shall be called: *for the last shall the world be made*. Used to failure, he thinks to himself, the actual work has not yet begun, it will take society's breath away.[46]

Post-unification satire

Although several major shifts have taken place in the production of satire in eastern Germany following unification – most notably in a turn towards a more 'subjective' satire, greater grotesquery and an overt borrowing from Western authors' writing techniques[47] – connections can be drawn between GDR and post-unification texts.[48] The influence of Morgner's complex, multi-genre approach and Braun's linguistic experimentation and grotesque societal critiques can be seen, for example, in Kerstin Hensel's *Tanz am Kanal* (Dance on the Canal, 2004) and *Lärchenau* (2008), as well as Kathrin Schmidt's *Die Gunnar-Lennefsen-Expedition* (The Gunnar-Lennefsen Expedition, 1998). Braun's mockery of socialist rhetoric also has its counterpart in the exquisite wordplay in Thomas Rosenlöcher's *Wiederentdeckung des Gehens beim Wandern* (Rediscovery of Walking/Leaving by Taking a Hike, 1991) or Thomas Brussig's *Helden wie wir* (Heroes Like Us, 1995).

Other authors, like Christoph D. Brumme, with *Nichts als das* (Nothing but That, 1994) and *Tausend Tage* (A Thousand Days, 1997); Jens Sparschuh, with *Der Zimmerspringbrunnen* (The Indoor Fountain, 1995); or Ingo Schulze, with *Neue Leben* (New Lives, 2005), have adopted the picaresque or the 'naive gaze' to reduce complexity and point of view to the fate of a single individual. Tanja Nause describes the 'naive gaze' as resulting from east German authors' desire to depict insecurity as a character trait. As *Sonderlinge* – fools, eccentrics or others who do not consciously choose to play the roles they are given – they are viewed and treated as outsiders.[49] The increased use of the picaresque and the naive gaze embodies in narrative form an irrevocable shift from 'socialist' objectivity to 'capitalist' subjectivity as east Germans had to face unification's changes individually and no longer as part of a perceived collective.

Politically too the goals have changed. Eastern German authors no longer write with the intent to improve society overarchingly. The *Eulenspiegel* author and editor Reinhard Ulbrich described his satirical novel *Spur der Broiler* (Trace of Grilled Chicken, 1998) thus: 'It is not as grand as utopia as a whole. It is also no grand system. They drummed too many theories of social organization into me for me to want to teach a social theory. It moves in much smaller units.'[50] Matthias Biskupek sums up this difference more pessimistically: 'Earlier we were supposed to say as little as possible and yet change everything in society. Now we can say everything, but nothing will change.'[51]

GDR satire once served as a powerful warning against the baleful effects of socialist totalitarianism. Since 1989, east German authors continue to dismantle the past, in the form of personal and public GDR history, and an imperfect capitalist system, from the unique perspective of having experienced both systems first-hand. The identifiably GDR edge to post-*Wende* satire can be found in the combining of an east German *Alltagsgeschichte* (history of the everyday) with complex intertextual and subtextual references. Thus, it can be viewed as a kind of *Heimatliteratur* (literature of home) for east Germans, chronicling the turbulent transition from 'socialism' to 'capitalism' and helping readers laugh at circumstances they might perceive as fearful, threatening or depressing. While Brussig's and Schulze's novels became bestsellers in the 1990s, today the most popular satirical criticism from east Germany takes the form of cabaret shows and film comedies like Leander Haußmann's *Sonnenallee* (Sun Alley, 1999) and *Hotel Lux* (2011) or Andreas Dresen's *Halbe Treppe* (Grill Point, 2002); with graphic novels such as *Da war mal was . . .* (There used to be something. . ., 2009) by Flix and *Kinderland* (Land of Children, 2014) by Mawil representing the newest trend in post-Wall humour.

Notes

1. Karl Marx, *Early Political Writings*, ed. and trans. Joseph O'Malley and Richard A. Davis (Cambridge University Press, 1994), pp. 60–61.
2. Hans Heinrich's *Kahn der fröhlichen Leute* (DEFA, 1949) was based on Jochen Klepper's novel of the same title, and Georg Wildhagen's *Figaros Hochzeit* (DEFA, 1949) was a film version of Mozart's opera.
3. Compare Fritz Martini, 'Ironischer Realismus: Keller, Raabe und Fontane', in Albert Schaefer (ed.), *Ironie und Dichtung* (Munich: Beck, 1970), pp. 113–43.
4. Georgina Baum, *Humor und Satire in der bürgerlichen Ästhetik* (Berlin: Rütten & Loening, 1959), pp. 7–8; pp. 77–84.
5. Ibid., pp. 16–17.
6. Ibid., p. 65; p. 76.
7. Christoph Links, email to the author, 3 July 2011; Siegfried Lokatis, email to the author, 10 June 2011.
8. Werner Neubert, *Die Wandlung des Juvenal. Satire zwischen gestern und morgen* (Berlin: Dietz, 1966), p. 7.
9. Ibid., p. 16.
10. Mathias Wedel, 'Zu den Funktionen von Satire im Sozialismus', unpublished dissertation, Berlin: Akademie für Gesellschaftswissenschaften beim Zentralkomitee der SED (1986), p. 27.
11. Biskupek was forced to leave the Gera cabaret *Fettnäppchen* in 1984 for writing a controversial show. See Jill E. Twark, *Humor, Satire, and Identity: Eastern German Literature in the 1990s* (Berlin: de Gruyter, 2007), p. 329.
12. Matthias Biskupek and Mathias Wedel, *Streitfall Satire* (Halle and Leipzig: Mitteldeutscher Verlag, 1988), p. 15.
13. Ibid., pp. 90–91.
14. 'Socialist realism', a Soviet aesthetic doctrine adopted in the 1930s, demanded 'Parteilichkeit' (socialist conviction); 'das Volkstümliche' (knowledge and understanding of the spirit of fellow citizens); and 'Wirklichkeitstreue' (the realistic depiction of subjects using typical characters and situations). See

Edward Mozejko, *Der sozialistische Realismus: Theorie, Entwicklung, und Versagen einer Literaturmethode* (Bonn: Bouvier, 1977), pp. 88–99.

15. See Matthias Judt (ed.), *DDR-Geschichte in Dokumenten: Beschlüsse, Berichte, interne Materialien und Alltagszeugnisse*, 2nd rev. edn (Berlin: Links, 1998), pp. 54–55.

16. Joachim Jaeger, *Humor und Satire in der DDR. Ein Versuch zur Theorie* (Frankfurt/M.: R.G. Fischer, 1984), p. 120; Ulrich Schacht, 'Lachen als Aufbruch und Ausbruch: Zu einer Tagung über das Lachen in der Literatur der DDR', *Deutschland Archiv*, 3 (1985), 309–11; p. 311.

17. Barbara Meyer, *Satire und politische Bedeutung. Die literarische Satire in der DDR. Eine Untersuchung zum Prosaschaffen der 70er Jahre* (Bonn: Bouvier, 1985), p. 39.

18. Ibid., p. 53.

19. Ibid., p. 1.

20. Heinz Kersten, 'Stacheln und Pfeffer: Kabarett in der DDR', *Deutschland Archiv*, 6 (1979), 568.

21. York-Gothart Mix (ed.), *Ein 'Oberkunze darf nicht vorkommen'. Materialien zur Publikationsgeschichte und Zensur des Hinze-Kunze-Romans von Volker Braun* (Wiesbaden: Harrassowitz, 1993), p. 12.

22. Twark, *Humor, Satire, and Identity*, p. 319.

23. Günther Drommer, *Erwin Strittmatter – des Lebens Spiel* (Berlin: Aufbau, 2000), pp. 68–69, 85–86, 93, 161, 168–69.

24. Hans Jürgen Geisthardt, 'Entdeckung neuer Konfliktgrundlagen. Zu Erwin Strittmatters Roman: *Ole Bienkopp*', in Klaus Jarmatz et al. (eds.), *Kritik in der Zeit* (Halle: Mitteldeutscher Verlag, 1970), pp. 639–51.

25. Because Strittmatter openly expressed support for SED decisions, such as to construct the Berlin Wall in August 1961, he was reviled in the 1960s by West German authors, critics and publishing houses and is still more or less ignored today. Compare Drommer, *Erwin Strittmatter*, pp. 149–54.

26. Marcia Landy, 'Introduction', in Landy (ed.), *Imitations of Life: A Reader on Film and Television Melodrama* (Detroit: Wayne State University Press, 1991), pp. 13–30 (p. 14).

27. Marcia Landy, 'The Melodramatic Context', in Landy (ed.), *Imitations of Life*, pp. 3–12.

28. '"Landwirtschaft." Damals im Osten. Mitteldeutschland – 1945 bis heute', Mitteldeutscher Rundfunk, 9 March 2011: www.mdr.de/damals/lexikon/151 4449.html#absatz6.

29. Phil Leask, 'Humiliation as a Weapon of the Party: Fictional and Personal Accounts', in Mary Fulbrook and Andrew I. Port (eds.), *Becoming East German: Socialist Structures and Sensibilities after Hitler* (London and New York: Berghahn, 2013), pp. 237–56.

30. Ibid., pp. 251–52.

31. Werner Liersch, 'SS-Vergangenheit. Erwin Strittmatters unbekannter Krieg'. *faz.net* 8 June 2008: www.faz.net/aktuell/feuilleton/buecher/ss-vergangen heit-erwin-strittmatters-unbekannter-krieg-1540322.html.

32. See Klaus-Dieter Schönewerk on *Neue Herrlichkeit* in 'Festgefroren – es bewegt sich nichts', *Neues Deutschland*, 12/13 October 1985, p. 14, and Christoph Funke on *Die Legende vom Glück ohne Ende*, in 'Die Auferstehung der PAULA', *Der Morgen*, 22 November 1983.

33. Mix, *Ein 'Oberkunze darf nicht vorkommen'*, pp. 66–67.

34. Ibid., pp. 70–71.

35. Dennis Tate, *Günter de Bruyn in Perspective*, German Monitor 44 (Amsterdam: Rodopi, 1999).

36. Günter de Bruyn, *Neue Herrlichkeit* (Frankfurt/M.: Fischer, 1984 and Halle: Mitteldeutscher Verlag, 1985).

37. See Mikhail Bakhtin, *Rabelais and His World*, trans. Hélène Iswolsky (Bloomington, IN: Indiana University Press, 1984), pp. 92–94.

38. *The Life and Adventures of Trobadora Beatrice as Chronicled by Her Minstrel Laura*, trans. Jeanette Clausen (Lincoln, NE and London: University of Nebraska Press, 2000), p. 175.

39. Ibid., p. 176.

40. Ibid., pp. 175–76.

41. Thomas J. Rice, *Joyce, Chaos, and Complexity* (Urbana and Chicago: University of Illinois Press, 1997), pp. 112–40.

42. Ibid., p. 131.

43. Werner Neubert, 'Aus einem Gutachten zum Manuskript "Leben und Abenteuer der Trobadora Beatriz nach Zeugnissen ihrer Spielfrau Laura – Roman in dreizehn Büchern und sieben Intermezzos" von Irmtraud Morgner', *NdL*, 22.8 (1974), 103–5; p. 104.

44. Volker Braun, *Hinze-Kunze-Roman* (Frankfurt/M.: Suhrkamp, 1988), pp. 9, 11, 18 etc. (the phrase is repeated 31 times).

45. See Twark, *Humor, Satire, and Identity*, pp. 196–244.

46. Volker Braun, *Machwerk oder Das Schichtbuch des Flick von Lauchhammer* (Frankfurt/M.: Suhrkamp, 2008), p. 220.

47. For example, Thomas Brussig drew on Philip Roth's *Portnoy's Complaint* in *Helden wie wir* (1995) and Ingo Schulze adopted Ernest Hemingway's short story/composite novel format in *Simple Storys* (1998).

48. Astrid Köhler, *Brückenschläge. DDR-Autoren vor und nach der Wiedervereinigung* (Göttingen: Vandenhoek & Ruprecht, 2007); see also Twark, *Humor, Satire and Identity*, pp. 286–310.

49. Tanja Nause, *Inszenierung von Naivität. Tendenzen und Ausprägungen einer Erzählstrategie der Nachwendeliteratur* (Leipzig: Universität Leipzig, 2002), pp. 37–41.

50. Twark, *Humor, Satire, and Identity*, p. 397.

51. Ibid., p. 335.

CHAPTER 8

The politics of dialogue
Poetry in the GDR

Gerrit-Jan Berendse

Poetry written in the GDR is characterized by dialogism, and for this reason it signifies the appropriate genre with which the stereotype of the GDR as a closed culture is denied. Dialogues consist of conversations and intertextual relationships in individual poems between both living and dead colleagues, but dialogue can also be identified as an intervention into public cultural and political matters. A dialogue with such dictatorial regimes as the GDR is always situated between being attracted to and distancing itself from the established cultural hegemony, that is, between adaptation and dissidence. Indeed, in its forty-year history GDR poetry showed a distinct critical engagement with the authorities. Even in times of extreme disengagement from national issues following the expatriation of Wolf Biermann in 1976, for example, and, again, in the 1980s, GDR poetry has shown a remarkable gravitational pull towards internal affairs and moreover has manifested a marked solidarity with the status quo. At the same time, however, poets have defined themselves as masters of deviation from the discourse of power and were agents of cultural transition in their roles as active translators. By incorporating 'foreign' voices in their work – literally crossing boundaries when travelling abroad and collaborating in cross-cultural projects – they represent what Stephen Greenblatt defined in 2010 as cultural mobility: a 'process of exchange across the borders of nations and cultures'.[1] For this reason, poetry written in the GDR must be characterized as a process of continuous oscillation between two extremes: that is, between, on the one hand, ambiguously engaging with authority's power discourse (also known as master discourse, or *Leitdiskurs*) and, on the other, the transcendence of domestic national issues with the aim of eliminating cultural provincialism.

In this chapter, I will present and analyse evidence of these opposing dynamics which, between 1949 and 1989, shaped the history of GDR poetry and influenced the cultural political discourse. It will be argued that both domestic and global qualities had an impact on the lyrical voice as Barbara Köhler articulated in the first strophe of her poem 'Rondeau Allemagne' (Rondo Allemagne):

> Ich harre aus im Land und geh, ihm fremd,
> Mit einer Liebe, die mich über Grenzen treibt,
> Zwischen den Himmeln. Sehe jeder, wo er bleibt;
> Ich harre aus im Land und geh ihm fremd.[2]

(I hold out in this country and go, estranged, / With a love that knows no borders, / Between the heavens. Every man for himself / I hold out in this country and go becoming faithless.)

There are three major phases in GDR poetry. The first is the foundation phase between 1949 and 1962, the period of what I call the 'Poet Laureates', or *Dichterfürsten* (namely, Stephan Hermlin, Erich Arendt, Johannes Bobrowski, Franz Fühmann, Bertolt Brecht and others). The second phase, up to 1979, consists of the generation of poets born around 1930, also known as the 'Saxon School of Poetry', or *Sächsische Dichterschule* (such as Volker Braun, Wolf Biermann, Sarah Kirsch, Karl Mickel, Elke Erb and Adolf Endler). Finally, I shall consider a younger generation of GDR poets writing from the end of the 1970s until the fall of the Wall, labelled the 'Prenzlauer Berg Connection' (including Bert Papenfuß-Gorek, Uwe Kolbe, Frank-Wolf Matthies, Durs Grünbein and Barbara Köhler).

The attitude of poets towards the state in these three periods has been described by Dieter Schlenstedt as a 'game of closeness and distance', even if the players were not aware of the game's rules.[3] According to Schlenstedt, the poets constantly oscillated between the extremes of being a loyalist engaged with the official cultural politics and a renegade which implicated the focusing on a wider European outlook. In other words, the poets can be classified by the level of their communication with power. In order fully to ascertain the political impact of poetry on GDR society this heterogeneous environment must be explored, as Mikhail Bakhtin argued in the 1930s in his studies on dialogism which were intended to counter Stalin's proposed primary cultural ownership.[4]

In dialogue with the master discourse

While returning from their exile either to the western zones or to the East, the Soviet Occupied Zone, German poets not only shared the same language but also were influenced by common, albeit diverse, pre-war cultural and political traditions. In the years immediately following the war, many of the returning exiled German intellectuals who were victims of the Third Reich decided to settle in the Soviet Occupied Zone, because they saw there the prospect for establishing a new, antifascist Germany, pursuing what Ernst Bloch called the 'Principle of Hope'.[5] Most of them had been communists since before Hitler gained power and had belonged to the League of Revolutionary Proletarian Writers, hence as John Flores has claimed '[t]o some extent literature and cultural politics in the DDR represent a continuation of this workers' movement tradition'.[6] The culture of the early years of the GDR was very much characterized by its intimacy with Marxist ideology.

The Cultural Union and its periodical *Die Aufbau* were the official forums that attempted to harness a common cultural spirit in the new socialist state in the first half of the 1950s, competing with the endeavours of the literary group *Gruppe 47* (Group 47) and its outlet *Der Ruf* in West Germany. Indeed, the Cold War can be defined as a series of oppositional rhetorical battles, fought between two articulate super powers in order to expose the ideological opponent's political and cultural weakness. The lyrical subjects in the poetry written in East and West Germany were placed in the centre of the discursive clashes in order to expose their presumed twisted ideologies.[7]

In East Germany many – including later critical poets – applauded Stalin's attempts to tighten communist politics and enrich the cultural élan of the Soviet Union. Marxism was seen as the only political 'medicine' to be taken seriously as a 'cure' for Germany's wrongdoings. As a consequence, several poems praising the building of the Wall in 1961 were published.[8] It did not take long for western conservative political and media circles to downgrade GDR poetry as a mere extension of socialist realism, that is, the poet was expected to have a responsibility towards the state or even reality in general and its political orientation.[9] Hence, in the early years of the Cold War GDR poetry was perceived exclusively as propaganda material. The best GDR poets, however, never surrendered to state communism or any other dogma. But instead its dominance has always provoked textual confrontations with official cultural politics and 'official pep purveyors', as East German cultural functionaries were labelled by Michael Hamburger.[10] Reading poems from the post-Wall era, or even earlier, by Brecht, for example, who responded to the 1953 uprising in his *Buckower Elegien* (Buckow Elegies), shows that the relation towards the state is much more complex and not caught in the dichotomy of either confirming or refuting the close relationship with power. Even if, as in the case of Brecht, these poems were published after the poet's lifetime, poetry was in constant dialogue with the state.

Research since the late 1980s has revealed that the firm engagement with and, at the same time, detachment from the state has contributed immensely to the quality of the poetic voice in the early years of the GDR. In his monograph *The Powers of Speech* (1995) David Bathrick detected the political dimension of the interchange between detachment and involvement, which GDR poets have capitalized on. For Bathrick, real provocation towards the state and its master discourse did not lie in any overtly dissident attitude but rather in the ambivalence to be found in the fluctuation between solidarity with Marxist ideas and the sharp and uncompromising critique of anything limiting intellectual activity. This fluctuation was misinterpreted as ambiguity, hence a lack of solidarity, and thus politically relevant.

In the twenty-first century, literary scholars no longer endorse the traditional view of a single stable or fixed national culture, and this has become paramount when writing new histories of a nation's literature, including that of the GDR. The nature of literature has always been dependent on both national and international contexts. However, as Homi K. Bhabha argues, 'all cultural statements and systems are constructed in [a] contradictory and ambivalent space'.[11] Poetry in particular is receptive to a much broader array of influences, by simultaneously responding to a wide range of dialogue partners, continuously crossing linguistic and thematic borders, and thus opening up the field of study as a more heterogeneous challenge.

This new research ultimately has an impact on the representation of East German culture in and beyond the academia. The variation in national and transnational interest in the GDR is reflected in, for example, two antholo- gies of GDR poetry published in the anniversary year of 2009: that is, in the volumes *100 Gedichte aus der DDR* (100 Poems from the GDR),[12] edited by Christoph Buchwald and Klaus Wagenbach, and *Lyrik der DDR* (Poetry of the GDR),[13] edited by Heinz Ludwig Arnold and Hermann Korte. Each of the anthologies demonstrates that the dialectic governing the lyric voice's involvement in internal affairs and its simultaneous desire for cultural mobility is a key component in the understanding of the specifics of GDR poetry. The first anthology, *100 Gedichte aus der DDR*, focuses exclusively on the poetry as an internal phenomenon. With its 170 pages, it draws a compact portrait of the poetic highlights of the GDR almost sealed off from the poetry of the rest of Europe; whereas in its 450 pages, the counter-anthology, *Lyrik der DDR*, addresses a more complex, transcultural mode. The editors Heinz Ludwig Arnold and Hermann Korte reflect a more accurate way of looking at cultural processes in a modern-day nation by identifying the overlapping, varied correspondences and differences from other cultures. In other words, they investigate the hybrid foundation of the cultural field.

The remainder of this chapter will focus on poems included in one or both of these two volumes and examine poetological matters referring to either the wider or the narrower context of the GDR.

GDR's *Poet Laureates*

For a nation recently risen from its ruins and congratulating itself on the transformation of Hitler's Germany into the first antifascist German state, it is perhaps surprising to see devotion to a new concept of *Heimat* (home) in its national anthem: 'Laß uns dir zum Guten dienen, / Deutschland, einig Vaterland.' (Let us serve your good will truly, / Germany, our fatherland.) At the same time, despite the forward-looking impetus of its title 'Auferstanden aus Ruinen' (Resurrected from the Ruins) this poem-turned-national anthem by Johannes R. Becher, who would become the first Minister of Culture in the GDR, is regressive in the sense that those who fall from grace will experience a return to the bad old days: 'Laßt das Licht des Friedens scheinen, / Daß nie eine Mutter mehr / Ihren Sohn beweint!' (Let all path by peace be lighted, / That no mother shall again / Mourn her son!) The poem represents the GDR state's founding myth: that the nation at once turned into an antifascist collective, and the idea that disloyalty to the new ideals threatens to turn back the clock. The poem advocates warmth and a sense of community, yet, at the same time, Becher sets loose a sense of fear in case the status quo is violated. The powerful images conveyed in Becher's text have been challenged by a varied range of poetic responses to the anthem.[14] The anthology *100 Gedichte aus der DDR* clarifies this by presenting miscellaneous variations on the political and cultural context from the first half of the 1950s. They are often more realistic than Becher's anthem, since they also seek to convey Germany's dark past appropriately. These poems must be read as critical responses to the narrow view that was the official dogma of the ruling Socialist Unity Party, the SED, and thus also as an attempt to undermine the state's obsession for a single truth, in other words, monosemia.

The omission of the Holocaust in Becher's patriotic depiction of post-war Germany motivated Stephan Hermlin's response in 'Die Asche von Birkenau' (The Ashes of Birkenau). The first part of the final verse reads as follows:

> Die da *Frieden* sagen
> Millionenfach,
> Werden die Herren verjagen,
> Bieten dem Tode Schach,
> Die an die Hoffnung glauben,
> Sehen die Birken grün,

Wenn die Schatten der Tauben
Über die Asche fliehn[15]

(Those who say peace / A million times over, / Will chase away the rulers, /
Checkmate death, For those who believe in hope, / The birch will be green, /
When the shadows of doves / Fly over the ashes)

On the one hand, Hermlin supports Becher's utopian sense of hope by
emphasizing the word *Frieden* (peace) and his bid to change the course of
post-war European history which is conveyed in the second strophe of the
national anthem. On the other hand, this is set against the background of
the horrific past reality (as conveyed by the name 'Birkenau') which Becher
ignores. Hermlin's interjection and other responses, many of them published in the anthology *100 Gedichte aus der DDR*, did not replace Becher's
optimistic outlook on the future, but rather indicated the need to enter
into dialogue with one of the nation's most influential poems, Becher's
hymn, by adding historical information that was politically delicate in
order to query the choice of words of a key representative of power.

Shortly after the end of the Second World War, poetry offered a further
alternative to the monosemy of cultural hegemony when the first translation
programmes were established. In 1947 the former exile Hermlin published a
volume of translated poems by Paul Éluard with Volk und Welt in Berlin.
The same publishing house, which specialized in presenting foreign cultures,
launched Erich Arendt's translations of the Cuban poet Nicolás Guillén and
also made Pablo Neruda's poetry available. Both Germans were key promo-
ters of poetry from various Romance languages and it was on Hermlin's
initiative that a concerted project of versioning foreign poetry began around
1955.[16] In the 1960s and 1970s, this programme of *Nachdichtung* was developed and sustained by the younger poets of the *Sächsische Dichterschule*. It
became a substantial component in the cultural exchange of poems on both
sides of the border.

In the anthology *Lyrik der DDR* the direct impact of the (in many
instances translated) foreign poets on GDR poetry is made apparent.
A good example is Johannes Bobrowski's 'Holunderblüte' (Elderberry
Blossom), in which the Soviet poet Isaak Babel features as a fictional
character. Using Babel's fearsome memories of his ordeal during Stalin's
Great Purge, Bobrowski warns the reader never to lose sight of the dangers
which can be caused by any kind of dictatorship in any period of history.
During the same period Erich Arendt and Peter Huchel both openly displayed their lyrical correspondence with colleagues in the Federal Republic
of Germany. In Huchel's poem 'Widmung' (Dedication) to Hanns Henny

Jahn, for example, the writer from Hamburg is presented as a constant stimulus for Huchel's own writing, typified as 'Die leicht erlöschende, ruhlose Glut' (The easily dying, restless ember).[17] It is clear in these intertextual references that GDR poets have fought against the danger of being cut off from cultural developments in other areas of Europe and in history. However, this was an affront to those in power because it made evident the fact that the reach of the master discourse was limited after all.

Stepping beyond the East German sphere, an arsenal of newly acquired images and a new lexis could be opened. Here dialogism had the ability to 'open windows' to foreign cultures, to borrow a term used by Simone Barck and Siegfried Lokatis, to indicate the transcultural endeavours in GDR poetry.[18] After cultural exchange programmes between the GDR and other Western European countries became a reality in the early 1970s, most of the so-called *Poet Laureates* and representatives of younger generations were able to travel abroad and realize their cosmopolitan aspirations.

Saxon School of Poets

In late 1962 Peter Huchel, one of GDR's *Dichterfürsten*, was sidelined by the SED for his supposedly international ambitions while working as managing editor of the journal *Sinn und Form*, the official forum of the Academy of Arts. As a reaction, his colleague Stephan Hermlin organized a poetry reading on the evening of 11 December 1962 in which the as yet unheard poetic voices of a younger generation of poets were introduced. The new texts Hermlin presented that evening appeared to be as seditious as Huchel's editorship. As secretary of the Poetry Section of the Academy of Arts of the GDR (Sektion Lyrik der Akademie der Künste der DDR), Hermlin launched his protest by demonstrating that this new generation of poets, born around 1930, had similar deviant aesthetic intentions as Huchel had as editor of *Sinn und Form*. For the first time, young and outspoken poets such as Wolf Biermann, Karl Mickel, Volker Braun and Sarah Kirsch, among others, read in public from their mostly unpublished work. This generation of poets was later named the Saxon School of Poets, or *Sächsische Dichterschule*, by Adolf Endler,[19] not only because many of the representatives were born and raised or studied in Saxony but also because Endler emphasized the concept of a 'school' of poetry. This manifested itself in the continuity of teaching and learning within the group and a process of dialogue with both the GDR and the European cultural heritage, as demonstrated in the legendary anthology *In diesem besseren Land* (In This Better Country), edited by Endler and Mickel in 1966.[20]

Both the readings at the Academy of Arts in 1962 and the publication of the anthology *In diesem besseren Land* four years later sparked off an unprecedented wave of interest in poetry, or *Lyrikwelle*, around the country. At the same time, a public debate was initiated about the importance of poetry and poets in a state that was to become a technological power house in Eastern Europe in the 1960s.[21] The public debates between poets, technocrats and cultural functionaries were published in the student magazine *Forum* in 1966.[22] Simultaneously, poets published texts which questioned the rise and supremacy of scientific progress, industrialization and rationalization. They did this in a number of ways, for example, by favouring hedonism in their textual dialogue in stark contrast to state asceticism. This attitude was also politically significant because through the poetry, their deviant voices were heard, thus demonstrating an alternative to the official agenda. Moreover, dialogism was the generation's trademark as can be read in a series of poems about eating and drinking. Poets conversed with each other through their writing, as poems by both Heinz Czechowski and Rainer Kirsch illustrate. In 'Erfahrungen mit Karpfen' (Experiences with Carp) Czechowski sets out detailed instructions on how to prepare a carp in the fourth verse of his poem:

> Den Vierpfünder trag ich im Netz in die Küche, bereit
> zum uralten Ritus, der Mordtat.
> Pfannen und Töpfe stehn auf dem Tisch. Ich prüfe
> Noch einmal die Vollständigkeit der Gewürze:
> Ruhmsüchtige Lorbeerblätter, Rosinen, Korinthen,
> Mandeln, süße und bittre, Gewürzkörner, Knoblauch,
> Paprika, Suppengrün, Salz und Zitrone.[23]

(The four pounder I carry in the net to the kitchen, ready / for the ancient ritual, the kill. / Pots and pans set on the kitchen table. One last time / I check if all the herbs are there: / Fame-seeking bay leaves, raisins, currants, / almonds, sweet and bitter, allspice berries, garlic, / paprika, stock-vegetables, salt and lemon.)

In 'Ernste Mahmung 75' (Serious Warning 75) Kirsch replies by inviting his fellow poets to a meal prepared by their colleague Czechowski in the final two lines of the poem. In order to realize this, however, fiction should interact with reality.

> CZECHOWSKI, STATT DER ODEN AUF DEN KARPFEN
> GIB UNS DEN KARPFEN, GLEICH! Die Stimme bricht mir.[24]

(CZECHOWSKI, INSTEAD OF THE ODE ON THE CARP / GIVE US THE CARP FOR REAL, NOW! My voice is breaking.)

Volker Braun displayed the relationship with reality in a different way, most of the time as an uncomfortable interaction with the state, since he was eager to uncover the hidden agenda behind the language of his government's bureaucracy. Braun's critique of the power discourse often ended up in ambiguous phrases such as 'Sprich lauter, Genosse, sind wir Illegale' (Talk louder, comrade, are we illegals) in the poem 'Die Geräusche meines Lands' (The Noises of My Country). The line can be read in three different ways, as a statement, an order or a question which can be interpreted as an attempt to unveil the discursive fragility of the system.[25] In the poetry of the *Sächsische Dichterschule* an entire network of dialogues can be seen to unfold in which praise, criticism, small-talk, love stories, polemics and affairs of state are presented and discussed openly. In this way poetry functions as an engine that starts public debate, indeed an act of engagement with the state.

The historical significance of this literary group is associated with its efforts to create alternative spaces for public speech in the GDR in the 1960s and 1970s. The poetry produced by this group opened up new ways of communication, and poets such as Karl Mickel, Heinz Czechowski, Volker Braun, Elke Erb and Adolf Endler were at the centre of some of the most profound cultural debates: the discussions in *Forum* in 1966, for example, and in *Sinn und Form* in 1972. Further, in their lyrical dialogues they managed to offer an alternative to the cultural politics in their country, particularly after the expatriation of Wolf Biermann in November 1976, which was a caesura in GDR's cultural history.

Apart from their constant 'conversation' with each other and their interventions in domestic cultural affairs, the poets of the *Sächsische Dichterschule* went beyond the local in other ways, through the creation, for example, of alternative milieus and though relating these fictional worlds to the existing situation in the GDR. The creation of new fantasy worlds was a particular hallmark of the poet Uwe Greßmann. He invented alternative societies such as the one portrayed in his so-called *Schilda* poems which questioned the mentality of the petit-bourgeois, known as Gothamite, or *Schildbürger*, in the socialist state.[26]

The international prospect of a poetry that provided the means to cross boundaries and detach poets from 'fixed geographical places' and their connected identities and transport them to places of imagination[27] was accompanied in the 1960s and 1970s by an enhanced programme of the *Nachdichtung* already begun in the 1950s. Indeed, the poet-translator became a common feature in the Saxon School of Poets. In addition to any aesthetic advantages, *Nachdichtung* also became an important source of income. Russian-language poetry had become a special focus for this generation of poets as Heinz Kahlau correctly observed.[28] The reception of translations of Russian poets not only helped to focus on new aesthetic concepts, it also familiarized poets and readers with a new culture of political engagement in a socialist country. Particularly significant was the emergence of a reaction against Stalinism in the Soviet Union and the subsequent public distance from the terror established in his name. In a hedonistic way, typical of the *Sächsische Dichterschule*, these foreign discourses were consumed and reproduced by the GDR poets – a poetic cannibalism of sorts.

Fritz Mierau, in particular, the scholar of Slavonic literatures, played a preeminent role in the reception of Russian and Soviet poets in the GDR. With his anthology *Mitternachtstrolleybus. Neue Sowjetische Lyrik* (Midnight Trolleybus. New Soviet Poetry, 1965), Mierau had not only presented contemporary Russian-language poets but had also introduced the new generation of GDR poets who had acted as translators. In his afterword, Mierau points out the significance of the relationship between translator and the translated poet and the significance of crossing the border – in geopolitical and cultural terms. For the generation writing in the final decade of the GDR a complete change of direction in the poets' attention became apparent; it was the United States that became their focus, although not for political reasons.

Prenzlauer Berg Connection

The dynamic poetic correspondence between fellow poets, both living and dead, was associated with those poets who were at the height of their powers in the 1960s and 1970s, but also became a 'weapon' for those publishing in the wake of the so-called Biermann affair. Poems by representatives of the Saxon School of Poets, for example, not only made an attempt – albeit an unsuccessful one – to persuade the state to revise its decisions concerning one of their colleague's fate and undo the cultural political mutilations in the post-Biermann era; they also functioned as whistle-blowers, exploiting their strong connections beyond the borders of the GDR to make the situation known to the international community. This open criticism of the state led to further isolation for those younger poets, born in the 1950s and 1960s, who were 'born into' the established GDR state, or *hineingeboren*, to borrow Uwe Kolbe's phrase.[29] Their cultural preconditions were radically different from the previous generations, and one of the most drastic actions taken by the cultural politicians was to introduce further restrictions on the permission to print, or *Druckgenehmigung*.[30] In order to avoid criminal charges, and also construct a more autonomous identity with regard to the state, various artistic scenes in many big cities in the GDR, such as Berlin, Dresden, Leipzig and Halle, were organizing groups with painters, artists, musicians and poets who worked together on artistic projects and avoided close contact with official institutions and agencies.

For the West, the Prenzlauer Berg scene, dubbed 'Prenzlauer Berg Connection' in the late-1980s,[31] became a countercultural model in its obvious juxtaposition of a bohemian lifestyle with overt political disengagement from the omnipresent state. With hindsight, any attempt to isolate itself from the state proved to be an illusion, partly due to the activities of the poets Sascha Anderson and Rainer Schedlinski as *Inoffizieller Mitarbeiter* (IM), or informants for the secret police.[32] Moreover, the poets' attempt to marginalize themselves socially and reject any involvement in the doctrine of socialist realism was in itself a political act: engagement through disengagement. This attitude was to a great extent adopted from Western colleagues who – in the tradition of the modern avant-garde movements in the first half of the twentieth century – used language as a means to unmask the power discourses in their respective countries. Since the majority of the young poets had no ambitions to become active political dissidents, their alternative means of expression was linguistic anarchy. The anthology *Lyrik der DDR* uses the poem 'ABWANDLUNG des DEUTSCHEN oder HERLEITUNG eines DEUTSCHEN' (ADAPTATION of the GERMAN or DERIVATION of a GERMAN) by Michael Wüstenfeld to portray this indirect confrontation with the state via a severe critique of language. In the first three lines it highlights the connection between language and power:

Deutsch	der Positiv	deutsch
Deutscher	der Komperativ	deutscher
Deutscherst	der Superlativ	DDR[33]

(German Positive German / More German Comparative More German / Most German Superlative / GDR)

Even more obvious in their linguistic anarchy are the poems of Bert Papenfuß-Gorek, who introduced the made-up term *Kwehrdeutsch* (slant German) as an indication of his aversion to authority of any kind, including that of the grammatical rules enshrined in the German dictionary *Duden*.

However, the Prenzlauer Berg Connection worked through the paradox that despite its disavowal of any dialogue with the state, its persistent aesthetic revolt and the loathing of the ambitions of somebody like Volker Braun, an engagement with power was unavoidable.[34] In his *Archaeology of Knowledge* (1972), Michel Foucault warned that nobody can be beneath the radar of the master discourse, or what Michael Thulin (alias Klaus Michael) later called 'the authoritarian institution of meaning'. David Bathrick stresses precisely this failure of an entire generation of poets:

> One might choose to parody, critique, destabilize, or even attempt to transform [narrative patterns], as many writers did, but in order even to mock one had to partake in the paradigm.[35]

The discursive imprisonment set out here was a result of the adaptation of neo avant-garde forms in the poetry of the Prenzlauer Berg scene and other metropolitan groups in the GDR. One of the key inspirations was the United States. The translation and republishing of North American poetry associated with the Beat Generation was one of the main programmes of the East Berlin publisher Galrev, for example. This counter-cultural scene in the 1950s and 1960s in the United States, featuring the work of Allen Ginsberg, William S. Burroughs, Andy Warhol and Charles Bukowski, had been passed on to the protest generation in the Federal Republic of Germany through anthologies such as *Silversceen, Acid* and *Fuck You*, edited by the West German poet Rolf Dieter Brinkmann in the late-1960s. Eventually – thirty years on – it reached the east.[36] As Hans Magnus Enzensberger has argued of the cultural context of the 1980s in the GDR, this meant the recycling of the already recycled: the 'elements of congruence and even imitation' recycled avant-garde material.[37]

However, the mediation of Brinkmann himself was also important. Brinkmann's own poetry was introduced in the GDR in 1986 by Chris Hirte in the famous 'Weiße Reihe' from the publishing house Volk und Welt, entitled *Rolltreppen im August* (Escalators in August), in which the young GDR poets of the 1980s welcomed Brinkmann's apolitical attitude as an antidote to the over-politicized milieu. Brinkmann's mode of action was indirect because he introduced new ways of seeing, that is, new methods of involvement with reality. Through his poetry he aimed at confronting the reader with new possibilities of dealing with the situation in which they found themselves. Another factor was also significant with regard to Brinkmann's frenetic reception in the subcultural scene in many major East German cities; this was related to the aggressive tone and remorseless tirades of insults, or *Hasstiraden*, with which Brinkmann addressed everybody and everything institutionalized.[38] His admonishment of authority touched a nerve with the young East German poets' own thinking. At the same time, and this is an important sign of dialogism in this generation, Brinkmann's radicalism and destructive psychological position influenced Papenfuß-Gorek's texts, in the sense that he radically transformed conventions. The new wild forms, the *Kwehrdeutsch*, as Papenfuß-Gorek called his anti-*Duden* grammar, were partly adopted from the intolerant writings of his Western contemporaries, as is demonstrated by the final cascading language-driven verses of the poem 'ihr seid ein volk von sachsen' (you are a nation of saxons), which is directed against those who initiated the peaceful revolution of 1989:

> ihr seid ein pack von fischköppen
>   radebergern, nordhäusern, richtenbergern
>   pritzwalkern, flämingen & wittstöcken
> genauso könntet ihr
>   ein volk von nacktspeichern
>   aus der traufe zu heben trachten[39]

(you are a pack of fish heads / you from radeberg, nordhausen, richtenberger / from pritzwalk, flaming & wittstock / you could just as well / have striven to lift a nation of *naked night storage heaters* / out of the eaves)

The transcultural adaptation of texts such as Brinkmann's goes further than simply translation or even *Nachdichtung*. The direct result is the absorption of another attitude and worldview. However, as in the case of translation and *Nachdichtung*, the influence is second-hand and the relation between source and target is static in contrast to face-to-face confrontations which became increasingly significant from the early years of the 1970s – the ultimate stage of cultural mobility.

Beyond the local

Those writers who belonged to those privileged to travel abroad, or *Reisekader*, were not the only ones to be invited to western countries as part of international cultural exchange programmes which were established after the GDR became a member of the United Nations in 1972. Higher education institutions in western Europe, in particular, welcomed GDR writers to augment their teaching of East German literature and culture. In the United Kingdom, academics such as Ian Wallace, Martin Kane, Rhys Williams and Karin McPherson took the initiative in inviting different generations of GDR poets, including Peter Huchel, Volker Braun and Reinhard Jirgl. Other European academics who welcomed GDR poets are Jean Mortier in France, Anna Chiarloni in Italy and Alexander von Bormann in the Netherlands. It is not only with hindsight that we may see the mobility and wider dissemination of the East German cultural context as a sign of the beginning of the state's decline. In the 1980s Uwe

Kolbe, for example, foresaw the state's collapse in his 'Am Ende der Zeit' (At the End of Time) by linking it with the increase of free movement. The three final lines in the poem are thus:

> .   Am Ende der Zeit schlafen
> alle Reisenden. Die Heimat
> wartet, das Ende der Zeit.[40]

(At the end of time all / travellers sleep. *Heimat* / awaits, the end of time.)

The Netherlands was altogether a special case, not only because it bordered West Germany, thus enabling convenient access to family, friends, colleagues and publishers, but also because many Dutch universities were employing German lecturers and professors.[41] Alexander von Bormann, Gerd Labroisse and Gregor Laschen teamed up GDR poets with their colleagues in the Netherlands and West Germany for translation projects such as those published in Laschen's series *Poesie der Nachbarn* (Poetry of the Neighbours). These intercultural alliances provided GDR poets with the opportunity to become part of a wider European cultural project.[42]

For all the GDR poets who were frequently involved in this and similar projects (these were Stefan Döring, Adolf Endler, Elke Erb, Wolfgang Hilbig, Barbara Köhler, Uwe Kolbe, Kito Lorenc and Brigitte Struzyk), the experience of globalization was a giant step to participation in the process of cultural mobility. It also made them aware of the consequent loss of the notion of *Heimat*, at least according to Kerstin Hensel's poem 'Schatten Riß' (Out Line / Shadow Tear), published in *Lyrik der DDR*:

> Die Welten glichen und da lobten wir uns
> Unkenntlich lang
> Wuchsen wir und liefen
> Breit, taub und lichtlos, und da ist was
> Dazwischen
> Gekommen
> Und das geht mitten durch
> Uns.[43]

(The worlds resembled and we praised ourselves / Long unnoticed / We grew up and walked / Broad, deaf and blind, and then something / Came / Along / And it cuts straight through / Us.)

For the serious literary student of GDR poetry, the combination of the broadening of the literary field as represented in the anthology *Lyrik der DDR* with the poetic representation of internal affairs in *100 Gedichte aus der DDR* allows new insights into a traditionally sealed-off field of study.

Varying cultural approaches can be detected: the dialogue with the state and, at the same time, the withdrawal from it.

Indeed, GDR poetry was never confined to the relatively small geographical entity of the state itself but was, instead, very much a vital part of wider European cultural history, oscillating between diverse ways of corresponding with the political framework, both within the GDR itself and in a more global understanding. The dialectic between national and international mechanisms is put into words by the Prenzlauer Berg poet Uwe Warnke in his 'DIALEKTIK' (DIALECTIC):

international
internationa
internation
internatio
internati
internat
interna
intern[44]

Notes

1. Stephen Greenblatt et al., *Cultural Mobility. A Manifesto* (Cambridge University Press, 2010), p. 4.
2. Christoph Buchwald and Klaus Wagenbach (eds.), *100 Gedichte aus der DDR* (Berlin: Wagenbach, 2009), p. 129. See also Barbara Köhler, *Deutsches Roulette. Gedichte 1984–1989* (Frankfurt/M.: Suhrkamp, 1991), p. 63. All translations mine. The author thanks Paul Clements and Sabine Berendse for their help.
3. Dieter Schlenstedt, 'Integration-Loyalität-Anpassung: Über die Schwierigkeit bei der Aufkündigung eines komplizierten Verhältnisses', in Heinz Ludwig Arnold (ed.), *Literatur der DDR: Rückblicke* (Munich: edition text + kritik, 1991), pp. 172–89; p. 176.
4. For example, Mikhail Bakhtin, *The Dialogic Imagination*, trans. Caryl Emerson and Michael Holquist (Austin: University Press of Texas, 1981).
5. Ernst Bloch, *Werkausgabe. Band 5: Das Prinzip Hoffnung* (Frankfurt/M.: Suhrkamp, 1985).
6. John Flores, *Poetry in East Germany. Adjustments, Visions, and Provocations, 1945–1970* (New Haven and London: Yale University Press, 1971), p. 4.
7. Lynn Boyd Hinds and Theodore Otto Windt, Jr., *The Cold War as Rhetoric: The Beginnings, 1945–1950* (New York: Praeger Publishers, 1991), pp. 5–25.
8. See interview with Adolf Endler, *Die Sirren. Gespräche mit Renatus Deckert* (Göttingen: Wallstein, 2010), pp. 167–81.
9. Compare the chapter by Wolfgang Emmerich.

10. Michael Hamburger, 'Introduction', in Hamburger (ed.), *An Anthology. East German Poetry* (Oxford: Carcanet Press, 1972), p. xix.

11. Homi K. Bhabha, *The Location of Culture* (London: Routledge, 1994), p. 37.

12. Buchwald and Wagenbach (eds.), *100 Gedichte aus der DDR.*

13. Heinz Ludwig Arnold and Hermann Korte (eds.), *Lyrik der DDR* (Frankfurt/M.: Fischer, 2009).

14. Compare Stephen Brockmann's chapter in this volume.

15. Ibid., pp. 20–21; p. 21. See also Stephan Hermlin, *Gesammelte Gedichte* (Munich and Vienna: Hanser, 1979), pp. 84–85.

16. See Simone Barck, Siegfried Lokatis and Martina Langermann (eds.), *Fenster der Welt. Die Geschichte des DDR-Verlages Volk & Welt* (Berlin: Links, 2004), Michael Opitz and Michael Hofmann (eds.), *Metzler Lexikon DDR-Literatur* (Stuttgart and Weimar: Metzler, 2009), p. 235 and Ruth J. Owen, 'Freedom of Expression. Poetry Translations in the East Berlin *Poesiealbum*', *Translation Studies*, 2 (2011), 133–48.

17. Arnold and Korte (eds.), *Lyrik der DDR*, p. 71. See also Peter Huchel, *Gesammelte Werke in zwei Bänden*, vol. 1, *Die Gedichte* (Frankfurt/M.: Suhrkamp, 1984), pp. 134–35.

18. Barck, Lokatis and Langermann (eds.), *Fenster der Welt.*

19. Adolf Endler, 'DDR-Lyrik Mitte der Siebziger. Fragment einer Rezension', *Amsterdamer Beiträge zur neueren Germanistik*, 7 (1978), 67–95.

20. See Gerrit-Jan Berendse, 'Die Überlebensfigur Sächsische Dichterschule', *German Life and Letters*, 3 (2010), 280–94.

21. David Bathrick, *The Powers of Speech: The Politics of Culture in the GDR* (Lincoln: University of Nebraska Press, 1995). p. 126.

22. Anthonya Visser, *Blumen ins Eis. Lyrische und literaturkritische Innovationen in der DDR. Zum kommunikativen Spannungsfeld ab Mitte der 60er Jahre* (Amsterdam: Rodopi, 1994).

23. Buchwald and Wagenbach (eds.), *100 Gedichte aus der DDR*, pp. 92–93. See also *Tintenfish*, ch 8 (1975), 17–18; p. 17.

24. Buchwald and Wagenbach (eds.), *100 Gedichte aus der DDR*, p. 95. See also Rainer Kirsch, *Ausflug machen. Gedichte* (Rostock: Hinstorff Verlag, 1980), pp. 51–52.

25. Ibid., p. 100. See also Volker Braun, *Training des aufrechten Gangs. Gedichte* (Halle/S. and Leipzig: Mitteldeutscher Verlag, 1982), p. 9.

26. Uwe Greßmann, *Schilda Komplex*, ed. Andreas Koziol (Berlin: Edition qwert zui opü, 1998).

27. Sheldon Pollock et al., 'Cosmopolitanisms', in Carol A. Breckenridge et al. (eds.), *Cosmopolitanism* (Durham and London: Duke University Press, 2001), pp. 1–14.

28. Heinz Kahlau, 'Über die Kunst des Nachdichtens', quoted in Gerrit-Jan Berendse, *Die 'Sächsische Dichterschule'. Lyrik in der DDR der sechziger und siebziger Jahre* (Franfurt/M.: Lang, 1990), pp. 122–29. Kahlau declares the 1960s to be the renaissance of *Nachdichtung* in the GDR.

29. Uwe Kolbe quoted in Leeder, *Breaking Boundaries* (Oxford University Press, 1996), p. 4.

30. Peter Böthig, *Grammatik einer Landschaft. Literatur aus der DDR der 8oer Jahre* (Berlin: Lukas, 1997), p. 77.
31. Adolf Endler, 'Alles ist im untergrund obenauf, einmannfrei . . . Anläßlich einer Anthologie', in Endler, *Den Tiger reiten. Aufsätze, Polemiken und Notizen zur Lyrik der DDR*, ed. Manfred Behn (Frankfurt/M.: Luchterhand, 1990), p. 46.
32. See Alison Lewis, *Die Kunst des Verrats. Der Prenzlauer Berg und die Staatssicherheit* (Würzburg: Königshausen & Neumann, 2003).
33. Arnold and Korte (eds.), *Lyrik der DDR*, p. 263. See also Heinz Ludwig Arnold (ed.), *Die andere Sprache. Neue DDR-Literatur der 8oer Jahre* (Munich: edition text + kritik, 1990), p. 56.
34. Volker Braun, *Rimbaud. Ein Psalm der Aktualität* (Stuttgart: Franz Steiner Verlag, 1985).
35. Bathrick, *The Powers of Speech*, p. 17.
36. Thomas Ernst, *Popliteratur* (Hamburg: Rotbuch, 2001) and Gerrit-Jan Berendse, 'Beat am Prenzlauer Berg. Das Treffen zweier Subkulturen', in Berendse, *Grenz-Fallstudien. Essays zum Topos Prenzlauer Berg in der DDR-Literatur* (Berlin: Erich Schmidt, 1999), pp. 41–58.
37. Leeder, *Breaking Boundaries*, p. 174.
38. See Jan Röhnert and Gunter Geduldig (eds.), *Rolf Dieter Brinkmann. Seine Gedichte in Einzelanalysen* (Berlin: de Gruyter, 2012).
39. Arnold and Korte (eds.), *Lyrik der DDR*, p. 344. See also Bert Papenfuß-Gorek, *tiské* (Göttingen: Seidl, 1990), p. 69.
40. Ibid., p. 293. See also Uwe Kolbe, *Bornholm II. Gedichte* (Berlin and Weimar: Aufbau, 1986), p. 87.
41. Jacco Pekelder, *Nederland en de DDR. Beeldvorming en betrekkingen* (Amsterdam: Boom, 1998).
42. A selection of all the ten volumes has been published in 1999: Gregor Laschen (ed.), *Schönes Babylon. Gedichte aus Europa in 12 Sprachen* (Cologne: DuMont, 1999).
43. Arnold and Korte (eds.), *Lyrik der DDR*, p. 324. See also Kerstin Hensel, *Schlaraffenzucht. Gedichte* (Frankfurt/M.: Luchterhand, 1990), p. 7.
44. Ibid., p. 338. See also Uwe Warnke, *wortBILD. Visuelle Poesie in der DDR* (Halle/S. and Leipzig: Mitteldeutscher Verlag, 1990), p. 26.

CHAPTER 9

Underground literature? The unofficial culture of the GDR and its development after the Wende

Birgit Dahlke

2009 retrospective: an exhibition

On 20 November 2009 an exhibition entitled 'Underground Poetry. East Berlin's Art and Literature Scene 1979–1989' opened in Berlin's Prenzlauer Berg district. Curated by Uwe Warnke, Thomas Günter and Ingeborg Quaas, it was a comprehensive appraisal of the unofficial art and literature scene that flourished in the 1980s through a network of small magazines. This was a milieu that at the time of unification in 1990 had been touted by some journalists as representing the 'real', that is, 'alternative', art and literature of the GDR.[1] It subsequently underwent a process of radical re-evaluation, not least because of revelations about the role of the Staatssicherheit (secret police) within it. And ultimately, the brief inclusion of the unofficial culture of the GDR into the canon by literary scholars and art historians was followed by a descent into near obscurity.

The exhibition's curators had deliberately included the contested term 'underground' in their title. Without denying the revelation made public at the end of 1991 that two important protagonists of the literary scene were complicit with the Stasi, the organizers were able to document the vitality and richness of an artistic world that existed beneath the radar of state control and which persevered despite state opposition and attempts to criminalize participation. The accompanying readings, tours, film screenings and lectures succeeded not only in providing vivid contextualization of the works, but also in reuniting some of the original protagonists, now somewhat grey around the temples. The art historian Christoph Tannert began his opening address (which can be found at www.poesiedesuntergrunds.de) with the claim that the exhibition had enabled the original participants from that period to reclaim interpretative authority over their own history. His polemical gesture made clear that even two decades after

Translated by Emily Spiers.

the fall of the Berlin Wall many East German artists and authors still felt subject to the dominant judgement of West German museum curators and literary historians, who even now did not grant them due recognition. Tannert went on to observe that whilst the old guard saw their work collected in museums, its value steadily rising on the art market, many of those who had been denied cultural (and above all financial) recognition before the *Wende* were still excluded in post-unification Germany.

Escaping censorship: 1979–89

By the end of the 1970s, and especially after the expatriation of Wolf Biermann in 1976, the generally accepted understanding of literature's social function had been overturned, especially by the youngest generation of writers. By producing small magazines, artists' books and 'Lyrik-Graphik-Mappen' (portfolios of poetry and graphic art), they evaded attempts by the state to control and determine the direction of their work. Private homes were transformed into venues for dramatized readings and galleries; workshops in inner courtyards, cellars, loft spaces and later any number of church-owned premises became concert venues and theatres. Readings and performances, often followed by long discussions, took on the atmosphere of spontaneous 'happenings' and frequently developed into parties (Figure 6). Participants would drive out to derelict farms in order to take part in Plein-Air painting events, hold punk rock concerts and fashion shows or to witness body-art performances. It was precisely the non-institutional, anarchic nature of these events that attracted young people. However, in order to belong in a real sense, it was necessary to become actively involved in some artistic capacity. This led to many people trying their hand, producing an extremely heterogeneous array of art works, concerts or films. There were notable forerunners to these happenings: Siegmar Faust's so-called 'motorboat reading' in Leipzig in 1968 (an illegal commandeering of one of the river boats on the Elsterstausee), for example. In 1974 Jürgen Schweinebraden had established the EP-Galerie in Berlin's Dunckerstraße and there was the Bödickerclub, at Berlin's Ostkreuz station, run by Reinhard Zabka and Martin Hoffmann; or readings at the homes of Heidemarie Härtl, Gert Neumann and Lutz Nitzsche-Kornel in Leipzig or Erich Arendt, Frank-Wolf Matthies and Wilfriede and Ekkehard Maaß in Berlin (Figure 7).

In the sprawling, run-down suburbs of big cities, young people reinvented themselves as 'bohemians' and carved out their own self-determined, alternative public space. What such outbursts of playful experimentation

Figure 6 Invitation to the 'Zersammlung' event, 5–11 March 1984, using a
drawing by Cornelia Schleime (1984). Courtesy of Uwe Warnke. From 5–11 March
1984 poets from the avant-garde scene met in the second court yard of Lychener Straße 6,
for a marathon reading, dubbed 'Zersammlung' (dis-meeting)
organized by Bert Papenfuß and Stefan Döring. The invitation, using an image by
Cornelia Schleime, states 'Arrive alone with your poetry and food, yours Harry'.
The anthology *Berührung ist nur eine Randerscheinung* appeared a year later, but only in
the west.

and creativity represented should not be idealized in retrospect, though; they
were always met with enormous pressures to conform and were subject to
attempts to control or even criminalize them. Nevertheless, a sense of
autonomy was an indispensable illusion for many of these young people; it
enabled them to disentangle themselves from the tightly woven nexus of
social institutions and preordained paths through life that were planned
down to the last detail by the authorities. Such concerns not only shaped the
development of independent theatre companies like *Zinnober*, the cine-film
scene and the Indie music scene but also students' final-year projects at
universities of film and television.[2]

Early experiments with publication suffered from censorship or were
banned: such as Kurt Schraeck's *Papiertaube* (Paper Dove, 1979), or the
texts collected in Leipzig by Thomas Böhme and Thomas Rosenlöcher
under the title *Laternenmann* (Lantern Man), which consisted of a few,

Figure 7 'Writers in Wilfriede Maaß's studio for a reading organized by
Ekkehard Maaß, 20 September 1981' (1981). © Helga Paris VG Bildkunst. (Standing
from left to right: Eberhard Häfner, Jan Faktor, Heinz Kahlau, Uwe Kolbe,
Roland Manzke, Wolfgang Hegewald, Peter Brasch, Dieter Schule, Hans-Eckardt
Wenzel, Michael Rom, Leonhard Lorek, Lutz Rathenow; Sitting, from left to
right: Rainer Kirsch, Rüdiger Rosenthal Traudl Kulikowski, Sascha Anderson, Bert
Papenfuß, Stefan Döring.)

scarcely legible carbon copies of typewritten text assembled in an illustrated
folder. In another example from the beginning of the 1970s, Ulrich
Plenzdorf, Klaus Schlesinger and Martin Stade were successfully prevented
from publishing the anthology *Berliner Geschichten* (Berlin Stories). But by
the end of that decade the infamous 1979 law governing printed matter (the
so-called *Druckgenehmigungsgesetz*) was being evaded successfully by inte-
grating illustrations into the written text. This occurred in, for example,
Poe Sie All Bum (Dresden, Berlin, 1978–84), *Und* (Dresden 1982–84),
Entwerter/Oder (Berlin 1982–89) and *A3* (Karl-Marx-Stadt 1983–90). This
was because illustrations were governed by a different law from printed
text. Posters, for example, only required official approval when produced in
larger print runs. A virtue was made of necessity: unified works of art were
produced in which texts, illustrations, photography and the art of book
production stood on an equal footing. Over time, these one-off creations
have become collectors' pieces; even pre-*Wende* some of those involved
sold pieces for West German currency in order to live off the exchanged

sums. In doing so, they were constantly testing the boundaries of what was legal. At the same time, these artists, whether consciously or not, were continuing a literary tradition: Stefan George, to take one example, had played exclusivity off against techniques of mass production as early as 1900, when he brought out his small-circulation magazine *Blätter für die Kunst* in the 1890s – albeit under different social conditions.

Even their outward appearance contravened the formal conventions of literary journals: they were bound with roller grids, sandpaper, squeaking polystyrene egg cartons or roofing felt (clearly indicating periods of economic hard-times); they were like lucky dips, difficult to open, full of confetti, loose sheaves of paper filled with poetry or collages made up of all kinds of everyday materials. These works staged the juxtaposition of artistic design and whatever came to hand.

In the early stages in particular, the often collectively written texts abounded with avant-garde expressions of renunciation – of the institution of art, of meaning itself; they demolished conventional language and reconstructed it in challenging and creative ways. These features can be seen in the first numbers of *Schaden* (Berlin 1984–87) and in the collective manifesto 'Zoro in Skorne' printed in *Schaden* 4 (1985).[3] In the latter text, the authors employ programmatic words such as 'uncontrollability', 'excess' and 'temporary zones of autonomy'.[4] These poets, who were fighting for intellectual independence, developed a poetic language which challenged the referential capacities of language. Deconstruction was seized upon, not simply as a modish theoretical tool as in the west; rather, under living conditions shaped by a dominant ideology, it was both understood and practised literally. The language of propaganda and newspapers was demolished, dismantled, attacked, parodied and ironized. It was only by means of the most diverse language experiments that artists were able to express themselves, or even to conceive of a self to express. The 'East German School for Language Therapy', as Bernd Wagner dubbed it,[5] served the cause of emancipation from ideological oppression.

At the same time, state security officers interfered less with poets working with this deconstructive (apparently apolitical) method than with others who had a more explicitly political agenda. To what extent this language, with its multiple layers of meaning and systematic obfuscation, also bore the traces of structures common to the language of the authorities and the secret service – that is, precisely those institutions, from which it sought to extricate itself – was, and still is, hotly debated.[6] It was above all those women who were active in the art scene who avoided bohemian posturing. It also became evident after 1991 that women were less susceptible in general to attempts to recruit them by the Stasi. However, texts by women were also marginalized within the scene, and the denigration of their work in the Berlin scene, especially, was for the most part continued by literary historians writing after 1990.[7]

Taking their lead from the avant-garde impulses of modernism, artists sought a path that enabled them to escape from the system, establishing what some understood as a 'counter' or 'oppositional culture', and some as a culture and literature that were simply 'other'.[8] Futurism, Dadaism, Concrete Poetry – any anti-bourgeois impulse – was adapted to the social conditions and aesthetic conventions of the GDR setting. The resulting anthologies which, due to censorship in the GDR, could only be published in the Federal Republic, including *Berührung ist nur eine Randerscheinung* (Contact Is Merely a Marginal Phenomenon, 1985), *Mikado oder der Kaiser ist nackt* (Mikado, or the Emperor Is Naked, 1988) and *Sprache & Antwort* (Language & Answer, 1988), served to create an impression of political and aesthetic homogeneity within the unofficial art scene. In fact this impression was inaccurate. Political texts by Václav Havel were included in the Leipzig-based magazine *Anschlag* (1984–89), for example, which would have been inconceivable in *Schaden* or in the more theoretically oriented *Ariadnefabrik* (Berlin, 1986–89).

No one really 'owned' the few published copies of these magazines, except those involved in their production. They found their public by being distributed individually among friends or through private readings. As a result, the time and place of reception were fixed variables. An artistic form such as 'Mail Art', familiar from the international Fluxus movement, gained greater subversive currency as soon as it began to play with the borders between East and West. In view of the violation of postal privacy practised widely by state security forces (it is alleged that ten per cent of German-German postal exchanges were opened and monitored), the Fluxus 'game' became a political act. The rules were simple: a mail artist designed and sent an invitation card to an international database of addressees with a specific project as its theme. The sender would receive between 80 and 300 art cards in response, which he or she would have displayed in an uncensored, non-competitive exhibition. Those who responded could possibly expect to receive an exhibition catalogue or at least a list of all other participants, which would often lead to new projects. The cards and letters distributed between 1974 and 1989 not only blurred the boundaries between social systems, and those between life and art, but also, in the case of the East German protagonists, between artists and non-artists. This was due to the fact that many of the East German 'Mail Artists' in the circles around Robert Rehfeldt in Berlin and Jürgen Gottschalk in Dresden earned their living as printers or technicians.[9]

From the mid-1980s onwards the distinctions between 'official' and 'unofficial' became muddied. What had been niches of subcultural activity disbanded; many authors began to move in both official and independent circles simultaneously, while others vehemently rejected all forms of engagement with the state. They were no longer reliant upon publishers, editors or the membership of the Writers' Union. Heike Drews (later Willingham), Raja Lubinetzki, Andreas Koziol, Frank Lanzendörfer, Durs Grünbein, Jan Faktor, Bert Papenfuß, Stefan Döring, Heidemarie Härtl, Gert Neumann, Gabriele Kachold, Leonhard Lorek and Ulrich Zieger had made a name for themselves outside state-run institutions.

Between 1983 and 1984 large numbers of young people began to leave the GDR. The temporary travel visas granted to some writers and artists meant that the sense of group identity which had previously been so pervasive began to slacken, as did the closed circuit of communication. The decision whether to stay or go became a recurrent theme. 'Ich harre aus im Land und geh, ihm fremd' (I hold out in this country and go, estranged), wrote Barbara Köhler in her poem 'Rondeau Allemagne' (Rondo Allemagne).[10] For Peter Wawerzinek, it was a case of '[w]er schreibt der bleibt – wer schreit & schreibt Bleibendes, geht dann doch einfach weg' (those who write, stay – those who shout & write for keeps, just go in the end).[11]

Emancipation from dominant discourses was followed by the process of differentiation between poetological leanings. Coteries were established around magazines like *Glasnot* (Naumburg, 1987–89), *Koma Kino* (Berlin, 1987–89), *Zweite Person* (Leipzig, 1987–89), *Liane* (Berlin, 1988–90) and *Bizarre Städte* (Berlin, 1988–89). These groups worked side by side, or occasionally also in competition with one another; together, however, they formed an alternative cultural infrastructure. Many painters and writers were involved with more than one magazine at a time, even working with those who had opposing conceptions of the public sphere. In Berlin at any rate there were many scenes operating, as it were, alongside one another, each one with its own language and vocabulary. The journal *Kontext*, a publication protected by the Protestant church, was something of an exception in Berlin, as it printed literary texts by Gabriele Stötzer-Kachold, Bert Papenfuß, Rainer Schedlinski and Detlef Opitz along with political essays by the civil rights activists Konrad Weiß, Uwe Bastian and Sebastian Pflugbeil.[12]

Gradually this scene began to find official outlets. Saxony's state library in Dresden began to acquire individual copies of literary magazines like *Entwerter/Oder, usw.* or *A3* from 1987 onwards. In conjunction with the prestigious Aufbau publishing house, Gerhard Wolf and Tilo Köhler brought out several volumes by selected 'underground poets' in a specially created series ambiguously titled 'Außer der Reihe' (Out of Turn; also Outside the Series). Rainer Schedlinski, Jan Faktor, Bert Papenfuß, Stefan Döring and Gabriele Kachold, among others, made their long-delayed official debuts in the GDR after the fall of the Berlin wall. The title of the inaugural volume of the series, *Dreizehntanz* (Thirteen Dance) by Bert Papenfuß, gestured sarcastically to the poet's endless attempts to be published officially. This process had gone on for thirteen years; the 'debutant' was now thirty-three years old, had published six volumes of poetry independently and had long been a recognized author in both East and West Germany. By the time Christoph Hein spoke openly about censorship at the Tenth Writers' Congress in 1987,[13] several small but distinct public spheres (*Teilöffentlichkeiten*) had existed side by side for a long time. The Academy of Arts, where, in 1980, Franz Fühmann had attempted – and failed – to present hitherto unpublished works by young writers, became host to the 'Werkstatt junge Kunst' (Workshop for Young Artists), where artists as different as Asteris Kutulas, the publisher of the journal *Bizarre Städte*, perforation performance artists 'Die Autoperforationsartisten', the independent theatre company *Zinnober* and the experimental band 'Expander des Fortschritts' (Expanders of Progress) shared a platform.[14]

As the pressures exerted on artistic production decreased, so attempts to suppress those intellectual and artistic scenes that were politically opposed to the state increased. Journals such as *Arche Nova, Aufrisse, Grenzfall, Oder, Umweltblätter* and *Kontext*, in particular, became targets. While there were fewer high-profile cases of outright prohibition towards the end of the 1980s, such as had been seen in 1984 with the Dresden-based magazine *UND* or in 1986 with Halle's *Galeere*, engaging with the countercultural sphere entailed intimidation and fear for many. Factors such as the uncertainty concerning the laws themselves, the long and precarious wait for permission to travel outside the country and family ties, often including, in contrast to those of a similar age in the west, children, all meant that the act of confronting the state was anything but a 'game' for most people.

Berlin naturally played a special role in this activity. It not only provided the location for countless covert creative hotspots but also acted as a meeting point between East and West Germany and as a thoroughfare for artists forced out of the GDR to the west. However, many observers found the subcultural initiatives outside Berlin more concentrated and more intense. In Erfurt, Karl-Marx-Stadt, Dresden, Leipzig, Rostock or Halle, contact between political intellectuals and so-called 'apolitical aesthetes' was closer, participants in the scene were more reliant on one another and a sense of mutual respect was more prevalent.

Although the texts published in the unofficial magazines reveal a tendency to differentiate between generations, they were more than simply a homogeneous expression of a single generation's culture. In the first place, this generation consisted of artists working with different aesthetic concepts at the same time. Werner Karma, Steffen Mensching and Hans-Eckhardt Wenzel, for example, worked with the musical theatre group *Karls Enkel*, which was formed in 1977. They created exciting programmes consisting of song and political cabaret, such as the 'DaDaeR' sketches, 'Hammer-Rehwü' (Hammer Revue) and 'Sichel-Operette' (Sickle Operetta). Their politically explosive nature as well as their artistic quality entailed that these acts were the equal of anything produced on the highly acclaimed art scene.[15] The fact that the group identified themselves as critical Marxists, however, meant that they were largely excluded by the scene and were not popular in the west. Nevertheless, to categorize them as members of the official GDR art scene, as those who had opted out of political engagement did, is to miss the point.

Secondly, as well as exploring heterogeneous aesthetic practices, artists of the independent scene were often mentored by more established GDR authors, such as Christa and Gerhard Wolf, Franz Fühmann, Karl Mickel, Heiner Müller and Volker Braun. They not only provided financial support but also offered some protection from attempts to criminalize their younger colleagues' activities. Adolf Endler and Elke Erb were to all intents and purposes a part of the scene, and texts by Heiner Müller, Heinz Czechowski and Wolfgang Hilbig appeared in the unofficial magazines. Even where the disjuncture between the aesthetic approaches of the different generations became apparent, it was nevertheless always accompanied by a genuine sense of personal solidarity. An example of the conscious demarcation between generations is the many references made by younger writers to Volker Braun as the representative of a different approach. A real mark of difference between the generations was the profound lack of interest felt by the younger writers in precisely the kind of historical philosophical thinking which motivated the dramas of writers such as Heiner Müller, Peter Hacks, Karl Mickel and, indeed, Volker Braun. A further difference can be found in the younger generation's concept of language as a phenomenon of the moment, leaving aside its historicity. This understanding, however, was not shared by all experimental poets on the scene.

Developments after 1990

After Wolf Biermann's acceptance speech at the Büchner Prize ceremony in November 1991, at which he effectively outed the guru of the unofficial scene, Sascha Anderson, as an unofficial informer for the secret police or 'IM' and debunked the credentials of the autonomous scene,[16] the political, anti-establishment scene took the place of its celebrated literary counterpart in the spotlight. The explicitly political satires of, for example, Lutz Rathenow or attempts to document subjects which had been hitherto taboo, such as neo-Nazism, pollution or sexual abuse, were now being compared favourably with what many viewed as hermetic language games on the part of the experimental authors. Those who claimed to have mistrusted the elitism present in the 'Prenzlauer Berg texts' from the beginning became more stridently critical.[17] The sober and self-critical manner in which many protagonists from within the scene took stock of what had happened there seemed indeed to support with these judgements. Even before 1989, Jan Faktor, Annette Simon, Leonhard Lorek and Detlef Opitz had noted the ignorance and exclusory tactics inherent in some conceptual elements of the scene. Gabriele Stötzer-Kachold had written off the whole scene as a male power game, and Uwe Kolbe had distanced himself from the gimmickry of what he dubbed the 'language activists'. None of this criticism had reached a wider public before, although it could be found in the unofficial magazines.[18] Older writers such as Adolf Endler and the painter A. R. Penck (the alias of the renowned artist Ralf Winkler) preserved instead an ironic distance. In 1987, Penck had already announced the 'end of the underground' in issue three of *Ariadnefabrik*, claiming that 'the illusion was shattered'.[19]

Between 1989 and 1990, however, there was an outpouring of long-stifled creativity; new small publishing houses and magazines mushroomed almost weekly; and public spaces became vibrant centres for the arts, as in the case of Cafe Kyril in Prenzlauer Berg. The exhibition 'Neue Ostberliner Verlage' (New East German Publishers) that took place in Berlin's public library in February 1991 featured an already impressive number of disparate types of publishing house, all of which had been established within a one-year period.[20]

Documentary projects which began to take stock of the situation in the 1990s furnished artists in the 'independent' publishing scene with both an identity and a tradition which stretched into the future as well as the past. 'Bohemian', 'dissident' and 'avant-garde' were some of the labels attached to them, as in the high-profile exhibition 'Boheme und Diktatur' (Bohemia

and Dictatorship) showing between September and December 1997 at the
Deutsches Historisches Museum in Berlin. The categories could even be
applied a decade later when the scene had fallen into ignominy – though
under different auspices. The photographic portraits of Döring, Lorek,
Papenfuß, Böthig, Kolbe and Zieger taken by Thomas Florschütz for
Schaden in 1986 originally seemed like police mugshots. The black-and-
white photographs captured hollow-cheeked and profoundly solemn grave
diggers, janitors and boilermen, in the act of writing.[21] Florschütz's use of
perspective and framing not only helped to reveal a daily life overshadowed
by spying, threats of imprisonment and expulsion from educational institutions but also made apparent to what extent this 'game' of autonomy was an
existential one for those involved. In 1997, however, when the portraits were
blown up and hung above the entrance to the museum's exhibition, they
underwent a strange transformation. Given that this was an artistic movement which had concerned itself with the power of the symbolic and of
propaganda, presenting these artists as heroes in this manner was in any case
problematic. Moreover, the exhibition's photographs did not attest to the
role that graphic artists, painters, bookbinders, photographers, potters and
fashion designers had played in shaping the tangible texture of the scene.
They also obscured the fact that it was predominantly women who provided
the driving force behind the atelier and salon culture, frequently having to
scrape the money together for stews and red wine while their male partners
celebrated the rejection of mundane daily life. Displayed under glass, even
the most preposterously tiny scrap of paper accrued the status of a historical
document. Signatures on the photographs, such as 'Communard', 'Squatter'
or 'Woodstock', provided contexts for the circle of people around the well-
respected dissident Robert Havemann and his children, for example, which
only served to confuse the uninitiated visitor. Contextualizing the polemical
and quasi-ironic vocabulary, a process essential for its understanding, has
only become possible after a number of attempts to reprocess and re-present
the work. Nevertheless an astonishing number of artistic careers originated
in this busy, collaborative environment. Being monitored by state security
forces was a constant factor: for example, a Stasi document dealing with
punks that had been sent to SED politburo member Egon Krenz among
others was also exhibited at the Deutsches Hisorisches Museum; its authors
even speak of 'degeneracy' (*Entartung*),[22] using vocabulary familiar from the
language of the Third Reich.

Many publishers and magazines established in 1989 were soon caught
off-guard by unexpected economic difficulties. The end of the GDR's
official press distribution agency, or *Postzeitungsvertrieb*, which coincided

with the German monetary union of 1991, already signalled the end for many. Setting up adequate accounting, distribution and advertising mechanisms became obstacles which the majority of the magazine and publishing projects could not overcome. The ambitious schemes of a small publisher like *Kontext*, or the magazine *Sondeur*, did not prove lucrative. The only money to be made, it seemed, was in publication of instructions and reports for the Ministry of State Security (by *BasisDruck*), and that only in the short term. Galrev, a project begun in 1991 combining a publishing house, printing press and cafe, initially blossomed, selling exclusive small print runs of signed poetry volumes, affordable editions of poetry and art work, bilingual anthologies, a series of poetological works, postcards, records and CDs. However, the revelation that the company's co-director, Sascha Anderson, had been involved with the Stasi raised questions about the financial resources which had been used to establish the ambitious publishing project. Authors who did not leave Galrev after this episode, such as Bert Papenfuß, Ulrich Zieger and Andreas Koziol, paid a high price: their works were no longer reviewed in the biggest daily newspapers.

The fate of *Sklaven*, founded in 1994, can serve as an example of that of many of the contemporaneous small magazines of the period. Adopting Franz Jung's 1927 title made the left-wing anarchist agenda of the publication clear. The simple paper and binding and its text-heavy layout in small print provocatively presupposed an interest in the written contents. Black-and-white copy combined with a few poorly printed illustrations embodied the publishers' purist approach. Philosophical texts offering critiques of capitalism, essays, prose pieces dealing with everyday life and occasional poems worked together to create an overall concept, which was revealed even in the distinctive two-line excerpts on the title page. Like many of the magazine projects of this period, *Sklaven* was remarkable for its social dimension and thus followed in the footsteps of its unofficial predecessors. The Torpedokäfer pub, in an area of Prenzlauer Berg then untouched by developers, became the venue for readings, debates and, in November and December 1993, the spectacular 'Knochengeldexperiment' (Bone-Money Experiment).[23] Fifty-four artists designed and signed one hundred counterfeit notes which were thereafter accepted as valid currency in twenty-three local shops and pubs for a period of seven weeks. This initiative prompted a discussion of the function and history of money and, as a result, went right to the heart of the difficulties inherent in adapting to post-unification German-German relations. But the *Sklaven* project also came to an end in the 1990s.

Bert Papenfuß, one of its instigators, went on to establish what was at first another hub of subcultural activity. The club and bar Kaffee Burger in Torstraße became notorious as the venue for series of events such as 'Verbrecherversammlung' (Criminal Gathering) and 'Russische Zelle' (Russian Cell); it also offered the group of writers 'Reformbühne Heim und Welt' from the neighbouring Volksbühne theatre an alternative platform. The categories of east and west were supposed to fade into the background, even if an unequal dynamic did remain apparent: the former Eastern bloc provided both model and blueprint for an ironic performance style. The success story of Kaffee Burger transformed the scene's previously subcultural nature, for soon the infamous retro 'Russendisko' (Russian Disco) was appearing in every travel guide and would also provide the title of the novelist and journalist Vladimir Kaminer's breakthrough satirical bestseller.[24] As a result, it is no longer possible for the cafe's successor, Rumbalotte, to connect with earlier traditions.

A final example is the book-art project *Entwerter/Oder* – whose title is a play on 'entwerten' (to devalue or validate) and the phrase 'entweder oder' (either or) – by Uwe Warnke, which continues to be both prized by collectors and financially successful. Various forms of visual poetry, original graphic art, collages and sketches have been appearing in this publication since 1982. The editions are published in-house and combine roller-grid effects, linoleum cuts, etching and other techniques with experimental texts and expensive, one-off productions. These are sold via an established, well-maintained network of wealthy book-art collectors. Of all the strategies employed by post-1989 publishers and magazines following in the tradition of the once unofficial art and literature scene, this combination of aesthetic exclusivity and commercialization has proven to be the only one conducive to survival.

Conclusion

The 2009 Berlin exhibition revealed to what extent a certain paradox persisted even twenty years later: while the protagonists of the independent art scene insisted on the heterogeneous nature of their motives and poetic concepts, their insistence was attended by a still palpable need to belong to a group. The covert culture explored in the inner courtyards of the run-down East German housing stock had been forced to stand in for the outside world for a long time. But it appeared, after 1990 when they had access to it, as if very few of the artists involved actually preferred the real outside world to the familiar comforts of their neighbourhood scene.

The poet Bert Papenfuß, born in 1956, looked back in the first-person plural at what he called 'Entliebung' ('Loved-out'): 'We didn't feel like we owed the whole workers-and-farmers business anything. We grew up with the disappointment that preceded the "training to walk upright", and had as much fun as we possibly could'.[25] His contemporary, Andreas Koziol, employs laconic accumulation in two related poems to gesture ironically towards the idea of commonality in difference. In 'addition der differenzen' (adding up the differences), written in 1984 and revised slightly in 1989, a litany of contrasting, if not opposing, themes and patterns employed by artists in the scene unfolds. The layering is kept intentionally casual, with no long goodbye:

> einer versteht seine worte als zeugen
> einer als landesweit offenes grab
> einer als mittel sich drüberzubeugen
> einer verläßt gegen Mittag die stadt

(one sees his words as witnesses / one as a nationwide open grave / one sees a way of buckling down / one leaves the city around midday)[26]

Those in the know recognize immediately that here 'leaving the city' signifies more than just moving from one city to another. It connotes a move from one state to another, from one society to another diametrically opposed to it. The shocking nature of this line originates in the sense that a decision as monumental as this is so common as to be hardly worth mentioning. Monotonous syntax and the uniformity of reference to the impersonal pronoun 'einer' (one) replicate structurally the theme of the poem: the individual artists are disconnected, yet work side by side; they do not seek to establish connections with one another, although they are indeed connected by their struggle for self-discovery, self-expression and orientation.

Koziol refers back to this poem again in 1993 with his poem 'Tradition der Differenzen' (The Tradition of Differences). At this point he argues that the only thing still uniting this group of individualists is their explicit insistence on difference, contradictions and heterogeneity. It was therefore no accident that the curators of the 2009 exhibition selected these two poems by Koziol to be printed in full on the cover of the exhibition catalogue. In doing so they traced an arc between independent artists' early years, when they were working under the excessive pressures imposed by a closed and 'comprehensively controlled' (*durchherrscht*) society,[27] and their artistic maturity, which was influenced by post-unification pluralism. It *is* possible to find a concrete referent for every laconically presented

protagonist in the poem; more useful, however, is to take the simultaneously alienating and mournfully monotonous tone seriously. It is here
that the round dance performed by the poem's protagonists (who are still
called 'Einer'/'One', but at least now with a capital letter) is held up to
scrutiny:

> Einer geht rückwärts, merkwürdig aufrecht,
> Einer hob ab, doch er hatte kein Glück,
> Einer kommt vorwärts, wirkt aber unecht,
> Einer fällt hinter die Einheit zurück,
> [. . .]
> Einen hat selbst die Erinnrung verlassen,
> Einer, den glatt sein Gedächtnis erschlug,
> Einer ist nicht mehr mit Worten zu fassen,
> Einer ist still jetzt. Sonst geht es ihm gut.

(One goes backwards, head held strangely upright, / One has taken off, yet
still had no luck, / One's getting on, but seems somehow fake / One's falling
back behind this united front, / [. . .] / One has even been left by remembrance, / One, well, his memory beat him into line, / One can no longer be
captured in utterance, / One is quiet now. Otherwise, he's fine.)[28]

While the earlier character sketches enumerate forms of revolt, even in the
face of failure, the later ones resonate with resigned observation. One
character is 'still' on the street, another doesn't want to talk to anyone
'anymore'. Evaluative time adverbs, simple past, perfect, imperfect and
iterative constructions now dominate. It is not significant that one of them
is quiet, but rather that he is quiet 'now' (i.e. was not always so). The final
line intensifies the poem's conclusion: although the litany ends on a
positive note in formal terms, the particle 'otherwise' (sonst) sounds a
tragic chord. It describes the difference between an existence free from
catastrophe and a state of fulfilment and happiness – and the negation is a
distant reminder of the claim made in the final sentence of Georg
Büchner's *Lenz*: 'Und so lebte er hin' (And so he lived on).

Many former literary colleagues have been ignored in the process of
individuation characteristic of the bourgeois literary scene. In 2009 I
supervised a group of students from Berlin's Humboldt University while
they prepared bibliographies for the Berlin exhibition. Their research
yielded contradictory results: out of the approximately eighty authors
selected from the scene, only a handful had gained recognition in the
post-unification literary market. If literary prizes and publication by
esteemed publishing houses connote the criteria for recognition, then
Adolf Endler, Elke Erb, Jan Faktor, Annett Gröschner, Durs Grünbein,

Wolfgang Hilbig, Barbara Honigmann, Johannes Jansen, Barbara Köhler, Uwe Kolbe, Katja Lange-Müller, Gert Neumann, Lutz Rathenow and Peter Wawerzinek have doubtless achieved this. Grünbein und Hilbig even received the renowned Georg Büchner Prize in 1995 and 2002, respectively. However, such facts and figures say less about literary quality than is perhaps thought: the works of Andreas Koziol, Ulrich Zieger, Detlef Opitz or Bert Papenfuß do not receive anywhere near as much attention as they deserve. The reasons for this are multiple and varied – ranging from unhappy relationships with publishers to avant-garde poetics and anti-capitalist attitudes, which prove incompatible with literary marketing. Even if they have not become freelance authors, many of those formerly involved with the literary scene have opted for careers, related to the cultural industries: they are journalists, run literary centres, teach at universities or work in academies, archives and libraries. Those who were predominantly active in graphic art, photography or bookbinding are still occupied in those areas today. The artists from the scene have become musicians, or work in theatre and film, but they also run pubs or hotels. Some editors have become collectors and museum curators. Many of them paid for their excessive, boundary-breaking lifestyles with their lives: Frank Lanzendörfer, Peter Brasch, Gino Hahnemann, Matthias Holst and Michael Rom all died young.[29]

For a long time, categorizing authors as participants in the 'independent East-German literary scene' was a contributing factor towards the canonization of their works, regardless of objections by the authors themselves. Two decades after the fall of the Berlin Wall, this cultural capital has been exhausted; now every new book stands or falls in the literary market on its own merits. Nevertheless, there still exists substantial interest in this historical countercultural phenomenon; the Berlin exhibition was toured to Rheinsberg, Jena, Greifswald, New York, Neustrelitz and Basel.[30] University courses on the subject are still always full. However, what seems to be most important to young people today is not so much the texts and art works themselves, but having access to a group of artists whose work was, as they might say, 'about something', where a personal language became a necessary tool in talking back to dominant institutions. Engaging critically with the art and literature of that period is problematic due to the difficulties involved in gaining access to primary sources; original copies of the small magazines and editions of poetry and graphic art have disappeared into the drawers and display cabinets of collectors. Falling back on the publications by individual authors entails taking their work out of the very context in question; extricating the texts from their dialogue with illustrations and the bibliophilic context in which they emerged has the same effect. Facsimile editions are also difficult to acquire. Walter Schmitz's efforts in collaboration with the Sächsische Landesbibliothek to digitalize the artists' magazines and books have proved invaluable.[31]

The label 'underground' suits the independent literary scene in the GDR to a lesser extent than those in other socialist countries. Czech, Russian, Polish or Hungarian *samizdat* literature was much more politically radical, and their political and literary scenes were more closely linked. Opponents of the GDR system were furthermore the only ones who could leave for West Germany without having to abandon their native language. This was, of course, a factor of the upmost significance for writers, in particular. With this in mind, the history of unofficial GDR literature cannot be written without also taking into consideration the West German public sphere and the opportunities which existed to publish works there. 'The Underground Literature of the GDR' is therefore also a German-German phenomenon.

Notes

1. Compare, for example, Heimo Schwilk, 'Gegen den Strich. "Die andere" Literatur der DDR', *Die politische Meinung*, 241 (1988), 23–28; Ulf Christian Hasenfelder, '"Kwehrdeutsch". Die dritte Literatur in der DDR', *NdL*, 1 (1991), 82–93; Birgit Dahlke, *Papierboot. Autorinnen aus der DDR – inoffiziell publiziert* (Würzburg: Königshausen & Neumann, 1997), pp. 19–26.
2. Compare Dieter Kraft, *Traumhaft. Theater Zinnober. Improvisationen, Spiele, Protokolle* (Berlin, Weimar: Aufbau, 1991); Karin Fritzsche and Claus Löser (eds.), *Gegenbilder. Filmische Subversion in der DDR 1976–1989. Texte Bilder Daten* (Berlin: Janus Press, 1996); Ronald Galenza and Heinz Havemeister (eds.), *Wir wollen immer artig sein. Punk, New Wave, Hiphop, Independent-Szene in der DDR 1980–1990* (Berlin: Schwartzkopf & Schwartzkopf, 1999).
3. Stefan Döring, Bert Papenfuß and Jan Faktor, 'Zoro in Skorne', reprinted in Klaus Michael and Thomas Wohlfahrt (eds.), *Vogel oder Käfig Sein: Kunst und Literatur aus unabhängigen Zeitschriften in der DDR 1979–1989* (Berlin: Galrev, 1992), pp. 14–25.
4. In German: 'Unkontrollierbarkeit', 'Zügellosigkeit', 'temporäre autonome Zone'. See also Bert Papenfuß in discussion with Birgit Dahlke on 3 December 1991. Published in *Deutsche Bücher*, 1 (1991), 3–17; p. 6.
5. Bernd Wagner, 'Tod der Intelligenz. Das Jahrzehnt nach der Biermannausbürgerung', in Wagner, *Der Griff ins Leere. Elf Versuche* (Berlin: Transit, 1988), pp. 110–24; p. 114.
6. Jan Faktor, 'Intellektuelle Opposition und alternative Kultur in der DDR', 'Aus Politik und Zeitgeschichte', supplement in *Das Parlament*, 10 (1994), 30–37; Uwe Kolbe, 'Die Heimat des Dissidenten. Nachbemerkungen

zum Phantom der DDR-Opposition', *Freitag,* 40 (1991), p. 20; Detlef Opitz, 'Die Fremdheit des Beobachters. Eine Erwiderung auf Uwe Kolbes Kritik an der DDR-Opposition im Freitag Nr. 40', *Freitag,* 41 (1991), p. 17; Kurt Drawert, 'Sie schweigen. Oder sie lügen. Von der Beschaffenheit einer gescheiterten Elite', in Peter Böthig and Klaus Michael (eds.), *MachtSpiele. Literatur und Staatssicherheit im Fokus Prenzlauer Berg* (Leipzig: Reclam, 1993), pp. 74–82.

7. Dahlke, Papierboot, pp. 26–35 and pp. 42–51.
8. Compare chapter by Gerrit-Jan Berendse in this volume.
9. Compare Lutz Wohlrab, 'Mail-Artisten am Prenzlauer Berg', in Uwe Warnke and Ingeborg Quaas (eds.), *Die Addition der Differenzen. Die Literaten- und Künstlerszene Ostberlins 1979 bis 1989* (Berlin: Verbrecher Verlag, 2009), pp. 222–27; Claudia Petzold and Paul Kaiser, 'Mysterien des Postwegs. Frankierte Kommunikation: Eine Mail Art-Gruppe sorgte Anfang der 80er Jahre in Dresden für Furore – bis die Staatssicherheit ein Exempel statuierte', in Kaiser and Petzold (eds.), *Boheme und Diktatur in der DDR. Gruppen Konflikte Quartiere 1970–1989.* Catalogue to the Museum of German History's exhibition between 4 September and 16 December 1997 (Berlin: Fannei & Walz, 1997), pp. 183–90.
10. Barbara Köhler, *Deutsches Roulette. Gedichte 1984–1989* (Frankfurt/M.: Suhrkamp, 1991), p. 63.
11. *Bizarre Städte,* 2 (1988). Compare also Peter Wawerzinek, *Das Kind, das ich war. Mein Babylon* (Frankfurt/M.: Fischer, 1997), pp. 133–224.
12. Available in Torsten Metelka (ed.), *'Alles ist im Untergrund obenauf, einmann-frei . . . ': Ausgewählte Beiträge aus der Zeitschrift Kontext 1–7* (Berlin: Edition Kontext, 1990), pp. 18–31, pp. 108–14, pp. 115–34. The film director and publicist Konrad Weiß was one of the first to broach the issue of neo-Nazism among young people in the GDR and also to sign up to the campaign 'Democracy Now' in September 1989; Uwe Bastian wrote about alternative sources of energy provision; the physicist Sebastian Pflugbeil was a critic of the GDR's nuclear energy policy and was a co-founder of Neues Forum (New Forum) in 1989. Compare Erhart Neubert, *Geschichte der DDR-Opposition* (Bonn: Bundeszentrale für politische Bildung, 1997).
13. Schriftstellerverband der DDR (ed.), *X. Schriftstellerkongress der DDR 24.–26. November 1987. Arbeitsgruppen* (Berlin and Weimar: Aufbau, 1988), pp. 224–47 (pp. 228–31).
14. *Werkstatt junge Kunst 1988. Arbeitsmaterial der Akademie der Künste* (Berlin: Akademie der Künste der DDR, 1989).
15. Compare, for example, Steffen Mensching, Hans-Eckardt Wenzel, *Allerletztes aus der DaDaeR. Hundekomödie* (Leipzig: Mitteldeutscher Verlag, 1991); David Robb, *Zwei Clowns im Lande des verlorenen Lachens. Das Liedertheater Wenzel & Mensching* (Berlin: Links, 1998).
16. Wolf Biermann, 'Der Lichblick im grässlichen Fatalismus der Geschichte', Büchner Prize Speech, in Biermann, *Der Sturz des Dädalus oder Eizes für die Eingeborenen der Fidschi-Inseln. Über den IM Judas Ischariot und den*

Kuddelmuddel in Deutschland seit dem Golfkrieg (Cologne: Kiepenheuer & Witsch, 1992), pp. 48–64.

17. Iris Radisch, 'Dichter in Halbtrauer. Junge Autoren nach dem Ende der DDR', *Die Zeit*, 4 June (1993), p. 11; Dirk von Petersdorf, 'Was ist an Kitzbühel so schlimm? Junge Lyrik. Fünf Porträts, ein Essay, ein Gedicht', *Neue Rundschau*, 3 (1993), p. 93.

18. Compare Jan Faktor and Annette Simon in *Ariadnefabrik*, 4 (1987). The text was not published in Andreas Koziol and Rainer Schedlinski (eds.), *Abriss der Ariadnefabrik* (Berlin: Galrev, 1990), but, instead, Faktor's acutely critical retrospective appeared in Böthig and Michael (eds.), *MachtSpiele*, pp. 91–111. See also Leonhard Lorek in *Schaden*, 9 (1986) and later *Machtspiele*, pp. 112–25; Kolbe in *Bizarre Städte*, Sonderheft, 1 (1989) and intensified in *Machtspiele*, pp. 84–90 or Kachold in *Kontext*, 5 (1989). Kachold's critique is reprinted in Torsten Metelka (ed.), *Alles ist im Untergrund obenauf; einmannfrei*, pp. 64–72 and (an edited version) in *MachtSpiele*, pp. 129–37.

19. A. R. Penck, 'Das Ende des Untergrunds', in Koziol and Schedlinski (eds.), *Abriss der Ariadnefabrik*, pp. 57–78 (p. 57).

20. For example: Katzengraben-Presse, Construktiv, Bonsai-Typart, Linksdruck, Galrev, BasisDruck, das Autorenkollegium, die Unabhängige Verlagsbuchhandlung Ackerstraße, Kontext, Corvinus-Presse, Thomas-Müller-Verlag, Warnke & Maas, Fischerinsel-Edition.

21. Reproduced in Kaiser and Petzold (eds.), *Boheme und Diktatur in der DDR*, pp. 72–73.

22. The adjective 'degenerate' (*entartet*) is familiar from the National Socialists' use of it to denounce tendencies in modern art, music and literature as un-German, for example, Expressionism or Dadaism.

23. 'Knochengeld-Experiment' was an ambitious, satirical art action initiated in Prenzlauer Berg by the o zwei gallery and the group oë Bsaffot (Bert Papenfuß, Wolfgang Krause, Nils Chlupka, G. P. Adan). The alternative currency (a single note was worth twenty DM) lost five per cent of its value per week if unused. Compare the website of the gallery www.ozwei.net/knochengeld/ or Christoph Tannert, Knochengeld', in Kathleen Krenzlin (ed.), *Wochenmarkt und Knochengeld* (Berlin: Lukas, 2006) pp. 122–23.

24. Vladimir Kaminer, *Russendisko* (Munich: Goldmann, 2000).

25. Bert Papenfuß, 'Entliebung', in Warnke and Quaas (eds.), *Die Addition der Differenzen*, p. 15. The quotation 'Training des aufrechten Gangs' (Training to walk upright) alludes to the title of Volker Braun's 1976 volume of poetry and beyond that to Ernst Bloch.

26. Andreas Koziol, *mehr über rauten und türme* (Berlin: Aufbau, 1991), p. 48.

27. The term was coined by the historian of everyday life Alf Lüdtke and was taken up by the contemporary historian Jürgen Kocka to characterize GDR society. See Alf Lüdtke, in Hartmut Kaelble, Jürgen Kocka, Hartmut Zwahr (eds.), *Sozialgeschichte der DDR* (Stuttgart: Klett-Cotta, 1994), p. 188; and Jürgen Kocka, in ibid., p. 547.

28. Andreas Koziol, *Sammlung* (Berlin: Edition qwertzuiopü, 1996), p. 29.

29. Compare the bio-bibliographies in Warnke and Quaas (eds.), *Die Addition der Differenzen*, pp. 306–18.
30. Compare also the 2010 exhibition 'Ohne uns! 8060 Dresden/7050 Leipzig/ 9040 Karl-Marx-Stadt. Nonkonforme Kunst und alternative Kultur in Sachsen vor 1989' (www.ohne-uns-dresden.de) organized in Dresden by Paul Kaiser and Frank Eckhardt.
31. Searching for the term 'Künstlerzeitschriften'/ 'artists' magazines' at the following addresses at least gives an impression of the editions: www.deutsche fotothek.de or www.slub-dresden.de/sammlungen/deutsche-fotothek.

CHAPTER 10

Tinker, tailor, writer, spy
GDR literature and the Stasi

Alison Lewis

Reconsidering the impact of the Stasi twenty-five years on from the scanda-lous revelations of widespread collaboration with the secret police among East Germany's writers calls for some careful rethinking of a number of aspects of the relationship between history and literature, fiction and non-fiction as well as culture and power. New interdisciplinary perspectives on the GDR and the Stasi in particular can be of assistance here as well as methods adapted from cognate fields such as trauma studies, autobiography and narratology. This is not to diminish the importance of those initial shocks after the fall of the Wall about the extent to which writers, even those in the underground, had collaborated with the Stasi, but rather to seek to arrive at a more sober assessment of the complex and fraught relationship between the Stasi and literature. Recent research has contributed to this, by shifting the focus away from a concern with totalitarianism to an engage-ment with society and the daily intersubjective exercise of power. More nuanced terms such as 'the dictatorship as safe-haven' (Wolle), a 'welfare dictatorship' (Jarausch) and a 'participatory dictatorship' (Fulbrook) are representative of this new approach to writing GDR history, which in turn has led to a more differentiated interpretation of the workings of the Stasi.[1] The Stasi is seen less as an all-powerful, omnipresent 'state in a state', as was the custom in the early 1990s, than as a 'nerve system and brain centre' within the communist body politic.[2] If conceived as an integral part of the state's functioning, the Stasi becomes a permanent and distinctive feature of GDR society without being elevated to the dominant force within the social structure. It has now become evident that the Stasi's system of surveillance was not able to function without deep penetration into the social body – into professional organizations as well as informal networks of friends and family – and without a range of largely secret 'technologies of power' that defined and divided loyal citizens from dissenters.

In the early 1990s Wolfgang Emmerich argued persuasively for the need for a paradigm shift in GDR studies, in which texts were evaluated less as political statements than in terms of their literariness, textuality and aesthetic value.[3] This literary turn is now well established and recent research continues to exploit an expanding array of theoretical approaches – from psychoanalysis, social theory or systems theory to the sociology of culture. Of particular relevance here are approaches that seek to adapt Pierre Bourdieu's sociology of culture to cultural production. By reconfiguring literature as a heteronomous cultural field which intersected on virtually every level with the field of power, it is possible not only to reconceptualize the literary field as a 'dynamic site of struggle' but also to reconceive writers in terms of 'social agents'.[4] As agents they operated in the complementary and frequently antagonistic fields of literature and power, often competing with one another 'to secure and exchange capital in its various forms'.[5] If writers can be thought of as possessing value in terms of capital, it follows that this capital can be used as currency: it can, for instance, be accumulated, invested, reinvested or lost, as the case may be, in their struggles with power. These insights can be helpful for analysing the impact unification has had on writers in terms of their literary capital. Writers experienced massive changes to their social capital (i.e. their social networks),[6] their cultural capital (in the cultural caché of their ideas)[7] and their symbolic capital (in their status and prestige),[8] all of which affected the ways they broached the topic of the Stasi.

This approach to writers and their works can be usefully brought to bear on post-1989 writing by those writers born and socialized in the GDR. Many established writers of the formative and middle generations lost their previous positions of privilege (symbolic capital) in the restructuring of the literary field after 1990 during which literature lost its constitutive connections to the field of politics and power. Writers had to renegotiate their position with publishers, win back old readers and find new ones. One of the more successful ways in which GDR writers have maintained their standing has been through the marketing of their lives. Not only have publishers like Aufbau rediscovered the lives of forgotten writers; they have also discovered a healthy appetite for autobiographical works of living writers. Indeed, it seems as if today the lives of GDR writers are of greater interest than their fictional works. Or, rather, the GDR writer is valued most of all as a writer of his or her own life. The collapse of the GDR has had the curious effect of creating empty spaces for writers to fill, not with their fiction, but with life-writing. This shift has seen the writer of the GDR transformed from a public institution into an eyewitness of history.

East German life-writing published after 1989 arguably belongs to the type of writing Thomas Anz calls 'literary autobiographics'.[9] According to Anz, it can often be difficult to draw strict boundaries between a writer's autobiographical writing and his or her fictional works. When literature is largely autobiographical, and letters and diary writing are about the creative process, both fiction and non-fiction could be seen as belonging to the same overarching genre of 'literary autobiographics'.[10] Anz's categorization makes it possible to read non-fictional, referential forms of writing such as diaries and letters less as explanations or documentary evidence of a writer's fiction than as parallel textual media, or as literature in their own right. Life-writing becomes a medium of intense self-expression and self-reflection that thematizes the life of the self, as it writes it. As Leigh Gilmore argues, the authors of autobiographies 'weave testimonial texts from disparate discourses'.[11] While genres such as biographies, memoirs, letter-writing and diaries are referential genres that refer to real people, real times and real places, they are also genres which are mediated through language and can benefit from 'tropological' readings that are sensitive to the figurative use of language.[12]

In most autobiographical writing the topic of the Stasi is a central pre-occupation, although writers' approach to the Stasi files varies enormously. Victims of the regime are, for instance, happy to consult and quote from Stasi sources, and in some cases, the file performs the dominant role of structuring the autobiographical narrative. For those writers accused of collaborating, however, the topic of the Stasi and the archive of the files are far more problematic. Before presenting a few representative examples along the victim–perpetrator spectrum of Stasi narratives, some clarification of the nature of the Stasi archive is necessary.

Today there is general agreement that the Stasi files represent a unique resource and an immensely rich source of information about the surveillance practices of a defunct secret service and a defunct society. Not only are the Stasi files an extremely detailed archive of what was one of the most extensive and highly organized secret police outfits of the modern era, they also archive social practices and mentalities that made up the peculiar kind of dictatorship that was the GDR. The files are for that reason a rather special kind of archive: an archive of secrets which is also an archive of the secret life of the population. In particular, they are material evidence of the social practices of policing and informing but also of resistance and civil courage. The Stasi archive is by no means the only or the entire archive of the GDR past – its rich body of literature and theatre is surely another infinite archive of the past – but it is a crucial component of the overall anatomy of the dictatorship of the GDR. With the opening of the Stasi Behörde (Stasi Archives) in 1992, however, the archive of the files has emerged as a privileged archive of the past, moving out of the shadows into the light of public scrutiny. Many of its secrets have been exposed and demystified, and what was previously covert or secret – such as the wholesale surveillance and control of cultural production – made public. With the setting up of a government agency to regulate and oversee access to the files, the burden of proof for a writer's relationship to the communist regime has shifted from the individual to the files. This has meant that denials of involvement with the Stasi, which were taken at face value in 1991, were rapidly superseded by hard facts in the evidence of the files. The truth became encapsulated in the informer's file, as Iris Radisch famously argued in desperation at the chronic lying of Sascha Anderson before his file was known: 'The truth is a file.'[13] Since that time the files have become invested with the authority that Jacques Derrida says is always located in the archive, or the *arkhē*, as both the origin and the home or place of the law.[14] On the border between the public and the private, the authoritarian past and the democratic present, the Stasi files are the sorts of secrets that 'make you tremble'.[15] They arouse fear when their contents are not known and fear when they are, lest the trauma they represented is repeated.[16] With the opening of the files the dominant scene of reconciliation in Germany has become not a public spectacle, as we see with the South African Truth and Reconciliation Commission, but instead an introspective, private 'scene of writing and reading'.[17]

This is not to say that the files are not, like any text, susceptible to misinterpretation. As Barbara Miller has argued, they have the potential to 'dispel and to create myths' about the past.[18] Their usefulness depends therefore on the purposes for which they are deployed, the contexts in which they are used and their discursive framing. While the contexts of writing and reading the files differ enormously today from communist times, it can be useful to talk of the files, both past and present, as belonging to a particular genre, or cluster of genres, of writing. The modern secret police file, as developed by communist regimes of Europe in the Soviet model, is, as Cristina Vatulescu argues, similar to a detective narrative.[19] There is one major difference, however, in that the file is less concerned with solving a crime than with profiling the suspect. There is no real riddle to be solved; instead the secret police file is concerned with compiling 'arresting biographies' to be used in the eventuality of an arrest. The detective stories in the Stasi files were above all bureaucratic tales produced and deployed for purely political purposes. In this respect the files acted as 'technologies of power' designed to discipline, punish and prevent politically undesirable behaviours. As key components of the security Panopticon that the Stasi instituted for population surveillance, the files also served as 'technologies of loyalty' for inculcating self-discipline in those loyal subjects the Stasi enlisted as officers in its ministry or as informers (IMs).

In the spheres of literature, the Stasi was especially vigilant, even setting up a separate operative unit in 1976 for the surveillance of intellectuals called the Special Branch XX/OG (*Hauptabteilung XX/Operativgruppe*). The ratification of bilateral as well as international exchange treaties meant that the regime needed a new and more subtle approach to the problem of growing internal dissent.[20] This entailed recruiting increasing numbers of undercover agents who could plausibly infiltrate 'enemy bases' and prevent the spread of 'political-ideological diversion', which might otherwise lead to the establishment of a political underground.[21] By the late 1970s most of the nation's officially unionized writers were either under some sort of surveillance or, alternatively – and this occurred far less frequently – had been enlisted as recruits themselves. In 1980 the elite unit ran high-level operations on 36 writers, employing 21 full-time officers and 108 informants.[22]

In the policing of culture the Stasi produced two basic types of files: files on individuals called 'person-related files' (*Personalbezogene Akten*) and files on groups, trends or movements called *Sachbezogene Akten*. The files on people represent a peculiar hybrid form of writing, made up of many different intersecting and complementary genres, usually with one main organizing author – typically the case officer (*Führungsoffizier*) – and many sub-authors in the various informants recruited to work in the field. The files also follow a specific format, consisting in the main of reports (*Treffberichte*) filled out during or after meetings and assessments of the overall operation and action plans (*Maßnahmepläne*). Both the officers' sections and the informers' reports have a rather specific structure of address, involving asymmetrical communications or conversations between a sub-ordinate and a superior. For instance, the framing files by the case officers are addressed to their superiors further up the line, and the informer reports embedded in the meeting reports are addressed directly to the case officers. As conversations, the writing employs different modalities and forms of reporting: some are records of real conversations (held in safe houses) and others are conversations at a distance (much like letter writing) that are written up prior to actual meetings.

The Stasi files constituted, or so the Stasi thought at the time, permanent or even absolute secrets, rather than conditional ones, which could be disclosed under certain circumstances. The knowledge in the files could wield immense power; it could empower writers and commissioning officers and could be used against victims in law courts. Of course, when the time was not deemed opportune for an arrest, the files were often left to languish in the archives, while the secret business of collection, documentation and accumulation often continued unabated. In these cases, the files reverted to being what they in essence always were: bad forms of writing, coarse character profiles, repetitive works of denunciation, trivial pieces of gossip, unfounded speculation and generally inadmissible acts of hearsay.

Today the files are rich evidence of collusion and collaboration. They document, moreover, the many varied reasons for working as an informer. The conscious motives could range from coercion and blackmail to loyalty and idealism whereas the unconscious motives could vary from an urge to compensate for loss or lack, to social envy and the desire for revenge.[23] Collaboration with the Stasi often imparted informers with a sense of performing a useful social service, especially those who were motivated by idealism.[24] Particularly for long-term collaborators the act of writing state secrets bestowed upon the author covert social and symbolic capital and secret prestige and status. For many informants, who were willing participants, the files were writing exercises in subservience, proof of ideological conformity but also of the desire to please authority.

With the political rupture of 1989 the files have thankfully been divested of their previous power. Removed from their secret settings, the files could be considered to have reverted to being mere texts or historical artefacts. However, some claim they are now no less innocent than before, and it should be noted that the exposure of their contents has not been without controversy. For many, their outing as informers has been painful and even traumatic. Many have been shocked by the hostile response from the media and feel unfairly treated or victimized. Some are plagued by feelings of guilt, while others have no sense of wrongdoing.[25] For the victims, too, the opening of the files after 1992 has not always been a blessing. Although access to the files is highly regulated, the files are now more or less free to circulate in the public sphere. In the new democratic fields in which they circulate, in the fields of economics, literature, history and the law, they are now read for new purposes – for reconciliation, restorative justice and personal healing. They are being reclaimed, reappropriated and rewritten by the victims.

Whether as incriminating or exonerating evidence, the files quickly took their place at the centre of testimonial writing about the Stasi, offering a unique opportunity to 'recreate the biography of a lost state'.[26] In one of its earliest official publications, the Stasi Archive (BStU) endorses the reading of files by victims in terms of 're-appropriation of one's biography'.[27] The Archive argues that access to the files is vital for healing and achieving justice, but it cautions against applicants having too high expectations from viewing the files.[28] In line with this official description, I have suggested that it can be useful to read the files on suspects, in particular the sections dedicated to profiling the suspect, as 'hostile, unauthorized biography'. These biographies were written by an unsympathetic author from an external perspective, or to be more precise, they were written by a series of hostile authors with similar negative views on their suspect.[29] If we consider the files as referential texts which complement texts such as life-writing, rather than only as source texts or explanatory documents, their inclusion in authors' autobiographies and memoirs presents us with an intriguing set of conundrums.

If the circumstances in which the files were produced were so inimical to artistic expression, how can these hostile biographies be useful for victims' testimony? Can they be translated into a new and less violent language – for instance, the language of the self in memory – and incorporated into new textual entities such as autobiographies or are they destined to remain inimical to all 'fictions of the self'?[30] Is it possible to recuperate the stories in the files and reinscribe them as less sinister alternative biographies? And finally, can the files be of use in restoring writers' damaged cultural and symbolic capital in post-authoritarian contexts?

In the afterlife of the Stasi file, the exposed Stasi secret is no less troubling. For victims, reading the revelations contained in the files can be a deeply empowering and therapeutic experience, although their toxicity still lingers on.[31] By the same token, it is easy to see how, once divulged, confessed or exposed, the Stasi secret can also be a source of shame and humiliation. This is the case for many writers who have discovered they have a perpetrator file.

At one extreme of the spectrum of non-fiction about the Stasi is Reiner Kunze's hybrid work *Deckname 'Lyrik'* (Code Name 'Poetry') named after the Stasi's surveillance operation (*Operativer Vorgang*) on him.[32] Although subtitled a documentation, and consisting virtually entirely of a selection from the 3,491 pages of the twelve volumes of his Stasi file, Kunze's work is patently much more than just a documentation. It tells in extremely economical fashion the powerful story of the Stasi's nine-year-long campaign against the poet. In this David and Goliath narrative, Kunze was first subjected to low-level Stasi security checks during the Prague Spring of 1968 and later to a full-scale security operation, following the publication of so-called 'antisocialist works'. The operation aimed at convicting Kunze of incitement to subversion and defamatory statements against the state. Not only was the Stasi intent on compiling an 'arresting biography' against him; it also devised proactive measures – which it called 'liquidation' or 'corrosion' (*zersetzen*) – to destroy his circle of influence. By the end of 1976 Kunze was identified alongside Wolf Biermann and Robert Havemann as one of the three main internal threats to national security.[33]

Kunze's documentation is also a powerful form of testimony, although it substitutes the personal 'I' of autobiography with a third-person narrative in which the author is the main protagonist. Throughout, Kunze leaves the third-person narrative form of the Stasi file, which refers to him mostly as 'Kunze' or even as 'Deckname Lyrik', unchanged. The authorial 'I' is replaced by the multiple 'Is' of the informers and officers writing the reports. Although Kunze only reveals the identity of one of his informers, it is obvious that his main intention is to hold up these unrelentingly and uniformly *hostile* perspectives on himself to scrutiny. He offers no commentary or authorial narrative to guide the reader through the plot (apart from a one-page prologue and an epilogue about one informer).

Instead, he presents his secret other life in unadulterated form to his reading public, confident, as it were, that his readers will share his perspective of the story. Kunze could be seen as placing his Stasi narrative under quarantine, in an attempt to contain his secret other life in its own poisonous discursive world to prevent leakage or contagion. It is almost as if his strategy were to seal this other narrative off in its own hermetic world, to wall off and encrypt the trauma of this episode in its own self-contained narrative. It seems significant for this reason that the Stasi file is placed in direct rather than indirect discourse. It is, moreover, almost as if his kangaroo court of law were only in the evidence-gathering phase and were planning to reconvene later to pass judgment. And because this judgment is suspended, it is left up to the reader to assume the role of judge and jury. It falls to the files to assume the task of bearing witness to the wrongs committed against Kunze, whereby the 'documentation' becomes a literary court of reckoning which puts the Stasi, and its many willing helpers, on trial.

Kunze's aim with this work is to cancel out and overwrite the original plot of his Stasi file, which cast him as a heretical writer engaged in dangerous dissident activity. He effectively reframes the files and inserts them into a new post-traumatic narrative about how he was persecuted by the regime. This technique of reworking the Stasi file into a new text bears similarities to the technique of 'detournement' used by political activists, or 'culture jamming', in which a work is turned against its original intention. Kunze's aim is similar, turning the file against itself by breaking the spell of its secrecy, taking public possession of those secret weapons that were once used against him. At the same time, the reappropriation of the files for telling his story could also be seen as an act of recuperation. This applies both in the medical sense of the word 'recuperation' as convalescence and rehabilitation – Kunze's writing starts a healing process – and in a semiotic sense of the word, whereby recuperation refers to the act of making something incomprehensible intelligible.[34] A key aspect of this 'turning away from its dedicated function' in the case of the Stasi file is the use of genre, in which the original genre undergoes a transformation into a new genre of writing.[35] Ross Chambers has called this a form of 'generic catachresis' or 'making do with another genre'.[36] The original bureaucratic genre of the Stasi file is thus overwritten, its meaning reinscribed and its toxic contents rendered comprehensible as 'hostile biography'.

One of the genres Kunze 'makes do' with is the diary. The work has no chapters, consisting only of a sequence of dated entries in chronological order, all of which are written by different, anonymous subjects. The narrative thus possesses a temporal structure that partly resembles a diary. The diary can be defined, as Philippe Lejeune suggests, at its simplest, as 'a series of dated traces' or, alternatively, as a 'narrative of traced dates'.[37] According to this definition Kunze's work could be read as a secret police diary that has been de-bureaucratized, reclaimed and re-personalized by the victim. Kunze filters, selects and records his victimization by the Stasi through the medium of his file, thus creating continuity out of the mass of discontinuities in his life much in the way that the diary does.[38] The work does not summarize or group instances of surveillance together, listing them instead individually and in order. This technique serves to underscore the sustained nature of the Stasi's effort not only to watch the movements of its 'enemy' but to take control of every aspect of its life. What is remarkable about this operation is its scale and severity, with the Stasi reserving its full arsenal of 'technologies of power' for him, from travel bans, telephone tapping, bugging, censorship of mail to confiscation of parcels, house searches and cloak-and-dagger operations to tamper with Kunze's medical records. Kunze's re-presentation of his file material serves, moreover, to indict the many willing informants who all played their part in the orchestrated campaign against him. In Kunze's case, the number and range of recruits the Stasi enlisted is quite remarkable: there were students, writers, literary reviewers, editors, publishers, neighbours, colleagues, librarians, pensioners and even doctors, who all actively proved their loyalty to the state by writing reports. Through the collage of file passages, from informant reports to the operative plans for his liquidation, Kunze effectively re-creates the Stasi file as victim's diary, thereby reversing the perspective of the original text, subverting its genre and inverting its political purpose. Rather than his disloyalty to his state, it is his victimization that is the topic of the newly inscribed work: the unrelenting surveillance of all aspects of his life, the systematic violation of his privacy and the state-engineered campaign to destroy his health, his family and his professional reputation. *Deckname 'Lyrik'* is thus able to expose previously invisible parts of the 'anatomy of a dictatorship', in particular of the 'nerve system and brain centre' of the Stasi.[39]

Günter Kunert's memoir *Erwachsenenspiele* (Adult Games), published in 1997, represents another interesting case of victims responding to their files. Kunert belongs to the middle generation of reform-socialist writers like Christa Wolf and others whose loyalty was put to the test by the draconian freezes in cultural politics in the 1970s. Kunert first came to the attention of the Stasi in 1957 during the Hungarian uprising when he was suspected of being in cahoots with counterrevolutionaries Wolfgang Harich and Walter Janka.[40] At first he was placed under surveillance under the codename of 'OV Benjamin', which intensified under the code 'OV Cynic' to new levels in the wake of the Biermann Affair. In a rare commentary on his file, Kunert compares reading his file to a belated encounter with the 'invisible third man', who provided the Stasi with information on him. He likens the act of reading these files to receiving lost letters addressed to him, in which he learns 'who and what I was in the eyes of Big Brother'.[41] Kunert is both fascinated and repelled by Big Brother's image of him and cites from numerous informer reports, from their assessments of his poetry, his character ('politically unaligned and labile')[42] as well as the Stasi's numerous conjectures about his movements. As narrator Kunert rarely engages directly with the contents of his files, and only occasionally lashes out at informers such as the '"sensitive poet" Uwe, [who], although languishing close to death, transforms himself sporadically into the IM "Uwe" and in that guise spies on and denigrates his colleagues'.[43] Kunert has this to say about the Stasi's characterization of himself: 'in them [the files] I am the "one-dimensional man" outlined by Herbert Marcuse who mixes with other one-dimensionalities'.[44] Like Kunze, Kunert also cites from his files in direct discourse, as if to contain these belatedly delivered letters within the frame of the secret police file and quarantine them within their own discursive space.

In Kunert's memoirs the file material serves various functions. On the one hand, its re-presentation serves to symbolically neutralize those original secret police settings by deliberately 'quoting them out of context'. The power the Stasi held over Kunert in the past can thus be broken and destroyed. On the other hand, the excerpts can be seen as providing testimony in a legal sense of how deeply affected Kunert was by his treatment at the hands of the regime. Kunert, like Kunze, creates a literary courtroom, over which he as author presides, calling on his Stasi files as expert witnesses. But these statements are not produced as evidence of Kunert's intention to undermine the state or to defect, as they were originally. Rather, the witness statements are reread instead as testimony of Kunert's systematic hounding by the secret police. The Stasi texts remain the same and yet we are invited to read them differently. By embedding his Stasi files in his own autobiographical text, Kunert is also, along with his implied readers, the all-powerful judge of the past and the prosecutor of each of his informants, for whom he has only the utmost contempt. And it is precisely because this work is authored by the victim that we can be sure in advance that Kunert's case for his defence will win. He gives us a clue as to his intentions when he writes of his wife's insistence in 1976 on being present during visits from authorities. She was, he says, his muse and his 'crown witness' to the threats and intimidation, bullying and harassment.[45] By analogy, the files could be considered to be Kunert's crown witnesses in the case he presents to the reader for the restoration of his dignity. Ironically, he lets his crown witnesses take the witness box more frequently towards the end, even allowing the Stasi's 'overwrought bureaucratic language' to 'overwhelm [his] natural idiom'.[46] But his strategy in allowing his story to be swamped by the Stasi's wildly distorted perspective on events is deliberate. In the end the hostile, one-dimensional biography the Stasi penned might appear to be the winner in the one-sided battle for memory. And yet, the reader knows with the benefit of hindsight that the Stasi loses the historical battle for control of the hearts and minds of GDR intellectuals, and Kunert escapes from the 'mental and intellectual coma' of East Berlin, taking his considerable literary capital with him to the West.[47]

A radically different approach to the Stasi file is taken by Monika Maron, a younger dissident writer who had a fleeting association with the Stasi as an informer before becoming a victim. When she was outed by the weekly magazine *Der Spiegel* in 1995, Maron was quick to defend her actions and published the two reports she wrote for the foreign espionage branch of the Stasi under the name of 'Mitsu' in a volume of essays.[48] The reports were so strident in their criticism of the GDR that they should have exonerated Maron completely, if the climate in Germany had been different at the time. Maron's other response was to write a family biography about the fraught nature of personal and intergenerational memory. In *Pawels Briefe* (Pawel's Letters, 1999) she places her own story of dissidence in a larger context: that of the story of her grandparents, who were victims of the Holocaust and her mother, a survivor of the Holocaust and a supporter of the communist regime.[49]

In the memoir, Maron's reluctance to engage with her brief episode of collaboration as well as with her thin perpetrator file is striking. She provides no reason for not including excerpts from her file or for not tackling the topic more directly than she does. We can only conjecture that the files could present her life in a misleading or unfavourable light, and possibly reinforce the public's overly simplistic view of collaboration. As evidence, they could be considered too incriminating to risk incorporation into the narrative of her family's biography. That secret narrative of betrayal, collusion and moral weakness that the perpetrator files could unlock – whether they do is another story – is possibly considered by Maron to be too explosive and damaging to reveal. In *Pawels Briefe* Maron is puzzled by her mother's forgetting of crucial details of the trauma of losing her parents, and yet Maron herself is inexplicably forgetful when it comes to her own past. She is unable to specify her reasons for collaborating: 'Whatever it was that motivated me – curiosity, thirst for adventure, the dream of a meaningful deed – I did not say no, and instead enquired about a Spanish course.' Instead she relies on her mother's recollections that her reason was that she wanted to leave the GDR.[50] She summarizes her involvement as a 'curious and odd episode [. . .] which I am not particularly proud of but also not ashamed of because it wasn't just a spy-affair'.[51]

Deirdre Byrnes argues that Maron was 'determined to avoid any further accusations of repression' and deliberately included her involvement with the Stasi in her family biography, but to little avail.[52] As Andrew Plowman has pointed out, there is a palpable tension in the work between the imperatives to remember created by the use of the confessional mode of the autobiography and the narrator's desire to conceal.[53] Maron deploys the opposite strategy to Kunze and Kunert and does not defer to her Stasi file, although to do so would be to exonerate her from any major wrong-doing, as a close analysis of the archival evidence reveals. The Stasi was so keen to secure Maron as a source that her case officer granted her far more freedom than was prudent, which Maron was only too happy to exploit.[54] Instead of mobilizing this file material in her defence as proof of her cavalier attitude to the Stasi, Maron hides behind her mother's recollections of the time and delegates the witnessing function to others.

It is ironic that Maron's Stasi story is so insignificant that it could have provided sufficient evidence to salvage her post-unification reputation as a dissident – and also to restore the market value of her literary capital – if only she had chosen to include it. Maron's refusal to satisfy her readers' curiosity suggests that there are other reasons for keeping the details secret, which may have to do with the fact that the episode was a source of deep personal shame as well as the cause of her public humiliation that it was impossible for her to confess to the real nature of her involvement with the Stasi.

The case of Sascha Anderson represents a far more extreme form of disavowal of the Stasi archives. Like other writers such as Hermann Kant, Anderson eschews all material from his Stasi file, insisting, as Sara Jones has remarked, on the 'superiority of his memories over the secondary biography of the files'.[55] Anderson was considered one of the leading intellectuals of the group of bohemian writers, artists, musicians and activists that became known by the name of the East Berlin suburb in which they lived in the 1980s: Prenzlauer Berg. His response to being exposed as an informer in 1991 was to write a third-person autobiography, in which the author's name is also the title of the work.[56] This rather irritating technique distances the auto-biographical self from the protagonist of the autobiography, effectively driving a defensive wedge between the writing self and the written self. This is despite the fact that a close reading of Anderson's personal Stasi file reveals that, apart from writing copious amounts of reports on virtually all of his close friends and associates, he was for a number of years also the victim of the Stasi's dogged attempts to enlist him. If we read his file from the underground's early years of 1977–80, and read for the plot as Vatulescu suggests, we are able to construe Anderson, initially at least, as a reluctant collaborator who only agreed to inform after considerable coercion.[57] This reluctance is paradoxically not reflected anywhere in his autobiography. Instead Anderson construes himself in Romantic and mythical terms as a Faustian character, caught between good and evil, locked in battle with his own security Mephisto.[58] Occasionally the topic of the Stasi surfaces from beneath the facade of postmodern pastiche and the tone of the writing becomes justificatory and defensive but never confessional.

In the post-unification era it is as eye-witnesses rather than as creators of fictional worlds that GDR writers are valued most. As they find themselves more and more consigned to history, and marginalized in the post-unification literary field, many have turned to testimonial forms of writing and writing about themselves as eyewitnesses of recent history. Their memoirs and autobiographies have acquired a testimonial insistence about them that asks to be read in close conjunction with the life of the author rather than with their works. These autobiographical texts are far more than source documents for reading and interpreting literary works; instead they are examples of 'literary autobiographics' that write the creative self as the eyewitness of extraordinarily testing historical circumstances. In this project, the archives of the Stasi play a curious role, emerging in some cases as the primary, privileged tools for writing the post-traumatic self and in others as the stigmatized inadmissible evidence of past mistakes and public humiliation. Where the files provide clear evidence of victimization the files are recuperated as the victim reclaims the agency lost through persecution. The files are translated from witness statements for the prosecution into witness statements for the defence, and their original genre is deflected or even hijacked for more humane purposes. The Stasi's hostile biographies about enemies of the state are rewritten from a subjective perspective and reinterpreted by the victims as biographies of unfair persecution, whereby the hostile account is subverted in the services of restorative justice. However, where the files provide incontrovertible evidence of the writer's fatal alliance with power – where the writer was an informer – the Stasi files are kept at arm's length in the writing process, excluded from the autobiographical plot, as evidence that is too damning and too incriminating to be incorporated into the life story of the writer. In both of these cases, the Stasi files hold the key to the remaking of the GDR author as historical witness and to the repositioning and reinvestment of his or her literary capital in the radically changed conditions of the literary field after 1989, either as evidence presented of the destruction of a career in the case of Kunze and Kunert or as evidence withheld of dubious compromises and shameful collusion. While this must seem like a lost opportunity, particularly in the case of Maron and Anderson, it must be acknowledged that in a post-authoritarian, liberal democracy it is ultimately an author's prerogative to use life-writing as he or she sees fit. The author is free to use writing as a literary court of reckoning to restore tarnished reputations and to reconstitute lost symbolic and cultural capital, just as the reader too is free to accept or reject these incomplete accounts of collaboration and, ultimately, to reserve judgement.

Notes

1. Stefan Wolle, *Die heile Welt der Diktatur: Alltag und Herrschaft in der DDR 1971–1989* (Berlin: Links, 1998); Konrad Jarausch, 'Care and Coercion: The GDR as Welfare Dictatorship', in Jarausch (ed.), *Dictatorship as Experience: Towards a Socio-Cultural History of the GDR* (New York, Oxford: Berghahn, 1999), pp. 47–72; Mary Fulbrook, *The People's State: East German Society from Hitler to Honecker* (New Haven, CT: Yale University Press, 2005), p. 12.
2. Mary Fulbrook, *Anatomy of a Dictatorship: Inside the GDR 1949–1989* (Oxford University Press, 1998), p. 53.
3. Wolfgang Emmerich, *Kleine Literaturgeschichte der DDR: Erweiterte Neuausgabe* (Leipzig: Gustav Kiepenheuer Verlag, 1996), pp. 11–28.

4. Stephen Parker and Matthew Philpotts, *Sinn und Form: The Anatomy of a Literary Journal* (Berlin, New York: de Gruyter, 2009), p. 5.
5. Ibid., p. 4.
6. Pierre Bourdieu, *Distinction: A Social Critique of the Judgment of Taste*, trans. Richard Nice (London: Routledge, 1984), p. 358.
7. Ibid., p. 81.
8. Ibid., p. 172.
9. Thomas Anz, *Franz Kafka: Leben und Werk* (Munich: Beck, 2009), p. 29.
10. Ibid., p. 22.
11. Leigh Gilmore, *Autobiographics: A Feminist Theory of Women's Self-Representation* (Ithaca: Cornell University Press, 1994), p. 125.
12. Ibid., p. 17.
13. Iris Radisch, 'Warten auf Montag', *Die Zeit*, 22 November 1991, p. 40.
14. Jacques Derrida, *Archive Fever: A Freudian Impression*, trans. Eric Prenowitz (Chicago and London: University of Chicago Press, 1995), pp. 1–2.
15. Jacques Derrida, *The Gift of Death and Literature in Secret*, trans. David Wills (Chicago and London: University of Chicago Press, 2008), p. 54.
16. Ibid., pp. 54–56.
17. Alison Lewis, 'Contingent Memories: The Crisis of Memory in Florian Henckel von Donnersmarck's *Das Leben der Anderen*', in Franz-Josef Deiters, et al. (eds.), *Limbus* 1 (2008), *Erinnerungskrisen / Memory Crises* (Freiburg i. Br.: Rombach, 2008), p. 152.
18. Barbara Miller, *Narratives of Guilt and Compliance in Unified Germany: Stasi Informers and Their Impact on Society* (London and New York: Routledge, 1999), p. 131.
19. Cristina Vatulescu, 'Arresting biographies: The Secret Police file in the Soviet Union and Romania', *Comparative Literature*, 56.3 (2004), 243–61; p. 244.
20. Joachim Walther, *Sicherungsbereich Literatur: Schriftsteller und Staatssicherheit in der Deutschen Demokratischen Republik* (Berlin: Links, 1996), pp. 182–83.
21. Ibid., pp. 186–87.
22. Ibid., pp. 184–86.
23. See Ingrid Kerz-Rühling and Tomas Plänkers, *Verräter oder Verführte: Eine psychoanalytische Untersuchung Inoffizieller Mitarbeiter der Stasi* (Berlin: Links, 2004), pp. 128–32.
24. Ibid., pp. 83–86.
25. Kerz-Rühling and Plänkers, *Verräter oder Verführte*, pp. 116–17.
26. Miller, *Narratives of Guilt and Compliance*, p. 132.
27. Roger Engelmann, *Zu Struktur, Charakter und Bedeutung der Unterlagen des Ministeriums für Staatssicherheit* (Berlin: BStU, 1994) [BF informiert Nr. 1], p. 53.
28. Engelmann, *Zu Struktur, Charakter und Bedeutung*, p. 53.
29. Alison Lewis, 'Reading and Writing the Stasi file: On the Uses and Abuses of the File as (Auto)Biography', *GLL*, 56.4 (2003), 337–97; pp. 383–85.
30. James Olney (ed.), *Autobiography: Essays Theoretical and Practical* (Princeton University Press, 1980).

31. Detractors of opening the files argued that the 'poison of the Stasi' might be perpetuated whereas victims claimed their 'poison' would last if the Stasi's crimes were not unearthed and publicized. See Hans Joachim Schädlich, 'Vorwort', in Schädlich (ed.), *Aktenkundig* (Berlin: Rowohlt, 1992), p. 7.

32. Reiner Kunze, *Deckname 'Lyrik': Eine Dokumentation* (Frankfurt/M.: Fischer, 1990).

33. Ibid., p. 89.

34. Irena R. Makaryk, *Encyclopedia of Contemporary Literary Theory: Approaches, Scholars, Terms* (Toronto, Buffalo, London: University of Toronto Press, 1993), p. 617.

35. Ross Chambers, *Untimely Interventions: AIDS Writing, Testimonial and the Rhetoric of Haunting* (Michigan: Ann Arbor Press, 2004), p. 29.

36. Chambers, *Untimely Interventions*, p. 29.

37. Jeremy D. Popkin and Julie Rak (eds.), *Philippe Lejeune on Diary* (Manoa, Hawaii: Biographical Research Centre, 2009), p. 179.

38. Ibid., p. 175.

39. Fulbrook, *Anatomy of a Dictatorship*, p. 53.

40. Günter Kunert, *Erwachsenenspiele: Erinnerungen* (Munich: Hanser, 1997), pp. 197–99.

41. Ibid., p. 200.

42. Ibid., p. 311.

43. Ibid., p. 368.

44. Ibid., p. 361.

45. Ibid., p. 385.

46. Owen Evans, *Mapping the Contours of Oppression: Subjectivity, Truth and Fiction in Recent German Autobiographical Treatments of Totalitarianism* (Amsterdam, New York: Rodopi, 2006), p. 200.

47. Ibid., p. 435.

48. Monika Maron, *Quer über die Gleise: Essays, Artikel, Zwischenrufe* (Frankfurt/M.: Fischer, 2000), pp. 24–33.

49. Monika Maron, *Pawels Briefe* (Frankfurt/M.: Fischer, 1999).

50. Ibid., pp. 196–97.

51. Ibid., p. 199.

52. Deirdre Byrnes, *Rereading Monika Maron: Text, Counter-Text and Context* (Bern: Lang, 2011), p. 143.

53. Andrew Plowman, 'Escaping the Autobiographical Trap? Monika Maron, the Stasi and *Pawels Briefe*', in Paul Cooke and Andrew Plowman (eds.), *German Writers and the Politics of Culture. Dealing with the Stasi* (London: Palgrave Macmillan, 2003), p. 228.

54. For a more detailed account of the contents of her files see Alison Lewis, 'Erinnerung, Zeugenschaft und die Staatssicherheit: Die Schriftstellerin Monika Maron', *Der Deutschunterricht*, 6 (2005), 22–33.

55. Sara Jones, 'Conflicting Evidence': Hermann Kant and the Opening of the Stasi Files', *GLL*, 62.2 (2009), 203.

56. Sascha Anderson, *Sascha Anderson* (Cologne: DuMont, 2002).

57. See the sections of Anderson's file held in the Stasi Archives in BStU, ZA, AIM, 7423/91, 1. Beifügung.

58. Ironically the officer's name is Faust but Anderson refers to him as his Mephisto: 'I called him Mephisto'. Anderson, *Sascha Anderson*, p. 125.

Intellectuals and the Wende
Missed opportunities and dashed hopes
Carol Anne Costabile-Heming

The *Wende* (peaceful revolution) in the fall of 1989 should have afforded writers and intellectuals in the GDR the long-sought opportunity to become active players in the creation and development of a society for which they had advocated so staunchly in their writings throughout the GDR's forty-year existence. Instead, because the *Wende* primarily was a grass-roots effort that first took hold within the circles of the *Friedensgebete*, or prayers for peace, the intellectuals in the GDR, who normally occupied a place of prominence in the public sphere, were to a large extent forced to the margins throughout the entire revolutionary process. Prominent writers such as Christa Wolf (1929–2011), Volker Braun (b. 1939), Stefan Heym (1913–2001) and Heiner Müller (1929–95) had often participated openly and vocally in critical societal debates throughout the GDR's history. By the late 1980s, however, the voices of these writers had become increasingly marginalized. In the period after unification, they were woefully silent on matters of social and political importance in the united Germany. Indeed, this silence that has persisted in post-unification Germany points to a crisis of intellectual engagement among those who previously had occupied the front lines of debate.

For GDR writers, unification brought about an end to the immediate and important role that they had played in the public sphere. Moreover, the change to a market economy meant that writers and most especially their literary works no longer occupied the position of esteem that they had in the GDR. In the immediate post-unification years prominent GDR writers published essays and autobiographies rather than fiction. Fiction, it seems, was no longer a suitable form for the stories the GDR writers wanted to tell. Indeed, one of the first fictional works, Christa Wolf's

I am indebted to Dr Rachel Halverson and Dr Caryn Connelly for their insightful reading of this manuscript.

Was bleibt (What Remains, 1990), detailing a day in the life of a writer under surveillance, was unable to find resonance with critics and readers, meeting instead with intense criticism and launching a literary debate. More than twenty-five years later, some of these same once critical authors have yet to let go of the past. In her *Stadt der Engel oder The Overcoat of Dr. Freud* (2010; *City of Angels: or, The Overcoat of Dr. Freud*, 2013), Wolf's protagonist reflects on the post-unification years, but rather than coming to terms with the GDR's demise, it becomes clear that the main character continues to mourn the end of the socialist utopian dream.[1]

Conceived as a survey of writers' engagement in the *Wende* and beyond, this chapter proposes that the relative silence of the intellectuals in the months leading up to the fall of the Berlin Wall on 9 November 1989 has roots in earlier attitudes and structures. As GDR citizens' success at demanding reforms progressed, the writers maintained a steadfast adherence to a socialist utopian ideal, manifest particularly in the months following the fall of the Wall. As the path to unification became imminent, the writers' special status and privileges evaporated, as did the need for their texts to create an alternative public sphere. This chapter analyses key speeches, political texts and newspaper articles by the most prominent GDR writers in the period leading up to the fall of the Wall and immediately thereafter. In addition, the chapter reassesses the most immediate post-*Wende* literary texts, in particular, Christa Wolf's *Was bleibt* and Volker Braun's poem 'Das Eigentum' (Property). The *Literaturstreit* (literary debate) following the publication of *Was bleibt* in 1990, as well as the subsequent revelations about collusion between writers and the Stasi, contributed significantly to the further distancing of the writers from their readers. Finally, the chapter will address the continued silence of these writers on matters of sociopolitical significance in the unified Germany.

It is perhaps instructive to begin the discussion by examining the officially sanctioned role of literature in the GDR. In 1990, the writer Jurek Becker stated bluntly what he saw as the differences in the literatures produced in the two Germanys: 'Without a doubt, literature played a different role in the GDR than in the West, a larger and more important role. Books always had the opportunity to give rise to disquiet, or to intervene in social conflicts, indeed to ignite them in a way that was unimaginable in the West.'[2] Here Becker emphasizes the importance of literature for creating social change. This was a belief that many East German writers shared, and it was a perspective often focused on by Western media. In hindsight, however, we can question whether or not Becker's statement is really true. Stephen Brockmann, for instance, has proposed that literature enjoyed a high status in the GDR because of its 'backwardness and authoritarianism'.[3] Because the ruling party, the SED, tightly controlled most aspects of the public sphere, literature and writers became elevated in the eyes of the people. The historian Timothy Garton Ash has stated that 'East Germany [was] clearly a totalitarian state in the sense that it *aspire[d]* to occupy and direct its citizens' every waking moment',[4] an aim that included controlling what citizens read, even fiction. The rigid mechanisms of the *Druckgenehmigungsverfahren* (the process for authorizing books for printing) ensured multiple levels of review and approval, with the result that the most critical texts never reached the hands of their intended readers. These differing perceptions are key background to understanding the writers' inability to foresee and respond to the momentous events of 1989.

From their own point of view, GDR writers took their role very seriously, and they viewed themselves and their texts as integral partners in helping to shape and reform GDR society. The significance of the events of the fall of 1989 was not lost on them, though many struggled to find a voice amidst the din of the protests. Christoph Hein, for instance, cautioned thus:

> We, the writers, the members of Artists' Unions and academies, the country's intellectuals, we will one day have to answer the question: 'So where were you when this was happening? Where did you demonstrate your resolve? Where can we find your responses, no matter how impotent?' And then no answer, however clever or smart it might be, will protect us from the shame, if we continue to remain silent today.[5]

In this speech before the Bezirksverband Berlin (Berlin district association) in September 1989, Hein articulates the need for writers and intellectuals to overcome their silence, find their voices and participate in the changes that were occurring in the GDR. He writes against what he perceives as paralysis gripping the intellectuals, who have failed to grasp the imperative nature of the protests and the inevitable changes that they were to provoke. Yet, the writers had not always been silent.

Prior to the public protests in GDR cities in 1989, criticism of state socialism in the GDR took the form of critical exchange in open forums and official congresses, and many GDR writers figured prominently in these debates. At the Tenth Writers' Congress in November 1987, writers and political leaders assessed the developments in GDR literature during the previous five years. While writers voiced mounting concerns about contradictions, their concerns often were overlooked by Party functionaries. In his greeting to the delegation, SED General Secretary Erich

Honecker praised the writers as 'reliable partners and active comrades of the working class and their Marxist-Leninist Party'.[6] As president of the Writers' Union, Hermann Kant chose to emphasize the continuity of present-day GDR literature with the literature of previous generations: 'The peculiarity of GDR literature, being close to the heart of things, and the strength of literature, to be in constant dialogue, have not changed with the generations.'[7] Yet, during this same meeting Christoph Hein forcefully demanded reforms and an end to censorship. In his speech before the 'Arbeitsgruppe IV Literatur und Wirkung' (Working Group IV Literature and Agency), Hein stated, 'The approval process, the state control, in a nutshell, the censorship of publishing houses and books, publishers and authors is obsolete, useless, paradoxical, inhumane, hostile to the people, illegal and culpable.'[8] In the plenary session, Günter de Bruyn echoed Hein's sentiments, stating bluntly that 'if nothing changes in the realm of cultural politics, writers or journalists will not be participants in societal improvements'.[9] De Bruyn addressed the question of censorship directly, proposing that the 'authorization process diminishes the enlightening impact of GDR literature. A society that does not abandon this practice in a timely fashion, damages its image, promotes doubt about its ability to reform and robs itself of criticism's driving force'.[10] This is one of the few instances where the writers and intellectuals played a central role in demanding change in the GDR prior to the *Wende*.

It is often misconstrued that because the GDR was viewed from the outside as a *Leseland* (country of readers), writers and other intellectuals enjoyed a particularly high regard. Yet, Hein warned his fellow writers in 1987 stating, 'More problematic is the high level, and as I interpret it, too high level of meaning that one imputes to writers in this country. One tends, willingly or unwillingly, to place them on a pedestal and grant the writer an overarching authority. But it is difficult to work on a pedestal, because one cannot experience anything there, without which our work is impossible.'[11] Hein's warning is prescient: there is no doubt that writers became increasingly distant (at least ideologically) from their readers, a fact that became most obvious during the tumultuous protests of 1989. Disappointingly, these auspicious provocations from 1987 were followed by relative silence during the turbulent summer and fall of 1989.

Hindsight affords us the possibility to review historical events, and, though they may not have been as apparent at the time, it is now possible to point out early signs that things in the GDR were destined to transform, and that writers did not necessarily have their fingers on the pulse of this change. Throughout the latter half of the 1980s, a number of contentious events point to the changing mood among the GDR populace, a mood characterized by an increasing lack of tolerance towards the government's heavy-handed control. In addition to the outspoken calls for an end to censorship in the GDR at the Writers' Congress, 1987 also witnessed protests about the Stasi actions against the environmental library at the Zion Church in East Berlin in November (concurrent with the Writers' Congress). In January 1988, a public demonstration commemorating Karl Liebknecht and Rosa Luxemburg resulted in the arrest and expulsion of protestors, most notably Stephan Krawczyk and Freya Klier. The pace of protest accelerated in 1989, beginning with accusations of fraud in the communal elections in May 1989. In June, Hungary opened its border with Austria; in September, Hungary allowed East Germans to pass through the border to Austria. Increasing numbers of refugees occupied the West German embassies in Prague and Warsaw, and eventually reached the West. Demonstrators began gathering at the Nikolaikirche in Leipzig; the first Monday demonstration took place on 25 September. Groups began founding alternative political parties such as *Demokratischer Aufbruch* and *Neues Forum*. In all of these venues, the voices of the writers were conspicuously absent. By the time renowned writers like Hein, Christa Wolf, Stephan Heym and Heiner Müller spoke at the Alexanderplatz demonstration in Berlin on 4 November, an event that was televised throughout the GDR, the demise of the socialist state was imminent. Yet even here, the intellectuals were unable to fathom the people's desire for radical change.

At Alexanderplatz, Wolf speaks of a state of 'crisis'[12] and of fear. She cautions the crowd that 'we know we must practice the art of not letting the ambivalence degenerate into confrontation'.[13] She implores the demonstrators to dream of socialism for all ('Socialism arrives and no one goes away!').[14] Heym rejoices in the courage of the people who have taken to the streets, but continues to plead for socialism: 'The socialism that we finally want to construct for our benefit and for the benefit of all of Germany, this socialism is not imaginable without democracy.'[15] Müller appeals for an end to privileges for the artists, writers and intellectuals, asking for solidarity with the people. Hein's message strikes a more sombre tone: 'Let us be wary of confusing the euphoria of these days with the changes yet to be achieved. The excitement and the demonstrations were and are helpful and essential, but they are no substitute for the work [that lies ahead].'[16] Hein warns against rapid decision-making 'that we don't create structures now, at the mercy of which we will one day find ourselves'.[17] The acclamation which the writers received from the Alexanderplatz masses was short-lived.

Four days after the Alexanderplatz demonstration, Wolf appeared on television imploring her fellow citizens to stay and help to build a democratic society: 'We are aware of the powerlessness of words against the will of the masses, but we have no other means than our words. Those who still leave now diminish our hope. We beg you, stay in your homeland, stay with us!'[18] Wolf continues her appeal: 'We are just at the beginning of the fundamental changes in our country. Help us to create a truly democratic society, which preserves the vision of a democratic socialism.'[19] Like the speeches on 4 November, in which the writers and intellectuals promoted 'socialism', Wolf speaks of a concept which had long lost its promise of a better life for the general population. Wolf's biographer, Jörg Magenau, suggests that the writers and intellectuals were the only ones who held on to this illusion, for the majority of the population was interested in democratic engagement.[20]

Throughout the autumn of 1989, writers found themselves sought-after partners in dialogue and they assumed a quasi-political function – in essence they were able to expand their engagement in the public sphere. Shortly thereafter, however, the writers became superfluous as conversation partners, for East Germany after the fall of the Wall quickly adopted Western ways, granting the media the role of the public sphere, which it enjoys in democratic states, but which writers had previously occupied in the GDR.

Following the fall of the Wall, many intellectuals held fast to their belief in the socialist utopia, an ideal far removed from the very real consumption-driven desires of the general populace. On 26 November 1989, the resolution 'Für unser Land' (For Our Country) was published. Signed by Frank Beyer, Volker Braun, Heym, Friedrich Schorlemmer, Konrad Weiß and Wolf, among others, this resolution was an attempt by the intellectuals to become involved in the creation of a post-Wall GDR in ways that offered an escape from the period of crisis. Close examination of the language of this resolution reveals the extent to which the split between many of the writers and their public had grown, for these intellectuals steadfastly believed that they still had a voice and could influence the direction that future developments would take. Moreover, these signatories viewed the current situation as a crisis, a perspective not shared by the general populace.

The resolution polarized the choices which the signatories saw for the future of the GDR: either the GDR remains as an independent state or it succumbs to the 'selling off of our material and moral values' and becomes subsumed by the Federal Republic.[21] The choice for the intellectuals is clear: to choose an independent GDR as a socialist alternative to the Federal

Republic, a decision that demonstrated just how out of touch they were with the needs and wants of the citizenry. The outcry against the intellectuals was almost immediate. Arno Widmann's critique of 'Für unser Land' published in the West German newspaper the *taz* accused the signatories of 'criminal arrogance', in attempting simply to sweep under the rug seventy years of experiences with socialism.[22] Egon Krenz, the successor to Erich Honecker, also then signed 'Für unser Land', an action which further served to discredit the resolution and those who stood behind it. Indeed, numerous writers refused to sign the appeal, among them Hein and de Bruyn. For ordinary citizens, it appeared that the intellectuals had lost touch with reality as they lived it, particularly with regard to their insistence on a socialist path. Moreover, the refusal by Hein and de Bruyn gave the appearance that the intellectuals were divided and disorganized, a further signal to the general populace to view them with scepticism.

The appeal also was not well received by writers in the West. Monika Maron published a retort to 'Für unser Land', in which she decried the inability of the writers to see how their society and their role in it were changing: 'the German writers were unable to come down from the podium', from which they proclaimed 'the promise of the next wonderful future for the people'.[23] Maron condemns the writers' inability to comprehend the actions of the people, berating them for turning their backs on their readers because the readers are not following the writers' wishes. Maron writes from a particular position: though she had lived in the GDR until 1988, her works were only published in the West. In this case her unforgiving stance toward her former writer colleagues serves to drive the wedge between them and their readers even further.

By February 1990, even Wolf had to admit that many of the speeches and texts she penned during the autumn of 1989 already were out of date.[24] Looking back, she admitted that she felt compelled to work on 'Für unser Land' because both East Germans and West Germans had contacted her about their concerns regarding the push for rapid unification. Yet, Wolf also admitted that she was afraid that the message was already too late.[25] Wolf's predicament underscores the antagonistic position writers experienced, as they struggled to come to terms with the rapid changes occurring in their society, yet were still hesitant to abandon their worldview.

Wolf, Braun, Hein and others enjoyed considerable privileges not accorded to the general populace, a fact that further served to distance the writers ideologically from their readers. Indeed, we can argue that this separation also occurred on a basic materialistic level, promoting a class-based distancing in

an ideologically 'classless' society. Peter Uwe Hohendahl has argued that the
writers viewed the autumn of 1989 as their opportunity to represent the people
and their wishes to the Party effectively.[26] Yet, an unanticipated outcome of
the people's new-found participation in the public sphere was an undermining of the writers' position as mouthpiece for the people.

The writers' position was weakened as early as October, when GDR
citizens dared to take to the streets to proclaim their dissatisfaction with the
GDR regime. Countless newspaper articles written by intellectuals underscore the extent to which writers had lost touch with their readers. Heym
presents perhaps the best example, for he was particularly vocal in the
month of October. In an article in *Die Zeit* Heym proclaimed: 'a socialist
state on German soil is necessary that will guarantee its citizens true
freedom and those rights to which all free citizens are entitled. And it is
not only for the people who choose to live and to persevere in the GDR, a
rationally functioning GDR socialism would also be essential for those
outside the GDR's borders, for the Left is suffering from the fiasco of the
SED throughout the world'.[27] Heym's comment here, although in essence
a plea for an alternative socialist German state, also points to the need for
democratic socialism in the world as an alternative to democracies such as
the Federal Republic of Germany. This comment underscores the role that
the leftist intellectuals played in the GDR and the perceived role that they
saw for themselves on the world stage. Heym continued to hold fast to his
belief in the need for a socialist state on German soil in December 1989:
'The GDR's raison d'être is socialism, whatever form it takes, in order to
offer an alternative to the privateering state with the harmless name of
Federal Republic.'[28] Despite the apparent disconnect between Heym and
readers at the time of the *Wende*, he pursued a political career as a member
of the PDS (Party of Democratic Socialism) and was elected directly to the
Bundestag in 1994 as a representative for Berlin-Mitte and Prenzlauer Berg.
His decision to join the PDS, a successor party to the SED, is further
evidence of his unfaltering adherence to a socialist utopian ideal.

While many intellectuals remained active in the grass-roots political
parties that emerged immediately following the fall of the Wall, it was
obvious by the time of the *Volkskammerwahl* (Parliamentary elections) on
18 March 1990 that the majority of the GDR populace was no longer
interested in the socialist utopian ideals espoused by the writers. Heym
resignedly admitted as much on GDR television: 'There will be no more
GDR. It will be nothing more than a footnote in world history.'[29] Indeed, in
these first free elections in the GDR, the intellectuals were dealt a resounding
blow, as the populace voted overwhelmingly for the Christian Democrat

Party. This unambiguous rejection of the intellectuals denotes 1990 as a significant turning point, heralding the end of political engagement that Wolf and others heretofore had known.

Most writers were active drafting speeches and essays during the weeks immediately preceding and following the fall of the Wall. However, the first literary text published prior to unification was Wolf's *Was bleibt* which appeared in June 1990. Originally written in 1979 and revised for publication in 1989, the short novel chronicles one day in the life of a writer (with a biography similar to Wolf) who is under intense observation by the East German secret police, the Stasi. Its publication unleashed a furor in the feuilleton press, making it abundantly clear that readers and critics in both East and West had little tolerance for the lamenting tone of the formerly highly acclaimed author. The ensuing *Literaturstreit* changed Germany's literary landscape forever. More importantly, it called into question whether it was even possible for GDR writers to have been critical of the system from within.

Critics were quick to point out that Wolf had enjoyed countless privileges under the GDR regime, privileges to which ordinary citizens were denied access. Moreover, they accused her of taking advantage of the political situation, and publishing the text at a time that was deemed 'safe'. Newspaper critics branded her 'Staatsdichterin' (state poet). Ulrich Greiner's review in *Die Zeit* took particular issue with the timing of the publication: 'That she publishes it now reveals a lack not of courage, for there are no more threats, but of sincerity to oneself and one's history, a lack of sensitivity to those whose lives were destroyed by the SED.'[30] For Greiner, the publication of *Was bleibt* in 1990 was simply embarrassing, in contrast to the sensation it could have been prior to 9 November. Indeed, Greiner views Wolf's timing of this publication as a cowardly attempt to ingratiate herself with those who had protested against the regime. Similarly, Frank Schirrmacher characterized the book's post-Wall publication as 'meaningless, anachronistic' and 'laughable'.[31] Wolf's supporters tried to counter the attacks, emphasizing the years that she had spent criticizing the SED in various formats. Moreover, Thomas Anz points out that the discourse of this debate evoked the post-Second World War rhetoric that pitted exiled authors against those in inner emigration,[32] an argument that Wolf herself employed while she was visiting the United States.

This critical reception stunned Wolf, who had done readings from the book in 1989. Her surprise was a further indication of the extent to which she was out of touch with her readers and the changes in her society. While the newly reformed structures within the GDR afforded writers the opportunity to publish texts that previously had languished in desk drawers, readers no longer were interested in texts that presented tensions and conflicts that had existed in the GDR. In many respects, writers, particularly those such as Wolf, who were perceived of as supportive of the GDR, were viewed with suspicion by the reading public following the fall of the Wall. Prior to November 1989, all works were a direct product of state control, and, for this reason, readers began to identify the authors of these works with the GDR and the SED, regardless of whether or not the writers were true supporters of the regime. It is no surprise then, that Wolf's presentation of repression faced by the writers in the GDR in the fictional form of *Was bleibt* did not find resonance with readers.

With the initial critical reception of *Was bleibt* focusing intently on Wolf as author, the literary quality of the novel remained mostly untouched. Now, more than twenty-five years after its publication, this narrative provides us with key insights into the relationship between writers and their readers and writers and the state in the GDR, as the writers themselves perceived them. A young woman visits the narrator to show her a manuscript that she had written. The young woman has had a chequered past: the reasons are not specified in the text, but the woman was expelled from the university and spent a year in jail. Although the narrator believes that the manuscript is good, she encourages the young woman not to show it to anyone, fearing another jail sentence as punishment. In essence, the narrator advises her to pack her text away in a desk drawer, to practice self-censorship (much as Wolf had done with her own manuscript). Despairingly, the narrator knows that the young woman has written the truth, and likely will not keep this truth to herself. While this scene underscores the struggles that accomplished and novice writers faced in bringing their texts into the public domain, precisely such scenes no longer found resonance with readers in 1990. The perceived cowardice of the writers stands in stark contrast to the fearlessness of the demonstrators who marched in the Monday demonstrations, unsure if the state would retaliate against them.

A subsequent incident brings the protagonist into direct contact with her readers. As she presents her unpublished manuscript at a public reading, she reflects 'I wanted to implant my world [in their minds].'[33] This statement unabashedly describes the wishes and desires of the writing elite both during and immediately after the *Wende*. Perceiving their readers as unworldly, the writers viewed themselves not only as spokespeople for the populace, but also relished the power they possessed to mould the thoughts and actions of their readers. This scene very clearly depicts the relationship between writers and their readers in the GDR, for in the act of reading to her audience, the author assumes a position of privilege over her audience. She is allowed to express her thoughts openly; the audience is not. The presence of the Stasi at the reading poses a very real danger to the audience members, should they choose to be outspoken.

Despite the presence of Party functionaries and the Stasi, such readings functioned as a quasi-alternative public sphere, where the reading public could interact directly with both the text and the author. Typically, the act of writing and the act of reading are solitary acts. The writer produces a product, the text; through the process of reading, the reader interprets the product by bringing his or her own perspective to the work and by reading between the lines. In *Was bleibt* a question and answer session follows the reading, providing an opportunity for genuine openness and dialogue. A young woman asks 'how a liveable future for ourselves and our children was going to grow out of this present situation'.[34] Although posed in 1979, this question is equally relevant in 1989, at the time that Wolf was revising the text, and signals a clear shift in thinking on the part of the audience and an acute awareness that things were changing. The narrator's reply indicates that she too is aware that change is imminent: 'for now the real questions had surfaced – the ones which give us life and can mean death if taken away from us'.[35] This scene depicts the possibility for dialogue that the venue of a public reading could create. As the public became increasingly empowered in the autumn of 1989, however, the need for and ability of the writers to serve as catalysts for open exchange began to diminish.

A second literary text, Volker Braun's poem, 'Das Eigentum', published in *Neues Deutschland* (under the early title of 'Nachruf' (Obituary)) and then in *Die Zeit* in August of 1990, was widely read and reprinted, a reception completely different from that accorded Wolf's short novel. Braun's poem lays bare an internal conflict for Braun, which corresponded to the reality for readers: 'Da bin ich noch: mein Land geht in den Westen' (I'm still here: my country is going West).[36] This first line situates the poem squarely within the sociopolitical crisis of 1989. The lyric subject speaks of loss: 'Was ich niemals besaß wird mir entrissen. / Was ich nicht lebte, werd ich ewig missen.' (What I never possessed is ripped away. / What I have not lived, I will eternally miss.), the loss of the utopian vision. This line points decisively to the divide between writers and their readers. The writers held fast to the belief in the prospect of the socialist utopia, while their readers abandoned those beliefs for the instant gratification offered by the West. By holding on to hope, which 'lag im Weg wie eine Falle' (stood in the way like a trap), the writers sealed their fate: they experienced a sense of detachment, as they perceived their readers turning their backs on the utopian message that they had preached for so long. Characteristic of Braun's poetry, this poem is open-ended: 'Wann sag ich wieder *mein und meine alle*' (when will I again say mine, and mean everyone's), leaving room for the continued wish for utopia. Much like the appeal 'Für unser Land', this last line underscores Braun's unwillingness to surrender his utopian vision.

Braun always probed and questioned. 'Das Eigentum' recalls an earlier poem 'Das Lehen' (Fiefdom), of 1987. Beginning with the line 'Ich bleib im Lande und nähre mich im Osten' (I remain in my country and nourish myself in the East), this earlier poem expresses the author's resolve to remain in the east, and his dedication to utopian socialism 'Die Bleibe, die ich suche, ist kein Staat' (the shelter that I seek is no country). Braun uses the poem to critique the GDR:

> Partei mein Fürst: *sie hat uns alles gegeben*
> Und alles ist noch nicht das Leben.
> Das Lehen, das ich brauch, wird nicht vergeben.[37]

(The Party my prince, *who gave us everything* / And everything does not include life / The fiefdom that I need cannot be awarded.)

In the autumn of 1989, GDR citizens abandon the quest for the socialist utopia and choose to find their 'fiefdom' in the west. In essence, the reading public has turned its back on the author, Braun, leaving him alone: 'Und ich kann *bleiben wo der Pfeffer wächst*' (literally: And I can *remain where the pepper grows*).[38] The quotation, an idiom meaning 'to get lost, go to hell', is a direct reference to Greiner's article in *Die Zeit* (22 June 1990), just weeks after the publication of *Was bleibt*, in which he concluded: 'Die toten Seelen des Realsozialismus sollen bleiben, wo der Pfeffer wächst' (The dead souls of really existing socialism can take a running jump).[39] By quoting Greiner, Braun clearly places himself on the side of Wolf as a target of Greiner's criticism. And Braun recognizes that his texts no longer resonate with the readers: 'Und unverständlich wird mein ganzer Text' (And my whole text becomes incomprehensible). Not only does this line underscore the isolation that writers felt, it signals Braun's ultimate despair and his anger that his whole life now seems to be for nought.

Following the unification of Germany, tension remained between the reading public and the writers from the former GDR, and economic and social changes played a key role. As the controversy surrounding *Was bleibt* illustrated, GDR authors were viewed suspiciously by western literary critics, a circumstance unknown during GDR times, when writers such as Wolf, Müller and Braun were held in high regard. Readers in the east also were drawn to books and writers that previously were forbidden. The currency reform of July 1990 radically changed production and distribution. Such external factors were beyond the control of the writers, and may well have contributed to the sense of isolation and despair which they experienced. And, while the division of Germany and the existence of two German literatures led to the development of similar institutions on both sides of the German-German border (such as two national bibliographies, two PEN organizations), this double existence became superfluous following unification.[40] The discussions about the possible dissolution of East German agencies and entities, along with the tendency to merge the eastern institutions with those in the west (exemplified in the political unification), called the very legitimacy of those eastern organizations into question and as a by-product, the legitimacy of the writers as well. This further reinforced the sense of solitariness among the writing elite, as their institutions abandoned their socialist roots.

The status of the writers grew even more precarious after Wolf Biermann exposed one of the leaders of the Prenzlauer Berg alternative scene, Sascha Anderson, as an *inoffizieller Mitarbeiter* (unofficial operative) or IM for the Stasi in his Büchner Prize Acceptance Speech in 1991. This revelation set off a witch hunt, seeking to discredit the leftist leaning intellectuals even more, and represents a further amplification of the literary debate from the summer of 1990. The media seemed to relish its ability to topple former cultural icons, as evidenced by its attempt to discredit Heiner Müller. On 21 January 1993, Christa Wolf made a pre-emptive move and divulged to the *Berliner Zeitung* that she had been an IM between the years of 1959 and 1962.[41] Wolf had repressed all memory of this activity, until she was confronted with it when she examined her own Stasi file in May 1992. Thomas Anz defends Wolf by suggesting that even though she had worked for the Stasi, her literary texts all were composed after that time period, and were critical of the system, thus attempting to dilute any damage done by the revelation.[42] In her final publication, *Stadt der Engel oder The Overcoat of Dr. Freud*, Wolf investigates her ability to remember, her disillusionment with the unification process, and her inability to shake her loyalty to the dream of a socialist utopia.

Given the severity of these public attacks, it is no wonder that these formerly very civically engaged intellectuals have retreated considerably from the public eye. Their active engagement on the world stage in public debates about human rights has been all but non-existent. In 1991, the writers, among them Wolf and Braun, wrote an appeal to the United

Nations against the first Gulf War. But they have done little to participate in subsequent global civil rights debates. Even on the home front, they have maintained their silence. In 2010, the SPD and the Green Party supported former Federal Commissioner for the Files from the Ministry of State Security, Joachim Gauck as candidate for President of the Federal Republic. As a pastor in the GDR active in the grass-roots movement in 1989, Gauck would seem to have been a figure around which other former GDR intellectuals could rally. When asked in an interview with *Der Spiegel* about her opinion of Gauck as candidate for President of the Federal Republic, Wolf responded evasively: 'I will not allow myself an opinion on this question, because I would not be able to justify it.'[43]

And so, we ponder what remains of the legacy of GDR writers and intellectuals. By 1994, Wolf again was celebrated by the reading public in Leipzig on the occasion of her sixty-fifth birthday. Magenau attributes this to the fact that she survived both the literary debate about *Was bleibt* and the revelation about her Stasi past. Magenau suggests that she removed herself from the 'open' public sphere, seeking instead, only the company of the likeminded.[44] We can thus view this behaviour as an ultimate retreat from public engagement. In a post-socialist world, writers like Wolf and Braun have continued to publish, but have done so from a decidedly GDR point of view and perspective.

Wolf's *Stadt der Engel* reads more like a lament for the 'good old days' of the GDR than a coming to terms with the past, as critics had expected. It revisits the period of 1992–93, the time of her visit to the Getty Centre in Santa Monica, California, and the high point of the Stasi revelations. It highlights the extent to which Wolf at this point still could not move past the end of the GDR. As the protagonist reflects on her life and ponders how much things have changed, she repeatedly ponders why she stayed in the GDR. The answer is simple: 'We loved this country.'[45] She was unable to rejoice at the fall of the Wall, for she viewed it as surrender, the surrender of the belief in a socialist future.

In order to conclude, let me return to Jurek Becker's comment about the differences between literature in East and West Germany. Becker emphasizes the importance of literature and books; he does not mention anything about the importance of the writers. This is perhaps the key to understanding why the writers were so far removed from the actual process of change as it unfolded in the GDR. Indeed, writers did not begin to occupy the spotlight until June of 1990, with the publication of *Was bleibt*. The debate that followed, however, did not focus at all on the literary and aesthetic quality of the text, but rather primarily on the person of Christa

Wolf, as representative for an entire institution of privilege. As Stephen Brockmann has argued, 'both literary debates were characterized by [a] high level of abstractness'.[46] Moreover, he writes, in the united Germany at this time, 'authors were important only as representatives of posited institutional discourse'.[47] The authors' lack of engagement in the post-Wall world confirms that they needed the manipulated public sphere offered under really existing socialism in order to project their voices. Without the protective cover of the GDR, their voices no longer are valued as social critics. The impact of the *Literaturstreit* was indeed far reaching, for it served not only as an indictment of socialist writers. While on the face of it, Greiner and Schirrmacher attacked Christa Wolf, they also called the very idea of *Gesinnungsästhetik* (aesthetic based on convictions) into question, leading ultimately to a revision of West German socially critical literature as well. In terms of GDR literature's place in literary history, we must read these texts (and the writers' biographies) both within the context during which they were written and against the knowledge that post-unification revelations brought and continue to bring.

Notes

1. Christa Wolf, *Stadt der Engel oder The Overcoat of Dr. Freud* (Berlin: Suhrkamp, 2010).
2. Jureck Becker, 'Die Wiedervereinigung der deutschen Literatur', *The German Quarterly*, 63 (1990), 359–66; p. 359. Unless otherwise noted, all translations are my own.
3. Stephen Brockmann, 'The Written Capital', *Monatshefte*, 91.3 (1999), 376–95; p. 382.
4. Timothy Garton Ash, *The Uses of Adversity: Essays on the Fate of Central Europe* (New York: Vintage Books, 1990), p. 9.
5. Christoph Hein, 'Rede auf der Versammlung des Bezirksverbandes Berlin des Schriftstellerverbandes der DDR (14.9.1989)', *NdL*, 38.1 (1990), 146–53; p. 152.
6. Erich Honecker, 'Grußadresse des Zentralkomitees der Sozialistischen Einheitspartei Deutschlands', *X. Schriftstellerkongreß der Deutschen Demokratischen Republik. Plenum* (Cologne: Pahl-Rugenstein, 1988), pp. 18–20; p. 19.
7. Hermann Kant, 'Rede', *X. Schriftstellerkongreß der Deutschen Demokratischen Republik. Plenum*, pp. 21–52; p. 37.
8. Christoph Hein, 'Arbeitsgruppe IV: Literatur und Wirklung', *X. Schriftstellerkongreß der Deutschen Demokratischen Republik. Arbeitsgruppen* (Cologne: Pahl-Rugenstein, 1988), pp. 224–47; p. 228.
9. Günter de Bruyn, 'Rede', *X. Schriftstellerkongreß der Deutschen Demokratischen Republik. Plenum*, pp. 128–31; p. 128.

10. Ibid., p. 129.
11. Hein, 'Arbeitsgruppe IV: Literatur und Wirkung', p. 243.
12. Wolf, 'The Language of the Turning Point', in Wolf, *Parting from Phantoms: Selected Writings, 1990–1994*, trans. Jan van Heurck (University of Chicago Press, 1997), pp. 3–5; p. 3.
13. Ibid., p. 4.
14. Ibid.
15. Stefan Heym, 'Rede', in Annegret Hahn, Gisela Puchler, Henning Schaller and Lothar Scharsich (eds.), *4. November '89: Der Protest, die Menschen, die Reden* (Frankfurt/M.: Ullstein, 1990), pp. 162–65; pp. 164–65.
16. Christoph Hein, 'Rede', in Hahn, Puchler, Schaller and Scharsich (eds.), *4. November '89: Der Protest, die Menschen, die Reden*, pp. 195–96; p. 195.
17. Ibid.
18. Christa Wolf, 'Erklärung', in Wolf, *Reden im Herbst* (Berlin: Aufbau, 1990), pp. 169–70; p. 169.
19. Ibid., p. 170.
20. Jörg Magenau, *Christa Wolf. Eine Biographie*, 2nd edn (Berlin: Kindler, 2002), p. 386.
21. 'Aufruf für eine eigenständige DDR vom 26. November 1989', in Charles Schüddekopf (ed.), *'Wir sind das Volk!' Flugschriften, Aufrufe und Texte einer deutschen Revolution* (Reinbek bei Hamburg: Rowohlt, 1990), pp. 240–41; p. 240.
22. Quoted in Thomas Anz, 'Der Streit um Christa Wolf und die Intellektuellen im vereinten Deutschland', in Peter Monteath and Reinhard Alter (eds.), *Kulturstreit – Streitkultur. German Literature since the Wall* (Amsterdam: Rodopi, 1996), pp. 1–17; p. 6.
23. Monika Maron, 'Die Schriftsteller und das Volk', *Der Spiegel*, 12 February (1990), pp. 68–70; p. 68.
24. Christa Wolf, 'Nachtrag zu einem Herbst', in Wolf, *Reden im Herbst*, p. 7.
25. Ibid., p. 13.
26. Peter Uwe Hohendahl, 'Wandel der Öffentlichkeit. Kulturelle und politische Identität im heutigen Deutschland', in Claudia Mayer-Iswandy (ed.), *Zwischen Traum und Trauma – Die Nation. Transatlantische Perspektiven zur Geschichte eines Problems* (Tübingen: Stauffenburg, 1994), pp. 129–46; p. 136.
27. Stefan Heym, 'Ist die DDR noch zu retten? Aus dem real existierenden muß ein wirklicher Sozialismus werden', *Die Zeit*, 13 October 1989: www.zeit.de/1989/42/ist-die-ddr-noch-zu-retten.
28. Stefan Heym, 'Aschermittwoch in der DDR', *Der Spiegel*, 4 December 1989 (1989), pp. 55–58; p. 58.
29. Hannes Bahrmann, Christoph Links, *Chronik der Wende. Stationen der Einheit. Die letzten Monate der DDR* (Berlin: Links, 1995), p. 174.
30. Ulrich Greiner, 'Mangel an Feingefühl', in Thomas Anz (ed.), *'Es geht nicht um Christa Wolf.' Der Literaturstreit im vereinigten Deutschland*, Erweiterte Neuausgabe (Frankfurt/M.: Fischer, 1995), pp. 66–70; p. 70.

31. Frank Schirrmacher, '"Dem Druck des härteren strengeren Lebens standhalten". Auch eine Studie über den autoritären Charakter: Christa Wolfs Aufsätze, Reden und ihre jüngste Erzählung *Was bleibt*', in Anz (ed.), *'Es geht nicht um Christa Wolf'*, pp. 77–89; p. 87.

32. Anz, 'Der Fall Christa Wolf und der Literaturstreit im vereinten Deutschland', in Anz, *Es geht nicht um Christa Wolf*, pp. 7–28; p. 10.

33. Christa Wolf, *What Remains and Other Stories*, trans. Heike Schwarzbauer and Rick Takvorian (New York: Farrar, Straus and Giroux, 1993), pp. 231–95; p. 285.

34. Ibid., p. 286.

35. Ibid., p. 287.

36. Volker Braun, 'Das Eigentum', in Braun, *Lustgarten Preußen: Ausgewählte Gedichte* (Frankfurt/M.: Suhrkamp, 1996), p. 141.

37. Volker Braun, 'Das Lehen', in Braun, *Lustgarten. Preußen*, p. 74.

38. Braun, 'Das Eigentum', p. 141.

39. Ulrich Greiner, 'Der Potsdamer Abgrund. Anmerkungen zu einem öffentlichen Streit über die "Kulturnation Deutschland"', *Die Zeit*, 22 June 1990, p. 59.

40. The PEN merger was particularly controversial, and a number of writers resigned their membership. A main point of contention was the collusion between some of the East German writers and the Stasi.

41. Hermann Vinke (ed.), *Akteneinsicht Christa Wolf. Zerrspiegel und Dialog*, 2nd edn (Hamburg: Luchterhand, 1993).

42. Anz, 'Der Fall Christa Wolf und der Literaturstreit im vereinten Deutschland', pp. 13–14.

43. Volker Hage and Susanne Beyer, 'Wir haben dieses Land geliebt', *Der Spiegel*, 24 June 2010, pp. 135–38; www.spiegel.de/spiegel/print/d-70940417.html.

44. Magenau, *Christa Wolf*, p. 437.

45. Christa Wolf, *City of Angels: or, The Overcoat of Dr. Freud*, trans. Damion Searls (New York: Farrar, Straus and Giroux, 2013), p. 51.

46. Stephen Brockmann, 'German Literary Debates after the Collapse', *German Life and Letters*, 47.2 (1994), 201–10; p. 202.

47. Ibid., p. 202.

CHAPTER 12

After-images – afterlives
Remembering the GDR in the Berlin Republic

Karen Leeder

Twenty-five years after the fall of the Berlin Wall, a wide variety of competing memories, interpretations and representations of the GDR have emerged. Indeed, contrary to predictions that the GDR would be a mere 'footnote in history' (see Introduction), the writers, artists and filmmakers of the Berlin Republic (and beyond) have dedicated huge energies to reimagining the socialist state, to the point that one can speak of East Germany enjoying a distinctive, if curious, afterlife. Society has moved definitively beyond the halfway point of the 'forty years' that Günter de Bruyn and others claimed would be needed to come to terms with the forty years that the socialist state existed on German soil.[1] It also means that a generation has come to adulthood with the GDR only as an inherited memory. Attempting to sketch an authoritative overview of this afterlife goes beyond the scope of this chapter. This is partly due to the sheer volume of material and the number of competing approaches, but also, simultaneously, because it is all as yet simply too close for any clear and final shape to have emerged.

For one, the quarter of a century that has elapsed has seen distinct 'phases and modes of cultural remembering'.[2] That is to say that the process of coming to terms with the legacy of East Germany has itself already been historicized in ways that have found broad consensus, even though they represent a complex interplay of factors. This schema has chiefly been governed by, but also complicated by, a generational paradigm (see also Wolfgang Emmerich's chapter in this volume) that has seen three or four distinct generations each bring their own perspective to bear, the youngest of whom have only a childhood memory of the GDR. This development in turn has been influenced by, and responded to, the larger political events of the intervening years of various different kinds: the German literary debate of 1990, the ongoing revelations from the Stasi archives, the introduction of the notorious Hartz IV welfare reforms, the financial straits ushered in by the global economic downturn, the events of

9/11 and the large-scale commemorations of German unity in 2009 and 2014.

Alongside this temporal axis, it is important not to forget the geographical differences at play. Writers, artists and filmmakers from West Germany have played a prominent part in shaping the retrospective memory of the GDR, along with the significant number of East Germans who had already left the GDR before the fall of the Wall and offer a different perspective again. Beyond this, in some sense, local response, it must also be remembered that perhaps more quickly and more extremely than any other event of recent history, the fall of the Berlin Wall and its aftermath became a global media phenomenon, accessed and 'experienced' by hundreds of millions of people. This has raised particular issues about the mediatization of memory; and it is noticeable that responses to the end of the GDR have been prominently associated with discussions of 'prosthetic memory' and 'post-memory'. In academic terms GDR Studies, or 'Transitional Studies' as it has also been dubbed, is a boom area in universities across the world. And, of course, many of the key cultural documents that have come to represent the GDR in the global consciousness have come from outside the GDR – none more so perhaps than Florian Henckel von Donnnersmark's Oscar-winning Hollywood film *The Lives of Others* (2006), which caught the attention of audiences around the world.

What is more, the period under scrutiny also coincides with what has been widely diagnosed as a shift towards globalization more generally, with much (East) German culture looking beyond the narrow confines of its own history and negotiating its place in a much larger, more conflicted or hybrid realm, and arguably losing a particular East German slant. In this sense the literature and film seeking to address the legacy of the GDR is itself part of a 'battle ground of memories' and contested projections, but is also simply one strand within the larger 'memory contests' that have set about negotiating the place of German history, culture and political identity after unification within a global context.[3]

It has also become part of what I have called a larger renegotiation of modernity and the modernist project per se. The 'sense of an ending', to borrow Frank Kermode's resonant title, which has marked a good deal of cultural production, especially in the wake of the millennium, has left its mark on approaches to the former East German state.[4] Commentators have diagnosed a sense of 'end times' thinking, symbolized in various forms: from the fairy to the ghost, or the ruin.[5] But, at another level, it also chimes with a number of philosophical interventions that have sought to locate society in a state of terminal decline, such as Slavoj Žižek's *Living in the End Times*, for example, or have tried to speculate with, even reinvent, futures from a Marxist perspective, amid the bric-a-brac of the present, such as Fredric Jameson's *Archaeologies of the Future* (2005).[6] Ultimately, this kind of terminal thinking is associated in political and philosophical terms with the passing of 'mass utopia' more generally, of which the end of GDR is simply a single example. In its wake has come a kind of catastrophic vision of the present as a moment marked more broadly by 'afterness'.[7]

This brief introduction gives a sense of the problem. Commentators have been rightly cautious; insisting on the end of a single interpretive paradigm and reinforcing the need to allow for 'multiple memories and plural authenticities' in addressing the legacy of the east.[8] In this spirit, what must inevitably only be soundings offered here will attempt to highlight some of the salient lines of investigation. Cumulatively it is hoped that documenting a series of discrete, though interconnected, 'after-images' of the GDR in the Berlin Republic will go some way to sketching its contested afterlife, while all the time foregrounding the processes that go into creating that image or memory. Given that many of the popular discussions of this period focus only on prose, this chapter will also attempt to redress the balance by foregrounding some of the other genres.

The lost country

The *Wende* of autumn 1989 has sometimes been compared to the 'Zero hour' of 1945, as a moment of new beginnings, of possibilities, of historical agency. Volker Braun recalled a moment of 'fantastical repose, as if to decide about the whole future': 'History / Turns on its heels and is / For one moment / Determined.'[9] In retrospect this seems a curious idea, given the profound continuities across the date and the extent to which the legacy of the now-defunct state would dominate German consciousness.[10] In fact, as Klaus Scherpe observes, the idea of the zero hour was itself a 'productive delusion, a historical phantasy, promoted by intellectuals', who clung on to the idea of a moment of calm between the ruined past and a hopeful future, and an outdated understanding of their own role.[11] In reality, as was almost immediately apparent, the 'beautiful moment' (Helga Königsdorf) was an illusion, and the hopes of the intellectuals gathered to promote the resolution 'Für unser Land' (For Our Country) at the Alexanderplatz demonstrations on 4 November 1989 (see the previous chapter) were in retrospect seen to be little more than 'a theatrical experiment'.[12] The intellectuals who had advocated a reformed utopian socialism had by this moment largely forfeited their privileged status as mouthpieces of the people. Indeed Thomas Brussig wickedly depicts Christa Wolf, 'Our Christa', spontaneously sitting down to write a new GDR constitution in his best-selling satire *Helden wie Wir* (Heroes Like Us, 1995). The governing tenor of the mood after unification moved seamlessly to loss. Alongside the many concrete losses – rights, pensions, housing, jobs and so on – there were also more invasive losses, for all that they were less immediately tangible (Marion Titze's title of 1993 *Unbekannter Verlust* [Unknown Loss] is relevant here), but ultimately one is speaking of the loss of history, of dreams, of hopes – of the self. This is worth setting out here because the crisis of loss that quickly followed the hopes of unification set the tenor of what was to come. Writers too lost their habitual status as 'hero' and were unceremoniously toppled from their pedestals just like the many decommissioned statues seen across the Eastern bloc. Everyone – even those who had created their identity in opposition to the state – had the coordinates that had governed their lives removed at a stroke. This led to a kind of implosion in the early years after the *Wende*, in which many writers were thrown back on themselves in an intense scrutiny of their actions, their beliefs and their lives. It is no chance that the central line of Volker Braun's poem 'Eigentum' (Property) became so resonant: 'Und unverständlich wird mein ganzer Text' (And my whole text becomes incomprehensible). In this image the word 'text' surely stands for the concrete literary work, but, beyond that specific reference, also a life lived, a history and the very utopian aspirations on which the GDR was founded. For younger writers, especially those who had felt alienated from, or indifferent to, their GDR context, that disengagement was easier. Durs Grünbein notes, already in his diaries for 'the first' year after unification, 'Utopia is a hysterical category'; and Thomas Rosenlöcher provocatively titles his ironic anecdotes about GDR life of 2001 'Eastern whining'.[13]

Ostalgie

The caricature of the 'Jammerossi' (whining East German) – along with his opposite number the 'Besserwessi' (know-it-all West German) – quickly became established. It was Wolfgang Emmerich, the author of the standard western literary history of the GDR, who memorably put this onto an intellectual footing when, discussing Albrecht Dürer's famous etching 'Melancholia I' (1514), he identified a 'furor melancholicus' as the defining characteristic of GDR writers and intellectuals after the fall of the Wall (1991).[14] Following Alexander and Margarete Mitscherlichs's analysis of the post-war German 'inability to mourn' (1967), Emmerich interpreted the post-1989 writing as the beginning of a process of separation from the 'ego-ideal' of the GDR: the self-conscious attempt to begin the mourning process.[15] In this, it can be argued, ex-GDR authors were also picking up the threads of the truncated 'work of mourning' of 1945 and beyond, and creating spaces where (necessary) elegiac structures could unfold.

A literature of elegy in the broadest sense has been a constant strand of German literature since 1990. And a pervasive 'Tristesse' has found its way into works of many writers, especially, but not confined to, those who invested most heavily in the utopian promise of GDR. So it is that several of the most high-profile works of the Berlin Republic by authors like Monika Maron, *animal triste* (1996), and Christa Wolf, *Die Stadt der Engel: oder, The Overcoat of Dr. Freud* (City of Angels: or, the Overcoat of Dr. Freud, 2010), for example, were still attempting to extricate themselves retrospectively from their GDR identification years, even decades, down the line.

But elegiac structures can be seductive. And this thread of writing arguably gave legitimacy to the pervasive nostalgia for the East that brought a new word into the German language: 'Ostalgie'. *Ostalgie* is not of course only a GDR phenomenon; 'a post-communist nostalgia' has been part of responses to the disappearance of socialism across the Eastern bloc and indeed in the West.[16] It is arguably also a symptom of our age, or at least the bowdlerized 'nostalgia mode' identified presciently by Fredric Jameson already in 1991. This is persuasively iterated by the likes of Mark Fisher, who, in *Ghosts of My Life* (2014), uses Jameson as a springboard and detects ubiquitous signs of exhaustion, finitude, deflation of expectations, temporal disjuncture and formal nostalgia in twenty-first-century popular culture.[17]

However, in remembering the GDR such nostalgia has a real and immediate focus. It is not simply a matter of a broad-brush 'Requiem for Communism', as Charity Scribner put it, in an influential work of 2003, nor indeed the nostalgia for pre-1989 West Germany – a less prominent but also significant phenomenon.[18] Rather, much literature has been concerned to remember, preserve and uphold particular facets of 'everyday life' in the GDR: symbolized by, for example, the distinctive East German traffic lights (Ampelmännchen), GDR foodstuffs, or particular cultural icons such as the East German children's bedtime animation, *Unser Sandmännchen* (Our Sandman), begun in 1959 and continued even after unification. This is nowhere clearer than in the controversy surrounding those films such as *Sonnenallee* (Sun Alley, Leander Haußmann, 1999, after the novel by Thomas Brussig) and, especially, *Goodbye, Lenin!* (Wolfgang Becker, 2003), which assert the rights of individuals to uphold and even celebrate aspects of their own past. As Mischa concludes in *Sonnenallee*, 'and if you ask me what it was like: it was the best time of my life, because I was young and in love'.[19]

At the macro-level, the historical diagnosis of GDR totalitarianism led to an act of dispossession vis-à-vis former East Germans: it robbed them of their past. Everyday memories risked being eclipsed, decreed sentimental or suspected of attempting to mitigate the brutalities of the regime. In response, then, at the micro-level, the retrospective iteration of aspects of that everyday life, or 'Alltagsleben', set out to 'tell it as it was' and reclaim that past. This has become an important response in GDR works to this day, carrying with it a vital recuperative effect. But it also potentially carries a political charge: implying the nurturing of a visceral 'Trotzidentität' (identity based on resistance), a form of 'writing back' against the hegemonic, possibly colonizing, assumptions of the united Germany that Paul Cooke has identified.[20] It is striking, nevertheless, that aspects of this approach have continued several decades after the end of the GDR, and also that they can be seen across generations and even in the very youngest writers, whose identification with a state that they experienced only as children is one of the more remarkable phenomena of recent years. Here, besides the perils of sentimentality, there is another danger, however, for the GDR heritage has also become recuperated by the market. While various iconic GDR goods have earned themselves an aura of 'retro-chic' beyond the borders of the new Bundesländer, even beyond Germany, they also run the risk of becoming a grotesquely commodified symbol, rather than any true after-image, of life in the GDR.

Generations

As Wolfgang Emmerich has set out in Chapter 1 of this volume, the paradigm of generational experience has a much greater force in German literature (and especially in the far more homogenous GDR sphere) than in other parts of the world. It was clear after 1990 that the literary scene would largely be dominated by older writers such as Heiner Müller, Volker Braun, Stefan Heym, Wolfgang Hilbig, Günter de Bruyn and Christa Wolf. For them the often painful coming to terms with the end of the GDR and the 'arrival in the West' (in André Brie's phrase) meant also rethinking their own lives. What is more, for them, the epochal caesura was intimately bound up with their own biological ageing, but also a wider apprehension of end times set out above. Theirs are late works in every sense of the word.[21]

The infirmities of old age and illness are conspicuous anxieties, for example, in Wolf's *Leibhaftig* (In the Flesh, 2002) and *Stadt der Engel*: 'I knew that I must die. I know how fragile we are. Old age was beginning';[22] while Müller, in an extraordinary body of late poetry, much of which has only recently been collected, charts his epochal disillusionment under the sign of his own illness and early death with characteristic dryness.[23] While the ageing process prompts an autobiographically-inspired life review, it is also seen as a symptom of increasing social redundancy and obsolescence. Günter de Bruyn contends, with a nod to Nietzsche, that 'growing older also means to no longer feel yourself to be the child of the age'.[24] Likewise, the slightly younger Monika Maron's post-1989 work – for example, *Endmoränen* (End Moraines, 2002) – explores feelings of superfluity in the debilitating emptiness of the present. In all these works, the individual experience is mapped onto the collapse of the state and end of history implied in its demise. Braun's important poetry collection *Tumulus* (1999) is quite literally founded on death (the title meaning hill of the dead, or sepulchral mound) and performs a kind of last rites of the GDR. The end of his 'Lagerfeld' famously projects the sense of uncontrolled descent into a cul de sac of historical aftermath (late capitalism) against a classical backdrop.

> In der Wegwerfgesellschaft
> Das Stadion voll letzter Schreie Ideen
> Roms letzte Epoche des Unernsts
> Sehn Sie nun das Finale ICH ODER ICH
> Salute, Barbaren
>
> (In the Throwaway Society
> The arena full of the last screams Ideas
> Rome's last era, unseriousness
> Now watch the finale ME OR ME
> Greetings, barbarians)[25]

He is not the only one to employ this trope. The years after end of the GDR saw an intense preoccupation with classical models, used both to diagnose the decline and also to model ways for the future. This had already been a distinctive aspect of GDR literature, but after 1990 not only Braun, Müller and Wolf but also younger authors (e.g. Durs Grünbein and Barabra Köhler) continued to mine classical sources to very great effect, using the affinities across the ages to shed an often-corrosive light on the present.[26] That this has also been marked by a kind of crisis about the efficacy, indeed point, of literature in the age of the market is perhaps inevitable, and *Mommsens Block* (1992/3) delineates Müller's own experience of writer's block against the classical historian Theodor Mommsen's failure to write the projected fourth part of his *History of Rome*: about the experience of the Roman Empire.

By common consensus 1994/1995 has been understood to mark a turning point. Iris Radisch published an influential article in the newspaper *Die Zeit* which heralded a 'second zero hour', as she called it, triggered by a 'change in generations'. Younger writers did not, she claimed, have any interest in remembering, reworking or revisiting the past: 'The third post-war generation has simply closed the great book of history [. . .]. There are many stories, but no history any longer'.[27]

Works by writers like Brussig, Grünbein but also Ingo Schulze and Kerstin Hensel heralded a different, and more distanced, way of approaching the legacy. Many highlighted that they had not felt connected to the utopian vision of the East German state and as a consequence neither perceived themselves as victims of it nor mourned its demise.[28] Their work focused primarily on the struggles and issues of everyday people and everyday life in the present of the united Germany with little sense of a specific generational experience, nor of any representative function. Unification, as an historic event, is notably marginal to their work, although its effects are still felt and examined. Kerstin Hensel, in a book combining stories from her past with photographs from GDR times, insisted on the importance of 'stories of the everyday' as the only way to access the past.[29] And the tone is not one of nostalgia, nor does it speak of a retrospectively constructed GDR identity. These writers are 'free', as Radisch claims, not to construct exemplary narratives in the model of post-war literature, but to express their own lives, liberated from any historical burden.[30] However, the effects of such freedom are not exclusively positive and these 'stories' also tell of an erasure of identity and history that leaves individuals anchorless in the east and the west. Perhaps the best example is Ingo Schulze's acclaimed *Simple Storys* (1998). With an acute eye for detail and a sometimes biting humour, he depicts a population in the provinces of the new Republic struggling to come to terms with capitalism: the people portrayed live precariously, at the mercy of the market, in perpetual fear of betrayal, failure, dismissal and ruin; and the work, for all its humour, offers a dismal vision of a 'condition post-communiste' (Boris Groys).[31]

But generational change and the shift of vision it implies reoccur at regular intervals, and Lutz Rathenow, introducing the journalist Robert Ide's *Geteilte Träume: Meine Eltern, die Wende und ich* (Divided Dreams: My Parents, the Wende and Me) in 2007, declares another such juncture.[32] In his work Ide (b. 1975) makes the point that the division between East and West is only one of the significant divisions at stake in contemporary

Germany. Another, of equal importance, are the 'divided dreams' entertained by different generations. Ide pinpoints the emergence of the so-called 'Zonenkinder' generation, a label borrowed from the best-selling book by Jana Hensel (b. 1976), which has since become shorthand for the 'confessions from an East German childhood and the life that came next' – as the book was subtitled in its English edition.[33] These are young authors (e.g. Jakob Hein, Claudia Rusch), who were only children when the Wall came down, but whose first literary works in the Berlin Republic identify their socialization within the GDR regime as their formative influence. It is clear that for these younger writers their experience of the GDR and of integration into the society of the Berlin Republic is fundamentally different from that of their parents and that they must constitute a 'last literature of the GDR'. Their existence between identities and times has led to them being thought of as a 'lost', even 'hermaphrodite' generation, and the success of this phenomenon has been dogged by controversy.[34] Nevertheless, in its reportage quality, pop-cultural references and turn towards global themes, aesthetically some of this literature provides a pendant to the pop literature of the West German 'Generation Golf' (Florian Illies) constituting a 'GenerationTrabi' of sorts.

Genre

This is the stage at which to interject a necessarily brief reflection on genre. It is striking that over the course of the last quarter of a century different genres have developed in different ways in approaching the afterlife of the GDR. What is more, different genres have had their own particular historical moment. One of the striking continuities, however, is preeminence of the autobiographical as a mode. This was of course one of particular facets of GDR writing (compare Dennis Tate's chapter in this volume) but it has also, perhaps unsurprisingly, played a major role in attempts to secure identity after 1990, even if that mode has sometimes been experimental: involving splicing autobiographical material with lyric, and theatrical modes, as well as reportage, photography, and in film the use of old GDR camera stock.

The urgency of the situation immediately after the *Wende*, however, privileged short forms: poetry, essays, journalistic pieces, resolutions, notes, interviews, speeches and open letters. During the bewildering first year, the sudden acceleration of history after decades of stagnation, writers felt the need to participate in the events, to help shape them, and to articulate their concerns as quickly as possible.[35] Interestingly women, often marginalized in the larger public forum, were particularly visible at this time.

With time came a second wave of essays, letters, more substantial dialogues, but also protocols, and fragments of memoir. This is a largely experiential literature with its roots in the work of documentary. It set about presenting the material of experience as recorded at a sub-literary stage and brought information to the public realm about lives often unsanctioned in the repressive context of the GDR. A category which is in many ways linked, but which can usefully be separated off for the purpose of discussion, is the historical memoir. Much of the memoir-writing dealt with the past at one remove; for example, treating childhood as a prominent theme, as in Christoph Hein's *Als Kind habe ich Stalin gesehen* (As a Child I Saw Stalin, 1992). From here one need not go very far to identify the beginnings of a new wave of 'Vaterliteratur' (literature dealing with the fathers). Kurt Drawert's *Spiegelland* (Mirror Land, 1992) is probably the most notable example, though one could point to many more. But more important (as Hein's title makes explicit), very many texts resisted the immediacy of the dislocation around them by dealing instead with events from a more distant past, especially Fascism and Stalinism. One of the more problematic results of this belated reckoning was the implied comparison of the 'two dictatorships' that many of these writers had lived through. However this category of documentary and memoir leads to an even more specific and controversial area: the publication of 'Stasi' files (dealt with in detail in Alison Lewis's contribution to this volume). This might be thought of as a genre in and of itself and, taken in toto, an alternative autobiography of the GDR.

The Berlin Republic was for a long time haunted by the search for the 'novel of unification'. It is worth pointing out, however, that the fractured forms and discontinuous aesthetics of the late 1990s and early 2000s offered for many a more aesthetically appropriate means to engage the contemporary historical moment. Schulze's *Simple Storys*, discussed above, is a case in point. At first glance his 'novel' of the East German province, set in Altenburg, where Schulze lived for some time, looks like twenty-nine isolated miniatures, each of which could be read as an autonomous short story. No one character's life is followed; there is no central I; and there is constant reflection on the notion of stories told, untold, fabricated and forgotten. In the American short story (especially that of Ernest Hemingway and Robert Carver) Schulze claimed to have found a model for what he called the 'short-story sound', the 'right frequency' to write about the experience of the new Germany: 'stories capture history [in German: "Geschichten treffen Geschichte"] more accurately. I could only recount it as stories'.[36] This was an experience and an aesthetic approach shared by others such as Katja Lange-Müller, Kerstin Hensel and Kathrin Schmidt. In their work the

snapshots of life, the humour and the often eccentric plot or mode (sometimes magic realist) serves 'to decentre the grand drama of history', and
aesthetically enact, as it were, the widespread feeling of instability.[37]

It was only later and at a relative temporal distance from the events of
unification that the lived reality of socialism and its aftermath finds its form
in realist aesthetics and epic narrative. Authors like Schulze himself, and
also Thomas Brussig, *Wie es leuchtet* (How It Shines, 2004); Uwe Tellkamp,
Der Turm (The Tower, 2008), Wolfgang Hilbig, *Das Provisorium* (The
Stop-Gap Measure, 2000); or "*Ich*" ("I", 1993) look to the form of the
novel to offer the space to reflect on the complex and multifaceted reality.[38]
Especially in Reinhard Jirgl's *Abtrünnig: Roman aus der nervösen Zeit*
(Renegade: Novel of the Nervous Time, 2005), we see a radical rethinking
of epic form. The many hyperlinks included serve as a vehicle for a discussion
of reading practices, linearity and structures of narrative and memory, while
also challenging the format of the traditional, printed book and how the
after-image of history can be reconstructed.

One aspect of this development is the much-discussed 'generational' or
'family novel', which has in many ways become the defining genre of the
Berlin Republic in recent years (for writers from East and West Germany)
and has already provoked much discussion: Monika Maron's *Pawel's Briefe*
(Pawel's Letters, 1999) or more recently Eugen Ruge's much-garlanded *In
Zeiten des abnehmenden Lichts* (In Times of Fading Light, 2011) have turned
to this genre to offer a more sustained reflection beyond the contemporary.
And important works like Reinhard Jirgl's epic and convoluted *Die Stille*
(The Silence, 2009) or Jenny Erpenbeck's *Heimsuchung* (Visitation, 2008)
go even further. Here the GDR reality is historicized within a much larger
historical trajectory: Jirgl's massive novel covering a century or so and
Erpenbeck situating the GDR and indeed the century within the vastness
of implacable geological time.

The theatre, stymied perhaps by the sheer drama of history itself, has by
and large found it harder to find a distinctive role in this period – notwithstanding several notable incarnations of GDR novels, a lively engagement
with GDR heritage and the debuts of a number of younger dramatists (e.g.
Anne Rabe).[39] Heiner Müller famously reflected on his inability to confront
history in theatrical form after 1990. And it is noticeable that his final play
Germania 3: Gespenster am toten Mann (Germania 3: Ghosts at the Dead
Man, 1996) is a singularly 'undramatic' drama (even within the context of
post-dramatic theatre): a (controversial) palimpsest of texts and citations that
sites itself after the death of the GDR and drama.[40] Instead, it is arguably
film that has become the key vehicle for remembering the GDR. Tate makes

the important point that many of the best-known novels of the period owe their success in part to subsequent celebrated film adaptations.[41] The liveliness of the post-GDR film scene has already been the subject of detailed discussion.[42] But it is worth also highlighting the influence of films like *Goodbye, Lenin!*, discussed earlier, but also West German filmmaker Christian Petzold's well-received reflections on GDR reality *Yella* (2007; one of his *Gespenster* or 'Ghost' Trilogy) and *Barbara* (2012). In this film, as with the other big hit of this period, von Donnersmark's *Lives of Others*, however, the reality of GDR existence has become identified with an image of the secret police. For all their virtues, and despite correcting the *Ostalgie* of earlier films, it is clear that in the global popular imagination the GDR has become identified as a 'Stasiland'.

Heimat

Anna Funder's memorable label for a country remembered through its structures of power, its security network, is one version of GDR *Heimat* that has, especially outside Germany, fascinated and disconcerted in almost equal measure.[43] Timothy Garton Ash, in an influential analysis of the film *Lives of Others*, distinguished modern Germany's singular if perverse achievement as being to have identified itself in the world's imagination with the 'darkest evils' of the century: 'The words "Nazi", "SS", and "Auschwitz" are already global synonyms for the deepest inhumanity of fascism. Now the word "Stasi" is becoming a default global synonym for the secret police terrors of communism'.[44] If David Bathrick applied the Brechtian term 'Greuelmärchen', that is, 'fairy-tales-of-horror' to Germany's filmic attempts to deal with Fascist past, von Donnersmark's film has been read as a 'fairy-tale of redemption', one of Hollywood's many attempts to find the 'good German', here the good Stasi officer.[45] It is, however, only one example of a large body of work (both film and prose) that has struggled in different ways to come to terms with this most corrosive legacy. Notable examples are Kerstin Hensel's *Tanz am Kanal* (Dance at The Canal, 1994), Hilbig's *"Ich"*, Brigitte Burmeister, *Unter dem Namen Nora* (Under the Name Nora, 1995), along with the films *Der Tangospieler* (The Tango Player, dir. Roland Gräf, 1991) or *Der Verdacht* (The Suspicion, dir. Frank Beyer, 1991). But the issue shows no signs of abating: a good deal of more recent work continues to worry at the schizophrenic consciousness underpinning the GDR, and in *After the Stasi*, Annie Ring persuasively demonstrates that these concerns feed directly into issues of sovereignty and surveillance that continue in the Berlin Republic.[46]

But this is only one version of the many reimaginings of an East German *Heimat* that have been constructed over the years. Early sentimental versions of a lost idyll, propagated by the likes of Erwin Strittmatter, very soon made way for very different visions. Some of these have been analysed as attempts to conjure 'community' in the face of the atomized society and human disenfranchisement of the moment. Jens Sparschuh's *Der Zimmerspringbrunnen* (The Room Fountain, 1995), for example, explicitly subtitled *Ein Heimatroman*, is a double-edged narrative ironizing a nostalgically remembered 'Heimat DDR' but also highlighting lack of human rootedness in the hyper-commercialized new Germany.[47] Others go further and continue the tradition of satire (analysed in this volume by Jill Twark) to launch savage attacks on the xenophobic politics and welfare programmes of the Berlin Republic: notably Volker Braun's *Machwerk oder Das Schichtbuch des Flick von Lauchhammer* (Botched Job or the Shift Book of Flick of Lauchhammer, 2008), at once a blistering assault on the times, but also an elegy for the dignity of work.

Two things are immediately apparent in surveying the multiple constructions of home. The first is a competing sense of where that home might be; something that has coincided with a topographical turn in contemporary criticism, which has in effect made this a very rich seam of contemporary criticism. On the one hand, Berlin, as the capital of the new Republic has become an enduring symbol of the new Germany, one might even say of the new Europe. But if some commentators have identified a 'farewell' to East Berlin in the city literature and art since 1990 as the statues, buildings and streets disappear to make way for a citadel to finance,[48] others have diagnosed the opposite. Maxim Biller's provocative notion of an 'Ossifizerung des Westens' (an Ossification of the West) is answered to some degree by the pre-eminence of certain GDR icons in representing the new Germany as a whole.[49] A case in point is the Berlin Fernsehturm (Television Tower, Figure 8), which, without moving an inch, has arguably metamorphosed into the symbolic shorthand for Berlin abroad, replacing the Brandenburg Gate in recognizability.[50] What is more, it appears on the cover of any number of works in this period, not only works by those from the former east. In short, it is argued that 'Berlin both preserves the old GDR (whether ironically as *Ostalgie* and tourism, or in the concrete forms which remain in the city) *and* draws its contemporary image from the 'Hauptstadt der DDR' (capital of the GDR) and [. . .] thus persists in the city in two ways, as past and present'.[51]

On the other hand, there has also been a move to locate after-images of *Heimat* far from the central locus of the new Germany. As Patricia Anne Simpson notes, 'East Germany no longer exists as a country: it persists as an

Figure 8 Christian Rudat, 'Berliner Fernsehturm' [Berlin Television Tower].
Courtesy of Christian Rudat.

intellectual "borderland", although no longer policed in any literal sense.'
In the absence of 'the collective locality of international socialism', the
ground of identity is instead displaced into 'regional affiliations'.[52]

This perhaps accounts for the pronounced interest in marginal identities
and liminal topographies ('Novel from the East German Province' is the
subtitle of Schulze's *Simple Storys* after all). One aspect is the fascination
with Dresden as an alternative locus for the imagination, but one that also
issues into a contemplation of a longer and traumatic history, as in
Tellkamp's *Der Turm* or Grünbein's *Porzellan: Poem vom Untergang meiner
Stadt* (Porcelain: Poem about the Destruction of My City, 2005) and *Die
Jahre im Zoo* (The Zoo Years 2015). However, it also appears in exemplary
fashion in Jenny Erpenbeck's *Heimsuchung* (Visitation, 2008), the haunting
and haunted chronicle of a house in the Brandenburg countryside; Lutz
Seiler's elegy for the disappeared mining villages of Gera in *pech & blende*
(pitch & blende, 2000); or Julia Schoch's bleak distillation of love, suicide
and provincial boredom in *Mit der Geschwindigkeit des Sommers* (With the
Fleetingness of Summer, 2009).[53]

The second point is linked. One of the striking things is the degree to
which the sense of imagined GDR *Heimat* in the Berlin Republic is frankly
dystopian. Seiler's villages, for example, which might in other hands be the
subject of rural elegy, are in fact poisoned by radiation from the uranium
mines there and surrounded by slagheaps. And a landscape of landfill,
garbage, dereliction and ruin, 'a broken world', is a notable aspect of much
more recent work, for example, young Leipzig author Clemens Meyer's
(b. 1977) *Als wir träumten* (As We Were Dreaming, 2006).[54] But so too are
descriptions of abject creatureliness. Grünbein's 'Porträt des Künstlers als
junger Grenzhund' (Portrait of the Artist as a Young Border-Dog] might
stand as a single example. A linked dystopian topos is that of emergent
monstrosities: Thomas Hettche's *Nox* (1995), Lange-Müller's *Die Letzten*
(The Final Ones, 2000) and Grünbein's own essays and poems all feature,
for example, the singular anatomical collections of defective births in the
Museum der Charité.[55] In short the *Heimat* conjured by post-1990 literature
is in essence an 'unheimliche Heimat' (unhomely/uncanny Heimat), which
plays out in many different forms and modes.[56]

Haunted states: the spectral existence of GDR
in the Berlin Republic

This uncanny nature of the afterlife of the GDR in the Berlin Republic can
be read in line with a 'spectral turn' identified more broadly in modern

culture.[57] The forgotten, suppressed or overwritten things from the past have manifested themselves in the plethora of spectres, ghosts, *doppelgänger*, vampires and undead, which can be identified in recent work across the spectrum. Commentators have been quick to diagnose a 'Post-Wall Gothic' or 'Post-*Wende* Uncanny'.[58] Traditionally a ghost is seen as the sign of 'unfinished business': a disturbance in the symbolic, moral or epistemological order that can be resolved once the ghost has delivered its message and fulfilled its mission. The widespread manifestation of spectres in the culture of the Berlin Republic can thus be read as symptomatic of a profound crisis, as unauthorised histories destabilize the present and remain unresolved. This speaks especially to the agitated legacy of the fascist past in Germany as a whole. But they also have an acute and overriding significance in addressing the death and afterlife of the GDR. In the first place it was a state founded on the spectre of communism (recalling the first sentence of the *Communist Manifesto*: 'A spectre is haunting Europe'). Nevertheless, one might argue, as Slavoj Žižek has done, that the GDR had only a spectral existence in any case. 'Really existing socialism' was thus actually a perverted reflection of an ideal socialism, beneath which a generally intact desire for a not yet-existing socialism played its utopian role. Tellingly Peter Thompson has called it a 'reverse-vampire syndrome', in which there is a reflection but no reality.[59] And finally, the GDR is now a spectre itself: one that haunts the imagination of a culture that tries, almost obsessively, to remember, reimagine or reconstruct it.

The power of its suggestiveness is demonstrated by the number of literal spectres, phantoms, ghosts, vampires and manifestations of the undead which have appeared in post-1989 work by GDR film-makers, artists, writers and photographers, but also, significantly, by those from outside writing about the GDR. Interrogating these spectres for what they have to say (or conceal) about the GDR and the other pasts and intertexts they mobilize can reveal many different things: nostalgia, trauma, lost ideals or ideological critique. Moreover, they open the way to a discussion of an aesthetic which has moved beyond the realisms explored in the section on genre.

What I have called a spectral vision is at the heart of one of the very first cultural events of the new Germany. Heiner Müller's *Hamlet/Maschine* (his 8-hour production of his own play within his own translation of Shakespeare's *Hamlet*) was in rehearsal during the tumultuous events of 1989. *Hamlet* itself thematizes 'times out of joint' and Müller felt that it was the play best-suited to pinpoint the tension of the moment. Moreover, he identified the key question arising from the play as 'Who is the ghost?' By the time the play appeared in 1990, however, the GDR no longer existed, and the answer to that question (Communism or the Deutsche Bank) is symptomatic of a bitter recognition echoing Shakespeare's play: 'Something is rotten in this age of hope.'[60]

As a symptomatic reflection on the end of the GDR, this fascination with spectral afterlife is particularly marked and particularly suggestive. Key texts such as Christa Wolf's *Leibhaftig* or Irina Liebmann's *In Berlin* (1994) have already attracted attention and deal with the pathologically haunted subjects of a post-*Wende* world, themselves rendered liminal by the experience of haunting.[61] A notable characteristic is the prevalence of 'doppelgänger': for example, in Klaus Schlesinger's *Trug* (Betrayal, 2000); Inka Parei, *Die Schattenboxerin* (The Shadow Boxer, 1999); Norman Ohler, *Mitte* (Centre, 2001); or split personalities: Hilbig's divided protagonist in *"Ich"* and the postmortem fantasy of Petzold's *Yella* offer further examples. What is more, many of these works are also haunted by previous bodies of literature (especially from a Romantic tradition).[62] This is also true of the various reanimations of the medieval 'danse macabre', which have been a fascinating aspect of contemporary German culture. In Braun's 'Totentänze', for example, we see the GDR tradition among others fed into a deathly landscape haunted by the ghosts of GDR ideology.[63]

Further investigation would focus on the 'spectral topographies' of the post-*Wende* landscape in some of those works already mentioned. Erpenbeck's slyly titled *Heimsuchung*, for example, sports a number of ghostly figures associated with the ice, and Schoch's *Mit der Geschwindigkeit des Sommers* might in many ways be thought of as peopled by ghosts. Furthermore, this offers a new way of reading the 'ghosts of others' in film and literature: that is, the 'spooks' of the Stasi, the unseen but observing instance which officially did not exist in the GDR but which has enjoyed a spectacular afterlife in post-1990 culture.

The analysis of spectres suggests a way of making a decisive intervention in a number of key contemporary debates about the legacy of the GDR. For example, although the political tensions within *Ostalgie* are a central concern of criticism, there is a danger that they are seen as simple binary poles: the curiously sterile bifocal perspective on the GDR as 'Stasiland' or 'Ostalgie'. In a spectrally split mode, we can have a vision that recognizes the hopes that animated the past, the complicity of history in what went wrong and the bankruptcy of what resulted. It also rejects the tyranny of the present and, more importantly, the high-tech amnesia that is the terminal malady of capitalist culture.[64] To return to Braun again speaking about his *Totentänze*: 'The arts are the grandiose dance of those ghosts that have emerged from the great departures of our existence.'[65]

Finally, it offers an aesthetic alternative to the privileging of the real. A spectral aesthetic might range from the intertextual dialogue with the dead to techniques of intertextuality, lacunae, deferral, the uncanny, undecidability, doubling and repetition (the essential hallmark of the ghost, as Derrida points out). In this it explicitly gives back a role to art, not simply as passive reflection, but rather as providing an alternative vision to the obsessively iterated trope of the authentic.

There is a further point to be made, however. What I have set out here as a kind of spectral afterimage of the GDR also raises questions of its own. I would like to finish with a literal 'afterimage' of the GDR that pinpoints the dilemma: one of West German photographer Michael Wesely's (b. 1962) extreme long exposure shots of Berlin.

This image (Figure 9) is one of a series of twelve of Potsdamer Platz, the central Berlin square, which once marked the trajectory of the Berlin Wall, now almost completely obliterated, like so many historical remains of the GDR. It is part of a series begun in 1997 and at that point his longest exposures to date: a single camera shot of over two years duration from five fixed cameras.[66] The extreme long exposure allows the demolition and

Figure 9 Michael Wesely, 'Potsdamer Platz' (1990). Courtesy of Galerie Fahnemann, Berlin.

construction that occurred over the course of months to appear as a ghostly apparition in the final single frame of the photograph. For example, in one shot the Brandenburg Gate and the dome of the Reichstag under construction can be seen on the horizon, through the translucent armature of the new buildings rising in the background: literally superimposing the new on the old his photo creates a unique representation of Berlin's historical transformation. This, then, is a profoundly haunted project and in an interview Wesely speculated about a similar shot which might last forty years – coincidentally perhaps the length of time that the GDR existed. Yet the image is also troubling. Individuals are completely eliminated (and would certainly be over an even longer exposure), but so too are natural phenomena including the sun.[67] Its path appears as a ghostly trace of parallel lines in the sky interrupted only by patches of bad weather, which uncannily enough reoccur in successive years when the Earth is in the same position – as if the sun were orbiting the Earth. Henri Cartier Besson in 1932 talked of the decisive moment of the photograph: a single, essential moment seized by the photographer. This is extrapolated here in an endless repetition of moments that renders the singular insignificant. The present, the past, blurs into one, thus opening onto a post-human vision in which the particularities of history are eclipsed. Might this signal the future of the afterlife of the GDR? In a sense, it represents an ultimate normalization and is an extreme version of tendencies already visible in literature by some of the authors (of all generations) already discussed, such as Müller, Grünbein, Erpenbeck and also Barbara Köhler's *Niemands Frau* (Nobody's Wife, 2007): the memory of the GDR simply as historical oddity, a brief stage in a much longer trajectory. Looked at from far enough away this singular period becomes smaller and smaller until is it eclipsed to almost nothing. Indeed in Wesely's more recent portraits of the GDR landscape, *Ostdeutschland East Germany* (2004), the even longer exposures render geological particularities into nothing more than blocks of colour, like an abstract painting.[68] But even if literature, art and film do not embrace a dystopian or frankly post-human perspective, it is clear that the contours of the GDR will change and fade. In the work of one of the most interesting young writers to emerge from this context, poet and short story-writer Ulrike Almut Sandig (b. 1979), that reality is never named, but is present none the less as an undelineated longing for elsewhere, a careful iteration of the missing and a deep-seated scepticism for ideological certainties. Her most recent publication is the tellingly entitled prose collection *Buch gegen das Verschwinden* (Book against Disappearing, 2015). This can no longer be called GDR literature in any real sense but perhaps gives a taste of what the

GDR will become in contemporary culture. And yet, certainly while those are still alive who experienced the GDR as historical reality, we can be pretty sure that its contested afterlife will continue.

Notes

1. Günter de Bruyn, *Vierzig Jahre: Ein Lebensbericht* (Frankfurt/M.: Fischer, 1996).
2. Compare Dennis Tate's useful overview in his Introduction, 'The Importance and Diversity of Cultural Memory in the GDR Context', in Renate Rechtien and Dennis Tate (eds.), *Twenty Years On: Competing Memories of the GDR in Postunification Culture* (Rochester, NY: Camden House, 2011), pp. 1–19.
3. See especially Martin Sabrow, *Erinnerungsorte der DDR* (Munich: Beck, 2009), p. 15, p. 20 and Anne Fuchs, Mary Cosgrove and Georg Grote (eds.), *German Memory Contests: The Quest for Identity in Literature, Film, and Discourse since 1990* (Rochester, NY: Camden House, 2006).
4. Frank Kermode, *The Sense of an Ending: Studies in the Theory of Fiction with a New Epilogue* (Oxford University Press, 1966 [2000]).
5. Anne Fuchs, *Phantoms of War in Contemporary German Literature, Films, and Discourse. The Politics of Memory* (Basingstoke and New York: Palgrave Macmillan, 2008); Julia Hell and Andreas Schönle (eds.), *Ruins of Modernity* (Durham and London: Duke University Press, 2010).
6. Slavoj Žižek, *Living in the End Times* (London, New York: Verso, 2010); Fredric Jameson, *Archaeologies of the Future: The Desire Called Utopia and Other Science Fictions* (London, New York: Verso, 2005).
7. Susan Buck-Morss, *Dreamworld and Catastrophe: The Passing of Mass Utopia in East and West* (Cambridge, MA, London: MIT Press, 2002); James Berger, *After the End: Representations of Post-Apocalypse* (Minneapolis, London: University of Minnesota Press, 1999); Gerhard Richter, *Afterness: Figures of Following in Modern Thought and Aesthetics* (New York: Columbia University Press, 2011).
8. Debbie Pinfold and Anna Saunders (eds.), *Remembering and Rethinking the GDR: Multiple Perspectives and Plural Authenticities* (Basingstoke: Palgrave Macmillan, 2012).
9. The poem is Volker Braun's 'Wende'; he cites and comments in his *Wir befinden uns soweit wohl. Wir sind erstmal am Ende. Äußerungen* (Frankfurt/M.: Suhrkamp, 1988), p. 153.
10. The continuities are sketched out in Astrid Köhler, *Brückenschläge: DDR-Autoren vor und nach der Wiedervereinigung* (Göttingen: Vandenhoeck & Ruprecht, 2007) or Holger Helbig (ed.), *Weiterschreiben: Zur DDR-Literatur nach dem Ende der DDR* (Berlin: Akademie Verlag, 2007).
11. Klaus Scherpe, 'GDR Literature beyond the GDR', in Konrad H. Jarausch (ed.), *United Germany: Debating Processes and Prospects* (New York, Oxford: Berghahn, 2013), pp. 183–204, p. 185.

12. Helga Königsdorf, *1989; oder Ein Moment der Schönheit* (Berlin: Aufbau, 1990), and *Aus dem Dilemma eine Chance machen* (Hamburg and Zürich: Luchterhand, 1991), p. 8.

13. Durs Grünbein, *Das erste Jahr. Berliner Aufzeichnungen* (Frankfurt/M.: Suhrkamp, 2001), p. 44; Thomas Rosenlöcher, *Ostgezeter. Beiträge zur Schimpfkultur* (Frankfurt/M.: Suhrkamp, 1997).

14. Wolfgang Emmerich, 'Status melancholicus. Zur Transformation der Utopie in der DDR-Literatur', in *Literatur in der DDR. Rückblicke* (Munich: Text+ Kritik, 1991), pp. 232–45.

15. Alexander and Margarete Mitscherlich, *Die Unfähigkeit zu trauern: Grundlagen kollektiven Verhaltens* (Munich: Piper, 1967).

16. Maria Todorova and Zsuzsa Gille (eds.), *Post-Communist Nostalgia* (New York: Berghahn, 2010).

17. Fredric Jameson, *Postmodernism, or, The Cultural Logic of Late Capitalism* (Durham, NC, Duke University Press, 1991), p. 18; Mark Fisher, *Ghosts of My Life: Writings on Depression, Hauntology, and Lost Futures* (Winchester, Washington: Zero Books, 2014).

18. Charity Scribner, *Requiem for Communism* (Cambridge, MA; London: MIT Press, 2003).

19. Leander Haußmann, *Sonnenallee. Das Buch zum Farbfilm* (Berlin: Quadriga, 1999). On these films and the issues see Nick Hodgin, *Screening the East: Heimat, Memory and Nostalgia in German Film since 1989* (New York, Oxford: Berghahn, 2011) and Paul Cooke, *Representing East Germany since Unification: From Colonization to Nostalgia* (Oxford: Berg, 2005).

20. Cooke, *Representing East Germany.*

21. On Wolf see Stuart Taberner, *Aging and Old-Age Style in Günter Grass, Ruth Klüger, Christa Wolf, and Martin Walser: The Mannerism of a Late Period* (Rochester, NY: Camden House, 2013).

22. Christa Wolf, *Stadt der Engel: oder, The Overcoat of Dr. Freud* (Frankfurt/M.: Suhrkamp, 2010), p. 335.

23. Heiner Müller, *Warten auf der Gegenschräge: Gesammelte Gedichte*, ed. Kristin Schulz (Berlin: Suhrkamp, 2014).

24. Günter de Bruyn, *Unzeitgemäßes: Betrachtungen über Vergangenheit und Gegenwart* (Frankfurt/M.: Fischer, 2001), p. 71.

25. Compare Volker Braun, *Tumulus* (Frankfurt/M.: Surhrkamp, 1999), p. 41.

26. Heinz-Peter Preußer, *Mythos als Sinnkonstruktion: Die Antikeprojekte von Christa Wolf, Heiner Müller, Stefan Schütz und Volker Braun* (Cologne: Böhlau, 2000).

27. Iris Radisch, 'Die zweite Stunde Null', *Die Zeit*, 7 October 1994, Literaturbeilage pp. 1–2: www.zeit.de/1994/41/die-zweite-stunde-null.

28. Michael Neubauer, 'Gefeit vor Utopien: Thomas Brussig und Ingo Schulze Erfolgsautoren der Nachwendegeneration im Gespräch über die DDR und den Osten, über Literatur und die Schwierigkeit, den Westen zu verstehen', *TAZ*, 5 October 1998, p. 15.

29. Thomas Billardt, Kerstin Hensel, *Alles war so. Alles war anders. Bilder aus der DDR* (Leipzig: Verlag Gustav Kiepenheuer, 1999), p. 7.

30. Radisch, 'Die zweite Stunde Null', p. 2.
31. Ingo Schulze, *Simple Storys. Ein Roman aus der ostdeutschen Provinz* (Berlin: Berlin Verlag, 1998).
32. The same point is made in Lutz Rathenow's article on Ide's 2007 novel: '"Ostdeutscher Generationsbruch": Robert Ide: *Geteilte Träume. Meine Eltern, die Wende und ich*', *Deutschland Kulturradio*, 28 May 2007.
33. Jana Hensel, *Zonenkinder* (Reinbek: Rowohlt, 2002); *After the Wall: Confessions from an East German Childhood and the Life That Came Next*, trans. Jefferson Chase (New York: Public Affairs Books, 2004).
34. Compare Jennifer Beerich-Shahbazi, 'The Zonenkinder Debate', in Donald Backmann and Aida Sakalauskaite (eds.), *Ossi Wessi* (Newcastle: Cambridge Scholars Publishing, 2008), pp. 57–74; Corinna Khanke '*Generation Golf* meets *Zonenkinder*: Gender (N)ostalgia and the Berlin Republic', in Margaret McCarthy (ed.), *German Pop Literature: A Companion* (Berlin and New York: de Gruyter, 2015), pp. 57–74.
35. Two notable anthologies of *Wende* poems came out very quickly. See Ruth Owen, *The Poet's Role: Lyric Responses to German Unification by Poets from the GDR* (Amsterdam and New York: Rodopi, 2001). The titles of various prose publications reflect the urgency: *Klartexte im Getümmel* (Wolf Biermann, 1990), *Jubelschreie Trauergesänge* (Günter de Bruyn, 1991).
36. Neubauer, 'Gefeit vor Utopien', p. 15.
37. Scherpe, p. 193. A useful comparison might also be with West German Judith Hermann's popular *Sommerhaus, später* (also 1998), which echoes the forms and feeling of many of these works. It is worth noting that later novels too, e.g. Schulze's own *Neue Leben* (2005) or Kathrin Schmidt's *Königskinder* (2002), are also based on a fragmentary structure.
38. For a good discussion see Scherpe, pp. 194–202.
39. For an overview and contrary view see Denise Varney (ed.), *Theatre in the Berlin Republic: German Drama Since Unification* (Berne: Lang, 2008).
40. Jonathan Kalb, '*Germania 3: Gespenster am toten Mann*: Heiner Müller and the Art of Posthumous Provocation', *New German Critique*, 98 (Summer 2006), 49–64.
41. Tate, 'Introduction', p. 8.
42. Hodgin, *Screening the East*; Cooke, *The Lives of Others and Contemporary German Film: A Companion* (Berlin, Boston: de Gruyter, 2013).
43. Anna Funder, *Stasiland. Stories from behind the Berlin Wall* (London: Granta, 2003).
44. Timothy Garton Ash, 'The Stasi on Our Minds', *The New York Review of Books*, 54.9, 31 May 2007. www.nybooks.com/articles/20210.
45. Daniela Berghahn, 'Remembering the Stasi in a Fairy Tale of Redemption: Florian Henckel von Donnersmarck's *Das Leben der Anderen*', *From Stasiland to Ostalgie*, 321–33 and Cooke (ed.), *The Lives of Others. The Good German*.
46. Annie Ring, *After the Stasi: Collaboration and the Struggle for Sovereign Subjectivity in the Writing of German Unification* (London: Bloomsbury, 2015).
47. Jens Sparschuh, *Der Zimmerspringbrunnen: Ein Heimatroman* (Cologne: Kiepenheuer & Witsch, 1995). Georgina Paul analyses this and works by

Hensel, Königsdorf, Maron, Burmeister and Annett Gröschner in 'The Privatization of Community: The Legacy of Collectivism in the Post-Socialist Literature of Eastern Germany', *From Stasiland to Ostalgie*, 288–98.

48. Katherina Gerstenberger, *Writing the New Berlin: The German Capital in Post-Wall Literature* (Rochester, NY: Camden House, 2008); see Chapter 4 'Goodbye to East Berlin'; Simon Ward, 'Encountering Lateness in Post-Unification Berlin' in Karen Leeder (ed.), *Figuring Lateness in Modern German Culture*, NGC 125 (2015), 115–135.
49. Maxim Biller, 'Die Ossifizierung des Westens: Deutsche deprimierende Republik', *FAZ*, 2 October 2009: www.faz.net/aktuell/feuilleton/debatten/die-ossifizierung-des-westens-deutsche-deprimierende-republik-1920987.html.
50. Compare Annett Gröschner, *Parzelle Paradies: Berliner Geschichten* (Hamburg: Nautilus, 2008), p. 48.
51. Lyn Marven, 'Berlin ist bekannt [...] für die Mauer, die es aber nicht mehr gibt': The Persistence of East Berlin in the Contemporary City', *From Stasiland to Ostalgie*, 299–309.
52. Patricia Anne Simpson, 'Dystopian Socialism: The Postmodern Topography of East German poetry', in Tobin Siebers (ed.), *Heterotopia: Postmodern Utopia and the Body Politic* (Ann Arbor: University of Michigan Press, 1994), pp. 122–48, p. 129.
53. Compare also Seiler's poetological essay 'Heimaten' in his *Sonntags dachte ich an Gott: Aufsätze* (Frankfurt/M.: Suhrkamp, 2004).
54. See Gillian Pye's thought-provoking 'Matter Out of Place: Trash and Transition in Clemens Meyer's *Als wir träumten*', in Rechtien and Tate (eds.), *Twenty Years On*, pp. 126–38.
55. For further information see Ring, *After the Stasi*, Ch. 5 and Gerstenberger, *Writing the New Berlin*, Ch. 4, respectively.
56. Peter Thompson, '"Die unheimliche Heimat": The GDR and the Dialectics of Home' in *From Stasiland to Ostalgie*, 278–87.
57. Jacques Derrida, *Specters of Marx. The State of the Debt, the Work of Mourning and the New International*, trans. Peggy Kamuf (New York, London: Routledge, 1994).
58. Catherine Smale, *Phantom Images: The Figure of the Ghost in the Literature of Christa Wolf and Irina Liebmann* (London, MHRA, 2013).
59. Thompson, 'Unheimliche Heimat', p. 284
60. Christoph Rüter, *Die Zeit ist aus den Fugen*, DVD, absolut Medien GmbH, 2009.
61. Smale, *Phantoms Images*.
62. Smale explores this in detail in *Phantom Images*. See also Elke Gilson, 'Doppelgänger in Post-*Wende* Literature: Klaus Schlesinger's *Trug* and Beyond', in Pinfold and Saunders (eds.), *Remembering and Rethinking the GDR*, pp. 83–100.
63. Hubert Kästner ed., *Neue Totentänze. Holzstiche von Karl-Georg Hirsch. Mit Gedichten von Volker Braun, Peter Gosse, Kerstin Hensel, Richard Pietraß, Hubert Schirneck und Kathrin Schmidt* (Frankfurt am Main, Leipzig: Insel, 2002).

64. Andreas Huyssen, *Twilight Memories: Marking Time in a Culture of Amnesia* (New York and London: Routledge, 1995).

65. Braun, quoted in *Neue Totentänze*, p. 110.

66. Michael Wesely, *Open Shutter* (New York: Museum of Modern Art, 2005).

67. A significant consequence of the process for long exposures is that once a given area of the negative has reached maximum density by exposure to strong light, the corresponding area in the positive print will be white.

68. Michael Wesely, *Ostdeutschland/East Germany* (Berlin: Die Deutsche Bibliothek, 2004).

Guide to further reading

This is a selection of available reading, with the emphasis on English-language works. The 'General reading' section is followed by brief lists for each chapter, though duplication has been avoided.

General reading

Ahbe, Thomas, *Ostalgie. Zum Umgang mit der DDR-Vergangenheit in den 1990er Jahren* (Erfurt: Landeszentrale für politische Bildung, 2005).

Arnold, Heinz Ludwig (ed.), *DDR-Literatur der neunziger Jahre* (Munich: edition Text + Kritik, 2000).

Literatur der DDR: Rückblicke (Munich: edition Text + Kritik, 1991).

Arnold de Simine, Silke, *Memory Traces: 1989 and the Question of German Cultural Identity* (Frankfurt: Lang, 2005).

Balbier, Uta A., Cristina Cuevas-Wolf and Joes Segal (eds.), *East German Material Culture and the Power of Memory*, Bulletin of the German Historical Institute, Supplement 7 (Washington, DC: German Historical Institute, 2011).

Barck, Simone, *Antifa-Geschichte(n). Eine literarische Spurensuche in der DDR der 1950er und 1960er Jahre* (Cologne: Böhlau, 2003).

Barck, Simone and Siegfried Lokalis (eds.), *Zensurspiele: Heimliche Literaturgeschichten aus der DDR* (Halle/S.: Mitteldeutscher Verlag, 2008).

Bathrick, David, *The Powers of Speech: The Politics of Culture in the GDR* (Lincoln: University of Nebraska Press, 1995).

Beattie, Andrew H., *Playing Politics with History. The Bundestag Enquiries into East Germany* (New York: Berghahn, 2008).

Biermann, Wolf, et al., *Die Ausbürgerung; Anfang vom Ende der DDR*, ed. Fritz Pleitgen (Berlin: List, 2006).

Bradley, Laura and Karen Leeder (eds.), *Brecht & the GDR: Politics, Culture, Posterity*, Edinburgh German Yearbook, vol. 5 (Rochester, NY: Camden House, 2011).

Brockmann, Stephen, *Literature and German Unification* (Cambridge University Press, 1999).

Brockmann, Stephen, *The Writers' State: Constructing East German Literature, 1945–1959* (Rochester: Camden House, 2015).

Buck-Morss, Susan, *Dreamworld and Catastrophe* (Cambridge, MA: MIT Press, 2000).

Clarke, David and Ute Wölfel (eds.), *Remembering the German Democratic Republic: Divided Memory in a United Germany* (Basingstoke: Palgrave Macmillan, 2011).

Cooke, Paul, *Representing East Germany since Unification: From Colonization to Nostalgia* (Oxford: Berg, 2005).

Dahlke, Birgit, Martina Langermann and Thomas Taterka (eds.), *LiteraturGesellschaft DDR. Kanonkämpfe und ihre Geschichte(n)* (Stuttgart, Weimar: Metzler, 2000).

Emmerich, Wolfgang, *Kleine Literaturgeschichte der DDR*, Erweiterte Neuausgabe (Berlin: Aufbau, 2000).

Engler, Wolfgang, *Die Ostdeutschen. Kunde von einem verlorenen Land* (Berlin: Aufbau, 1999).

Fröhling, Jörg, Reinhild Meinel and Karl Riha (eds.), *Wende-Literatur: Bibliographie und Materialien zur Literatur der Deutschen Einheit* (Frankfurt/M.: Lang 1996; 3rd edn, 1999).

Fulbrook, Mary, *Anatomy of a Dictatorship: Inside the GDR 1949–1989* (Oxford University Press, 1998).

Fulbrook, Mary, *The People's State: East German Society from Hitler to Honecker* (New Haven: Yale University Press, 2005).

Geyer, Michael (ed.), *The Power of Intellectuals in Contemporary Germany* (Chicago and London: University of Chicago Press, 2001).

Goodbody, Axel and Dennis Tate (eds.), *Geist und Macht: Writers and the State in the German Democratic Republic, German Monitor* 29 (Amsterdam: Rodopi, 1992).

Grix, Jonathan and Paul Cooke (eds.), *East German Distinctiveness in a Unified Germany* (Edgbaston: University of Birmingham Press, 2002).

Haase, Horst, et al. (eds.), *Geschichte der deutschen Literatur von den Anfängen bis zur Gegenwart*, vol. XI: *Literatur der Deutschen Demokratischen Republik* (East Berlin: Volk und Wissen, 1976).

Hermand, Jost and Marc Silberman (eds.), *Contentious Memories: Looking Back at the GDR*, German Life and Civilization 24 (New York: Lang, 1998).

Jäger, Wolfgang and Ingeborg Villinger (eds.), *Die Intellektuellen und die deutsche Einheit* (Freiburg i. Br: Rombach, 1997).

Jarausch, Konrad H. (ed.), *Dictatorship as Experience: Towards a Socio-Cultural History of the GDR*, trans. Eve Duffy (New York, Oxford: Berghahn, 1999).

United Germany: Debating Processes and Prospects (New York, Oxford: Berghahn, 2013).

Köhler, Astrid, *Brückenschläge: DDR-Autoren vor und nach der Wiedervereinigung* (Göttingen: Vandenhoeck & Ruprecht, 2007).

Kummer, Michael, *Der kurze Sommer der Anarchie: Der Einfluß der Wende von 1989 auf die Biographien junger Ostdeutscher* (Hamburg: Diplomica Verlag, 2010).

Major, Patrick, *Behind the Berlin Wall: East Germany and the Frontiers of Power* (Oxford University Press, 2010).

Naughton, Leonie, *That Was the Wild East: Film Culture, Unification, and the New Germany* (Ann Arbor: University of Michigan Press, 2002).

Opitz, Michael and Michael Hofmann (eds.), *Metzler Lexikon DDR-Literatur: Autoren – Institutionen – Debatten* (Stuttgart: Metzler, 2009).

Parker, Stephen and Matthew Philpotts, *Sinn und Form: The Anatomy of a Literary Journal* (Berlin, New York: de Gruyter, 2009).

Reid, J. H., *Writing without Taboos: The New East German Literature* (New York, Oxford: Oswald Wolff Books, Berg, 1990).

Robinson, Benjamin, *The Skin of the System: On Germany's Socialist Modernity* (Stanford, CA: Stanford University Press, 2009).

Ross, Corey, *The East German Dictatorship: Problems and Perspectives in the Interpretation of the GDR* (London: Hodder Arnold, 2002).

Sabrow, Martin (ed.), *Erinnerungsorte der DDR* (Munich: Beck, 2009).

Sabrow, Martin et al. (eds.), *Wohin treibt die DDR-Erinnerung? Dokumentation einer Debatte* (Göttingen: Vandenhoeck & Ruprecht, 2007).

Saunders, Anna and Debbie Pinfold (eds.), *Remembering and Rethinking the GDR: Multiple Perspectives and Plural Authenticities* (Basingstoke: Palgrave Macmillan, 2012).

Schubbe, Elimar, *Dokumente zur Kunst-, Literatur-, und Kulturpolitik der SED, 1946–1970* (Stuttgart: Seewald, 1972).

Silberman, Marc (ed.), *The German Wall: Fallout in Europe* (Basingstoke, New York: Palgrave Macmillan, 2011).

Tate, Dennis, *The East German Novel: Identity, Community, Continuity* (New York: St Martin's Press, 1984).

Franz Fühmann: Innovation and Authenticity (Rodopi: Amsterdam, 1995).

Todorova, Maria and Zsuzsa Gille (eds.), *Post-Communist Nostalgia* (New York: Berghahn, 2010).

Webber, Andrew J., *Berlin in the Twentieth Century: A Cultural Topography* (Cambridge University Press, 2008).

Wedeking, Volker (ed.), *Mentalitätswandel in der deutschen Literatur zur Einheit (1990–2000)* (Berlin: Erich Schmidt, 2000).

Wolle, Stefan, *Die heile Welt der Diktatur. Alltag und Herrschaft in der DDR 1971–1989* (Berlin: Links, 1998).

The Emergence of GDR Culture

Brockmann, Stephen, *German Literary Culture at the Zero Hour* (Rochester, NY: Camden House, 2004).

Davies, Peter, 'Hanns Eisler's 'Faustus' Libretto and the Problem of East German National Identity', *Music & Letters*, 81.4 (November 2000), 585–98.

Dietrich, Gerd, *Politik und Kultur in der SBZ 1945–1949* (Bern: Lang, 1993).

Gansel, Carsten, *Parlament des Geistes: Literatur zwischen Hoffnung und Repression 1945–1961* (Berlin: BasisDruck, 1996).

Haug, Wolfgang Fritz (ed.), *Historisch-Kritisches Wörterbuch des Marxismus*, vol. IV (Hamburg: Argument, 1999).

Klemperer, Victor, *Kultur: Erwägungen nach dem Zusammenbruch des Nazismus* (Berlin: Neues Leben, 1946).

Orlow, Dietrich, 'The GDR's Failed Search for a National Identity, 1945–1949', *German Studies Review*, 29.3 (October 2006), 537–58.

Schivelbusch, Wolfgang, *Vor dem Vorhang: Das geistige Berlin 1945–1948* (Frankfurt/M.: Fischer, 1997).

Ulbricht, Walter, *Reden und Aufsätze* (Hamburg: Blinkfüer, 1968).

Antifascism and DEFA

Ahbe, Thomas, *Der DDR-Antifaschismus: Diskurse, Generationen, Kontexte und Identitäten* (Leipzig: Rosa-Luxemburg-Stiftung, 2007).

Allan, Seán and John Sandford (eds.), *DEFA. East German Cinema, 1946–92* (Oxford: Berghahn, 1996).

Barnert, Anne, *Die Antifaschismusthematik der DEFA. Eine kultur- und filmhistorische Analyse* (Marburg: Schüren, 2005).

Berghahn, Daniela, *Hollywood behind the Wall. The Cinema of East Germany* (Manchester, New York: Manchester University Press, 2005).

Brockmann, Stephen (ed.), *A Critical History of German Film* (Rochester, NY: Camden House, 2010), esp. Part Five, pp. 213–82.

Byg, Barton, 'The Antifascist Tradition and GDR Film', in *Proceedings, Purdue University Fifth Annual Conference on Film* (West Lafayette, IN: Purdue University Press, 1980), pp. 115–24.

Hake, Sabine, 'Political Affects: Antifascism and the Second World War in Frank Beyer and Konrad Wolf', in Paul Cooke and Marc Silberman (eds.), *Screening War. Perspectives on German Suffering* (Rochester, NY: Camden House, 2010), pp. 102–22.

Kannapin, Detlef, *Antifaschismus im Film der DDR: DEFA-Spielfilme, 1945 bis 1955/6* (Cologne: Papy-Rossa, 1997).

Theatre in the GDR

Barnett, David, *Literature versus Theatre. Textual Problems and Theatrical Realization in the Later Plays of Heiner Müller* (Frankfurt/M.: Lang, 1998).

Bradley, Laura, *Cooperation and Conflict: GDR Theatre Censorship, 1961–1989* (Oxford University Press, 2010).

'From Berlin to Prenzlau: GDR Theatre in Literature and Film', in Nick Hodgin and Caroline Pearce (eds.), *The GDR Remembered: Representations of the East German State since 1989* (Rochester, NY: Camden House, 2011), pp. 19–36.

Funke, Christoph, 'The Activist Legacy of Theater in the German Democratic Republic', *Contemporary Theatre Review*, 4.2 (1995), 7–11.

Kalb, Jonathan, *The Theater of Heiner Müller*, 2nd revised edn (Chicago: Academic Publishers, 2001).

Kruger, Loren, '*Wir treten aus unseren Rollen heraus*: Theater Intellectuals and Public Spheres', in Michael Geyer (ed.), *The Power of Intellectuals in Contemporary Germany* (Chicago and London: University of Chicago Press, 2001), pp. 183–211.

Kuberski, Angela (ed.), *Wir treten aus unseren Rollen heraus: Dokumente des Aufbruchs Herbst '89*, Theaterarbeit in der DDR, 19 (East Berlin: Zentrum für Theaterdokumentation und -information, 1990).

Lennartz, Knut, *Vom Aufbruch zur Wende: Theater in der DDR* (Velber: Erhard Friedrich, 1992).

Robb, David, *Zwei Clowns im Lande des verlorenen Lachens: Das Liedertheater Wenzel & Mensching* (Berlin: Links, 1998).

Simpson, Patricia Anne, 'Crossing Bridges and Borders: Independent Theatre in the GDR', *PAJ*, 11.1 (1988), 39–45.

Stuber, Petra, *Spielräume und Grenzen. Studien zum DDR-Theater* (Berlin: Links, 2000).

Autobiographical Writing in the GDR Era

Dahlke, Birgit, Dennis Tate and Roger Woods (eds.), *German Life Writing in the Twentieth Century* (Rochester, NY: Camden House, 2010).

De Bruyn, Günter, *Das erzählte Ich: Über Wahrheit und Dichtung in der Autobiographie* (Frankfurt/M.: Fischer, 1995).

Fühmann, Franz, 'Gespräch mit Wilfried F. Schoeller', in Hans-Jürgen Schmitt (ed.), *Franz Fühmann: Den Katzenartigen wollten wir verbrennen: Ein Lesebuch* (Munich: DTV, 1988), pp. 273–301.

Heukenkamp, Ursula (ed.), *Deutsche Erinnerung: Berliner Beiträge zur Prosa der Nachkriegsjahre* (Berlin: Erich Schmidt, 2000).

Krauß, Angela, *Die Gesamtliebe und die Einzelliebe: Frankfurter Poetikvorlesungen* (Frankfurt/M.: Suhrkamp, 2004).

Olney, James, *Memory and Narrative: The Weave of Life-Writing* (Chicago: University of Chicago Press, 1998).

Preußer, Heinz-Peter and Helmut Schmitz (eds.), *Autobiografie und historische Krisenerfahrung* (Heidelberg: Winter, 2010).

Tate, Dennis, *Shifting Perspectives: East German Autobiographical Narratives Before and After the End of the GDR* (Rochester, NY: Camden House, 2007).

Wolf, Christa, 'Lesen und Schreiben', in Wolf, *Essays, Gespräche, Reden, Briefe 1959–1974, Werke*, vol. IV (Munich: Luchterhand, 1999), pp. 238–82.

Gender in the GDR

Dueck, Cheryl, *Rifts in Time and the Self. The Female Subject in Two Generations of East German Women Writers* (Amsterdam, New York, NY: Rodopi, 2004).

Hell, Julia, *Post-Fascist Fantasies. Psychoanalysis, History, and the Literature of East Germany* (Durham and London: Duke University Press, 1997).

Kaufmann, Eva, 'Women Writers in the GDR, 1945–1989', in Chris Weedon (ed.), *Post-War Women's Writing in German. Feminist Critical Approaches* (Providence, RI: Berghahn, 1997), pp. 169–209.

Kuhn, Anna K., *Christa Wolf's Utopian Vision. From Marxism to Feminism* (Cambridge University Press, 1988).

Lewis, Alison, *Subverting Patriarchy. Feminism and Fantasy in the Works of Irmtraud Morgner* (Oxford: Berg, 1995).

Linklater, Beth V., *'Und immer zügelloser wird die Lust'. Constructions of Sexuality in East German Literatures* (Bern: Lang, 1998).

Lukens, Nancy and Dorothy Rosenberg (eds. and trans.), *Daughters of Eve. Women's Writing from the German Democratic Republic* (Lincoln and London: University of Nebraska Press, 1993).

Martens, Lorna, *The Promised Land? Feminist Writing in the German Democratic Republic* (Albany: State University of New York Press, 2001).

McLellan, Josie, *Love in the Time of Communism. Intimacy and Sexuality in the GDR* (Cambridge University Press, 2011).

GDR Satire

Biskupek, Matthias and Mathias Wedel, *Streitfall Satire* (Halle and Leipzig: Mitteldeutscher Verlag, 1988).

Klötzer, Sylvia, *Satire und Macht. Film, Zeitung, Kabarett in der DDR* (Cologne: Böhlau, 2006).

Leask, Phil, 'Humiliation as a Weapon of the Party: Fictional and Personal Accounts', in Mary Fulbrook and Andrew I. Port (eds.), *Becoming East German: Socialist Structures and Sensibilities after Hitler* (London and New York: Berghahn, 2013), pp.237–56.

Liersch, Werner, 'SS-Vergangenheit. Erwin Strittmatters unbekannter Krieg', faz. net 8 June 2008.

Meyer, Barbara, *Satire und politische Bedeutung: Die literarische Satire in der DDR. Eine Untersuchung zum Prosaschaffen der 70er Jahre* (Bonn: Bouvier, 1985).

Mix, York-Gothart (ed.), *Ein 'Oberkunze darf nicht vorkommen': Materialien zur Publikationsgeschichte und Zensur des Hinze-Kunze-Romans von Volker Braun* (Wiesbaden: Harrassowitz, 1993).

Neubert, Werner, *Die Wandlung des Juvenal. Satire zwischen gestern und morgen* (Berlin: Dietz, 1966).

Poumet, Jacques, *La Satire en R.D.A.: Cabarets et presse satirique* (Lyon: Presses universitaires de Lyon, 1990).

Twark, Jill E., *Humor, Satire, and Identity: Eastern German Literature in the 1990s* (Berlin: de Gruyter, 2007).

Wedel, Mathias, 'Zu den Funktionen von Satire im Sozialismus', unpubl. diss. Berlin: Akademie für Gesellschaftswissenschaften beim Zentralkomitee der SED, 1986.

Wilhelm, Frank, *Literarische Satire in der SBZ, DDR 1945–1961: Autoren, institutionelle Rahmenbedingungen und kulturpolitische Leitlinien* (Hamburg: Kovač, 1998).

GDR Poetry

Berendse, Gerrit-Jan, *Die 'Sächsische Dichterschule'. Lyrik in der DDR der sechziger und siebziger Jahre* (Frankfurt/M.: Lang, 1990).
Grenz-Fallstudien. Essays zum Topos Prenzlauer Berg in der DDR-Literatur (Berlin: Erich Schmidt, 1999).
Böthig, Peter, *Grammatik einer Landschaft. Literatur aus der DDR der 8oer Jahre* (Berlin: Lukas, 1997).
Endler, Adolf, *Den Tiger reiten. Aufsätze, Polemiken und Notizen zur Lyrik der DDR*, ed. Manfred Behn (Frankfurt/M.: Luchterhand, 1990).
Flores, John, *Poetry in East Germany. Adjustments, Visions and Provocations. 1945–1970* (New Haven and London: Yale University Press, 1971).
Geist, Peter (ed.), *Ein Molotow-Cocktail auf fremder Bettkante. Lyrik der siebziger / achtziger Jahre von Dichtern aus der DDR* (Leipzig: Reclam, 1991).
Laschen, Gregor, *Lyrik in der DDR. Anmerkungen zur Sprachverfassung des modernen Gedichts* (Frankfurt/M.: Athenäum, 1971).
Leeder, Karen, *Breaking Boundaries. A New Generation of Poets in the GDR* (Oxford: Clarendon Press, 1996).
Visser, Anthonya, *Blumen ins Eis. Lyrische und literaturkritische Innovationen in der DDR. Zum kommunikativen Spannungsfeld ab Mitte der 6oer Jahre* (Amsterdam: Rodopi, 1994).
Wolf, Gerhard, *Sprachblätter Wortwechsel. Im Dialog mit Dichtern* (Leipzig: Reclam, 1992).

Underground Literature

Berbig, Roland, Birgit Dahlke, Michael Kämper-van den Boogart and Uwe Schoor (eds.), *Zersammelt. Die inoffizielle Literaturszene der DDR nach 1990*, Recherchen: 6 (Berlin: Theater der Zeit, 2000).
Böthig, Peter, *Grammatik einer Landschaft. Literatur aus der DDR in den 8oer Jahren* (Berlin: Lukas Verlag, 1997).
Böthig, Peter and Klaus Michael (eds.), *MachtSpiele. Literatur und Staatssicherheit im Fokus Prenzlauer Berg* (Leipzig: Reclam, 1993).
Dahlke, Birgit, *Papierboot. Autorinnen aus der DDR – inoffiziell publiziert* (Würzburg: Königshausen & Neumann, 1997).
Felsmann, Barbara and Annett Gröschner (eds.), *Durchgangszimmer Prenzlauer Berg. Eine Berliner Künstlersozialgeschichte in Selbstauskünften* (Berlin: Lukas Verlag, 1999).
Grundmann, Ute, Klaus Michael and Susanne Seufert (eds.), *Die Einübung der Außenspur. Die andere Kultur in Leipzig 1971–1990* (Leipzig: Thom Verlag, 1996).

Günther, Thomas (ed.), *Poesie des Untergrunds*, Catalogue for the Consulate General of the Federal Republic in New York City: 9 December 2010–3 March 2011 (Berlin: Edition Galerie auf Zeit, 2011).

Kaiser, Paul and Claudia Petzold, *Boheme und Diktatur in der DDR. Gruppen Konflikte Quartiere 1970–1989*, Catalogue for the Museum of German History's exhibition: 4 September–16 December 1997 (Berlin: Verlag Fannei & Walz, 1997).

Koziol, Andreas, *Vortrag. Staatsgeheimnis und Sprachgeheimnis. Zur Untergrunddichtung der späten DDR*, Franc-Tireur Heft 10 (Kirchseeon: Verlag Peter Ludewig, 2010).

Lewis, Alison, *Die Kunst des Verrats: Der Prenzlauer Berg und die Staatsicherheit* (Würzburg: Königshausen & Neumann, 2003).

Michael, Klaus and Thomas Wohlfahrt (eds.), *Vogel oder Käfig sein. Kunst und Literatur aus unabhängigen Zeitschriften in der DDR 1979–1989* (Berlin: Galrev, 1992).

Warnke, Uwe and Ingeborg Quaas (eds.), *Die Addition der Differenzen. Die Literaten- und Künstlerszene Ostberlins 1979 bis 1989* (Berlin: Verbrecher Verlag, 2009).

Intellectuals and the Wende

Anz, Thomas (ed.), *'Es geht nicht um Christa Wolf'. Der Literaturstreit im vereinigten Deutschland*, Erweiterte Neuausgabe (Frankfurt/M.: Fischer, 1995).

Becker, Jurek, 'Die Wiedervereinigung der deutschen Literatur', *The German Quarterly*, 63 (1990), 359–66.

Brockmann, Stephen, 'German Literary Debates after the Collapse', *German Life and Letters*, 47.2 (1994), 201–10.

'The Written Capital', *Monatshefte*, 91.3 (1999), 376–95.

Garton Ash, Timothy, *The Uses of Adversity: Essays on the Fate of Central Europe* (New York: Vintage Books, 1990).

Greiner, Ulrich, 'Der Potsdamer Abgrund. Anmerkungen zu einem öffentlichen Streit über die "Kulturnation Deutschland"', *Die Zeit*, 22 (June 1990), 59.

Hahn, Annegret, Gisela Puchler, Henning Schaller and Lothar Scharsich (eds.), *4. November '89: Der Protest, die Menschen, die Reden* (Frankfurt/M.: Ullstein, 1990).

Hohendahl, Peter Uwe, 'Wandel der Öffentlichkeit. Kulturelle und politische Identität im heutigen Deutschland', in Claudia Mayer-Iswandy (ed.), *Zwischen Traum und Trauma – Die Nation. Transatlantische Perspektiven zur Geschichte eines Problems* (Tübingen: Stauffenburg, 1994), pp. 129–46.

Magenau, Jörg, *Christa Wolf. Eine Biographie*, 2nd edn (Berlin: Kindler, 2002).

Maron, Monika, 'Die Schriftsteller und das Volk', *Der Spiegel* (12 February 1990), 68–70.

Monteath, Peter and Reinhard Alter (eds.), *Kulturstreit – Streitkultur. German Literature since the Wall* (Amsterdam: Rodopi, 1996).

Schüddekopf, Charles (ed.), *'Wir sind das Volk!' Flugschriften, Aufrufe und Texte einer deutschen Revolution* (Reinbek bei Hamburg: Rowohlt, 1990).

Vinke, Hermann (ed.), *Akteneinsicht Christa Wolf. Zerrspiegel und Dialog. Eine Dokumentation*, 2nd edn (Hamburg: Luchterhand, 1993).

The Stasi

Anderson, Sascha, *Sascha Anderson* (Cologne: DuMont, 2002).

Byrnes, Deirdre, *Rereading Monika Maron: Text, Counter-Text and Context* (Bern: Lang, 2011).

Cooke, Paul and Andrew Plowman (eds.), *German Writers and the Politics of Culture: Dealing with the Stasi* (Basingstoke: Palgrave Macmillan, 2003).

Evans, Owen, *Mapping the Contours of Oppression: Subjectivity, Truth and Fiction in Recent German Autobiographical Treatments of Totalitarianism* (Amsterdam, New York: Rodopi, 2006).

Jones, Sara, *Complicity, Censorship and Criticism: Negotiating Space in the GDR Literary Sphere* (Berlin: de Gruyter, 2011).

Kerz-Rühling, Ingrid and Tomas Plänkers, *Verräter oder Verführte: eine psycho-analytische Untersuchung Inoffizieller Mitarbeiter der Stasi* (Berlin: Links, 2004).

Kunze, Reiner, *Deckname 'Lyrik': Eine Dokumentation* (Frankfurt/M.: Fischer, 1990).

Lewis, Alison, 'Erinnerung, Zeugenschaft und die Staatssicherheit: Die Schriftstellerin Monika Maron', *Der Deutschunterricht*, 6 (2005), 22–33.

'Reading and Writing the Stasi file: On the Uses and Abuses of the File as (Auto)Biography', *German Life and Letters*, 56.4 (2003), 337–97.

Maron, Monika, *Quer über die Gleise: Essays, Artikel, Zwischenrufe* (Frankfurt/M.: Fischer, 2000).

Miller, Barbara, *Narratives of Guilt and Compliance in Unified Germany: Stasi Informers and their Impact on Society* (London and New York: Routledge, 1999).

Vatulescu, Cristina, 'Arresting Biographies: The Secret Police File in the Soviet Union and Romania', *Comparative Literature*, 56.3 (2004), 243–61.

Walther, Joachim, *Sicherungsbereich Literatur: Schriftsteller und Staatssicherheit in der Deutschen Demokratischen Republik* (Berlin: Links, 1996).

Wolle, Stefan, *Die heile Welt der Diktatur: Alltag und Herrschaft in der DDR 1971–1989* (Berlin: Links, 1998).

GDR Literature and the Berlin Republic

Bathrick, David, 'Crossing Borders: the End of the Cold War Intellectual', *German Politics and Society* (Fall 1992), 77–87.

Betts, Paul, 'The Twilight of the Idols: East German Memory and Material Culture', *Journal of Modern History*, 72 (2000), 731–65.

Boym, Svetlana, *The Future of Nostalgia* (New York: Basic Books, 2001).

Brüns, Elke, *Nach dem Mauerfall: Eine Literaturgeschichte der Entgenzung* (Munich: Wilhelm Fink Verlag, 2006).

Cooke, Paul (ed.), *The Lives of Others and Contemporary German Film: A Companion* (Berlin, Boston: de Gruyter, 2013).

Costabile-Heming, Carol Anne, Rachel J. Halverson, and Kristie A. Foell (eds.), *Textual Responses to German Unification* (Berlin, New York: de Gruyter, 2001).

Fischer, Gerhard and David Roberts (eds.), *Schreiben nach der Wende. Ein Jahrzehnt deutscher Literatur 1989–1999* (Tübingen: Stauffenburg, 2001).

Gerstenberger, Katherina, *Writing the New Berlin: The German Capital in Post-Wall Literature* (Rochester, NY: Camden House, 2008).

Helbig, Holger (ed.), *Weiterschreiben: Zur DDR-Literatur nach dem Ende der DDR* (Berlin: Akademie Verlag, 2007).

Hodgin, Nick, *Screening the East: Heimat, Memory and Nostalgia in German Film since 1989* (New York, Oxford: Berghahn, 2011).

Hodgin, Nick and Caroline Pearce (eds.), *The GDR Remembered: Representations of the East German State since 1989* (Rochester, NY: Camden House, 2011).

Jones, Sara, *The Media of Testimony: Remembering the East German Stasi in the Berlin Republic* (Basingstoke: Palgrave Macmillan, 2014).

Kane, Martin (ed.), *Legacies and Identity. East and West German Literary Reponses to Unification* (Oxford: Lang, 2002).

Leeder, Karen (ed.), *From Stasiland to Ostalgie: The GDR – Twenty Years After, Oxford German Studies*, 38.3 (November 2009).

Ludwig, Janine and Mirjam Meuser (eds.), *Literatur ohne Land? Schreibstrategien einer DDR-Literatur im vereinten Deutschland* (Freiburg: Förderungsgemeinschaft wissenschaftlicher Publikationen von Frauen e.V., 2009).

Literatur ohne Land II (Freiburg: Förderungsgemeinschaft wissenschaftlicher Publikationen von Frauen e.V., 2014).

Monteath, Peter and Reinhard Alter (eds.), *Kulturstreit – Streitkultur: German Literature since the Wall* (Amsterdam, Atlanta, GA: Rodopi, 1996).

Owen, Ruth, *The Poet's Role: Lyric Responses to German Unification by Poets from the GDR* (Amsterdam and New York: Rodopi, 2001).

Philpotts, Matthew and Sabine Rolle (eds.), *Contested Legacies: Constructions of Cultural Heritage in the GDR*, Edinburgh German Yearbook 3 (Rochester, NY: Camden House, 2009).

Rechtien, Renate and Dennis Tate (eds.), *Twenty Years On: Competing Memories of the GDR in Postunification German Culture* (Rochester, NY: Camden House, 2011).

Reimann, Kerstin E., *Schreiben nach der Wende – Wende im Schreiben. Literarische Reflexionen nach 1989/90* (Würzburg: Königshausen & Neumann, 2008).

Ring, Annie, *After the Stasi: Collaboration and the Struggle for Sovereign Subjectivity in the Writing of German Unification* (London: Bloomsbury, 2015).

Scribner, Charity, *Requiem for Communism* (Cambridge, MA: MIT Press, 2005).

Simpson, Patricia Anne, 'Dystopian Socialism: The Postmodern Topography of East German Poetry', in Tobin Siebers (ed.), *Heterotopia: Postmodern Utopia and the Body Politic* (Ann Arbor: University of Michigan Press, 1994), pp. 122–48.

Smale, Catherine, *Phantom Images: The Figure of the Ghost in the Literature of Christa Wolf and Irina Liebmann* (London: MHRA, 2013).

Starkman, Ruth A. (ed.), *Transformations of the New Germany* (Basingstoke: Palgrave Macmillan, 2006).

Wilke, Sabine (ed.), *Legacies of German Unification: Literature and Culture in the New Republic*, special edition of *Literatur für Leser*, 10.2 (2011).

Index

Rump, Bernd, 83
Rusch, Claudia, 222
Rushdie, Salman, 29

Saeger, Uwe, 122
    Nöhr, 122
Sagert, Horst, 77, 83
Sakowski, Helmut, 74
    Weiberzwist und Liebeslist, 74
Salomon, Horst, 76, 78
Sandig, Ulrike Almut, 232
    Buch gegen das Verschwinden, 232
Sartre, Jean-Paul, 71
Sasuly, Richard, 55
satire, 126–140, 169, 217, 226
'Saxon School of Poetry' (Sächsische
    Dichterschule), 19, 144, 149–152
Saxony, 9, 10, 101, 149, 166
Schacht, Ulrich, 141n16
Schädlich, Hans Joachim, 19, 24, 27, 130
    Versuchte Nähe, 24
Schedlinski, Rainer, 28, 153, 166, 167
Scherpe, Klaus, 216
Schicht-Theater (cabaret), 83
Schiller, Friedrich, 24, 53, 70
    Kabale und Liebe, 53
Schirmer, Bernd, 131
Schirrmacher, Frank, 205, 211
Schleime, Cornelia, 162
Schlenstedt, Dieter, 144
Schlesinger, Klaus, 24, 26, 99, 130, 163, 230
    Alte Filme, 24
    Fliegender Wechsel, 99
    Trug, 230
Schmidt, Jochen, 29
Schmidt, Kathrin, 139, 223
    Die Gunnar-Lennefsen-Expedition, 139
    Königskinder, 235n37
Schmitz, Walter, 176
Schmitz-Köster, Dorothee, 117
Schneider, Rolf, 79
Schoch, Julia, 228, 230
    Mit der Geschwindigkeit des Sommers, 228, 230
Schönemann, Horst, 80
Schopenhauer, Arthur, 128
Schorlemmer, Friedrich, 16, 202
Schraeck, Kurt, 162
    Papiertaube, 162
Schroth, Christoph, 80, 81, 84
    Entdeckungen, 81
Schubert, Helga, 120
Schule, Dieter, 163
Schulz, M. W., 18
Schulze, Ingo, 29, 139, 140, 221, 223–224, 228
    Neue Leben, 139

Simple Storys, 221, 223–224, 228
Schütz, Stefan, 25, 81
    Fabrik im Walde, 81
Schwab, Sepp, 57
Schwartz, Michael, 122n2
Schwarz, Jaecki, 63, 64
Schwarz, Yevgeni, 77
Schweikart, Hans, 53
    Das Fräulein von Barnhelm, 53
Schweinebraden, Jürgen, 161
Scribner, Charity, 218
Second World War, 8, 14, 18, 35–38, 39, 40, 42,
    46, 49, 90, 97, 126, 148, 205
SED (Socialist Unity Party), xiv, xv, 8, 11, 15–17,
    19, 23, 40–41, 48, 54, 56–57, 58, 59, 61,
    72–73, 75, 77–79, 81, 96, 98, 107, 108, 115,
    130, 132, 133, 138, 147, 149, 170, 199,
    204, 205
    Central Committee (Eleventh Plenum), xiv,
    23, 61, 62, 77, 78, 82, 96
Seghers, Anna, 12, 18, 22, 48,
    49, 90
    Das siebte Kreuz, 48
    Der Ausflug der toten Mädchen, 90
    Der Mann und sein Name, 49
    Die Toten bleiben jung, 48
Seidel, Georg, 82
Seiler, Lutz, 18, 228
    pech & blende, 18, 228
self-censorship, 20, 95, 206
self-realization, 95–98, 99
Senftenberg Miners' Theatre, 74
Seven-Year Economic Plan, 74
Seyfahrt, Ingrid, 79
Shakespeare, William, 75, 76, 83, 229
Sholokhov, Mikhail, 74
    Neuland unterm Pflug, 74
'Sichel-Operette', 168
'Sieger der Geschichte', 14
Silberman, Marc, 68n17
Silesia, 35
Simon, Annette, 169
Simpson, Patricia Anne, 226
Sinn und Form, 78, 131, 149, 151
Sinngebungsliteratur, 25
Skupin, Vera, 72
Slánský, Rudolph, 65
Smale, Catherine, 236n58
small magazines, 160, 161, 171, 175
socialist realism, xiv, 10, 12, 19, 22, 46–47, 49, 60,
    62, 70, 71, 73, 74, 76, 83, 89–90, 95, 108,
    112, 129, 130–131, 132, 145, 153
Soja, Edward W., 28
Soldovieri, Stefan, 59
Sophocles, 76